CHINESE THROUGH POETRY

An Introduction to the Language and Imagery of Traditional Verse

AUTHOR'S BIOGRAPHY

Archie Barnes was born in 1931 in Holmwood, Dorking, Surrey, Archie was the eldest child of a large family. He always had a natural aptitude for languages - he won a scholarship to Dorking Grammar School. With the encouragement of a local church minister; and aged only 17, he passed the London Matriculation exam in Chinese.

At SOAS, University of London, he graduated with a First in Chinese in 1952. In 1961, Archie joined the University of Durham to lecture in Chinese, where he remained until his early retirement through ill-health. He died in 2002 after completing "Chinese Through Poetry", a book which was built on a lifetime of learning and teaching.

Translated works by Archie Barnes include:

"Red Sun" by Wu Chiang
"Morning in Shanghai" by Zhou Erfu
"Sunrise" by Tsao Yu
"Schoolmaster" by Yeh Sheng-Tao
"Taming the Dragon and the Tiger" by Tuan Cheng-Pin and Tu Shih-Tsun
"Songs of the Red Flag" by Kuo Mo-Jo and Chou Yang
"Thunderstorm" by Tsao Yu (translated with Wang Tso-Liang)

CHINESE THROUGH POETRY

An Introduction to the Language and Imagery of Traditional Verse

by

A. C. BARNES

Formerly Senior Lecturer in Chinese
University of Durham

with a foreword by

K. PRATT

University of Durham

First published in Great Britain 2007 by Alcuin Academics an imprint of WritersPrintShop

ISBN 1904623514

Cover Design: Dr Kevin McLoughlin

Cover images courtesy of the Oriental Museum, Durham

CONTENTS

AUTHOR'S PREFACE

This is a dual-purpose text book. While the sub-title *An Introduction to the Language and Imagery of Traditional Verse* is a description of the main contents, the main title *Chinese through Poetry* needs some explanation. It indicates the original motivation behind my approach.

It is usual to approach the study of Classical Chinese first through prose and only later (if at all) through verse. I am attempting to reverse this procedure in the hope that approaching Classical Chinese through a preliminary study of verse will be more effective for several reasons. First, the student is given confidence by learning to read complete, self-contained texts with a minimum of vocabulary. Second, the contents are mainly words used in their original concrete meanings rather than in the abstract extended meanings more common in prose. Third, the vividness, colour and emotional content of the poems should assist vocabulary absorption in memorable contexts. Fourth, poetry brings us closer to the essence of the Chinese psyche than the philosophical text straditionally used for learning Classical Chinese. It is for this reason that script, grammar and vocabulary are taught from scratch, enabling the work to be used as a first introduction to traditional literary Chinese by anyone with no knowledge of the language. The book can of course be used as an introduction to Chinese verse for its own sake, either independently or as part of a more general course.

To be more precise, this book is an introduction to the language and imagery of traditional Chinese lyrical verse, concentrating on the Tang dynasty (618–907) but ranging back to the Han (206 BC to AD 220) and forward to the Sung (960–1279) when appropriate.

The script used is the traditional one (繁體字), not the simplified version (簡體字). The system of transcription used is the standard 拼音 *pinyin*. Its primary purpose is not, of course, to indicate the medieval pronunciation of the Chinese texts but to enable the reader to use the Vocabulary Index and any Chinese-English dictionaries arranged by *pinyin*.

References are given for all Chinese verse texts quoted. Where possible I have given a reference to *The Three Hundred Tang Poems* (唐詩三百首) since it is often used as a source of texts for students.

Though I suppose that this course will be used mainly by students who are already familiar with at least the rudiments of modern Chinese and of the Chinese script, I have made provision for the absolute beginner with no knowledge of any kind of Chinese by including an introductory section on the Chinese writing-system. For such new-comers to Chinese I should suggest that this course be followed by a more advanced work: D. Hawkes, *A Little Primer of Tu Fu*, Oxford, 1967, reprinted 1987. A dictionary in traditional script will also be needed for further study, such as R. H. Mathews, *A Chinese-English Dictionary...*, Harvard UP, 1974.

In memory of
Archie Barnes

The Seagulls

Along the river's edge the cold gulls play,
with no other concern than doing as they please;
changing their minds, they turn their jade-white wings;
following their fancy, they dot the green rice-shoots.

When snow is dark they still must bathe;
when the wind rises, they drift, unresisting.
A few flocks over the blue sea,
pure figures daily uttering desolate cries.

Tu Fu (circa 784AD)

Translation: Archie Barnes (see also page 323)

Archie's favourite Tang Poem

Tu Fu's The Seagulls
in cursive calligraphic script

Acknowledgements

Archie's work, although completed before he passed away, could easily have been lost forever, were it not for his sons, John and Jim, rescuing it from the depths of his computer and were it not for Graham being willing to take on the task of final processing. Thank you. This book would not be here without your various input.

I would also like to take this opportunity to show my appreciation to Durham University for its support of this project, especially Professor Keith Pratt, a long time colleague and friend of my husband, who contributed the Foreword and to the Oriental Museum and Dr Kevin McLoughlin who put together the cover for the book.

Marie Barnes

Foreword

by
KEITH PRATT
University of Durham

FOREWORD

Change is an essential factor in our daily life. So frequently do we identify it with progress and improvement that stability, despite its comforting sense of familiarity, risks the charge of out-datedness. We have learned to live with Alvin Toffler's outlandish predictions which so alarmed many back in 1970 when they first read them in *Future Shock*. 1984 is past and gone, and we who inhabit a Brave New World look back beyond the age of Aldous Huxley with no more than a passing sense of nostalgia. Younger generations can hardly appreciate what it meant to live in a world that was not permanently aware of constant shifts and developments in technology, communications, medicine, culture, even climate. Are they, and we, the better for it? Yes of course, in many respects. Are we the happier? Possibly, though the risk that the questioning, re-examination and discrediting of inherited devices, traditions and values can sometimes result in doubt, uncertainty, and even cataclysm cannot be denied.

Traditional China also confronted change. If the pace of life was less frenetic than ours, it was none the less capable of throwing up plenty of developments and dilemmas to concern its thinking citizens. Political upheavals and rivalries were a frequent curse and the threat from beyond China's borders a real one. Ideological movements, economic fluctuations, and technical innovations periodically challenged social stability. In the face of constant ups and downs, people fostered a stoic attitude which today's affluent generation, whether in China or the wider world, finds largely incomprehensible. What they clung on to, the stability they trusted and valued most highly and that helped to define Chinese civilisation over so many centuries, was the culture enshrined in the arts of the brush. To them, ink, paint, paper and silk afforded continuity, security, and reassurance, and of all the arts associated with them poetry was the greatest. Some of the Chinese poets were among the greatest the world has ever known. The subjects they wrote (and sang) about – beauty in nature, the changing seasons, riverine scenery, absent loved ones, military campaigns, homesickness, drink, wistful music, female allure – still strike a chord with us today. We can marvel too at the sophistication of their literary structures and the subtlety of their allusive powers. That said, we can never hope to see things as they saw them through their own eyes, nor can even the best translation into modern English convey the depths of meaning imparted by the succinct phraseology of classical Chinese. The language they used was difficult. It made no concessions to the reader: indeed, the more abstruse the writer could make it, the greater the compliment he paid to his reader, who he knew would enjoy teasing out its hidden depths. Unlike today's writers churning out ephemera for the masses with an eye on the best-seller lists, he wrote for a tiny audience, perhaps no more than one. Some, especially the historians among them, may have hoped that their work would survive for the guidance of later generations, but none could envisage a readership outside their own elite circle of educated Confucian scholars. They would have greeted with incomprehension and incredulity the idea that what they wrote would be read and analysed by foreigners ('barbarians') more than a thousand years hence.

Classical Chinese (*wenyan*) was both nebulous and precise, capable of conveying philosophical concepts of the greatest profundity on the one hand and unexpected degrees of scientific exactitude on the other (Archie Barnes used to tell students that there were something like a dozen characters for blue/green in Chinese, and that the well-informed reader knew exactly what shade was being described by each of them). It was also liable to what we should call ambiguity. But when students were perplexed to discover that a phrase or sentence was susceptible to more than one or even two possible interpretations, Barnes would patiently explain that the writer knew exactly what he was doing, and that putting over two or more meanings at once was not so much a failing (as it might be regarded in a student's essay) as an intellectual plus. To try and pin a Chinese scholar down and expect that his words should be translatable into one exact, corresponding meaning in 20th-century English was, *au contraire*, a sign of the modern reader's own blinkered understanding.

We can never put ourselves in the position of a Confucian historian or a Daoist poet, and the world reflected in the classical Chinese language is long since past and gone. But as Archie Barnes grew up in the difficult 1930s the attractions of its apparently stable civilisation were seductive and it still exercised considerable sway, not only in China but increasingly in the West: its philosophy was exalted by Bertrand Russell, the humanism of its Confucian education by John Dewey, its literature by Arthur Waley, and its visual arts by the organisers of the great 1935 Royal Academy Exhibition. It was only natural that a born linguist like he (as a teenager he excelled at French, Latin and German, and had a working knowledge of Greek and Russian, which he taught himself from a book on his lap during French lessons) should be attracted by Chinese. His Religious Education teacher, an ex-China missionary, gave him lessons and he passed the London Matriculation examination in it at the age of 17. In 1952 he graduated with first Class Honours from the School of Oriental & African Studies, and was then called up to do his National Service in the Essex Regiment, which included a posting to Korea in the latter stages of the War there. Korean was duly added to his growing portfolio of languages. After his demob he became a freelance translator, some of the twelve books he translated in the late 1950s and early 1960s being published by the Foreign Languages Press.

In 1961 he took up a post as Spalding Lecturer in Chinese Language and Civilisation in the School of Oriental Studies at the University of Durham. There he entered a small, intimate community of older specialists into which, despite his youth, his linguistic voracity fitted him with ease: Tom Thacker (Egyptology), Heinz Kuhn (Coptic), Richard Hill (Sudanese studies), John Haywood (Arabic), Frank Bagley (Persian), C.G.Simpson (Turkish), Ray Thornhill (Hebrew), and Arabinda Basu (Indian studies). As well as the School, Elvet Hill House was home to the Oriental Section of the University Library, where a team of dedicated staff worked under the eye of the redoubtable Ian Foster. Discussions in the staff common room (the Spalding Room) were scholarly, wide-ranging and spirited, the kind of comparative multi-cultural exchange that provided Archie Barnes

with umpteen fascinating points to file away into his encyclopaedic memory, to
be brought out in the course of tutorial debate perhaps years later. (More mundane
matters of University administration were generally relegated to a smoke-filled
corner in the New Inn at lunch time.)

The syllabus Archie Barnes inherited from Ray Dawson in 1961 was modelled
on that of pre-war Oxford, and reflected the traditional Chinese respect for the
classical world and its literature. Set texts included portions of the *Analects* of
Confucius, the philosophers Mencius and Mozi, the history *Shiji*, and selections
from the great poets. Classical unseens were taken more seriously than modern
ones (Ray Dawson had famously told his students in 1959 that there was no point
in learning to speak Chinese because they would never be able to go there, whereas
there would never be any shortage of books written in classical Chinese in the
library). Archie was able to expand and modernise the syllabus, introducing some
of the books he himself had translated such as Cao Yu's *Thunder*. Composition
and translation into Chinese were exclusively concerned with the modern
language, because as late as the 1950s the syntactic analysis of wenyan was still
in its infancy, and the grammar of classical Chinese was generally deemed to
be either non-existent or largely inexplicable. The first attempt to formulate a
comprehensive grammatical description of the ancient language was W.A.C.H.
Dobson's *Late Archaic Chinese* (1959), and though Ray Dawson, as one of
Dobson's former students, made some use of it as a teaching tool, both he and,
at first, Archie preferred to initiate students in the time-honoured way, reading
simple texts like the *Xiaojing* (from H.G. Creel's *Literary Chinese by the Inductive
Method*, 1938) and commenting on grammatical particles as they occurred. Mrs
Liu's *Fifty Chinese Stories* was a useful primer, as familiar to students in Durham
as in London. Harold Shadick's *First Course in Literary Chinese* was based on a
broader sample of textual passages, including examples of poetry, and appeared
in the same year (1968) as Ray Dawson's *Introduction to Classical Chinese*. All
of these had their uses, but their approach was still basically inductive and Archie
was convinced that if classical Chinese was to be taken seriously, it had to be put
on a par with, say, Latin, and its grammar presented in logical and comprehensive
format. One of the obstacles hindering the easy appreciation of wenyan was its
lack of a proper system of punctuation. The first classics to appear in punctuated
form were the *Shiji* (1959) and Lanzhou University's edition of *Mencius* (1960),
and great excitement greeted the slow appearance of punctuated versions of the
dynastic histories through the 1960s and '70s. Archie, however, who had the
ability to skim through unpunctuated texts with uncanny ease, had already begun
hand-copying for his students his own punctuated recensions of their set texts in
his superb 'Golden' calligraphy (the style of Emperor Song Huizong), along with
vocabularies and grammatical notes. One of the first to come was the biography
of the Prince of Wei, chapter 71 of the *Shiji*. He set a high standard: students in
succeeding years expected similar privileged treatment long after he himself had
gone. In due course his years of study and experience were crystallised in the
beautifully handwritten and photocopied *Introduction to Wenyan Composition*
(1977), an unpublished text much used in Durham and one that contributes a

great deal to the present book. To the chagrin of his students, Archie never sought to publish such things during his working career, and it is appropriate that some of them – particularly Graham Ormerod and his widow Marie (herself a former student) – are working at making this the first book in an ongoing project to bring more of his unpublished trots and grammar work into the public domain. One of the modest achievements in which he took the greatest pride was the success of the system he devised for students to learn Chinese characters, known to all Durham graduates as VOLATS (Voluntary Learning and Teaching System). Archie tested it himself with Gaelic and Cornish before introducing the system in 1976, and his students subsequently exported it all over the world. Details can be found on the website of another (unrelated) alumnus, David Barnes, at http://www.earthcallingdavid.com.

In many ways, Archie Barnes' approach to scholarship and teaching was old-fashioned. He gave the same undeviating care to everybody, from interviewee to returning alumnus. Whoever requested his help received his total attention, whether it were in an evening class or the University's Gulbenkian Museum of Oriental Art, where he was often called on to help staff with a difficult inscription. Among those who visited him periodically with requests for advice, and into whose areas of own special interest Archie unhesitatingly dived with enthusiasm, were William Wheat (Chinese roof decoration), Sammy Chow (archaic bronzes), Arthur Cooper (etymology), and Richard Stephenson (astronomical records). But it was his undergraduate students who always came first, whether in class or tutorial period (either of which was likely to finish well past the allotted hour, thanks to some interesting idea or question cropping up just before its end, and resulting in frustration for the waiting teacher and a flying run for Archie down the path from one room to the next) or in the marking and assessment of their exam papers. Fairness was paramount for him. He told students that it took as long, or longer, to draw up an exam paper as it did to answer it: passages for translation had to be evaluated to the last character, every possible nuance in the wording of a question considered. And marking was just as slow, since the possible merits of every variant answer had to be considered, where many another reader would straightway have marked them wrong.

Archie Barnes was no traveller. His sole visit to China was as part of a delegation in 1960, and his disappointment at what he saw there later turned to disillusionment. He didn't attend conferences. He had no sabbatical leave in the twenty-plus years that he taught in Durham (until, that is, he took a year in 1983-4 and retired at the end of it), and through that long period of time he published virtually nothing. He was frequently heard to say 'There's an article in that', but never quite got round to writing it himself. He was, even so, held in the highest professional regard by his fellow sinologists. He was lucky to retire before the constant pressures of teaching and research assessment began to distort the true and logical pursuit of knowledge. The world of limited-duration undergraduate modules and fixed-term doctoral courses would have been anathema to him. He would have been horrified at the grade inflation tolerated in today's Final Honours examinations, and no better pleased at the thought that a scholar's true worth could be measured by compelling him to publish a set number of books or articles within a given time period. His own erudition knew no such artificiality.

Archie was a loving and committed family man. Himself the eldest offspring in a large family, he was intensely proud of his first wife Winnie and their four children. But tragedy struck, and following Winnie's early death Archie's health declined and he took early retirement in 1984. A second marriage brought great solace and he and Marie moved south. As he recovered his health he mastered computer languages and added programming skills; in order to help with his voluntary work he also learned Braille and sign language. In due course he returned to work on a project that had lain at the back of his mind for many years, a study of traditional China through its poetry. Rooted as his scholarship was in the outlook of gentler times, he was not blind to the potential of modern developments. He had been greatly excited when the University Library acquired a Chinese typewriter, and spent lots of time helping with the preparation of catalogue slips and spine titles and using it to type out exam papers. When he retired the School of Oriental Studies had only just acquired its first computer, and he was intrigued by the advantages this might eventually bring: just think, he would say – not really believing that such a thing would ever really be possible – what could be done if all the dynastic histories were put on to a computer and could be searched from end to end! And what might you not discover if the oeuvres of the great poets were put on disc! The present book, needless to say, was prepared by him on a computer and amply proves the point. It is a unique testament to a lifetime's passion, and a very special insight into the great intellect of a bygone era in one of the world's great civilisations.

Keith Pratt
Emeritus Professor
University of Durham
August 2006

INTRODUCTION

Layout of the units

The main text of the book falls into two parts: (a) Units 1 to 15 and (b) Units 16 to 40.

The first part is mainly concerned with basic grammar, though some further grammatical topics are treated in the second part. The vocabulary introduced in the first part is based on the nine poems in Units 7, 12 and 15, supplemented with other basic vocabulary required to construct exercise material. The exercises are progressive in that each is restricted to the vocabulary and grammar met so far. A key to the exercises is provided after Unit 40. To provide practice in writing, the written form (*kaishu*) is given before the printed form in the main vocabularies in part one; the nine exercise-poems are also given in written form in case you should want to copy them.

The second part consists of 57 poems for the reader to translate as an exercise; new vocabulary needed for this purpose is given in each unit. Romanization is provided so that previously met but forgotten vocabulary can be looked up in the vocabulary index. A key is provided for all translation exercises. In order to reduce the vocabulary burden, these poems are mainly taken from a restricted range of topics (the moon, separation in springtime, Buddhist temples, reclusion and flower-symbolism). Only the printed form of the characters is used in the second part since by then you should be able to transcribe from printed to written form without too much difficulty.

In both parts, lines and couplets, and occasionally whole poems, are quoted to illustrate features of language and imagery; in these examples four aids are provided *in situ:* romanization, vocabulary not included in the vocabulary index, grammatical analysis, and translations. This should enable linguists to use the material for comparative purposes without having to study the Chinese script. The main vocabularies include information about the radical number and the number of extra strokes for each character to facilitate the use of dictionaries arranged by this system.

Transcription (*pinyin*)

Where modern dictionaries of Chinese disagree over pronunciation I have elected to follow 現代漢語詞典, 香港, 1977, which is arranged in *pinyin* alphabetical order. The words in question are these (pronunciations in older dictionaries are given in parentheses):

壑 *hè* (*huò*) 寂 *jì* (*jí*) 期 *qī* (*qí*) 雖 *suī* (*suí*) 危 *wēi* (*wéi*) 微 *wēi* (*wéi*) 息 昔 *xī* (*xí*) 夕 *xī* (*xì*) 暫 *zàn* (*zhàn*)

I have used modern pronunciations of the following words where some transcribers use the 'classical' alternatives given in parentheses:

白 *bái* (*bó*) 百 *bǎi* (*bó*) 柏 *bǎi* (*bó*) 薄 ('thin', not 'approach') *báo* (*bó*) 比 ('next to') *bǐ* (*bì*) 車 *chē* (*jū*) 浮 *fú* (*fóu*) 黑 *hēi* (*hè*) 六 *liù* (*lù*) 綠 *lyù* (*lù*) 他 *tā* (*tuō*) 我 *wǒ* (*ě*).

Tang poets sometimes used alternative tones in certain words. I give the modern standard form in parentheses. I shall use the standard tone except where the rhyme or tonal pattern indicates the alternative:

場 *cháng* (*chǎng*) 過 *guō* (*guò*) 教 *jiāo* (*jiào*) 看 *kān* (*kàn*) 思 (noun) *sì* (*sī*) 聽 *tìng* (*tīng*) 忘 *wáng* (*wàng*)

Quite a large number of characters represent differently-pronounced words with different (but sometimes related) meanings, e.g.

宿 *sù* 'spend the night', *xiù* 'constellation'; 惡 *è* 'evil', *wù* 'hate'; 爲 *wéi* 'be, do', *wèi* 'for'; 重 *chóng* 'double', *zhòng* 'heavy; again'; 曲 *qū* 'bend', *qǔ* 'song'; 將 *jiāng* 'take, and', *jiàng* 'a general, to lead'.

For the names of dynasties I shall use not *pinyin* but the traditional English forms:

秦 'Chin', 晉 'Tsin', 宋 'Sung'.

The 'straight quote' (') is used as a syllable-separator, for example in 'Chang'e' and 'Xi'an'.

Tone-marks are omitted from personal and geographical names used outside transcribed texts.

For readers unfamiliar with *pinyin* here is a very rough guide to its pronunciation in terms of English sounds. Consonants: *c = ts*, *q = ch*, *x=sh*, *z = dz*, *zh = j*; the other consonants as in English. Vowels and diphthongs: *a* in *ian* or *yan* = *e* in *men*, otherwise = *a* in *father*; *e* after consonant = *e* in *father*, otherwise = *e* in *men*; *i* after *c/s/z* = *z*, after *ch/r/sh/zh* = *r*, otherwise = *ee* in *meet*; *ou* = *oh*, otherwise *o* = *aw*; *ü* after *l* or *n* (simplified to *u* after *j/q/x/y*) = French *u* or German *ü*, otherwise *u* = *oo*. The accents represent the tones, i.e. the musical movements up and down of the voice. All this is valid only for modern standard Chinese, not of course for the original pronunciation of traditional verse.

Grammar

This is a brief outline of my approach to the grammar of Chinese verse.

Grammar is about two things: word-classes (parts of speech) and the relationships between them. The more familiar languages of Eurasia indicate these to a greater or lesser degree, either together or separately, by the following devices:

(a) variations in the form of words, principally by the addition of prefixes such as the Russian perfective prefix *po-*, infixes such as the Latin inchoative infix *-esc-*, suffixes such as the English participial suffix *-ing*, and ablauts such as those of the English *sing, sang, sung, song* type;

(b) the use of separate words as markers of structures, such as the English 'if' to mark the beginning of a conditional clause, or 'the most … in the …' to mark the first space (slot) as containing an adjective and probably a following noun as well;

(c) word-order, e.g. 'John saw Bill' versus 'Bill saw John'.

The first of these is used not at all in Chinese (except that occasionally the choice of tone imposed by the tonal pattern of a poem may reveal that the word in question is a noun or a verb); overt markers are used to some extent in prose but not a great deal in verse; this leaves word-order as almost the only grammatical device available to us. But since word-classes are not marked, word-order cannot be discussed in terms of marked word-classes but only in terms of semantic classes. But even here there is little joy for the grammarian, for even if he decides to base his grammar on semantic classes he will still find that rules of word-order elude him; for example, the concept of 'returning to the woods' will now appear as 歸 林 *guī lín*, with the action before the destination, now as 林歸 *lín guī*, with the destination preceding the action. It helps little to be told that the former is the normal prose and verse order, and the latter an inversion used only in verse.

I have a suspicion that the wealth of grammatical clues under (a) to (c) above in the highly redundant languages that cover most of the globe outside China and mainland South-east Asia may sometimes blind us to the degree to which we rely on non-grammatical indicators to guide us through a sentence. One of the potential benefits of studying the language of Chinese classical verse is to make us vividly aware of how little we actually rely, or need to rely, on grammar for understanding language. Here we have a language that has long been characterised as 'without grammar' or '*supra grammaticam*' in the first two senses given above, yet one that has been in continuous literary use for at least three thousand years, hence basically comprehensible. The disagreements of Chinese commentators and the sometimes radically different translations of classical Chinese verse made into modern Chinese and other languages do not detract from the likelihood that the meaning of an ancient or medieval poem was perfectly clear to the poet's educated contemporaries.

I cannot help feeling that any attempt to impose a Western-style grammatical analysis upon Chinese verse can in fact be little more than a retrospective rationalization of something that has been first grasped intuitively by the analyst; in other words we usually decide that such-and-such a phrase is adjectival rather than adverbial only on the basis of how we have understood it using non-grammatical criteria.

This will not deter me from offering grammatical analyses throughout this course as an aid to making the transition from English to the very different language of traditional Chinese verse. A list of the symbols used for this purpose is to be found immediately before Unit 1, though each symbol will be explained and exemplified on its first occurrence.

Dates of authors

The precise dates of birth and death of the majority of Chinese poets are uncertain or unknown. For these, approximate or doubtful dates are usually given by writers on Chinese poetry, with considerable disagreement. In the minority of cases where there seems to be general agreement with no 'c.' or '?' I give the precise dates; otherwise I indicate only the century or part of a century ('early' and 'late' meaning mainly the first or second half respectively), particularly since this work is concerned not with biography but with linguistic features that in the main are valid for the whole imperial period.

THE CHINESE SCRIPT

This section has been included for readers with no knowledge of the Chinese script; it is hoped that it will be of some assistance in acquiring at least a passive (reading) knowledge of the characters.

1. The nature of the Chinese script

The fundamental unit of the Chinese script, at least for the 3,000-odd years since the earliest surviving records, has always been the 'character' representing a one-syllable word.

A word is a combination of sound and meaning, unlike a logo, which represents only meaning. Words are part of language, and writing is the representation of language; a logo is not a representation of language since it has no unique sound-value. It follows that the Chinese script, like all writing-systems, represents a combination of sound and meaning.

The world's earliest known script was Sumerian, used in Mesopotamia around 3000 BC. The earliest known Chinese script uses the same principles as the Sumerian (sound-elements plus discriminatory meaning-elements) but its earliest surviving inscriptions date from around 1300 BC, by which time the Near-Eastern scripts descended from the Sumerian had progressed to the alphabetic stage (North Semitic 1700–1500 BC). Even today, the Chinese script is structurally still at the stage that Sumerian had reached 5,000 years ago. The shapes of the signs have changed but the three basic principles have not.

The first principle is that a sign can represent a word, i.e. a sound with a meaning, e.g. a picture of a dog can represent the word for 'dog' in the local language. But this device does not get us very far, for very few words in any language can easily be represented by a picture: try writing this sentence in pictures if you have any doubt about this! So a writing-system, a representation of language, cannot be made using this device alone. Writing cannot come into existence until the phonetic principle is invented.

The second principle is that a word-sign can be used not just for its sound-plus-meaning but also for its sound alone, i.e. to write other similar-sounding words. This is the rebus-principle sometimes used to represent names in coats of arms and book-plates. This principle gives us, in the case of monosyllabic Chinese, a syllabary, where each sign represents a whole syllable, not just a phoneme as in the case of an alphabet. The key word here is 'similar', for the syllabic sign will represent not just the sound of the original word-sign but also that of any vaguely similar-sounding word. This by itself will naturally lead to a great amount of ambiguity.

The third principle is an attempt to remove this ambiguity by adding distinguishing signs. These are chosen for their class of meaning. The resultant combination will mean 'the word that sounds a bit like A and means something to do with B'. But this is only a kind of mnemonic: the whole character still has to be learned as meaning 'the word that has the precise sound X and the precise meaning Y'. But this principle was not used systematically: sometimes a meaning-element was added, sometimes not; sometimes a whole character was used to write a new word either as it was or else with the addition of a new meaning-element, but without removing the old meaning-element.

In order to demonstrate and discuss these three principles I shall use the following abbreviations:

'W' stands for 'word-sign', a sign having its original sound and meaning;

'S' stands for 'sound-element', a sign used purely for its sound-value;

'M' stands for 'meaning-element', a sign added to indicate the class of meaning;

'*' before a meaning indicates that it is unattested, i.e. that the sign has not been found with this meaning in any text and that this meaning has been deduced from what the sign seems to depict and/or from its sound-value;

'<' means 'developed from' and '>' means 'developed into';

'OB' means 'oracle-bone script' (c. 1300–1000 BC);

indented items are extended uses or developments of the head-item.

In principle, any primary sign can be used in any of these three ways, but in actual practice the largest number are used as an S, usually with the addition of an M, and only a minority of characters are used as a W or M.

Before illustrating the way these principles were applied to the Chinese script I should like to invite you to imagine the problems confronting the script-devisers in the ancient world, whether in the Near East or in the Far East. They were officials in city-states that needed to keep records of stores (food, weapons, tools, etc.), of land-tenancy and taxation (a city-state was dependent on rents and taxes from the surrounding cultivated countryside), of employees, etc. Their city's wealth attracted the envy of neighbours, especially the nomadic herdsmen from beyond the cultivated area, so they needed to keep in contact with their armies on the borders. These were but a few of the record-keeping and message-writing requirements of a city-state.

Where do they begin? Let us see what would have happened if their language had been English and they had needed to record that a tenant farmer, a Mr Arthur Jones, had been assessed for 85 bushels of grain in land-tax. This will require as a minimum 'Arthur Jones 85'. Since there is no obvious pictorial representation available either for the name or for the number (apart from 85 strokes!) their only solution will be to find something depictable that will sound something like them. What depictable object can they find that sounds vaguely like 'Arthur'? A drawing of a hearth might do, though that might also be taken as a depiction of a grate and so representing a name sounding something like 'grate', e.g. 'Graham'. For 'Jones' the best I can come up with is a picture of a pair of longjohns , though that might equally suggest 'Long' or 'Johnson'. For the sound of 'eight' we might find nothing closer than a picture of a gate or even of a hat, and a fife would seem to be the closest phonetic depiction we could find for 'five'. The latter two, being numerals, would be in constant use, so would quickly become abbreviated for ease of writing.

The sad fact is that phonetic distance is essential for any language: communication would become very difficult if too many words sounded alike or very similar. This means that finding similar-sounding words is already a difficult task, one which is made even more difficult if one is looking for a word which both sounds similar and also stands for a simply and unambiguously depictable object or activity. The rebus-method is a very unpromising start for a script.

It is only against this background that one can truly appreciate the enormous leap represented by the invention of the alphabet in the ancient Near East: the Semitic unvowelled alphabet and the Greek vowelled alphabet. Suddenly any word that can be distinguished in speech can be written down unambiguously. The Chinese have been aware of the existence of Indian alphabets for two thousand years but have never switched to alphabetic writing. This is not the place to go into the reasons for this conservatism since we are concerned here only with the structure of the traditional Chinese script.

Now, since our imaginary English-speaking bronze-age scribes never have occasion to write about hearths, longjohns, gates (or hats) or fifes in their official records and correspondence, there will be no possibility of ambiguity: the picture of a hearth no longer means 'hearth', but only 'Arthur', and similarly with the other signs. When their distant descendants begin writing down their oral literature and wish to write the word for 'hearth', they will have to add the sign for 'fire' to distinguish it from 'Arthur'.This is the kind of problem all early script-makers must have had. Now let us see what traces of this process survive in the Chinese script. In the following, the ancient characters preceded by '<' are oracle-bone script unless otherwise stated.

(a) Word-signs

Let us begin with some characters used as W:

人 < 𣎿 *rén* 'person'

木 < 𣎿 *mù* 'tree'

林 < 𣎿𣎿 *lín* 'a wood, forest'

鳥 < 🦅 *niǎo* 'bird'

日 < ⊟ < ⊙ *rì* 'sun, day'

月 < 𝄞 < 🌙 *yuè* 'moon, month' (90° rotation to the left)

山 < 𝄞 < 𝄞 *shān* 'hill, mountain' (90° rotation to the left)

水 < ⅋ *shuǐ* 'water, river' (a winding river with splashes of water)

雨 < ⻗ *yǔ* 'rain' (rain falling from the ⁼ sky)

竹 < 𝄞𝄞 *zhú* 'bamboo' (bamboo leaves hanging down: not OB but a later form)

The shapes of these characters have changed a great deal in the past 3,000 years and so of course have their sounds, but their original meanings have remained intact and they have not been used for other purposes as words, but only (in some cases) to write foreign names (e.g. 山 *shān* was once used to write the third syllable of 'Alexandria' and 林 *lín* is used to write the first syllable of 'Lincoln').

(b) Word-signs doubling as sound-elements

Some primary signs were used both as W and as S, though not necessarily in that order (see **(g)** below):

W 云 *yún* 'cloud' (< 𝄞 a cloud hanging from the ⁼ sky)
    S 云 *yún* 'say'

W 耳 *ěr* 'ear' (< 𝄞)
    S 耳 *ěr* 'only'

W 烏 *wū* 'crow' (a bird without an eye: the crow's dark eye does not show up against its black plumage)
    S 烏 *wū* 'how?'

W 女 *nǚ* 'woman' (< 𝄞 a woman kneeling with arms crossed to cradle baby)
    S 女 *rǔ* 'you'

W 且 *zǔ* 'male ancestor' (< 𝄞 phallus)
    S 且 *qiě* 'also'

W 然 *rán* 'burn' (does not occur in OB: consists of 'flesh', 'dog' and 'fire')

S 然 *rán* 'thus'

(c) Meaning-elements

The signs used as M run into several hundreds. They largely overlap with the 214 'radicals' used to classify characters in traditional dictionaries (see the 'Table of radicals' at the very end of this introduction to the script). These meaning-elements may occur anywhere in a character, but especially on the left (e.g. 舟 in 船, 木 in 杜, 人 in 住). Some occur mainly or exclusively on the right (e.g. 鳥 in 鴻, 力 in 動) or on top (e.g. ⺾ in 草) or underneath (e.g. 皿 in 盅), even split between left and right (e.g. 行 in 衙) or between top and bottom (e.g. 衣 in 裏).

Their class-indication is sometimes very vague, e.g. 木 'tree' may indicate a kind of tree or something made of wood; 氵 'water' may indicate a body of water, or actions performed by or with water, or qualities associated with water; 心 or 忄 'heart' is used to mark all kinds of mental activities and emotional states.

(d) Sound-plus-meaning combinations

These form the bulk of the Chinese character-set. One S may be used to write a large number of different words, which may or may not be distinguished by the addition of Ms.

W 皮 *pí* 'skin' (< 𐅀 later than OB, depiction unknown, but seems to be seated figure with mouth open upwards as in 𐅀 (> 祝 *zhù* 'pray'), with a hand added)

S 皮 + M 氵 'water' > 波 *bō* 'wave'

W 爿 *chuáng* 'bed' (< 𐅀 the original picture rotated 90° to the right)

S 爿 + M 士 'knight' > 壯 *zhuàng* 'strong, heroic'

W 介 *jiè* 'armour' (< 𐅀 man with armour around him)

S 介 + M 田 'field' > 界 *jiè* 'boundary'

W 古 *gǔ* 'ancient' (< 𐅀 unknown depiction)

S 古 + M ⺾ 'grass, herb' > 苦 *kǔ* 'bitter'

(e) Irrelevance of meaning-elements

Do not expect the M in an 'S+M' combination always to indicate the current area of meaning, because the whole character may subsequently have been used as an S to write an unrelated word.

W 勺 *sháo* 'ladle' (no OB form but depiction is clear)

　　　S 勺 + M 白 'white' > 的 *dí* 'target' (with white bull's-eye)

　　　S 的 *dí* 'indeed' ('white' now irrelevant)

W 女 *nǔ* 'woman' (< 𡥩)

　　　S 女 + M 氵 'water' > 汝 *rǔ* 'River Ru'

　　　S 汝 *rǔ* 'you' ('water' now irrelevant)

W 隹 *zhuī* 'kind of bird' (< 𥋇)

　　　S 隹 + M 忄 'heart' > 惟 *wéi* 'think'

　　　S 惟 *wéi* 'only' ('heart' now irrelevant)

(f) Accumulation of elements.

The processes of phonetic loan (using a character as S) and determination (adding M) may be repeated a number of times, leading to an accumulation of irrelevant Ms, so that a character may have been built up as S+M+M+M, where only the last M is relevant to the current meaning; but of course even the last one may be irrelevant to the current usage, as we saw under (e).

W 欠 *qiàn* 'yawn' (< 𣣦 　kneeling figure gaping)

　　　S 欠 + M 二 'two' > 次 *cì* 'second, next'

　　　S 次 + M 艹 'grass' > 茨 *cí* 'thatch' ('two' now irrelevant)

W 生 *shēng* 'grow' (< 屮 　plant growing out of ground)

　　　S 生 + M 目 'eye' > 相 *xiàng* 'observe'

　　　S 相 + M 雨 'rain' > 霜 *shuāng* 'hoarfrost' ('eye' now irrelevant)

W 鳥 *niǎo* (< *diǎo*) 'bird' (< 𪈈)

　　　S 鳥 + M 山 'hill' > 島 *dǎo* 'island'

　　　S 島 + M 扌 'hand' > 搗 *dǎo* 'beat' ('hill' now irrelevant)

W 工 *gōng* 'artisan' (< 工　unknown depiction)

　　　S 工 + M 氵 'water' > 江 *jiāng* 'river'

　　　S 江 + M 鳥 'bird' > 鴻 *hóng* 'swan-goose' ('water' now irrelevant)

W 古 *gǔ* 'ancient' (< 𠖾 unknown depiction)

　　　S 古 + M 肉 'flesh' > 胡 *hú* 'dewlap'

　　　S 胡 + M 氵 'water' > 湖 *hú* 'lake' ('flesh' now irrelevant)

(g) Possible primary sound-elements

Some signs have perhaps only ever been used as S, never as W. In the examples that follow, this doubt is indicated by the '?W' and the asterisk.

First, some characters whose conjectured original meaning is not found in texts but which occur as S with the addition of M in later spellings of the original word:

?W 西 *qī 'to nest' (< 甶 a bird's nest, seen also on a tree in 巢 cháo 'a nest')

    S 西 xī 'west'

    S 西 + M 木 'tree' > 栖 qī 'to nest'

?W 七 *qiē 'cut' (< 十 a vertical stick cut by a horizontal line)

    S 七 qī 'seven'

    S 七 + M 刀 'knife' > 切 qiē 'cut'

?W 樂 *lì 'oak' (< 𤴡 a tree surmounted by twists of silk thread (the wild silkworm (*Antherea pernyi*) lives on oak-leaves); later with the addition of 𝛉 an acorn)

    S 樂 lè 'joy'

    S 樂 + M 木 'tree' > 櫟 lì 'oak'

?W 永 *yǒng 'swim' (< 𣲘 a person enclosed in water)

    S 永 yǒng 'always'

    S 永 + M 氵 'water' > 泳 yǒng 'swim'

?W 又 *yòu 'right hand' (< 𠂇 a right hand)

    S 又 yòu 'again'

    S 又 + M 口 'mouth' > 右 yòu 'right hand'

The above examples take two stages to come full circle, but this process may involve three stages, with or without M being used at each stage:

?W 亦 *yè 'armpits' (< 夵 a person with a mark under each arm)

    S 亦 yì 'also'

    S 亦 + M 夕 'night' > 夜 yè 'night'

    S 夜 + M 肉 'flesh' > 腋 yè 'armpits'

?W 丁 *chéng 'city' (< ☐ outline of a square walled city)

    S 丁 dīng '4th day of decade'

    S 丁 + M 戊 'military' > 成 chéng 'victory'

    S 成 + M 土 'earth' > 城 chéng 'city'

?W 十 *zhī 'twig' (< | a stick)
    S 十 shí 'ten'
    S 十 + M 又 'right hand' > 支 zhī 'support'
    S 支 + M 木 'tree' > 枝 zhī 'twig'

?W 凵 *kū 'pit, hole' (< 凵 still pictorial!)
    S 凵 + M 止 'foot' > 出 chū 'go out'
    S 出 + M 尸 'sit still' > 屈 qū 'bend over'
    S 屈 + M 穴 'hole' > 窟 kū 'hole'

?W 戊 *wǔ 'military' (< 戈 a hand holding a kind of halberd)
    S 戊 wù '5th day of decade'
    S 戊 + M 止 'foot' > 武 wǔ 'big toe'
    S 武 wǔ 'military'

?W 來 *mài 'wheat' (< 𣏟 a plant with ears of wheat hanging down)
    S 來 lái 'come'
    S 來 + 夊 'arrive' > 麥 *lái 'come'
    S 麥 mài 'wheat'

Sometimes the process is halted and begun again with a different S:

?W 自 bí 'nose' (< 𦣻 a nose with a mysterious triangle across it)
    S 自 zì 'from'
    Replacement:
    W 畀 bì 'give' + M 自 'nose' > 鼻 bí 'nose'

?W 余 *chú 'hoe' (< 𠃌 a hoe held by a hand, later replaced by 木 'wood')
    S 余 yú 'I'
    Replacement:
    W 且 zǔ 'male ancestor' + M 力 'strength' > 助 zhù 'help'
    S 助 + M 金 'metal' > 鋤 chú 'hoe'

It is not known whether these '?W' signs were ever actually used as W or whether they were only used as S from the very beginning: 'armpits' at least is unlikely to have been a basic vocabulary-item in early administrative records!

(h) Word-families

These include words of two kinds:
    (1) extended meanings of the same word, e.g. 'spring' (jump, arise), 'spring' (season when plants rise) and 'spring' (water rising out of the ground); or 'fall' (descend) and 'fall' (autumn, when leaves fall);

(2) words which share a common root, e.g. 'fall' and 'fell' (a tree); or 'breath' and 'breathe'; or 'sit', 'seat', (bishop's) 'see', 'siege', 'session' and 'sedentary'.

Words with identical or similar sounds may belong to the same word-family or else the similarity may be coincidental or arise from a prehistoric kinship that can only be a matter of conjecture. Chinese characters sharing a sound-element may represent either related or unrelated words in the underlying language. In a minority of cases the choice of the same S may indicate an awareness (or presumption) of kinship on the part of the script-makers. Let us look briefly at one S which has been used to write both related and unrelated words.

?W 才 *cái 'cut timber' (< 丫 the top of a tree cut by a horizontal line)

W 才 + M 木 'wood' > 材 cái 'timber'

W 才 + M 戈 'halberd' > 㦮 zāi 'to wound'

W 㦮 + M 衣 'clothes' > 裁 cái 'cut out garments from cloth'

The 'W' above indicates that these characters are used to write extensions of the same word meaning 'cut'; in the following examples the 'S' indicates words that are apparently unrelated:

S 才 + M 土 'earth' > 在 zài 'be at'

S 才 + M 川 'river' > 巛 zāi 'flood disaster'

S 㦮 + M 口 'mouth' > 哉 zāi 'indeed!' (exclamatory final particle).

(i) Notes on the above

The above examples illustrating the principles underlying the structure of the Chinese script may give the impression that the history of any character can be fully explained, but this is far from the truth. All that can be said of the majority of characters is that the meaning of the latest M is usually explainable, whereas the S is of uncertain or unknown origin. Most of the characters in the oracle-bone script are of unknown depiction or structure, though a great deal of guesswork has gone into trying to interpret the inscriptions. My own feeling is that what we see in this earliest known form of the Chinese script is the end-product of a long period of development involving simplification and corruption, and that little further light can be shed upon it without the discovery of much older documents either in the Yellow River valley or perhaps in the south of China, from which agriculture and perhaps also civilisation spread northwards in prehistoric times. Only further archaeological discoveries can tell us more about this.

The figures given in the vocabularies represent the radical number of the character followed by the number of extra strokes, e.g. '72.5' means 'consisting of radical 72 (日) with five additional strokes'. This will enable you to find the character in the index of any traditional dictionary using this system, e.g. *Mathews*; but be warned: some more recent dictionaries have their own classification systems to match the 'simplified' reformed script.

   These figures are followed in the vocabularies by an indication of the etymological type of the character, viz. 'W', 'S', 'M' or 'X', where 'M' means 'S+M' followed by the actual M, and where 'X' means 'of unknown or uncertain structure'. Of the first 400 characters in the vocabularies of this course 14% are W, 13% are S without the addition of M, 58% are S+M, and 15% are X.

2. Variants of script-elements

A few script-elements take variant forms in different positions within the character but are treated as identical for the purpose of radical-classification in dictionaries. In the groups of characters given below the first character is the isolated form occurring as a complete character; the second is the form occurring (usually as M) in the position indicated; and the third is an example of the use of the second in a character. The 'R' stands for 'radical number'.

(a) On the left

R. 9, *rén* 'person' 人 亻 估   R. 61, *xīn* 'heart' 心 忄 忙

R. 64, *shǒu* 'hand' 手 扌 扣   R. 85, *shuǐ* 'water' 水 氵 江

R. 94, *quǎn* 'dog' 犬 犭 狂   R. 96, *yù* 'jade' 玉 王 珀

R. 113, *shì* 'revelation' 示 礻 祝   R. 130, *ròu* 'flesh' 肉 月 肝

R. 145, *yī* 'clothes' 衣 衤 袒   R. 170, *fù* 'hills' 阜 阝 阻

(b) On the right

R. 18, *dāo* 'knife' 刀 刂 別   R. 163, *yì* 'city' 邑 阝 郢

(c) Separated on left and right

R. 144, *xíng* 'travel' 行 彳 and 亍 衙

(d) On the top

R. 87, *zhǎo* 'claw' 爪 爫 爭

R. 118, *zhú* 'bamboo' 竹 ⺮ 竿

R. 122, *wǎng* 'net' 网 罒 罟

R. 140, *cǎo* 'grass' 艸 艹 苜

R. 173, *yǔ* 'rain' 雨 ⻗ 雲

(e) On the bottom

R. 86, *huǒ* 'fire' 火 灬 烈

R. 130, *ròu* 'flesh' 肉 ⺼ 背

(f) On the bottom beneath 𠆢

R. 61, *xīn* 'heart' 心 ⺗ 忝

R. 85, *shuǐ* 'water' 水 氺 泰

(g) Separated on top and bottom

R. 145, *yī* 'clothes' 衣 亠 and 𧘇 衷

(h) Notes

Distinguish 礻（示）from 衤（衣）.

As a left-hand element 月 may be 月 *yuè* 'moon' or (more often) 肉 *ròu* 'flesh'.

阝 on the left is R. 170 阜 *fù* 'hills' and on the right is R. 163 邑 *yì* 'city'.

As a top or bottom element 曰 may either be R. 73 曰 *yuē* 'say' or (more often) R. 72 日 *rì* 'sun'.

3. Written stroke forms

Whereas the font used in the greater part of this book is a normal printed style, the font used in this section and the following two is *kaishu*, based on brush-written characters. I have chosen this in case you wish to write Chinese characters as part of this course, in addition to reading them. The printed form is normally never used in writing. One of the most noticeable differences is that a printed square, □, is written as three strokes: 口, the left-hand side as one stroke, the top and the right-hand side together as one stroke, and finally the bottom. In the vocabularies of part one (Units 1–15) you will be able to compare the written and printed forms; here are some points to look out for:

(a) the printed form does its best to fill a square, whereas the written form is much freer in this respect;

(b) the printed horizontal strokes are truly horizontal, whereas the written horizontals are tilted slightly upwards from left to right;

(c) the printed verticals are noticeably thicker than the horizontals, whereas the written form makes no such distinction;

(d) some elements are quite different in the two styles, e.g. (printed form first) the lefthand side of 情 情, the top of 草 草, the lefthand side of 遠 遠, and the top of 曾 曾.

The basic element of Chinese writing is the stroke, a straight, curved or bent line with or without a final hook. In the writing of a stroke the pen does not leave the paper.

(a) There are five initial directions:

(1) → = horizontal from left to right;

(2) ↗ = slightly upward from left to right;

(3) ↓ = vertical from top to bottom;

(4) ↙ = left-oblique, i.e. simultaneously leftward and downward;

(5) ↘ = right-oblique, i.e. simultaneously rightward and downward.

(b) Excluding final hooks, a continuous stroke may have zero, one, two or three corners (changes of direction of 90° or more).

(c) A final hook (>) is clockwise on a straight stroke but is placed on the inside of a curved stroke or corner.

Strokes are modified in shape, size and direction to fit in with the overall composition of a character, so the following list cannot be complete in terms of such detail. You will notice that because of this my categories shade into one another. They are not meant to be watertight classes, merely a rough guide to get you initially familiar with the kind of shapes you will be dealing with.

Each of the stroke-types below is illustrated with one or more examples to show you how they are combined with other strokes and modified in the process. If you are using a Chinese brush or Japanese brush-pen you will be able to match the varying thicknesses but if you are using a pen or pencil this refinement will not of course be possible, nor is it necessary for legibility. Do not attempt to write the characters in this section until you have studied stroke-order in the next section, otherwise you may develop bad writing-habits.

(a) Horizontal

(1) 一　　　二 三 土 十 門 事 干 壽 佳

(2) 一 疋 皮 宀 冘 冥 尤 宀 宮

(3) ノ　　　又 久 夕 各 癸 五 令 互 丑 甬

Note that the end of this stroke tapers and curves when free (except

for 今), but is straight when blocked at a T-junction.

(4) 亅　　　司 冂 巾 月 永 卩

Note that the hook is omitted when blocked by a T-junction: 且 .

(5) 𠃌　　　刀 力 勹 勿 母

(6) 乀　　　气 虱 𠃌 飛

(7) 乚　　　几 凡 九

(8) 乙 乞

(9) 𠃌　　　𠬛 及 辶 (printed form 辶)

(10) 𠃌　　　乃

(b) Upward

(11) 一　　　七 斗

(12) ╱　　　孑 氵 扎 功 坡 珏

Note that bottom or intersecting horizontals in left-hand elements are often

tilted up in anticipation of the right-hand element.

(13). ㇆　　　水

(14) ㇀　　　也

(c) Vertical

(15) 丨　　　川 十 中 丫 土 半

(16) 丿　　　川 井 月 厂 儿 判 升 介 户

(17) 亅　　　事 于 寸 刂 小 乎 手

(18) ㇄　　　七

(19) ㇄ ㇖　　　凵 山 出 凶 匚 巨

(20) ㇄　　　以 民 改 卯 衣 比 叫

(21) ㇄　　　扎 匕 己 毛 兆 心

(22) ㇆　　　丐 焉 与 弓

(d) Leftward

(23) 丿 丶　　　人 八 杉 生 爻 少 必 心

(24) ╱　　　千 禾 采 斤 舌

(25) ㄥ ㇄　　　厶 糸 互 鄉 至 亥 母

(26) 〱 〱　　　巛 女

(27) ㄅ　　　孜 兮 (Not the same as two-stroke ㄅ)

(e) Rightward

(28) 丶 丶   卜 六 刈 益 矩 心 氵 州 然 寒
(29) 乀   人 八 衣 疋 豕
(30) 乚   弋 氐 戈 成
(31) 丿   了 子 狗 豕

4. Stroke- and element-order

If you intend to learn to write Chinese characters it is a sensible idea to write the strokes in the standard order from the very beginning. This will make the writing of a character a mechanical habit that will leave your attention free for other things. On the whole all Chinese write the strokes in the same order, though there are variations in some cases.

Fortunately the stroke-order of the majority of character-elements can be reduced to a few simple rules.

(1) 'Left before right'

The order of the three strokes of the element 川 is left-to-right. This rule applies however complex the elements, e.g. in the character 擲 the three elements 扌 奠 阝 are written in left-to-right order. 'Left before right' also applies to the individual strokes of 心 and 必 (丶 乚 丶 丿 丶). A major exception to this rule is the order of strokes in elements of the 厂 type, which is top-before-left; other elements of this type are 广 尸 户 虍 疒 (in this last element the two dots on the left follow the 广).

(2) 'Top before bottom'

The order of the three strokes of 三 is top-to-bottom, and in 蒽 the three elements 艹 田 心 are written in top-to-bottom order.

(3) 'Major division first'

This principle applies when three or more separate elements are not arranged in a straight line. A major division is a real or potential gap extending right across a character from left to right or from top to bottom. For instance, in the character 盟 there are three elements 日 月 皿 arranged as ⊞ but only one major division, viz. the horizontal one between 明 and 皿. The vertical division between 日 and 月 is blocked by the 皿, so it is not a major division. So the overall rule is 'top before bottom', i.e. 明 before 皿 across the major division. The 明, of course, is 'left before right' across the minor division, so the order for the whole character is 日 月 皿. The order of the character 萌 (⊞) will be 艹 日 月, and that of 昭 (⊞) will be 日 刀 口 (vertical major division).

(4) 'Arch before contents'

The 'arch' 冂 consists of two strokes, 丨 and 乛 in that order, like a Roman 'n', and the 'contents' are anything beneath the arch. Here the rule of 'top before bottom' applies, with the arch being treated as a top element. This means that 口 , 日 and 目 consist of an arch above 一, 二 and 三 respectively. The rule is applied twice to 回, which is written 冂 冂 一 一. In Chinese schools the arch-rule is illustrated with the character 囚, meaning 'prisoner': first you build your prison 冂, then you put your prisoner 人 inside, and finally you shut the door 一. Examples of other arches: 門 向. The arch-principle applies also to partial arches, e.g. 句 司 式 寸 厄 庇 尼 病.

(5) 'Contents before pit'

Just as the top and right side of the arch form one continuous stroke, so do the left side and bottom of the 'pit': 凵 consists of the two strokes 乚 and

丨 and resembles the Roman 'u'. Here the contents precede the pit according to the top-before-bottom rule, e.g. in 山 the central 丨 comes before the 凵. A bottom left-hand corner element is usually treated as bottom, not left, i.e. as a partial pit, e.g. 辶 in 過, 又 in 建 etc. This applies also to 止 (卜 丨 一), 匕 (丿 乚) and 也 (乛 丨 乚).

(6) 'Horizontal before vertical'

This applies only to intersecting lines, i.e. crossroads, not T-junctions, so that in 十 the 一 is written before the 丨. The rule applies however many lines are involved: 井 is 二 丿 丨, and in 事 the 亅 comes last of all. But an upward-tilted horizontal stroke crossing a left-hand vertical element is written *after* the vertical, e.g. in 扣孤.

(7) 'Left-oblique (丿) before intersecting right-oblique (丶)'

Examples: 爻 父 文 交 又 (丿 丶 two strokes). When the strokes are separate the normal rules of 'left before right' and 'top before bottom' apply, e.g. 丫 平 冫 氵. An exception to this rule and also to the previous one is 女 (く 丿 一). The same applies to the related character 母 (乚 𠃌 一 丶 丶).

(8) 'A T-junction has a gap'

As mentioned under (4) above, if a line merely touches another line but does not cross it, there is always a theoretical gap between them that can allow a division to pass beween them. In other words, 丁 consists of two strokes, 一 and 亅, separated by a notional gap (丁), so that the 'top before bottom' rule applies since we are dealing with the arrangement ☐. Similarly

with 天, where the top 一 precedes the bottom 大 ; this in turn involves
an intersection, so the middle horizontal 一 precedes the 'vertical' element
人 ,which follows the 'left before right' rule (✓ before ↘). More examples
of T-junctions: 土 王 山 出 . This last character is like the first of the
four except that the two horizontals are replaced by pits, five strokes in all.

(9) 'Arms before body before legs'

By 'arms' I mean symmetrical elements on either side of a vertical near the
top, and by 'legs' I mean the same feature near the bottom. An example is
坐, consisting of the 'arms' 人 人, followed by the 'body' 土 .
Another is 木, consisting of a 'body' 十 followed by the 'legs' 丿
乀 . The character 米 has both arms and legs. The element 火 can either
follow this rule or else the 'left before right' rule (丶 丿 ✓ 乀).
'Limbs' in central position are usually treated as 'legs', e.g. 小 水 (亅
𠃌 丿 乀), but 忄 is usually treated as 'arms before body' ('
丶 丨). In most cases of a 'double body' the order is 'left body, left limbs,
right body, right limbs': 非 (丿 三 丨 三), 兆 . But the 'limbs' of
亦 are treated as 'legs' added after the double 'body'.

(10) 'Top right-hand dot comes last'

Examples: 犬 弋 戈 甫 .

5. Shape-modification

Although quite a few elements are basically symmetrical, absolute symmetry is
avoided in calligraphy. This is done by various means. One is a natural product
of the Chinese writing-brush: the brush is normally held in the right hand (left-
handed calligraphers are rare), so that when the tip of the brush is applied to
the paper it produces a 'dot' 丶 , which is actually a very short ↘ -stroke,
the opposite slope from an Italic nib. The effect of this bias may be seen in the

two originally symmetrical strokes of 八 or those of 乂. But most asymmetry is deliberate, for the purpose of injecting life into what would otherwise be flat and dull. Simple examples of this are 三 and 川, where originally identical strokes have been modified to give the main weight to the final stroke and the least weight to the middle stroke. For more complex examples compare the following to see what happens to the size and shape of some elements in composition: 日 昌　火 炎　立 章 口 中 喉　魚 鲁. One very common example of artificial asymmetry that we have seen above is the writing of a square with three strokes, so that top and bottom are not identical, nor are the left and right sides.

In most characters there will be a noticeable difference in size as between left and right constituents or between top and bottom constituents. This is largely a natural consequence of the fact that the last-added M will be simple whereas the S will often be compounded of two or more elements. Most Ms are added on the left, so usually the left side is narrower than the right, e.g. 儒.

Other examples of asymmetry are writing the element 口 above the centre on the left-hand side, e.g. 呱, and the writing of the element 阝 low down on the right-hand side, e.g. 邱.

It is important to integrate the parts of a character into a harmonious whole. Apart from ensuring inequality of the kind we have just seen, mirroring the inequalities of Nature with her hierarchies of dominance and subordination, this means ensuring that the parts are internally cohesive. This in turn means two things: spacing and rhythm.

Spacing means (a) ensuring that the physical distances between the elements inside the character are shorter than those between characters, and (b) adjusting the spacing between and within elements to avoid cramping or gaping but introducing enough variety of spacing to avoid monotony.

Rhythm means making the strokes and elements flow into one another in such a way that as the eye follows the movement of the brush one experiences its varying tempos flowing together in a rhythm like the movements of a dance, strong and confident yet elegant. The great sin in Chinese calligraphy is weakness and uncertainty manifested in feeble strokes and characters that fall apart. One of the things that hold a character together is the network of invisible lines where the brush has moved without making contact with the paper. In more rapid styles the ends of these lines may be minutely visible where the brush leaves and rejoins the paper, and in the most rapid styles they may actually appear as thin connecting lines; but, whether they are visible or not, one is aware of these connecting movements between strokes or elements.

Considerations of spacing and rhythm have led to modifications of shape particularly in left-hand elements. Let us look at these one at a time.

(1) Abbreviation to reduce spacing affects final strokes of two kinds, viz. Nos. 21 (乚) and 29 (㇏) above.

(a) 乚 (with or without the hook) is narrowed to No. 20 (亅). Compare the following pairs of characters: 己 改　匕 比　光 輝 鹿 廊　七 切.

(b) ㇏ as the final stroke is shortened to No. 28 (丶): 木 相 禾 秋　矢 矩　夫 規　火 煙　皮 頗. The tops of the following are similarly affected: 金 鋼　舍 舒　余 斜. In the following the same happens and in addition the penultimate stroke (丿) is omitted: 長 髟　食 蝕　良 郎.

(2) The modification under (1a) not only allows closer spacing but also provides a rhythmical connection by pointing upward toward the beginning of the right-hand element. A similar modification occurs with final (bottom or intersecting) horizontal strokes (一 replaced by ㇀): 土 坦　工 功　王 珏　金 鋼　且 助　丘 邱　立 站 里 野　重 動　止 此 and also with the last stroke of 足 跟. Intersecting final horizontals: 子 孤　女 如　牛 牝.

(3) The left-hand modification we saw in 川 has a similar effect to that of the bold No. 29 (㇏) on the right of a character: it gives strength to an otherwise weak structure. We see it also with some other final verticals (丨 replaced by 丿): 羊 翔　半 判.

(4) Some left-hand elements extend their final 乚 or ㇏ beneath the right-hand element. This kind of unifying embrace may have been modelled on that of the elements 廴 and 辶, e.g. in 建 and 過. Examples are: 走 超　鬼 魁　是 題　麥 麵　爪 爬　瓜 瓞.

6. Table of radicals

	0	1	2	3	4	5	6	7	8	9	
0		一	丨	丶	丿	乙	亅	二	亠	人 亻	0
10	儿	入	八	冂	冖	冫	几	凵	刀 刂	力	10
20	勹	匕	匚	匸	十	卜	卩	厂	厶	又	20
30	口	囗	土	士	夂	夊	夕	大	女	子	30
40	宀	寸	小	尢	尸	屮	山	巛	工	己	40
50	巾	干	幺	广	廴	廾	弋	弓	彐	彡	50
60	彳	心 忄	戈	戶	手 扌	支	攴 攵	文	斗	斤	60
70	方	无 旡	日	曰	月	木	欠	止	歹	殳	70
80	毋	比	毛	氏	气	水 氵	火 灬	爪 爫	父	爻	80
90	爿	片	牙	牛	犬 犭	玄	玉 王	瓜	瓦	甘	90
100	生	用	田	疋	疒	癶	白	皮	皿	目	100
110	矛	矢	石	示 礻	禸	禾	穴	立	竹 ⺮	米	110
120	糸	缶	网	羊	羽	老 耂	而	耒	耳	聿	120
130	肉	臣	自	至	臼	舌	舛	舟	艮	色	130
140	艸	虍	虫	血	行	衣 衤	襾	見	角	言	140
150	谷	豆	豕	豸	貝	赤	走	足	身	車	150
160	辛	辰	辵 辶	邑 阝	酉	釆	里	金	長	門	160
170	阜 阝	隶	隹	雨	青	非	面	革	韋	韭	170
180	音	頁	風	飛	食	首	香	馬	骨	高	180
190	髟	鬥	鬯	鬲	鬼	魚	鳥	鹵	鹿	麥	190
200	麻	黃	黍	黑	黹	黽	鼎	鼓	鼠	鼻	200
210	齊	齒	龍	龜	龠						210
	0	1	2	3	4	5	6	7	8	9	

Note: Two radicals have special forms beneath a ⌒ shape: 61 ⺗ and 85 氺.

ABBREVIATIONS OF TEXT LOCATIONS
USED IN FOOTNOTES

楚	楚辭
杜	杜甫詳注
古	古詩箋
漢	全漢三國晉南北朝詩
舊	舊唐書
李	李太白全集
論	論語
全詩	全唐詩
詩	詩經
宋	宋詞三百首
唐	唐詩三百首
王	王摩詰集箋注
樂	樂府詩集
資	資治通鑒

The final number given with 詩經 references is the 毛 number; otherwise it is the 卷 number.

LIST OF GRAMMATICAL SYMBOLS

a	adverb
A	adverbial
c	conjunction
C	clause
C,C	equal-status clauses
C-C	movement- or resultative compound
C:C	main clause followed by object (clause or predicate) or added description
d	demonstrative
m	measure
n	noun
n2 (etc.)	two- (etc.) syllable noun
n-n	qualifier–head noun-phrase
n&n	additive noun-phrase
N	noun-phrase (uncommitted)
NN	verbless statement
Np	postpositional phrase
O	object
p	postpositional noun
prep	'prepositional' verb
q	quantifier
S	subject
v	verb
V	main verb, predicator
x	word of unspecified class
X	clause-component of unspecified function
1S2VO3 (usually /ASAVOA/)	relative positions within a clause
/.../	slashes enclose any grammatical analysis
/...=.../	word-class analysis followed by phrase-function analysis
[...]	understood element
(...)	attribute (adjectival or adverbial qualifier)
{...}	algebraic grouping of elements that belong closely together

UNIT 1

This unit is concerned with (a) nouns, that is words standing for things, e.g. 'trees', and for events and concepts treated as things, e.g. 'autumn', and (b) the ways in which two or more nouns can be combined to form a noun-phrase.

Vocabulary

Note: the first form given is the written form (*kaishu*) and the second is the printed form. Letters between slashes indicate the word-class (part of speech); /n/ means 'noun'. The figures are the radical-number and the number of extra strokes respectively. For the 'W', 'S' and 'M' in parentheses see the introduction to the script above; 'X' means 'character etymology unknown or uncertain'.

chūn /n/ spring (season) 72.5 (M 日 'sun')

fēng /n/ wind, breeze, draught 182.0 (S)

huā /n/ flower, blossom 140.4 (M ⁺⁺ 'plant')

lín /n/ a wood, forest, grove, trees 75.4 (W < 木 'tree' reduplicated)

mù /n/ tree 75.0 (W)

niǎo /n/ bird 196.0 (W)

qiū /n/ autumn 115.4 (M 禾 'grain'; S is abbreviation)

rì /n/ sun; sunlight; day 72.0 (W)

shān/n/ mountain, hill 46.0 (W)

shēng/n/ sound, voice 128.11 (M 耳 'ear'; the S consists of 士 尸 几 又)

shuǐ /n/ water; river 85.0 (W)

yè /n/ night 36.5 (M 夕 'night')

yǔ /n/ rain 173.0 (W)

yuè /n/ moon; moonlight; month 74.0 (W)

31

竹   竹   *zhú* /n/ bamboo 118.0 (W)

Notes on the vocabulary

春 *chūn* and 秋 *qiū*: in Chinese poetry spring and autumn are the two poetic seasons *par excellence*, for they are both seasons of change, whereas summer and winter are more extreme and static and hence far less useful as symbols of the changes in human life. Spring is associated with youth and renewal, and autumn with old age, decay and death, as one might expect; but for the Chinese poet spring can also be sad if it reminds him of lost youth or if he is far from home and unable to enjoy the springtime with his family. The two kinds of sadness that afflict the poet in these two seasons are called 傷春 *shāng chūn* 'wounded (i.e. heart-broken) by the spring' and 悲秋 *bēi qiū* 'saddened by autumn' respectively.

風 *fēng*: Symbol of freedom, for the wind 'bloweth whither it listeth', unlike the man trapped in exile as soldier or magistrate. The wind brings the scent of flowers or the voice of the brook; the wind then becomes a symbol of moral influence, whether for good or ill, spreading through the land, and hence of local customs. As a storm the wind is of course a symbol of dangers and obstructions.

花 *huā*: Flowers, particularly fruit-tree blossom, represent both the glory of springtime and youth and also 'the flower of grass that fadeth' when autumn and old age come. Flowers also represent able or virtuous people, especially those whose talents should be employed in government but who have been overlooked, so that their fragrance is wasted in the political wilderness.

林 *lín* can refer to (a) woods on the local hills, (b) forests on the distant mountains, or (c) the countryside as somewhere to retire to, away from the city but still close to the 漁樵 *yú qiáo* 'fishermen and woodcutters'. Retirement and more temporary escape is to 林泉 *lín quán* 'the wildwood and the burn'. Retirement is often referred to as 林居 *lín jū* 'living in the woods' or 歸林 *guī lín* 'returning to the woods', though this is not to be taken too literally.

鳥 *niǎo*: The most common birds in poetry are 雁 *yàn* 'wild goose' and 鴻 *hóng* 'swan-goose' (or often just 'wild goose') as symbols of homesickness or message-carrying (for which see Unit 16); 燕 *yàn* 'swallow' as a nest-builder and one of a pair, associated with spring; 鶯 *yīng* or 黃鳥 *huáng niǎo* 'golden oriole' as a song-bird, also associated with spring; and 鴛鴦 *yuān yāng* 'mandarin duck' as a symbol of marital love and fidelity.

山 *shān* can refer to (a) the hills around a village above the cultivated area, covered with woods, a source of timber and fuel, or (b) the mountains away from inhabited areas, the haunt of wild beasts, yetis (野人 *yě rén* 'wild people'), mountain demons (山鬼 *shān guǐ*), hermits in caves or monasteries, and airborne immortals (羽人 *yǔ rén* 'feathered people'). Mountains include the Five Sacred Mountains (五嶽 *wǔ yuè*) and others with spectacular scenery and hence objects of tourist pilgrimage.

聲 *shēng* is not only the sounds of Nature and music and noisy crowds, but also reputation (cf. English 'a big noise').

水 *shuǐ* 'water, river': most rivers in China flow eastward from the mountains in the west to the China Sea. They provided convenient east–west communication but, without adequate north–south roads, they and the ranges of hills and mountains between them also formed a barrier between the metropolitan north and the colonial south, so 江湖 *jiāng hú* 'rivers and lakes' becomes a symbol of the perils confronting civil and military officers from the capitals of the north (on the Yellow River) who have to travel to central or southern China.

In Chinese painting 山 *shān* and 水 *shuǐ* form a complementary pair, where the mountain represents the *yang* or male principle of solidity, immobility, upthrust and dominance while the river represents the *yin* or female principle of flexibility and submission. At the outset the mountain seems stronger than the river, which has to go around it, but in the course of time the river wears the mountain down, just as the passage of time destroys all things. So landscape painting, which represents the interaction of the two primal forces of *yin* and *yang*, is called 山水 *shān shuǐ* or 山水畫 *shān shuǐ huà* 'mountain and river painting'. Incidentally, it is a convention in Chinese painting that no two dominant mountains should be of the same height, for even males have to submit to a boss!

The mountain does not move, but the river never stops moving, so the river becomes a symbol of time going on forever, in contrast to the limited brief span of human life. The river carrying away the fallen blossom of springtime becomes a symbol of time eroding our youth.

夜 *yè*: night is often associated with loneliness (sleeping alone, looking at the moon etc.) but also, for instance, with spending the night drinking and talking with an old friend briefly encountered in 'exile'.

月 *yuè* usually refers to the full moon and hence the moon is often called 明月 *míng yuè* 'the bright moon'. Its roundness is a symbol of the reunion of the whole family circle, hence a reminder to a husband far from home that he is missing his family, and to the wife left behind that she is missing her husband.

In the sense of 'month' it refers to a lunar month or lunation; for details see Unit 20 'The Lunar Calendar'.

The sun and moon symbolize the *yang* and *yin* principles respectively. As we shall see later, the basic meaning of *yang* was 'sunlight', whereas *yin* meant 'overcast' or 'shade'. The male/female symbolism of these terms was a later development, as were their numerous other associations.

竹 *zhú* Bamboo can reach tree-height. It is an important material, being strong and flexible, hence it became a symbol for flexible strength.

1.1 Nouns

Chinese nouns are invariable: there are no modifications to indicate number or case as there are in most of the languages of Europe and Asia. So 山 *shān* is either a single 'mountain' or more than one 'mountainS'. It is true that one can, if necessary, distinguish the singular by prefixing the word 一 *yī* 'one', and the plural either by prefixing some such word as 眾 *zhòng* 'all the various' or else by using a compound such as 山嶽 (also written 山岳) *shān yuè* (two words for 'mountain' combined), but in general this is not done and it will be up to you as the reader to decide which is intended in any particular case, singular or plural.

A possessive form (made by adding the word 之 *zhī*, equivalent to English -'s) is not often used in verse, though it is common in prose; this can sometimes cause difficulties, as we shall see later in this unit.

1.2 Qualifier–head noun-phrases

A noun-phrase is a group of words operating as a major clause-component, for instance as the subject or object of a verb. The simplest noun-phrase consists of a single noun /n/ (the slashes enclose any symbolic notation in this course); the next simplest consists of two nouns /nn/.

The most common relationship between two nouns forming a noun-phrase in Chinese verse is when the first (the 'qualifier' or 'attribute') qualifies, limits or describes the second (the 'head') in various ways. As in the parallel English usage in compound nouns such as 'book-token', I shall use a hyphen to notate this relationship: /n-n/. In English and other European languages, by contrast, a qualifier may precede or follow the head according to the qualifier's structure. For instance, we can speak of 'an autumn day' (qualifier before head) or 'a day in autumn' (qualifier after head), whereas Chinese uses only the first form. Compare the following examples of these two word-orders in English (qualifiers in italics):

> (a) Single-word qualifier before the head:
> an *autumn* day (qualifier is a noun),
> a *gloomy* day (qualifier is an adjective),
> the *fading* day (qualifier is an active participle),
> the *new-born* day (qualifier is a passive participle),
> *my* day (qualifier is a possessive pronoun).

> (b) Phrasal qualifier following the head:
> a day *in autumn* (qualifier is a prepositional phrase),
> the day *(that) he died* (qualifier is a relative clause),
> a day *remembered by all* (qualifier is a participle plus a prepositional phrase),
> a day *to remember* (qualifier is an infinitive).

In Chinese, the equivalents of all the words in italics must precede the head (here 'day'), so that we get the literal equivalents of the following:

> an *in-autumn* day,
> the *he-died* day,
> a *remembered-by-all* day.

1.3 Qualification relationships in noun-phrases

Here are some examples of how Chinese nouns qualify a following noun, and some indication of the precise nature of the relationship.

But first a general word of caution. Chinese verse is very economical. You will have to go at least half-way towards meeting the poet. He will not spoon-feed you; in fact, at times you may feel he's doing his best to baffle you! You will not get much out of Chinese poetry unless you are prepared to visualize the scenery and its physical implications of location, shape, colour, sounds and sensations, filling in the gaps yourself, and also to empathize with the poet, to enter not just his physical world but also the world of his feelings, since that after all is the whole point of poetry as distinct from prose. It is strongly recommended that you practise doing this even with the simple phrases of these early units.

春 *chūn* X: spring(time) X; X in spring(time); X affected by spring (hence bright, active or growing).

> 春林 *chūn lín* the springtime woods; the forest in springtime (putting out leaves, filled with bird-song and flowers).
> 春鳥 *chūn niǎo* the birds in springtime (singing, nesting, swallows gathering mud).

秋 *qiū* X: autumn(al) X; X in autumn; X affected by autumn (dying, chilly, sad, lonely).

> 秋風 *qiū fēng* the autumn wind (chill, stripping the leaves from the trees, sad-sounding).
> 秋雨 *qiū yǔ* autumn rain (chilly and miserable).

夜 *yè* X: night(time) X; nocturnal X; dark X; X at night; X of the night; the night's X.

> 夜風 *yè fēng* the night wind; the wind in the darkness.
> 夜林 *yè lín* the woods at night; the forests in the darkness.

月 *yuè* X: moon X; lunar X; X of the moon; the moon's X; moonlit X; X in the moonlight; X illuminated by the moon.

> 月林 *yuè lín* the moonlit forest; the woods in the moonlight; the trees beneath the moon.

月夜 *yuè yè* a moonlit night.

風 *fēng* X: wind X; the wind's X; windy X; wind-swept X; X blowing in the wind (hence moving, rustling, creaking).

> 風林 *fēng lín* the trees tossing in the wind; the wind-blown woods.
> 風竹 *fēng zhú* bamboos swaying and rustling in the wind.

雨 *yǔ* X: rain X; rainy X; rain-soaked X; X in the rain (wet, cold, beaten down, sad etc).

> 雨竹 *yǔ zhú* bamboos in the rain; bamboos with rain dripping from the leaves; bamboos with wet, glistening leaves.
> 雨夜 *yǔ yè* a rainy night; a wet night; a night of rain; rain-filled darkness.

水 *shuǐ* X: water X; river X; X in/on/by the water/river.

> 水竹 *shuǐ zhú* river-side bamboos; bamboos by the water.
> 水鳥 *shuǐ niǎo* river-birds; water-birds; birds that live by the water.

山 *shān* X: mountain X; hill X; X among/in/on/above the mountains.

> 山花 *shān huā* mountain flowers; blossom on the hills.
> 山風 *shān fēng* mountain breezes; the wind blowing across the hills.

林 *lín* X: wood(land) X; in/above the woods/forest.

> 林風 *lín fēng* the wind through the woods; forest winds.
> 林月 *lín yuè* the moon over the woods; the moon shining through the trees.

One of the nouns in this unit is mainly used as a head, not as a qualifier:
X 聲 *shēng*: the sound of X.

> 林聲 *lín shēng* the sounds of the forest; woodland sounds (e.g. bird-song); the voice of the woods.
> 花聲 *huā shēng* the sound of falling blossom; the creaking of flower-stems in the wind.

If we analyse the relationships in the above phrases we find in the English not only nouns and adjectives used as qualifiers but also a range of prepositions ('of, at, in, on, among, above, beneath, with, by, across, through, over') and phrases involving participles ('affected, tossing, blowing, -lit, -blown, -soaked, swaying, rustling, creaking, dripping, shining'). In other words, English has the resources for much greater precision in specifying relationships than the language of Chinese verse has, but this can be a disadvantage: where English spoils the reader by over-specification, Chinese verse-language requires the exercise of imagination and empathy, a halfway step towards the poet, which can hardly be a bad thing.

It is quite common for compound nouns in other languages to show a wide range of relationships between the two nouns concerned, but Chinese verse seems to me to have a wider range than that of other languages; that, though, is something I must leave to others to determine. At least you have had due warning of the wide range of relationships connecting Chinese nouns in a qualifier–head relationship — and noun-phrases are very common indeed in Chinese verse.

1.4 Additive noun-phrases

A less common relationship between two nouns forming a noun-phrase is addition. This can be done by using the conjunction /c/ 與 *yǔ* 'and' between two nouns, e.g. 水與木 *shuǐ yǔ mù* /ncn/ 'rivers and trees', but on the whole verse omits the conjunction and simply puts two nouns together, giving in this case 水木 *shuǐ mù* /n&n/, where the '&' stands for the 'understood' conjunction meaning 'and'.

Does this not lead to confusion? Yes, it can: in verse you will find 水木 *shuǐ mù* either as /n&n/ in the sense of 'rivers & trees' that soothe the soul of an escapee from city life, like 林泉 *lín quán* 'woods and upland streams', or else as /n-n/ 'river-trees', i.e. 'trees by the waterside' (e.g. in Unit 21, first poem). Similarly, 山水 *shān shuǐ* most often means 'mountains and rivers' /n&n/, but sometimes means 'rivers in the mountains' /n-n/.

In additive compounds the two nouns represent members of the same semantic class of things, whereas the nouns in the qualifier–head compounds given above belong to different classes. For instance:

日夜 *rì yuè* 'day and night' (both are units of time),

山水 *shān shuǐ* 'mountains and rivers' (both are topographical features),

竹木 *zhú mù* 'bamboos and trees' (both are plants),

春秋 *chūn qiū* 'spring and autumn' (both are seasons),

日月 *rì yuè* 'sun and moon' (both are heavenly bodies),

日月 *rì yuè* 'days and months, the passage of time' (both are units of time).

In the case of 水木 *shuǐ mù* as an additive compound /n&n/, the rivers and trees are thought of as two equal sources of pleasure; as a qualifier–head compound /n-n/, they are thought of as a place and as things growing there, respectively. The same is true of 山水 *shān shuǐ* in its two meanings. The important thing about this is that semantic classes are subjective: whether or not two concepts belong to the same class depends on what criteria are being applied in order to classify them. So the rule given above for distinguishing '-' from '&' is only a rough guide, not a hard-and-fast one.

1.5 Noun-phrases of more than two words

Larger phrases may be built up of three or four nouns, though these are less common.

In the case of three nouns the first and second are usually more closely linked than the second and third, i.e. /nnn/ represents in algebraic terms /{nn}n/, not /n{nn}/; for instance, 風竹聲 *fēng zhú shēng* is 'the sound of bamboos-[rustling]-in-the-wind' /{n-n}-n/, not '*the-sound-of-bamboos [borne] on the wind' */n-{n-n}/. Similarly, 山水畫 *shān shuǐ huà* is 'paintings of rivers-and-mountains' /{n&n}-n/, not '*river-paintings in the mountains' */n-{n-n}/. I shall refer to this principle as the 'grouping-rule'.

Four-noun phrases may be /nn/ qualifying /nn/, as in 秋山風林 *qiū shān fēng lín* 'wind-swept woods on the autumn hills' /{n-n}-{n-n}/, or they may be /nn/ plus /nn/, as in 風花雨竹 *fēng huā yǔ zhú* 'wind-blown flowers and rain-drenched bamboos' /{n-n}&{n-n}/.

Exercise

Translate the following noun-phrases into English and check your version against the key at the end of the book. You should not of course expect your wording to be identical with that of the key; all that matters is that you have grasped the overall meaning of the phrase. The same will apply to all later translation exercises.

(1) 春風 (2) 風花 (3) 花林 (4) 林木 (5) 鳥聲 (6) 秋水 (7) 春日 (8) 山雨 (9) 水風 (10) 夜聲 (11) 雨夜 (12) 月林 (13) 竹日 (14) 山竹 (15) 山水 (16) 春月 (17) 風聲 (18) 林鳥 (19) 日夜 (20) 秋木 (21) 水鳥 (22) 山秋 (23) 秋聲 (24) 秋日 (25) 春山 (26) 山春 (27) 山風聲 (28) 秋山月 (29) 雨聲 (30) 水月 (31) 夜山 (32) 雨竹 (33) 月夜 (34) 竹林 (35) 春花 (36) 日月 (37) 竹風 (38) 夜木 (39) 山鳥 (40) 林花 (41) 春木 (42) 山日 (43) 雨花 (44) 水聲 (45) 山月 (46) 竹木 (47) 雨日 (48) 山木 (49) 春秋 (50) 夜鳥 (51) 秋月 (52) 夜花 (53) 竹風 (54) 山鳥 (55) 春水 (56) 秋水聲 (57) 春林月

UNIT 2

This unit is concerned with quality-verbs (stative verbs), that is verbs used to specify or describe what things are like rather than what they are doing.

Vocabulary

白 白 *bái* /v/ be white 106.0 (W)

長 長 *cháng* /v/ be long (in space or time) 168.0 (W)

此 此 *cǐ* /d/ this, these; this kind of; /n/ this thing; this place, here 77.2 (S)

大 大 *dà* /v/ be big 37.0 (W)

高 高 *gāo* /v/ be high, tall; have high social, political or moral status 189.0 (W)

谷 谷 *gǔ* /n/ valley 150.0 (W)

寒 寒 *hán* /v/ be cold, chilly; vulnerable 40.9 (M 冫 'ice')

空 空 *kōng* /v/ be empty; hollow; deserted (no people present); /a/ in vain, uselessly 116.3 (M 穴 'hole')

明 明 *míng* /v/ be bright, shining; clearly visible; clear-sighted; intelligent 72.4 (M 月 'moon')

青 青 *qīng* /v/ be blue or green (sometimes black, livid or pale) 174.0 (M 丹 'red')

人 人 *rén* /n/ person, people, human being; others (not self); someone, anyone 9.0 (W)

色 色 *sè* /n/ colour; facial expression of mood 139.0 (M 人 'person')

深 深 *shēn* /v/ be deep 85.8 (M 氵 'water')

苔 苔 *tái* /n/ moss 140.5 (M 艹 'plant')

天 天 *tiān* /n/ sky; Heaven; Providence; Nature (excluding the human race!) 37.1 (X)

39

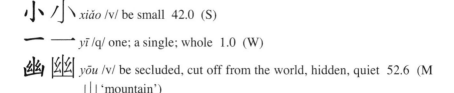

小 *xiǎo* /v/ be small 42.0 (S)

一 *yī* /q/ one; a single; whole 1.0 (W)

幽 *yōu* /v/ be secluded, cut off from the world, hidden, quiet 52.6 (M 山 'mountain')

Notes on the vocabulary

The letters between slashes ('/.../') above indicate the word-class (part of speech) of the vocabulary-item concerned: /a/ = adverb, /d/ = demonstrative, /n/ = noun, /q/ = quantifier, /v/ = verb.

高 *gāo* 'high' can refer not only to physical elevation (on a hill or tower or in the sky, for instance) but also to a high position in government or other walk of life, or to withdrawal from the world as a recluse; in the latter sense there are often overtones of moral purity, avoiding contamination by the despised world of politics.

寒 *hán* 'cold' has overtones of 'chilly, shivering, vulnerable, neglected, poor, pitiful, sad'.

空 *kōng* 'empty' has three main meanings in verse: (a) deserted, helpless, vulnerable, ignored by Nature; (b) empty of people hence peaceful and free; (c) (for Buddhist writers) a state of calmness achieved by suppressing painful emotions. This word encapsulates one of the basic paradoxes of Chinese poetry: seeking the peace and quiet of isolation yet at another level craving human company.

明 *míng* in its primary sense of 'bright' most often refers to the moon: 明月 *míng yuè*. Note that 明日 *míng rì* means not '*bright sun' but 'tomorrow'; the adjective used with the sun is 'white': 白日 *bái rì*. The adjectives 'bright' and 'white' attached to these two celestial bodies are so frequent as to have almost ceased to have any discriminatory function in these two phrases.

青 *qīng* is the colour of the sky and sea and hills and mountains and vegetation, i.e. the whole range from 'blue' to 'green', like the Gaelic and Welsh *glas*. It will be dealt with in more detail in Unit 22. As 'green' it is associated with springtime and youth. The 青龍 *qīng lóng* 'Green Dragon' of the east is a constellation whose heliacal rising marks the arrival of spring.

色 *sè* 'colour' was originally the space between the eyebrows, the focus of facial expression; from here its meaning was extended to mean other aspects of emotional expression such as blushing; from here it was an easy step to Nature's 'expression' of seasonal atmosphere and colour, and then to colour in general. Meanwhile another extension of meaning occurred: facial appearance led to the meaning of 'female beauty' and to 'the pleasures of sex'.

深 *shēn* 'deep' can be used of water in the sense of 'vertically deep', but more commonly refers to the distant sky or a long distance into the mountains or woods; with time-units such as night and the names of the seasons it means 'late,' and when referring to a courtyard it implies 'secluded, unvisited'. There is often a sense of deep feelings hovering around this word.

天 *tiān* 'sky' has a wide range of meaning: (a) the physical sky; the heavenly bodies whose movements control the seasons and hence agriculture; ditto as astrological indicators (Chinese astrology is political, not personal, and the constellations are associated with the imperial court and the various provinces); (b) Heaven, the abode of deceased ancestors, deified heroes and gods; (c) a supernatural controlling force, God (similar to the *New Testament* use of 'Kingdom of Heaven' as a euphemism for 'Kingdom of God', and to English expressions such as 'Good Heavens!'); and (d) Nature as opposed to mankind; natural as opposed to artificial. The emperor was 天 子 *tiān zǐ* 'the (adoptive) son of Heaven', on whose behalf he ruled. The Chinese world was called 天 下 *tiān xià* '(all) under Heaven'.

幽 *yōu* seems originally to have referred to distant, secluded valleys, judging by the 山 'mountain' element used as the meaning-element in the character. A 幽 人 *yōu rén* is a recluse. Like 高 *gāo*, 幽 *yōu* sometimes has overtones of moral purity.

2.1 Quality-verbs used as main verbs

In a Chinese clause (a statement centred around one main verb) the subject usually precedes the main verb, as it does in English, though we shall meet exceptions later. So 'The sky is blue' is simply 天 青 *tiān qīng* 'Sky be-blue'.

When I am speaking about the word-classes of individual words I shall use small (lower-case) letters, e.g. /n/ for 'noun' and /v/ for 'verb', and when I am considering the functions of phrases within the clause I shall use capital (upper-case) letters, e.g /S/ for 'subject'. I use the equals-sign (=), meaning 'functioning as', to separate these two levels of analysis. In terms of word-classes this clause 天 青 *tiān qīng* consists of a noun and a verb /nv/; in terms of function, these two words are functioning as subject and main verb (predicator) respectively /SV/. We can represent both levels of analysis in this case by /nv = SV/, meaning 'a noun and a verb functioning as the subject and main verb respectively'.

The sequence /nv/ is not always a subject followed by a main verb; it could also be used as /nv = AV/, where /A/ is an adverbial qualifying the main verb, and 天 青 *tiān qīng* would then mean 'is celestially blue, is sky-blue, is as blue as the sky', or it could be used as an uncommitted noun-phrase /nv = N/ 'the fact that the sky is blue, the blue(ness) of the sky.' For the time being, for practical exercise purposes, I shall treat /nv/ as a subject and a main verb /SV/, otherwise life will become unnecessarily complicated at this early stage.

Similarly with /nnv = Nv = SV/, where two nouns /nn/ form a noun-phrase /N/, which then functions as the subject /S/ of the statement:

(a) 山月明 *shān yuè míng* 'The moon over the hills is bright';

(b) 林苔青 *lín tái qīng* 'The woodland moss is green'.

There are three things to notice about the statement 天青 *tiān qīng*:

(a) There is no Chinese equivalent for the English 'the'. In some contexts, particularly in prose, the word 其 *qí* sometimes corresponds to the English definite article, but at this stage it is more important to get accustomed to the fact that, in general, Chinese has nothing like the obligatory English articles ('the, a, an, some, any').

(b) Since 青 *qīng* already means 'to BE blue,' not just 'blue,' there is no need for an equivalent of the verb 'to be' in any of its forms ('am, is, are, was, were, being, been' etc.) with 青 *qīng* or with any other quality-verb.

(c) It is possible to indicate tenses in Chinese by the use of adverbs meaning 'already', 'once', 'about to' and so on, but this is done far less frequently than in English, where all finite forms of the verb have to have their tense specified. So 天青 *tiān qīng* can equally mean 'The sky IS blue' or 'The sky WAS blue'. This can of course create significant ambiguities in a minority of cases.

2.2 Optional precision

This may be an appropriate point to introduce a very important feature of Chinese as compared to many other languages: the principle of 'optional precision'. In English we almost always have to specify whether a noun or pronoun is singular or plural, even when this is perfectly clear from the context. For instance, we have to say 'three dogS', where the '-s' means 'more than one'; but we already know from the 'three' that there are more than one, so from a logical point of view the plural '-s' is redundant in this case. The existence of cases like 'three sheep', where no '-s' is required, demonstrates this. But in general the obligatory distinction between singular and plural in English is something we feel more comfortable with, especially as it saves us deciding in each case whether the context has already made it clear whether we are dealing with 'one' or 'more than one' and whether that distinction is important in this case.

Another category of possible redundancy is the indication of tense. When describing a past event (unless we are using the 'historic present' as in 'so he says to me…') we put all the finite verbs into the past tense, usually by adding '-ed'. But once we have established that the story we are telling happened in the past we don't really need to keep reminding our listeners of the fact by using the past tense in every sentence.

Whereas English tends to err in the direction of over-redundancy in these and other ways, Chinese errs in the opposite direction and under-indicates distinctions that most languages find essential. The one that may well cause you the most difficulty in Chinese poetry is the tendency not to tell you who is doing something to whom, by the under-use of pronouns. See my remarks on the first line of the poem in Unit 31 for an example of the kind of ambiguity this may lead to. In lyrical poems it is most often 'I' or 'me' or 'my' that is not specified, but in narrative poems it is more likely to be a third person.

The problem is not that the Chinese language cannot clearly express tense, number and person, but that it is not obliged to, hence my use of the word 'optional'. Since economy of words (minimalism) is an ideal in Chinese poetry, one that is reinforced by the shortness of the lines (usually five or seven words), it is hardly surprising that poets take full advantage of this optionality, even if it reduces clarity for the Western reader (and often for the modern Chinese reader or translator as well). In fact, when the poems were written they probably caused few problems to contemporary readers because the latter would have been familiar with the kind of things that would be said in a poem written on a particular occasion. In other words, the real difficulty with Chinese poetry is not so much the language as the concepts and images, and especially the conventions, forming the cultural tradition within which the poems were written.

While we are on the subject of optional precision, let us look in passing at a poem that shows how far we have to go towards meeting the poet by supplying the relationship-markers and specifiers that he has not included. The poet is saying goodbye at the capital (Chang'an in present-day Shaanxi) to a friend who is going to take up post as assistant prefect in far-off present-day Sichuan province. First, the text:

Example text[1]

Wang Bo (late seventh century): 'Seeing off Assistant Prefect Du when he left to take up post at Shuzhou'

城闕俯[2]三秦 *chéng què fǔ sān qín*

風煙望五津 *fēng yān wàng wǔ jīn*

與君離別意 *yǔ jūn lí bié yì*

同是宦遊人 *tóng shì huàn yóu rén*

海內存知己 *hǎi nèi cún zhī jǐ*

---

[1] 王勃 杜少府之任蜀州 唐 3

[2] I adopt the variant reading 俯 *fǔ* since the usually-accepted reading 輔 *fǔ* makes nonsense of the first line and destroys the parallelism ('looking near and far') of the first couplet. Cf. Du Fu's 城上俯江郊 *chéng shàng fǔ jiāng jiāo* 'from the city walls we look down over the riverside suburbs' (杜甫 陪諸公上白帝城頭… 杜15)

天涯若比鄰 *tiān yá ruò bǐ lín*

無爲在歧路 *wú wéi zài qí lù*

兒女共霑巾 *ér nǚ gòng zhān jīn*

Note on the text

Shuzhou: present-day Chongqing county, west of Chengdu

Next, a literal translation:

> The walls of the capital look down over the Three Qin [= Shaanxi, where I shall be];
> wind and mist gaze afar towards the Five Fords [= Sichuan, where you will be].
> Feelings at saying goodbye to you
> share being official wanderers.
> China contains true friends,
> the ends of the earth are like the house next door.
> Let's not be, at the parting of the ways,
> children weeping together.

Clearly this is nonsense as it stands, for wind and mist do not gaze, feelings do not share anything, and the ends of the earth are anything but like the house next door; but if we insert the obviously intended connectives and specifiers (in square brackets below), the poem suddenly makes perfect sense:

> [From] the walls of the capital [we] look down over the Three Qin;
> [through] wind and mist [we] gaze afar towards the Five Fords.
> [My] feelings as I say goodbye to you
> [are that we] share being official wanderers (which brings us together rather than separating us).
> [While] China contains true friends
> the ends of the earth [will] be like the house next door.
> [So] let's not be, at the parting of the ways,
> children weeping together.

Note: for the overtones of wind and mist as symbols of separation cf. 茫茫 *máng máng* etc. in Unit 13.

The two versions of this poem will repay close study since they embody many of the differences between the language of Chinese verse and English: the non-specification of person ('my, I, we'), tense ('will'), prepositions ('from, through'), the copula ('are'), and conjunctions ('that, while, so'). But these omissions would have occasioned Wang Bo's friend no difficulty, since it would have been obvious to him from the sentiments expressed what these omissions were. In fact, he may not even have been conscious of them, since the remaining words would have been enough to trigger the ideas. The situation is rather like what we experience if we cover up the bottom half of a line of printed letters: we have no difficulty in reading the line and may not even notice that it has been half obscured.

The difference between Chinese verse and most of the world's literature is that this reconstructive capability of the human mind has been exploited to the full in China for literary purposes, not just for reading telegrams and headlines.

2.3 Quality-verbs qualifying nouns

We saw in Unit 1 that the Chinese equivalents of English relative clauses (introduced with 'which, that' etc.) have to precede the head-word. So how do we express 'blue sky' using the verb 青 *qīng* 'be blue'? Obviously we shall have to express it as 'sky which is blue', rearranged in the Chinese order 'which-is-blue sky'. Although the 'which' can be expressed in Chinese, especially in prose, it is usually omitted in verse, so that we are left with 'is-blue sky', viz. 青天 *qīng tiān* /vn/. This looks superficially very much like the English 'blue sky', but it is important to remember that 青 *qīng* is still a verb functioning like an English relative clause; we shall see in Unit 5 that other kinds of verbs, corresponding not to English adjectives but to English verbs, behave in exactly the same way.

As in the case of /nv/, the structure of /vn/ is also ambiguous: as well as being a verbal qualifier and a noun head functioning as an uncommitted noun-phrase /vn = N/ it can also be a verb and an object /VO/, in this case theoretically meaning 'blue the sky, make the sky blue, regard the sky as being blue'. For the time being I shall ignore this second alternative.

Here are some examples comparing predication /nv = SV/ with qualification /vn = N/:

(a) 山空 *shān kōng* 'The hills are empty' /nv = SV/; 空山 *kōng shān* 'the empty hills' /vn = N/;

(b) 林深 *lín shēn* 'The woods are deep (extend a long way, have hidden depths)'; 深林 *shēn lín* 'the deep woods,' confusingly used where English would say 'deep in the woods' or 'in the depths of the woods'.

We can combine both uses in one statement /vn v = S V/:

(a) 深林空 *shēn lín kōng* 'The deep woods are empty';

(b) 青山高 *qīng shān gāo* 'The blue mountains are high'.

When we use a verb–noun phrase to qualify a following noun /vn n = N/, e.g. 高山鳥 *gāo shān niǎo*, the meaning will be 'the birds on the high mountains', not 'the tall mountain-birds' because the usual grouping of /nnn/ is /{nn}n/, not */n{nn}/, as we saw in Unit 1, and /vnn/ as qualifier plus head follows the same pattern /{vn}n/, not */v{nn}/. The latter pattern occurs, of course, when /nn/ is the object of /v/, but for the moment we shall not be using this structure.

2.4 Numerals and demonstratives

As in English, numerals such as 'one' and 'first', and demonstratives like 'this' and 'that', can be used before nouns and noun-phrases to qualify them; the result is still a noun-phrase:

> (a) 一人 *yī rén* 'one (single) person' /qn = N/;
> (b) 一小鳥 *yī xiǎo niǎo* 'one little bird' /qvn = N/;
> (c) 此山 *cǐ shān* 'these hills' /dn = N/;
> (d) 此幽谷 *cǐ yōu gǔ* 'this secluded valley' /dvn = N/.

Note that in /qvn/ and /dvn/ the logical grouping is different from /{nn}n/ and /{vn}n/, viz. /q{vn}/ and /d{vn}/.

The uncommitted noun-phrase /N/ usually functions as the subject /S/ or object /O/ of a verb or as an adverbial /A/ qualifying the verb; in these cases it will be notated as /S/, /O/ or /A/ respectively. It also occurs in verbless clauses (see Unit 14), in which case it will remain /N/ and not be committed to any of these functions.

Exercise

All the items in the following exercise are of three Chinese words. Those that end in a noun are noun-phrases /xxn = N/, not complete statements; those that end in a quality-verb /xxv/ are complete statements (clauses) /xx v = S V/. They have been mixed to give you practice in distinguishing them.

(1) 幽竹青 (2) 深春色 (3) 明月白 (4) 谷竹青 (5) 春色明
(6) 高山人 (7) 秋水深 (8) 春水花 (9) 一花木 (10) 大水白
(11) 此雨苔 (12) 谷水聲 (13) 雨日長 (14) 空天色 (15) 此
高林 (16) 風聲高 (17) 空谷寒 (18) 寒水風 (19) 一山高
(20) 小水青 (21) 深林苔 (22) 一寒鳥 (23) 秋天高 (24) 幽
竹聲 (25) 寒雨長 (26) 大水聲 (27) 幽花色 (28) 一大山
(29) 小雨寒 (30) 雨竹青 (31) 夜風寒 (32) 青天鳥 (33) 春
山明 (34) 秋水鳥 (35) 此花白 (36) 小鳥寒 (37) 高林深
(38) 空天風 (39) 寒山色 (40) 風聲寒 (41) 一天明 (42) 此
高山

UNIT 3

This unit is concerned with (a) action-verbs and (b) adverbs.

Vocabulary

不 不 *bù* /a/ not 1.3 (X)

出 出 *chū* /v/ emerge, go out, come out; rise (of sun or moon); produce, emit 17.3 (M 止 'foot')

多 多 *duō* /v/ be much; be many; have many; /a/ mostly 36.3 (X)

歸 歸 *guī* /v/ return, return to; go home, come home 77.14 (M 止 'foot')

見 見 *jiàn* /v/ see 147.0 (W: 儿 = 人 'person' with enlarged 目 'eye')

來 來 *lái* /v/ come; come to; bring 9.6 (S)

流 流 *liú* /v/ flow, drift, float; wander; shed (tears or blood) 85.7 (M 氵 'water')

落 落 *luò* /v/ fall (e.g. of leaves); set (of sun or moon); settle (of bird) 140.9 (M 艹 'plant')

去 去 *qù* /v/ go away, leave; go 28.3 (X)

入 入 *rù* /v/ enter, go in, come in; set (of sun or moon) (distinguish from 人 *rén*) 11.0 (W)

少 少 *shǎo* /v/ be little (small amount); few; have few, be short of; /a/ rarely. (Note: 小 *xiǎo* 'small in size'; 少 *shǎo* 'small in number or amount') 42.1

未 未 *wèi* /a/ not yet, never yet 75.1 (X)

聞 聞 *wén* /v/ hear 128.8 (M 耳 'ear')

葉 葉 *yè* /n/ leaf 140.9 (M 艹 'plant')

已 已 *yǐ* /a/ already 49.0 (X)

47

雲 雲 *yún* /n/ cloud 173.4 (M 雨 'rain')

照 照 *zhào* /v/ shine; shine on, illuminate 86.9 (M 灬 'fire')

Notes on the vocabulary

雲 *yún*: Clouds moving in the sky often symbolize a wanderer, i.e. a husband, son or friend far from home, or else a contrast with one, as when clouds sail freely by but the wanderer does not return. Clouds shrouding mountains are a symbol of isolation and distance from the everyday world, so they are associated with monasteries and individual recluses. 雲 心 *yún xīn* 'cloud heart' means a mind that is free of worldly worries, as free as the clouds. From here they can become a symbol of mystery and magic, as in the 雲 文 *yún wén* 'cloud script' used to write some esoteric neo-Taoist documents. 青 雲 *qīng yún* 'blue clouds' means an elevated position, especially on the career-ladder.

3.1 Action-verbs

One basic feature of Chinese word-order is that (as in English) the performer of an action usually comes before the action, while the person or thing affected by or resulting from the action will usually come after the action, in the order of 'Who (the subject, abbreviated to /S/) does-what (the main verb, /V/) to-whom (the object, /O/)'. I shall treat this /SVO/ order as the 'normal' order. We shall see later that this is only the most common arrangement, not a universal one, for the arrangements /VS/ and /OV/ are also met. An example of the 'normal' order would be 月 照 林 *yuè zhào lín* 'The moon illuminates the woods', where both the Chinese and the English versions can be represented by the notation /SVO/. Reminder: capital (upper-case) letters are used to represent the order of major clause-components whereas small (lower-case) letters are used for word-classes.

If /V/ is a verb of movement, it will usually be followed (if by anything) by the end-point or destination of the movement, e.g. 風 入 谷 *fēng rù gǔ* 'The wind enters the valley' or 'The wind comes INTO the valley'. I shall follow the parallelistic practice of Chinese poets and treat such destinations, origins and routes directly following a verb as objects /O/.

The object of the main verb when the latter consists of a verb of perception, knowledge, thought, speech etc. may be either a noun, e.g. 見 月 *jiàn yuè*/vn = VO/ 'I saw the moon' or 聞 風 聲 *wén fēng shēng* /vnn = VO/ 'I hear the sound of the wind', or else a clause (SV or SVO or VO), e.g. 見 人 歸 *jiàn rén guī* /vnv = V:SV/ 'I see someone returnING'. Notice that when the object of a verb is a clause I shall not use /O/ but shall separate the main clause from the object-clause with a colon. The semantic class of the main verb may give an indication of the nature of the relationship between the two verbs, as it does in this case, where 'verb-of-perception n v' means 'perceive n v-ing'. But very often it is up to the reader to decide what the precise relationship is.

For the moment let us consider the possibilities of structure of /vnv/ apart from the /SV/ meaning in Unit 2. Let us see how some of these /vnv/ sequences translate into English. Since the following examples contain some unfamiliar vocabulary, a literal word-by-word translation (a trot) will be given before the English version.

(a) 有 人 來 *yǒu rén lái* (there-is person come =) 'There is someone WHO comes' or 'Someone is coming' /VO:V/.

(b) 見 月 出 *jiàn yuè chū* (see moon emerge =) 'I see the moon rise' (or 'risING') /V:SV/.

(c) 知 春 來 *zhī chūn lái* (know spring come =) 'I know THAT spring has come' /V:SV/.

(d) 請 人 來 *qǐng rén lái* (request person come =) 'I ask someone TO come' /VO:V/.

(e) 渡河來 *dù hé lái* (cross river come =) 'I come ACROSS the river' /VO-V/.

Clearly these are of different structures not only in the English wording but in the relationships implied: (a) implies 'There is a person AND that same person comes', but (b) is not identical because it implies that I actually see the rising of the moon, i.e. not just 'I see the moon, and it rises' but 'I see the-moon-rising'. We cannot rephrase the others in the same way: (c) is not 'I know the spring AND the spring has come' but 'I know a fact, and the fact is that the spring has come'; (d) is not 'I make a request to a person and that person comes', because he may decline the invitation; it means 'I issue an invitation to him, HOPING that he WILL come'; and (e) is not 'I cross the river and the river comes' but 'I cross the river and I come', i.e. 'I cross the river in this direction'.

These five examples all have different structures but the same surface appearance if we just think in crude terms of nouns and verbs, so that is not going to help us differentiate them, and we have none of the clues to their structure provided in the English versions by means of 'that', 'to' and '-ing'.

Yet no Chinese reader would be in doubt for a moment about their meaning. So what is happening here? Obviously the English markers are redundant, just as the plural '-s' is redundant in 'three pigs'. The Chinese reader deduces the structure of a verb's environment from some covert (unmarked) feature of each individual verb, namely the invisible framework it carries around with it, whereas the English reader has this framework overtly marked out in addition to being implicit. For example, the Chinese 請 *qǐng* actually conveys the implication of 'invite (someone) TO (do something)' if followed by a noun and a verb. It seems highly probable that all languages convey structural information by means of a mixture of such overt and covert markers; it just so happens that English has a higher proportion of OVERT (and redundant) markers than Chinese or the other 'Sinoid' languages that share most of the main structural features of Chinese (e.g. Thai, Cambodian and Vietnamese).

I am not pretending that the absence of clear overt markers does not sometimes lead to ambiguity: all I am saying is that on the whole the languages of China and mainland South-east Asia have managed perfectly well without the high density of overt markers considered indispensable in English, at least for the practical purposes for which they have been used hitherto. This is not to say that future heavier demands on these languages for scientific or philosophical purposes may not reveal a need for a wider range of overt markers and their more frequent use.

This all works well enough in everyday spoken language, especially since gesture and intonation help eke out the sparse grammatical indicators. But in traditional Chinese verse, thanks to the limited range of its subject-matter, the system has been pushed to its limits and far greater liberties are taken with grammatical economy and word-order than in spoken language, or even in prose. In these early units I shall be keeping as far as possible to 'normal' word-orders in order to ease your passage into a unique form of human communication that I do not pretend is easy in its more advanced forms.

Exercise

Here is some translation-practice involving a mixture of /SV/, /VO/ and /SVO/:

(1) 葉落 (2) 鳥歸 (3) 水流 (4) 日落 (5) 雲歸 (6) 人來 (7) 聞聲 (8) 落水 (9) 歸山 (10) 入林 (11) 去此 (12) 聞風聲 (13) 照夜林 (14) 多寒風 (15) 月照人 (16) 葉落水 (17) 月入山 (18) 見人來 (19) 聞人歸 (20) 月落 (21) 人歸 (22) 雲來 (23) 日出 (24) 鳥落 (25) 風來 (26) 見雲 (27) 照木 (28) 出林 (29) 來此 (30) 聞風 (31) 見高山 (32) 歸此山 (33) 入深林 (34) 鳥落木 (35) 人見天 (36) 鳥歸林 (37) 聞水落 (38) 見月出

3.2 Adverbs and nouns preceding and qualifying the verb

In this unit these are:

(a) Adverbs: 不 *bù* 'not', 多 *duō* 'mostly', 少 *shǎo* 'rarely', 未 *wèi* 'not yet', 已 *yǐ* 'already';

(b) Nouns: 日日 *rì rì* 'every day', 日夜 *rì yè* 'day and night', 深夜 *shēn yè* 'late at night', 夜 *yè* 'at night', 夜夜 *yè yè* 'every night'.

Apart from the three possible main components of a clause (S, V and O), there is a rag-bag of secondary components that are usually called 'adverbials'. The difference between /SVO/ and these secondary components is that whereas /SVO/ answers the question 'Who is doing what to whom?', adverbials /A/ answer all the other questions, such as when, where, why, how, with whom, for whom, how often, with what result etc. the action was performed.

'Main' and 'secondary' are used in a purely structural sense as a matter of convenience in exposition: they should not be understood as meaning more or less important for the meaning or point of the statement. Any component can function as the essential part of the answer to the question, whether real or imaginary, that prompted the statement to be made. To some extent there is a tendency in Chinese prose for the 'topic' of a statement to precede the 'comment', for the known to precede the unknown, for the background to precede the foreground, but this tendency is in competition with other structural requirements and by no means always prevails. In verse the greater freedom in word-order weakens this tendency even more, so that we have to be prepared for the emphatic components to occur in any position.

Adverbials consisting of adverbs usually occur immediately before the verb they are qualifying or before another adverbial in this position, so that we can have several such verb-qualifiers in a row, just as a noun can be qualified by a demonstrative, a quantifier and a verb. Other types of adverbials (non-adverbs) may occur in any of three positions: (1) before S ('position 1'), (2) between S and V ('position 2'), and (3) after O ('position 3'), giving the total possible range of main and secondary clause-components as: /1S2VO3/, for which I shall more often use the formula /ASAVOA/. The distribution of adverbials is freer in verse than in prose, mainly because poets need greater freedom in the arrangement of words, as we shall see in Unit 14.

An English clause illustrating /1S2VO3/ is '(1) Nowadays (S) we (2) never (V) see (O) him (3) alone', where each position is occupied by a single word. A longer example: '(1) Three days after that (S) John and I (2) both (V) telephoned (O) the suppliers (3) independently of each other', where some of the positions are occupied by phrases. This formula will be found useful for describing most of the clause-structures of Chinese verse and also for comparing Chinese and English structures.

Why this constant reference to English? Because I believe that adults can acquire a rapid grasp of another written language most effectively by working from the known to the unknown, unlike young children who can afford to spend several years of constant exposure in order to acquire their native spoken language by working from the unknown. Since the language of Chinese verse is in many ways very far removed from most other languages, a solid starting point in the structure of the reader's own language is obviously desirable, even though I hope that you will go on to make a full transition to seeing the poems, as far as it is possible, through ancient Chinese eyes, when English grammar will be of little help, as well as being no longer necessary. I should not talk about grammar at all if I did not think that such a bridge offers a more rapid and reliable transition than plunging straight into the chaos of white water. So I beg for a little patience on the part of the grammar-haters among my readers.

In English the adverbs under (a) usually come in position 2, while the phrases under (b) come in position 3, but in Chinese the usual place for any of these words or phrases is in medial position 2. Compare the Chinese and English word-orders of the following: Chinese 不來 *bù lái* /AV/ and English 'DOES NOT come', also /AV/; Chinese 日日來 *rì rì lái* /AV/ and English 'comes EVERY DAY' /VA/.

In clause-analysis notation all adverbials, whatever their position, will be represented by a capital /A/, so we can give the 'normal' sentence order as /ASAVOA/. The last two examples above may be represented as /av = AV/ and /nnv = AV/ respectively.

We mentioned in Unit 2 that /nv/ can stand for /SV/ or /AV/. This can happen with (among other things) nouns of time, e.g. 春來 *chūn lái* can mean either 'Spring comes' /nv = SV/ or 'He comes in the spring' /nv = AV/. For the moment I shall use nouns of time adverbially in this situation.

Exercise

(39) 日已高 (40) 天未明 (41) 人不少 (42) 鳥多小 (43) 夜夜白 (44) 日夜明 (45) 葉已落 (46) 日未出 (47) 月已出 (48) 人夜歸 (49) 人少來 (50) 夜夜落 (51) 深夜歸 (52) 未見人 (53) 已來此 (54) 花未多 (55) 山不高 (56) 月已明 (57) 山多青 (58) 水不白 (59) 日夜寒 (60) 日日青 (61) 日未落 (62) 人不歸 (63) 水不流 (64) 雲不來 (65) 鳥多去 (66) 日日來 (67) 日夜流 (68) 不入山 (69) 夜見月

UNIT 4

This unit is concerned with five-word lines of two kinds: (a) longer clauses of the /SAVO/ type, combining what we have covered in the preceding units, and (b) two short clauses combined in one line and how they relate to one another.

Vocabulary

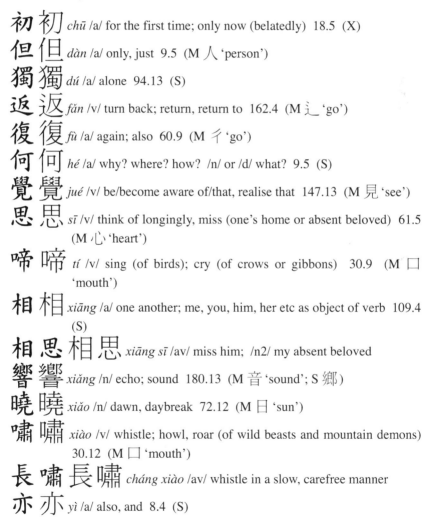

初 初 *chū* /a/ for the first time; only now (belatedly) 18.5 (X)

但 但 *dàn* /a/ only, just 9.5 (M 人 'person')

獨 獨 *dú* /a/ alone 94.13 (S)

返 返 *fǎn* /v/ turn back; return, return to 162.4 (M 辶 'go')

復 復 *fù* /a/ again; also 60.9 (M 彳 'go')

何 何 *hé* /a/ why? where? how? /n/ or /d/ what? 9.5 (S)

覺 覺 *jué* /v/ be/become aware of/that, realise that 147.13 (M 見 'see')

思 思 *sī* /v/ think of longingly, miss (one's home or absent beloved) 61.5 (M 心 'heart')

啼 啼 *tí* /v/ sing (of birds); cry (of crows or gibbons) 30.9 (M 口 'mouth')

相 相 *xiāng* /a/ one another; me, you, him, her etc as object of verb 109.4 (S)

相思 相思 *xiāng sī* /av/ miss him; /n2/ my absent beloved

響 響 *xiǎng* /n/ echo; sound 180.13 (M 音 'sound'; S 鄉)

曉 曉 *xiǎo* /n/ dawn, daybreak 72.12 (M 日 'sun')

嘯 嘯 *xiào* /v/ whistle; howl, roar (of wild beasts and mountain demons) 30.12 (M 口 'mouth')

長嘯 長嘯 *cháng xiào* /av/ whistle in a slow, carefree manner

亦 亦 *yì* /a/ also, and 8.4 (S)

影 影 *yǐng* /n/ shadow; dark image; bright image; reflection 59.12 (M
彡 'stripes')

Notes on the vocabulary

影 *yǐng*: The basic meaning seems to be 'a bright shape against a dark
background,' e.g. flowers glowing in the dusk, the gleam of a sunlit waterfall
against a dark hill, or sunbeams entering a dark wood. It can also mean 'a dark
shape against a light background,' e.g. the outline of dark trees against a
sunset sky or a shadow on the ground. It is also used for 'reflections' in a
mirror or in water, when of course either contrast is possible. See also the
section on its related verb 映 *yìng* in Unit 30.

相 *xiāng*: Note that although this will usually translate into an English object-
pronoun such as 'him' in position /O/, it is still an adverb in Chinese and will
occupy position 2 like any other adverb.

4.1 Line-length

Whereas Chinese prose prefers four-syllable units, Chinese verse for the last
two thousand years (but not before then) has preferred lines of five or seven
syllables. We are familiar with something like this rhythm in English nursery-
rhymes, e.g. the seven beats in 'MAry HAD a LITtle LAMB; its FLEECE was
WHITE as SNOW', or, at a rhythmically more sophisticated level, the five
theoretical beats of blank verse. For the moment we shall deal only with the
Chinese five-syllable line. Syntactically this normally divides into two plus
three syllables /xx xxx/; that is to say, a close-knit phrase will not usually
overlap this divide (sometimes misleadingly called the caesura) by occupying
the second and third syllables, which would mean a 1+2+2 /x xx xx/ grouping.
Sung dynasty song-style verse is an exception to this rule, and Tang dynasty
poets will break it for special effect.

So far we have worked with phrases of two or three syllables; for the rest of
this unit we shall work with five-word lines where the major division is
between the second and third words in order to encourage you to begin
thinking in this pattern before you are confronted with actual poems in Unit 7.
These exercise-lines (and those in exercises in future units) are not from actual
poems and lay no claim to any poetic quality, but have been made up solely to
give you practice in vocabulary, grammar and verse-rhythms at an elementary
level.

Exercise

(1) 秋花日日少 (2) 白日照青葉 (3) 寒風入空谷 (4) 不見一人歸 (5) 夜聞竹葉聲 (6) 日已出青山 (7) 夜見明月出 (8) 日未入高山 (9) 此人何不返 (10) 夜夜聞水響 (11) 曉鳥復長啼 (12) 未覺天已明 (13) 日夜長相思 (14) 此鳥何獨啼 (15) 日日獨長嘯 (16) 秋山多寒風 (17) 深夜聞人歸 (18) 白雲日日來 (19) 夜夜聞秋聲 (20) 寒日照山林 (21) 未見春山色 (22) 秋月照夜木 (23) 但聞一鳥啼 (24) 初覺日已落 (25) 日影入深林 (26) 何不歸高林 (27) 但聞山鳥響 (28) 相思何日歸

4.2 Two-clause lines

The five-word line may consist of two clauses, the first of two words and the second of three words /xx, xxx/, where I use a comma to separate the two clauses (classical Chinese uses no punctuation). We have already seen that two nouns can have different unmarked relationships, either qualifying or, if in the same semantic class, additive. The same sort of situation obtains here between two clauses. In English we usually distinguish these different relationships by means of conjunctions such as 'and, but, when, so that' etc., whereas Chinese more often leaves the relationship unstated. Here are the more common relationships, though the list is not exhaustive:

(a) The connection may be a simple 'and,' as in 天高山木落 *tiān gāo shān mù luò* 'The skies are high AND the mountain trees are shedding their leaves' /nv nnv = SV, SV/;

(b) it may be 'but' where a contrast is involved, as in 雲來人未歸 *yún lái rén wèi guī* 'The clouds come BUT he has not yet come home' /nv nav = SV, SAV/;

(c) it may be 'and then' for a simple sequence of events, as in 日落明月出 *rì luò míng yuè chū* 'The sun set AND THEN the bright moon came up' /nv vnv = SV, SV/;

(d) it may correspond to an English 'when' in the first clause, as in 天明人已去 *tiān míng rén yǐ qù* 'WHEN day broke, he had already gone' /nv nav = SV, SAV/.

(e) In the majority of cases the relationship between the two clauses is one of cause and effect, including reason or purpose or condition. In these cases the cause may come before the effect, as in 風高春花落 *fēng gāo chūn huā*

luò 'The wind is high WITH THE RESULT THAT the spring blossom falls,'
/nv nnv = SV, SV/;

(f) or the effect precedes the cause, as in 風寒春未來 *fēng hán chūn wèi lái* 'The wind is cold, FOR spring has not yet come' /nv nav = SV, SAV/.

It is left to the reader of Chinese verse to determine what exactly the relationship between two clauses is. This habit of going half-way to meet the poet should be cultivated as soon as possible, since it will be needed at deeper and deeper levels as we go on, both at the level of words and phrases and of whole poems. The succinct, non-explicit quality of literary Chinese should be seen not just as an inconvenience but as a guarantee that the reader will not gain much from the poet/reader interface without being willing to visualize and empathize within the framework of Chinese culture rather than the reader's own culture.

Exercise

(29) 雨大不見山 (30) 人去日已長 (31) 去此入幽谷 (32) 日落寒風來 (33) 日出照高林 (34) 夜深天未明 (35) 復來聞林響 (36) 水深鳥影明 (37) 出林初見日 (38) 相思不相見 (39) 長嘯入深山 (40) 天明人已去 (41) 天高山木落 (42) 出林見明月 (43) 鳥歸人未歸 (44) 鳥來落寒水 (45) 秋來鳥已去 (46) 曉出夜返山 (47) 雲來雨亦來 (48) 獨來復獨返 (49) 鳥啼人亦嘯 (50) 入林初聞鳥

UNIT 5

This unit is concerned with (a) expressions of place and (b) action-verbs qualifying nouns.

Vocabulary

邊 邊 *biān* /n/ side, edge; /p/ beside; at the edge of 162.15 (M 辶 'go'; the S consists of 自穴方)

步 步 *bù* /v/ walk 77.3 (W: 止 'foot' repeated in mirror-image)

處 處 *chù* /n/ place 141.5 (M 夂 'go')

何處 何處 *hé chù* /n/ what place? where? somewhere

處處 處處 *chù chù* /n/ every place, everywhere

此處 此處 *cǐ chù* /n/ this place, here

此 此 *cǐ* /n/ here

浮 浮 *fú* /v/ float, drift 85.7 (M 氵 'water')

河 河 *hé* /n/ river (distinguish from 何 *hé* 'what?') 85.5 (M 氵 'water')

後 後 *hòu* /n/ rear; following period; /p/ behind; after 60.6 (M 彳 'go')

湖 湖 *hú* /n/ lake 85.9 (M 氵 'water')

篁 篁 *huáng* /n/ bamboo-grove 118.9 (M 竹 'bamboo')

間 間 *jiān* /n/ interval, space between; /p/ between; among; in; at 169.4 (X)

江 江 *jiāng* /n/ river 85.3 (M 氵 'water')

居 居 *jū* /v/ live, dwell, stay 44.5 (M 尸 'sit still')

客 客 *kè* /n/ guest; stranger; an exile 40.6 (someone in 'exile', i.e. serving far from home); exile (the state of being in exile) (M 宀 'house')

來 來 *lái* /v/ come up to the present; /p/ in, during; for the last ... 9.6

裏 裏 *lǐ* /n/ lining, inside; /p/ in, inside 145.7 (M 衣 'clothing')

眠 眠 *mián* /v/ sleep 109.5 (M 目 'eye')

前 前 *qián* /n/ front, space in front; preceding period; /p/ in front of; before 18.7 (S)

沙 沙 *shā* /n/ sand 85.4 (M 氵 'water')

上 上 *shàng* /n/ upper part, surface; space above; /p/ on; above 1.2 (W)

石 石 *shí* /n/ stone, rock 112.0 (W)

外 外 *wài* /n/ exterior; /p/ outside; beyond 36.2 (S)

下 下 *xià* /n/ lower part; space below; /p/ under; below 1.2 (W)

中 中 *zhōng* /n/ middle, centre; interior; space among; /p/ in, inside; among 2.3 (W)

坐 坐 *zuò* /v/ sit 32.4 (X)

Notes on the vocabulary

The /p/ means 'when used as a postpositional noun' (see Section 5.2 below).
Rivers and lakes: 水 *shuǐ*, 河 *hé*, 川 *chuān* and 江 *jiāng* are general words for 'river', so that 'mountains and rivers' is expressed as 山水 *shān shuǐ*, 山河 *shān hé*, 山川 *shān chuān*, or 江山 *jiāng shān* (not *山江 *shān jiāng*).
河 *hé* is sometimes used specifically to refer to the 黃河 *huáng hé*, the Yellow River of North China, whereas 江 *jiāng* or 大江 *dà jiāng* is often used for the 長江 *cháng jiāng*, the Yangtse of Central China. (It is possible that 江 *jiāng* is a southern (Thai) word, for it comes from Old Chinese *klong*, which is similar to the Thai *khloong* 'canal'.) 河 *hé* has overtones of 'northern river', that is of the metropolitan area of the Yellow River, whereas 江 *jiāng* has overtones of the half-Sinicized South where less-favoured officials were sent as prefects and magistrates, so in a way 河 *hé* means 'the rivers of home' and 江 *jiāng* 'the rivers of exile', like 'the waters of Babylon'.
The great lakes of China are south of the Yangtse and so 湖 *hù* has also become associated with travelling and 'exile' in the distant, alien South, especially in the phrase 江湖 *jiāng hù* 'rivers and lakes'.

5.1 Phrases of place

Phrases of place at this stage are adverbials of two kinds: (a) ordinary noun-phrases, e.g. /nn = A/, and (b) postpositional phrases, e.g. /Np = A/.

We have seen the ordinary noun-phrase of place as an object in such expressions as 入深山 *rù shēn shān* /v vn = V O/. So far we have seen place-indicators of this kind only as the object of verbs of movement, but they can occur also as the object of verbs of position such as those meaning 'sit', 'lie', 'lean', 'live' etc, where the meaning is of course *at* a place, not *to* or *from* a place, as it is with verbs of movement. So whereas 入深山 *rù shēn shān* means 'go *into* the deep hills', 居深山 *jū shēn shān* means 'live *in* the deep hills'.

Phrases of this kind also occur as adverbials in position 1, e.g. 深山寒風多 *shēn shān hán fēng duō* /vn vn v = A S V/ '*In* the deep hills cold winds are numerous'.

Such ordinary noun-phrases are less common in position 2, though two kinds of place-expressions are very common here: (a) phrases such as 何處 *hé chù* 'where?', 處處 *chù chù* 'everywhere' and 此 *cǐ* 'here', e.g. 此人何處來 *cǐ rén hé chù lái* /dn dn v = S A V/ 'Where does he come from?' and (b) the postpositional phrases discussed in the next section of this unit.

Exercise

(1) 竹林春色來 (2) 大水白鳥落 (3) 青山白雲浮 (4) 深山人少入 (5) 何處聞啼鳥 (6) 夜夜獨步月 (7) 青山白雲出 (8) 深林不見日 (9) 竹林苔色明 (10) 空山白雲多 (11) 深林何人居 (12) 此客何處居

5.2 Structure of postpositional phrases

This clumsy expression (hereinafter abbreviated to its notation /Np/) is used to mean a noun-phrase followed by (and hence qualifying) one of the postpositional nouns /p/ given in the vocabulary above. A /Np/ is a noun-phrase mainly used adverbially, i.e. /Np = A/, and may occur at any of the three secondary positions. The list above is not complete and we shall meet other postpositions later in this course.

In European languages we have prepositions, such as 'in, under, between, beyond' etc., so-called because they precede a noun. Corresponding to these Chinese has three kinds of relationship-indicator: (a) prepositional verbs, (b) postpositional nouns, and (c) a combination of the two.

A /p/ stands for a part of an object (top, bottom, side, edge etc.) or the space adjacent to it (vicinity, space above it, space around it etc.).

Here are some examples of /Np/s, all /Np = A/:

木間 *mù jiān* literally 'the space between the trees', used where English would use 'between the trees' or 'among the trees';

林邊 *lín biān* 'the side of the forest', used like English 'beside the forest' or 'on the edge of the forest';

雲外 *yún wài* 'the far side of the clouds', used like English 'beyond the clouds';

石後 *shí hòu* 'the rear of the rock', used like English 'behind the rock';

山前 *shān qián* 'the front of the hill', used like English 'in front of the hill';

林裏 *lín lǐ* 'the interior of the woods', used like English 'in the woods';

山中 *shān zhōng* 'the middle of the mountains', used like English 'in' or 'among the mountains';

天上 *tiān shàng* 'the top of the sky', used like English 'in the sky' (literally 'on the sky');

山下 *shān xià* 'the bottom of the mountain', used like English 'at the foot of the mountain' (literally 'underneath the mountain', like Good King Wenceslas's peasant).

Note on 間 *jiān*, 裏 *lǐ* and 中 *zhōng*: in general 裏 *lǐ* and 中 *zhōng* are used interchangeably in the sense of 'in', e.g. 'in exile' can be expressed as 客裏 *kè lǐ* or 客中 *kè zhōng*. (The fact that 中 *zhōng* is a level-tone word whereas 裏 *lǐ* is in an oblique tone may have encouraged poets to retain both for use in different tonal contexts; examples are to be seen in the second poem in Unit 27 and in the third poem in Unit 33, in both of which these two words are used in parallel in opposite tonal environments.) There is another word 內 *nèi* (not practised here) meaning 'inside' or 'on this side of' as opposed to 外 *wài*. 間 *jiān* is basically 'between' or 'among' but is sometimes also used as 'in', e.g. 江間 *jiāng jiān* 'in the river', or even as 'at', e.g. 腰間 *yāo jiān* 'at the waist'.

Exercise

(13) 林中 (14) 水外 (15) 山前 (16) 天上 (17) 花間 (18) 竹裏 (19) 鳥邊 (20) 竹後 (21) 篁裏 (22) 湖上 (23) 河間 (24) 石上 (25) 江外 (26) 月下 (27) 木後 (28) 雪中 (29) 水邊 (30) 山外 (31) 風前 (32) 林邊 (33) 谷間 (34) 篁後 (35) 山上 (36) 河邊 (37) 湖裏

5.3 Occurrence of postpositional phrases

Like the noun-phrases in the first section above, these /Np/s may occur in either initial or final position, for example 天上白雲來 *tiān shàng bái yún lái* /np vn v = A S V/ 'In the sky the white clouds come' and 獨歸青山外 *dù guī qīng shān wài* /a v vnp = A V A/ 'He returns alone to beyond the green hills'.

In the middle of a five-word line (words 3 and 4) there are two possibilities: (a) before a noun the /Np/ will be qualifying the noun (see next section); (b) before a verb it will be an adverbial qualifying the verb. This should cause no difficulty since the same thing happens in English, except that in English the PREpositional phrase comes AFTER the noun or verb, e.g. (a) 不見水中月 *bù jiàn shuǐ zhōng yuè* /a v npn = A V O/ 'I do not see the moon (WHICH IS) IN THE WATER', (b) 魚龍水中居 *yú lóng shuǐ zhōng jū* /nn np v = S A V/ 'Fish and dragons live IN THE WATER'.

Exercise

(38) 白鳥沙上眠 (39) 湖水沙邊白 (40) 一人步湖邊 (41) 初見江中月 (42) 客亦雨中歸 (43) 復坐河邊石 (44) 獨坐苔石上 (45) 一葉風前浮 (46) 但思天邊客 (47) 獨居水聲中 (48) 月影湖中明 (49) 山前寒花落

5.4 Action-verbs qualifying nouns

We have met both quality-verbs and action-verbs as main verbs (predicators), e.g. 花白 *huā bái* 'the blossom is white' and 花落 *huā luò* 'the blossom falls', both /nv = SV/; we have met only quality-verbs as noun-qualifiers, e.g. 白花 *bái huā* 'white blossom' /vn = N/, but not yet action-verbs in this capacity, e.g. 落花 *luò huā* 'falling blossom' /vn = N/. This last combination has been delayed until now to avoid confusion between an action-verb qualifying a following noun to form a noun-phrase /vn = N/ and one taking a following noun as an object /vn = VO/.

Action-verbs may be subdivided into transitive (those which may take an object) and intransitive (those which do not).

Qualifying intransitive verbs correspond to an active participle in other languages (English *-ing*, German *-end*, French *-ant* etc.), but even here there is scope for ambiguity about tense: are 落葉 *luò yè* 'leaves which have fallen'('fallEN leaves') or 'leaves which are still in the process of falling'('fallING leaves')? Either is possible, and both uses of 落葉 *luò yè*

occur in verse. But 落月 *luò yuè* is 'the setting moon', not 'the moon which
has already set', and 歸鳥 *guī niǎo* are 'birds flying homewards', not 'birds
which have arrived home'. Just to complicate matters, 棲鳥 *qī niǎo* 'roosting
birds' and 宿鳥 *sù niǎo* 'birds staying the night' can also mean 'birds flying
home to roost', like a future participle in other languages such as Latin *-turus*
or Korean *-ŭl*.

   Qualifying transitive verbs correspond to passive participles in English.
They are fairly common in prose and in modern Chinese; in fact, there is one
modern (Cantonese) example that many English-speakers are familiar with:
炒麵 *chǎo miàn* 'chow mein', meaning 'fried noodles'. But in classical verse
qualifying transitive verbs are not very common.

Exercise

(50) 不見去人歸 (51) 春水多浮花 (52) 秋月照落木 (53)
歸鳥入夜林 (54) 流水花已去 (55) 空谷來人少 (56) 秋山
多落葉 (57) 落日照幽苔 (58) 夜聞葉落聲 (59) 浮雲日日
來 (60) 風林落花白 (61) 白沙多眠鳥 (62) 此處來客少

UNIT 6

This unit is concerned with (a) questions, (b) expressions of time, and (c) clauses qualifying nouns.

Vocabulary

故 故 *gù* /v/ be old, of long standing, original 66.5 (S)

會 會 *huì* /v/ meet, get together 73.9 (X)

幾 幾 *jǐ* /q/ how much? how many? a few 52.9 (X)

今 今 *jīn* /n/ today; now 9.2 (X)

久 久 *jiǔ* /v/ be a long time; /a/ for a long time 4.2 (X)

君 君 *jūn* /n/ gentleman; you (polite) 30.4 (S)

能 能 *néng* /v/ be able; be able to, can 130.6 (X)

年 年 *nián* /n/ year 51.3 (M 禾 'grain')

豈 豈 *qǐ* /a/ surely not? cannot possibly 151.3 (X)

琴 琴 *qín* /n/ lute 96.8 (M 珏 'musical instrument')

時 時 *shí* /n/ time 72.6 (M 日 'sun')

事 事 *shì* /n/ matter, affair, activity, event 6.7 (X)

誰 誰 *shuí* /n/ who? 149.8 (S)

所 所 *suǒ* /n/ place; (treated as /a/) the place where; that which; which 63.4 (S)

彈 彈 *tán* /v/ pluck (strings of musical instrument), play 57.12 (M 弓 'bow')

我 我 *wǒ* /n/ I, me, my; we, us, our 62.3 (X)

鄉 鄉 *xiāng* /n/ neighbourhood; village 162.10 (X)

63

遊 遊 *yóu* /v/ wander, rove; be away from home on service; tour (also written 游) 162.9 (M 辶 'go')

語 語 *yǔ* /v/ speak; talk, converse 149.7 (M 言 'speak')

者 者 *zhě* /n/ the person who, the one which 125.5 (X)

知 知 *zhī* /v/ know; understand; /v = A/ I wonder 111.3 (S)

昨 昨 *zuó* /n/ yesterday 72.5 (M 日 'sun')

Notes on the vocabulary

故 : There are four common words for 'old':

(a) 古 *gǔ* 'ancient; in ancient times; antiquity'. Nowadays refers mainly to the period BC. 古 人 *gǔ rén* 'the ancients, the sages of antiquity'.

(b) 故 *gù* 'of long standing, original'. 故 人 *gù rén* 'old friend, friend of long standing'. 故 鄉 *gù xiāng* 'home-town/village, native heath'. 故 林 *gù lín* 'home woods (of a bird); home village (of people)'.

(c) 舊 *jiù* 'previous, ex-, no longer in use'. 舊 人 *jiù rén* 'the previous favourite wife whom a new concubine (新 人 *xīn rén* 'new person') has replaced in her husband's affections'. 舊 *jiù* is also used like 故 *gù* in the sense of 'home'.

(d) 老 *lǎo* 'aged, elderly'. 老 人 *lǎo rén* 'elderly person, senior citizen' (entitled to respect). Early philosophers from Confucius onwards tended to be known by nicknames. There was a Taoist philosopher whose nickname was 老 子 *lǎo zǐ* 'the old fellow' (Laotzu); he was the supposed author of a famous work of the same name, later also known as the 道 德 經 *dào dé jīng* (Taoteching).

能 *néng* in the sense of 'can' is treated as an adverb in parallelism, though it translates as a verb in English. It will be treated as a verb in this course.

6.1 Noun-phrases as expressions of time

We have already met 日 *rì* and 日 日 *rì rì* 'every day, day by day', 日 夜 *rì yè* 'day and night', and 夜 夜 *yè yè* 'every night'; similarly, 年 年 *nián nián* 'every year, year by year'.

'Today' is 今 *jīn* or 今 日 *jīn rì*, 'yesterday' is 昨 *zuó* or 昨 日 *zuó rì*, but 'tomorrow' is 明 日 *míng rì*, not *明 *míng* alone. Similarly are formed 今 夜 *jīn yè* 'tonight', 今 春 *jīn chūn* 'this spring', 昨 夜 *zuó yè* 'last night' etc., 此

時 *cǐ shí* 'this time, now', 此 日 *cǐ rì* 'this day, today'. We shall also meet some longer expressions of time below in Section 4.

Expressions of 'time when' occur in positions 1 and 2, and occasionally in position 3; expressions of 'time how long' (e.g. 三 年 *sān nián* 'three years') occur mainly in position 3, but not infrequently also in 1 or 2. All are adverbials /n = A/, /nn = N = A/ etc.

6.2 Question-words

Most are formed from 何 *hé* /d/ 'what?' or 幾 *jǐ* /q/ 'how many?, how much?' followed by a noun: 何 事 *hé shì* (literally 'what matter?' /dn = N = A/) 'why?'; 何 處 *hé chù* 'where?'; 何 人 *hé rén* 'what person?, who?' /dn = N/; 幾 人 *jǐ rén* 'how many people?'.

Others include 誰 *shui* /n/ 'who?'; 多 少 *duō shǎo* /v2/ 'be how many?, be how much?'; 豈 *qǐ* /a/ 'surely not?'; 豈 不 *qǐ bù* /aa/ (literally 'surely-not not?') 'surely?'.

Note that 何 *he* may also be an adverb meaning 'where?' or 'why?' and 何 不 *hé bù* 'why not?'. 何 所 *hé suǒ* /na = N/ means 'what?' as the object of a verb, though located in position 2 (see Sections 6.4 and 6.7 below); it sometimes means 'where?' or 'how?' /a/.

6.3 Question-words of time

何 時 *hé shí* 'when?'; 幾 時 *jǐ shí* 'when?' in position 2, but 'how long?' in position 3; in the set phrase 能 幾 時 *néng jǐ shí* /v qn = V: [V] A/, literally 'can how long', meaning 'How long can it last?', i.e. 'It won't last long', a verb meaning 'last' or 'survive' is understood (I use square brackets to enclose an 'unexpressed' component).

Compare the use of 何 *hé* and 幾 *jǐ* in the following:

何 日 *hé rì* 'which day?, when?' versus 幾 日 *jǐ rì* 'how many days?'

何 年 *hé nián* 'which year?, when?' versus 幾 年 *jǐ nián* 'how many years?'

6.4 General remarks on questions

Chinese sometimes locates its question-words at the same position in the clause as the expected answering word, for instance, 遊人到何處 *yóu rén dào hé chù* /vn v dn = S V O/, literally 'Wanderer arrive WHERE?', where English would bring the question-word to the beginning of the question: 'WHERE has the wanderer got to?' The reason for the Chinese word-order is to match a possible answer such as 遊人到臨洮 *yóu rén dào lín táo* /vn v n2 = S V O/ 'The wanderer has arrived at Lintao'. Note: /n2/ means a two-syllable noun which may be analysed historically (in this case as /vn/) but which functions as an unanalysable unit.

Another example: 遊人何年歸 *yóu rén hé nián guī* /vn dn v = S A V/ 'Wanderer WHICH YEAR return?' because the answer could be 遊人明年歸 *yóu rén míng nián guī* 'Wanderer NEXT YEAR return'. Sometimes in Chinese verse the same thing is done as in English, which should cause you no difficulty. A half-way situation is where 何 *hé* or 何所 *hé suǒ* 'what?' as the object of the verb comes not in the usual position of /O/ but in position 2: /SOV/. This word-order is normal also in prose.

Except in quoted dialogue, e.g. in poems in imitation of folk-songs, questions in verse do not of course expect an answer, but have one of four uses:

(a) Meaning 'I wonder', especially when preceded by 不知 *bù zhī* 'I don't know', rather illogically abbreviated to 知 *zhī* (but still implying that I DON'T know), e.g. 知何處 *zhī hé chù* /v dn = A A/ 'I wonder where …', 'Where, I wonder, …';

(b) Rhetorical, i.e. equivalent to a negative, e.g. 誰能 … *shuí néng*… 'Who can …?', meaning 'Nobody can …';

(c) Exclamatory, meaning 'How …!' or 'What …!', e.g. 一何悲 *yī hé bēi* /a2 v = A V/ 'How sad!' or 何茫茫 *hé máng máng* /a v2 = A V/ 'How vast!' Note that the choice of 何 *hé* or 一何 *yī hé* depends on the number of syllables following, i.e. the 一 *yī* is metrical padding and has no meaning here.

(d) Indefinite, as when 何處 *hé chù* means 'somewhere' (see example in Section 6.6 below).

Exercise

In the following exercise we meet lines of seven syllables. Whereas the five-syllable line's major division is after the second syllable, that of the seven-syllable line is after the fourth syllable; in both cases the second half of the line is of three syllables:

The seven-syllable line: X X X X / X X X

The five-syllable line: X X /X X X

Most Chinese verse from Han to Tang (the first millennium A.D.) had lines of five or seven syllables, though during the Tang and Sung dynasties the 'song-style' verse (詞 *cí*) had lines of varied lengths from two syllables upwards, six syllables being quite common.

(1) 多少鄉人去不歸 (2) 所見所聞不能語 (3) 久遊天邊何不返 (4) 春風明月思故人 (5) 明年何時返故鄉 (6) 鳥遊江湖思故林 (7) 何事獨坐長彈琴 (8) 遊鳥返時木未青 (9)

多少秋葉落寒山 (10) 今日不見昨夜客 (11) 客居江湖知幾年 (12) 今春日日遊高山 (13) 獨步寒雨何所思 (14) 君遊山林何所見 (15) 久遊江外鄉思多 (16) 此事誰能久不語 (17) 聞琴初覺秋風寒 (18) 客中豈不思故鄉 (19) 春山處處聞鳥語 (20) 此人何事復來此 (21) 故人遊山不知處 (22) 獨眠豈能不相思 (23) 昨我來此今復去 (24) 久居深山誰能知 (25) 明年此時知何處 (26) 夜來何處彈琴聲 (27) 今夜相會復何年 (28) 秋來木葉豈能久 (29) 夜來琴聲知誰彈 (30) 此日見君復何日 (31) 山外幾人歸 (32) 雨後天復青 (33) 昨來今已去 (34) 明日返故鄉 (35) 今後歸何處 (36) 深夜聞語聲 (37) 何時復相會 (38) 君歸我不歸 (39) 故人幾時返 (40) 昨事今初語 (41) 春花能幾時 (42) 來時春木青 今去秋風寒 (43) 春林誰彈琴 (44) 此人何所知 (45) 久遊青山中 (46) 豈不年年來

6.5 Clauses qualifying nouns

You are already familiar with the minimal qualifying clause in Chinese, consisting of a single verb of quality or action and functioning as the qualifier of a following noun. In this unit we are concerned with more complex clauses.

You will remember from Unit 1 that a Chinese noun-qualifier may correspond, among other things, to an English relative ('wh-') clause or to an English participle or infinitive. For instance 飛鳥 *fēi niǎo* corresponds both to English 'birds which fly' and to English 'flying birds'. Since a Chinese clause qualifying a noun does not correspond ONLY to an English relative clause I shall avoid the latter term in this course except with reference to English.

In my notation I shall enclose a qualifying clause in parentheses (round brackets) if it consists of more than just a verb.

In principle, any clause may be used to qualify a noun, but in actual practice there are three main types of qualifying clause in Chinese verse: (a) subject-headed, (b) object-headed, and (c) adverbial-headed, depending upon how they are derived from a hypothetical underlying main clause.

6.6 The subject-headed qualifying clause

Let us begin with such a hypothetical underlying statement: 人見山 *rén jiàn shān* 'Someone sees a mountain', having the structure /nvn = SVO/. Now let us extract the subject and make it into the head-noun, and make the rest of the clause qualify it: 見山人 *jiàn shān rén* 'the person WHO SEES THE MOUNTAIN', having the structure /vn n = (VO) N/.

You may wonder how this meaning can be distinguished from that of the same 見山人 *jiàn shān rén* when it means 'sees the mountain-people', with the structure /v nn = V O/. The answer, of course, as in all cases where there are no grammatical indicators, is by looking at the context and the situation to see what makes sense. Let us look at two examples from Chinese poems. (Both involve two noun-phrases unconnected by any main verb, a structure to be dealt with in Unit 14, but here we are concerned only with the structure of the SECOND noun-phrase in each line, so please do not worry about the overall structure of the lines at this point.)

First, an example from the poem in Unit 30: 古木無人徑 深山何處 鐘 *gǔ mù wú rén jìng / shēn shān hé chù zhōng* /vn vnn vn dnn/ literally 'Ancient tree have-not people path, deep mountain what (or some) place bell'. Some translators have made of 無人徑 *wú rén jìng* 'without a human track', taking it as /v {nn} = V O/; but this couplet is a strictly parallel one, so 無人 徑 *wú rén jìng* is likely (but not absolutely certain) to have the same structure as the corresponding phrase in the following line, viz. 何處鐘 *hé chù zhōng* 'a bell somewhere', which can only be /{dn} n = N/, a noun-phrase. 無人徑 *wú rén jìng* as a noun-phrase can only be /{vn} n = (VO) N/ 'a path without people'. My own instinct is to translate the whole couplet as 'Ancient trees, a path without people; deep in the mountains, a bell somewhere'.

A similar, but not identical, case is a couplet from a poem by Li Bai: 月下 飛天鏡 雲生結海樓 [3] *yuè xià fēi tiān jìng / yún shēng jié hǎi lóu* /nv vnn nv vnn/ literally 'Moon descend fly sky mirror, cloud be-born build sea tower'. But this is not just a potential puzzle for the Western reader, for Chinese commentators and translators have also had trouble with this couplet, being misled by the occurrence of 天鏡 *tiān jìng* and 海樓 *hǎi lóu* as compound nouns elsewhere, the latter with a meaning ('mirage') not intended here. My own interpretation is 'The moon descends, a mirror floating in the sky; clouds are born, towers building on the sea' /SV, [V](VA)O/, i.e. 'The moon descends, [and it is] a mirror floating in the sky'.

The pronoun 者 *zhě*, meaning 'the person who' or 'the one which', seems to occur in verse only when qualified by a clause, e.g. 林居者 *lín jū zhě* /nv n = (AV) N/ 'those who live in the woods'; it usually refers to people rather than things.

---

[3] 李白　渡荊門送別　唐3

6.7 The object-headed qualifying clause

Here we run into a snag in Chinese, for if we extract the object as head and make the rest of the underlying clause qualify it, we get the clause we began with: 人見山 *rén jiàn shān*. This will not distinguish the noun-phrase /nv n = (SV) N/ 'the mountain WHICH SOMEONE SEES' from the clause /n v n = S V O/ 'Someone sees a mountain', so Chinese inserts the word 所 *suǒ* 'that which' in position 2 to distinguish the qualifying clause, giving 人所見山 *rén suǒ jiàn shān* 'the mountain WHICH SOMEONE SEES', /nav n = (SAV) N/. You will no doubt find this structure strange; in fact the word 所 *suǒ* (together with an older equivalent 攸 *yōu*) is unique in Chinese, constituting a word-class of its own, though I shall treat it for convenience as an adverb. It cannot be explained in terms of the rest of Chinese grammar and seems to be a relic from a prehistoric southern substratum, like the structure following '有 *yǒu* + O' in Unit 10. Whatever its origin, we are interested here only in its function, which will involve a slight but messy digression (skip it if you're not that interested in historical grammar).

Digression begins.

One meaning of 所 *suǒ* is as a noun meaning 'place', as in 得其所 *dé qí suǒ* /v dn = V O/ 'find one's (right) place'. The trouble is that when it is qualified by a verb, the verb usually FOLLOWS it instead of preceding it, as in 所居 *suǒ jū* /N(V)/, 'the place where he lives', though there are also examples of the 'normal' order, e.g. 無定所 *wú dìng suǒ* /v vn = V (V)O/ 'has no fixed place, has no fixed abode'.

To make things worse, if it is qualified by a following clause containing a subject, the subject PRECEDES the 所 *suǒ*, as in 人所居 *rén suǒ jū* 'the places where people live', where the structure seems to be a noun qualifying a noun-phrase which in turn consists of a noun qualified by a following clause.

From 'the place where' 所 *suǒ* somehow comes to mean 'that which', as in 人所知 *rén suǒ zhī* 'that which people know, what people know', with the same structure. So it may be that 人所見山 *rén suǒ jiàn shān* originally meant 'the mountain, [viz.] the one which someone sees', where 'the mountain' stands in apposition to the rest of the phrase.

Digression ends.

My solution to this jumbled mess of historically competing structures is to notate 所 *suǒ* as /a/, except where it is behaving 'normally' as a solitary noun or as a head-noun PRECEDED by a qualifier. This will entail supplying an 'understood' (unexpressed) head-noun in some cases, viz. [N], to remind you that 所 *suǒ* X is functioning as a noun-phrase. This should make life much simpler without detracting from the validity of the analysis. This will give us, instead of the above notation, 所居 *suǒ jū* as /av = (AV)[N]/, and both 人所居 *rén suǒ jū* and 人所知 *rén suǒ zhī* as /nav = (SAV)[N]/.

In actual poetic practice the most common form of object-headed relative clause is /av n = (AV) N/, e.g. 所見山 *suǒ jiàn shān* 'the mountain which [I, you etc.] see'.

6.8 The adverbial-headed qualifying clause

Here a whole clause, i.e. one in which both subject and object are permitted but not necessarily used, qualifies a noun which represents neither the subject nor the object of an underlying sentence, but is an adverbial of (1) time, (2) place or (3) something which in the underlying sentence would have some other relationship to the predicator, often difficult to specify exactly.

(1) When an attributive clause qualifies a noun of time, the connective in the corresponding English relative clause will not be 'who' or 'which' or 'that', but 'when' or even 'after':

明月照君時 *míng yuè zhào jūn shí* /vn vnn = (SVO)N/, which we may notate as /(SVO)A/ when it is functioning as an adverbial, literally 'bright moon shine on you TIME', meaning 'WHEN the bright moon shines on you';

遊人歸來日 *yóu rén guī lái rì* /vn vvn = (SV)N or (SV)A/, literally 'wandering person return come DAY', meaning '[ON] THE DAY WHEN the wanderer comes back home';

此人返鄉後 *cǐ rén fǎn xiāng hòu* /dn vnn = (SVO)N = SVO)A/, literally 'this person return home AFTER-TIME', meaning 'AFTER he has returned home'.

(2) When an attributive clause qualifies a noun of place, the English connective will not be 'which' but 'where':

此人獨居處 *cǐ rén dú jū chù* /dn avn = (SAV)N = (SAV)A/, literally 'this person alone live PLACE', 'meaning [AT] THE PLACE WHERE he lives alone'.

Nouns of place include buildings and so on WHERE something happens or roads ALONG WHICH people travel, for instance 'the path ALONG WHICH we came' will be either 來徑 *lái jìng* /vn = (V)N/ or 所來徑 *suǒ lái jìng* /(AV)N/ according to whether two or three syllables are required by the metre.

(3) Even when the head is not a noun of time, the English equivalent may include the word 'when', for instance 別情 *bié qíng*, literally 'say-goodbye feelings' may be thought of as 'the feelings I have WHEN I say goodbye'. It does NOT mean 'the feelings WHICH say goodbye'. There are several other words besides 情 *qíng* commonly used for one's feelings in such contexts, e.g. 思 *sì* (N.B. tone) 'yearning', 意 *yì* '(state of) mind, mood' and 心 *xīn* 'heart, feelings'.

A similar case is 行跡 *xíng jī* literally 'walk footprints', meaning 'the footprints WHERE he walked' or simply 'his footprints'. It does not mean 'the footprints WHICH walk'.

Similarly with 離杯 *lí bēi* 'a parting cup, a cup of wine which one drinks WHEN parting', not 'a cup WHICH departs'.

It will now be obvious that in order to decide the exact semantic relationship of a Chinese attributive clause to its head-noun you will not have the same same precise indications that you will find in an English relative clause but will have to rely upon common sense and imagination.

Exercise

(47) 但見江邊思鄉客 (48) 深山居者知風寒 (49) 不知深夜彈者誰 (50) 此豈昨夜所聞聲 (51) 何不復歸所居山 (52) 所見春花豈能久 (53) 故人去後未復聞 (54) 去時春花歸時落 (55) 遊人歸日多寒風 (56) 今日見月復何夜 (57) 歸鳥落處白沙寒 (58) 明月出照落水花 (59) 明月出時花影白 (60) 何年復見所思人

UNIT 7

In this unit we begin reading real poems in addition to the often very unpoetic made-up lines that we have been using for grammar and vocabulary practice. You should by this point be familiar with the vocabulary and grammar of these poems.

The suggested procedure in this and all similar 'real verse' units is:

(1) Make a literal translation of the first poem;

(2) Check your translation against the key to make sure you have got the sense right (the actual wording of your translation does not matter, of course);

(3) Read the discussion of the form and meaning of the poem;

(4) Then repeat the procedure for the second and third poems.

You may of course also wish to make 'literary' translations of the poems for your own amusement, though that has nothing to do with this language course.

If you wish to memorise the Chinese text you will find this a great help in reading other poems in the future, particularly in the matter of atmosphere and overtones.

Text 1[4]

Wang Wei (early eighth century): 'Luzhai'

空山不見人 *kōng shān bù jiàn rén*

但聞人語響 *dàn wén rén yǔ xiǎng*

返景入深林 *fǎn yǐng rù shēn lín*

復照青苔上 *fù zhào qīng tái shàng*

---

[4] 王維 （輞川集） 鹿砦 唐5

Notes on the text

Luzhai: a place-name, near Wang Wei's retirement cottage. In line 3 景 is here an alternative spelling of 影.

Discussion of Text 1

The five-syllable quatrain is the shortest form of Chinese poem. Its purpose is often to create an atmosphere or mood by minimalist means, requiring the reader to put real effort into getting into it: visualizing the scene, developing the implications, and feeling the overtones and resonances of the words. In poems as short as this, every word is important, and since the physical compass is small there is a better chance for the images to resonate with one another.

Some students find it helpful to hang a copy of a poem on a wall where it will catch the eye from time to time, so that as the days go by it will have a chance to unfold and display its deeper recesses.

Although I think that 'explaining' a poem in one's own language can be as deadening as explaining a joke, I'm going to use the poems in this course as teaching material both for language and culture, and that inevitably means a certain amount of explaining, for we are dealing with a language and culture far removed in space and time from the West, and even from modern China in time.

At first glance much Chinese verse may seem bland and innocuous, but there are always different levels of coding and disguise to get through. In general, these are three in number:

(a) the poet's own personality and experience of his world;
(b) the Chinese environment, physical, social and literary–cultural;
(c) deliberate coding or disguise.

Much of the first is beyond knowledge but not beyond conjecture from the internal evidence of the poems themselves; but since this is primarily a language course I shall not on the whole venture into the realms of biographical literary criticism, particularly since a great deal has been written on that topic, whereas the actual language of Chinese verse has attracted far less attention from academics. I shall concentrate on the second type of coding, which was the common, largely unconsciously absorbed heritage of a particular cultural group. I shall not concern myself with the third type of coding, which was adopted for the disguise of political or personal criticism or else as literary showing-off, for apart from the voluminous commentaries needed to explain it, it does not necessarily even produce good poetry.

However, to give you a taste of these other two types of coding I have given examples of deliberate coding in Unit 39 and of personal coding in Unit 40. I should not like to give the impression that the relatively straightforward verse in this elementary language course is the end of the story.

So what do we need to know about the cultural background of this particular poem?

In the first couplet we encounter a very common theme: the basic conflict of the Chinese civil servant in retirement. Someone who has grown up in the intensely socially-oriented environment of an extended Chinese family will inevitably take his need for company with him when he tries to be alone, so that a conflict arises between his conscious desire for solitude and his unconscious need to have other people around him. Wang Wei's solution is to sit in a wood on a hillside where he cannot see people and be disturbed by them but where he has the reassurance of their distant voices.

The word 空 *kōng* 'empty' is a key word in Chinese verse; here it means 'with no people around'. We shall meet it later as an adverb describing the rest of Nature's lack of interest in the human race and its concerns, but for the moment we are only concerned with its intra-human meaning: an empty hillside is one where one can avoid not just people in general but more particularly the political rat race and stressful social over-involvement in general. In the Buddhist sense 空 *kōng* was an attempt to escape conscious social stresses by 'emptying' the conscious mind (this was before Freud's discovery of the unconscious, remember). In another poem which we shall read later (in Unit 24) Wang Wei speaks of peaceful meditation to restrain his 'poisonous dragon', a rather more picturesque way of describing this attempt at escape.

But at the same time an empty hillside is unpitying, devoid of compassion for the poet, and any use of the word 空 *kōng* in the sense of escape will constantly be haunted by the theme of unfeelingness. This is something that goes back to early Taoism and Han-dynasty Confucianism, which make a clear division between mankind (人 *rén*) and the rest of Nature (天 *tiān*), and it recurs as a constant theme or undertone throughout Chinese poetry. An example is a line in a poem by Du Fu where he is saying goodbye to a departing friend: 青山空復情 [5] *qīng shān kōng fù qíng* 'The green hills emptily respond to our feelings'; we are sad at parting and we imagine that we see our sadness reflected in the face of the hills, but we know that the hills do not really share our feelings, and the realisation that we look in vain for some sympathy from Nature only makes our sadness and isolation the more poignant. This is of course the same feeling that Robert Burns expresses by 'How can ye chant, ye little birds, and I sae fu' o' care!'

The image of the second couplet is that of the poet being in the wood all day long, from early morning when the rays of the rising sun still penetrated beneath the canopy of the trees and made the mosses deep in the wood glow in the semi-darkness. During the day the high sun has been unable to penetrate the canopy and the moss has not glowed. Now it is evening and once again the sun is low enough for its rays to return to the depths of the wood and once

---

[5] 杜甫　奉濟驛重送嚴公四韻　唐3

again illuminate the moss. The two key words here are 返 *fǎn* 'return' and 復 *fù* 'again', for without them we should not be reminded of the similar situation at sunrise.

So much for the meteorology and the botany; but what is the poem really about? Here I can only say what it suggests to me personally, though you may relate the image to something else in your experience of life. I see the early morning, the hot daytime and the cool evening as symbols of early childhood, of working life and of retirement respectively. In childhood we see with unclouded eye the moss glowing like green fire, the summer meadows bright with flowers, the cotton-wool clouds in a sky as deep as the sea. Then the pressures of formal education and work tend to dim our vision of these things, just as the canopy of the trees blocks out the sunlight. In retirement we may recapture something of the child's naive, unobstructed perception of reality in all its vividness. And so the wheel comes full circle, the rooks return from their foraging, and dusk promises the ultimate rest and oblivion.

I have a suspicion that an important part of the aesthetic appeal of Chinese poetry lies in its use of simple, vivid images from the 'natural' world that restore to us briefly this childhood vision of non-human Nature (天 *tiān*) without the interposition of the moil and toil of life's scheming and competing.

Text 2[6]

Wang Wei (early eighth century): 'Zhuliguan'

獨 坐 幽 篁 裏 *dú zuò yōu huáng lǐ*

彈 琴 復 長 嘯 *tán qín fù cháng xiào*

深 林 人 不 知 *shēn lín rén bù zhī*

明 月 來 相 照 *míng yuè lái xiāng zhào*

Note on the text

Zhuliguan: another place-name in that area.

---

[6] 王維 （輞川集）竹里館 唐5

Discussion of Text 2

This poem is one of the same suite as the preceding one and takes the idea of escape a stage farther. This time the poet has a visitor, but not a troublesome human one. The moon demands nothing of him but it does take the trouble to come and shine on him, to show him some attention. The trouble with the moon is that the poet knows, consciously or unconsciously, that it may give light but it provides no warmth, being the ice-palace of the lonely, self-exiled moon lady Chang'e that we shall meet later. Like emptiness, moonlight reflects a conflict.

Text 3[7]

Meng Haoran (689–740): 'Spring dawn'

春眠不覺曉 *chūn mián bù jué xiǎo*

處處聞啼鳥 *chù chù wén tí niǎo*

夜來風雨聲 *yè lái fēng yǔ shēng*

花落知多少 *huā luò zhī duō shǎo*

Discussion of Text 3

Here we have an unusual use of the quatrain, though we shall see its mirror-image in the third poem in Unit 12. It describes the process of waking up in four successive stages: first, unconsciousness; second, the awakening of sensory perception; third, the awakening of memory; and fourth, the awakening of rational thought, giving full daytime consciousness.

I shall only mention that spring is the season of new growth, just as dawn is the coming of new light; but the fall of spring blossom from the trees is a common symbol of the brevity and evanescence of human life. The word 知 *zhī* 'I wonder' brings a note of helplessness in the face of heartless Nature; it was used in this way especially in the song-style poetry of the Sung dynasty.

---

[7] 孟浩然 春曉 唐 5

After this literary interlude we shall resume our confrontation with new grammar and vocabulary for the next four units before we meet more actual poems in Unit 12.

UNIT 8

This unit is concerned with verbs of movement and location.

Vocabulary

吹 吹 *chuī* /v/ blow 30.4 (M 口 'mouth')

到 到 *dào* /v/ arrive at, reach; to 18.6 (M 至 'arrive')

渡 渡 *dù* /v/ cross, pass over (esp. water); across (also written 度)
85.9 (M 氵 'water')

飛 飛 *fēi* /v/ fly; float in the air 183.0 (W)

孤 孤 *gū* /v/ be lonely; orphaned 39.5 (M 子 'child')

海 海 *hǎi* /n/ sea 85.7 (M 氵 'water')

徑 徑 *jìng* /n/ path 60.7 (M 彳 'go')

看 看 *kàn* /v/ look at, watch 109.4 (M 目 'eye')

上 上 *shàng* /v/ ascend, rise; up

松 松 *sōng* /n/ pine-tree 75.4 (M 木 'tree')

隨 隨 *suí* /v/ follow, go with 170.13 (M 辶 'go')

童 童 *tóng* /n/ boy 117.7 (M 辛 =?, S 重 *zhòng*, both abbreviated)

童子 童子 *tóng zǐ* /n2/ boy, servant-boy

翁 翁 *wēng* /n/ old man 124.4 (S)

下 下 *xià* /v/ descend; set; settle; down

行 行 *xíng* /v/ travel (of person, boat etc); walk, go; row or sail (a boat)
144.0 (W)

雪 雪 *xuě* /n/ snow 173.3 (M 雨 'rain')

遊人 遊人 *yóu rén* /n2/ wanderer, man travelling away from home
on civil or military service

78

遊 子 遊 子 *yóu zǐ* /n2/ = 遊人 *yóu rén*

在 在 *zài* /v/ be at; at; be alive, be still in existence 32.3 (M 土 'earth')

x 何 在 *hé zài* /nav = SAV/ 'Where is X?'

舟 舟 *zhōu* /n/ boat 137.0 (W)

舟 子 *zhōu zǐ* /n2/ boatman

子 子 *zǐ* /n/ person (polite), gentleman; you, sir 39.0 (W)

8.1 Compound verbs of movement

In Unit 4 we saw how one line of verse may consist of two statements with an unexpressed relationship between them. In this unit we look at one particular type of relationship, viz. that between two or more verbs of movement or location, either immediately adjoining one another or separated by other words, combining to describe one single movement. A combination usually consists of two or more of the following elements in the order given:

(a) Verb of MODE of movement, e.g. 步 *bù* 'walk', 行 *xíng* 'travel', 飛 *fēi* 'fly', 遊 *yóu* 'wander', 流 *liú* 'flow', 吹 *chuī* 'blow', 隨 *suí* 'follow';

(b) Object of (a) if it is a transitive verb, e.g. 葉 *yè* 'leaves' as the object of 吹 *chuī* 'blow' in 風吹葉 *fēng chuī yè* 'The wind blows the leaves …';

(c) Verb of OBJECTIVE direction, e.g.
出 *chū* ('emerge') 'out, out of, out into',
入 *rù* ('enter') 'in, into',
上 *shàng* ('ascend') 'up, up on to , up along',
下 *xià* ('descend') 'down, down to, down into, down along',
歸 *guī* ('return') 'back, back to',
返 *fǎn* ('return') 'back, back to',
渡 *dù* ('cross') 'across',
到 *dào* ('arrive, arrive at, reach') 'to'.

Note that these Chinese verbs in this position are translated as English adverbs if not followed by a destination, or as prepositions if followed by a destination.

(d) Object (destination) of the preceding verb, (also route or origin in some cases);

(e) Verb of SUBJECTIVE direction (direction relative to location of speaker, cf. German *hin-* and *her-* with verbs of movement), viz. 來 *lái* 'come, hither, to here, in this direction', and 去 *qù* 'go, go away, hence, thither, away'. An exception is the combination 來 到 *lái dào* 'come to' followed by a destination.

8.2 Compound verbs of location

These combinations are much more limited and consist of:

(a) Mode of location, e.g. 居 *jū* 'dwell', 坐 *zuò* 'sit';
(c) General verb of location, viz. 在 *zài* 'be at';
(d) Object of place.

8.3 Structure of the combinations

The five elements under (a) to (e) consist of three verbs, of which the first may be followed by an object and the second by an object of destination or place. I shall use hyphens instead of commas to connect any of these components that are present to emphasize that they are not three separate predications but are working together to describe one single movement. When all five of the above positions are filled, our notation for this will be: /VO-VO-V/. Examples of some such combinations:

a-c--: 流出 *liú chū* /V-V/ 'flow out'

a---e: 飛來 *fēi lái* /V-V/ 'fly hither'

a-cd-: 遊到海 *yóu dào hǎi* /V-VO/ 'wander to the sea'

--c-e: 歸去 *guī qù* /V-V/ 'go back, go home'

a-cd-: 飛上天 *fēi shàng tiān* /V-VO/ 'fly up into the sky'

--cde: 下山來 *xià shān lái* /VO-V/ 'come down the hill'

abcde: 吹葉渡河去 *chuī yè dù hé qù* /VO-VO-V/ 'blow the leaves away across the river'

a-cd-: 居在海邊 *jū zài hǎi biān* /V-VO/ 'live by the seaside'

Exercise

We shall practise the verbs of movement and location first in short phrases, then in complete lines mixed with general revision.

(1) 流出 (2) 飛入 (3) 步返 (4) 遊渡 (5) 流出 (6) 飛來 (7) 步來 (8) 遊去 (9) 出來 (10) 上去 (11) 歸來 (12) 渡去 (13)

上天 (14) 下海 (15) 渡山 (16) 返林 (17) 渡河 (18) 上山去
(19) 返谷來 (20) 入林去 (21) 流入海 (22) 飛上雲 (23) 吹
渡江 (24) 步下山 (25) 來到此 (26) 行到海 (27) 返到江
(28) 見人下山來 (29) 大風吹渡江 (30) 寒雪流入竹 (31)
昨夜眠中聞雨聲 (32) 獨行小舟下大江 (33) 故人歸來長
夜語 (34) 海水上天風高嘯 (35) 今年此處行人少 (36) 上
天下海日日飛 (37) 昨遊山前今山後 (38) 童子何事不歸
去 (39) 但見舟子坐空舟 (40) 去鄉居在幽谷里 (41) 遊人
未歸故鄉來 (42) 風來落花飛上天 (43) 竹徑鳥啼人不來
(44) 琴響到舟知誰彈 (45) 小舟出海不復返 (46) 但見白
雲相隨來 (47) 青天白鳥來去飛 (48) 孤翁行舟獨寒江
(49) 寒月來照松徑雪 (50) 風前松雪落幽徑 (51) 舟子坐
看白雲渡 (52) 風吹秋葉渡空山 (53) 河水流來復流去
(54) 客上小舟渡湖去 (55) 入山已久未出來 (56) 遊客在
此已一月 (57) 夜來高風吹葉下 (58) 孤翁已去幽徑在
(59) 童年故人今何在 (60) 何人獨坐青松下

UNIT 9

This unit is concerned with (a) prepositional verbs, (b) modal adverbs and (c) complete object-clauses.

Vocabulary

傍 傍 *bàng* /v/ be beside; /prep/ beside; along 9.10 (M 人 'person')

悲 悲 *bēi* /v/ be sad; be sad that 61.8 (M 心 'heart')

別 別 *bié* /v/ say goodbye, take one's leave, leave 18.5 (M 刀 'knife')

採 採 *căi* /v/ pluck, gather (fruit, flowers, mulberry leaves etc) 64.8 (M 扌 'hand')

釣 釣 *diào* /v/ fish with rod, angle 167.3 (M 金 'metal')

敢 敢 *gǎn* /v/ dare to 66.8 (S)

恐 恐 *kǒng* /v/ fear that 61.6 (M 心 'heart')

臨 臨 *lín* /v/ look down over/on; stand above, stand on the edge of; /prep/ above; on the point of, facing 131.11 (S 品, M 見 'see' bent over to look down)

泣 泣 *qì* /v/ weep 85.5 (M 氵 'water')

師 師 *shī* /n/ teacher, master 50.7 (X)

宿 宿 *sù* /v/ spend the night, lodge, put up 40.8 (W: person on mat under roof)

同 同 *tóng* /v/ have the same …; be in/from the same …(e.g. 同鄉 *tóng xiāng* /n2/ fellow townsman); /prep/ in the same …(e.g. 同舟 *tōng zhōu* /VO/ be in the same boat) 30.3 (X)

問 問 *wèn* /v/ ask ('enquire', not 'ask for') 30.8 (M 口 'mouth')

言 言 *yán* /v/ speak, say; speech; language 149.0 (X)

藥 藥 *yào* /n/ medicinal herbs, medicine 140.15 (M 艹 'plant')

依 依 *yī* /v/ rest on; /prep/ on 9.6 (M 人 'person')

82

應 應 *yīng* /v/ ought to, should, have a duty to; probably 61.13 (M 心 'heart')

欲 欲 *yù* /v/ wish to, want to; be about to; be almost 76.7 (M 欠 'gape')

蹤 蹤 *zōng* /n/ footprints, tracks 157.11 (M 足 'foot')

9.1 Prepositional verbs

In most European languages we have words and phrases that normally function as prepositions, e.g. 'in, on, at, beside, in place of, by means of' etc. These are combined with noun-phrases to form adverbials or adjectivals.

We have seen that the Chinese equivalent of some of these is the postpositional noun. We now see another type of Chinese equivalent, the prepositional verb followed by a place-expression and together with it forming a secondary (subordinate) clause. To some extent the two types overlap in meaning, e.g. 'beside the sea' can be expressed either as 海邊 *hǎi biān* /np = N/ '[at the]sea side' or 傍海 *bàng hǎi* /v n = V O/ 'being beside the sea'.

It is important to understand that I am using the term 'prepositional verb' merely because we are starting from English, and English often has prepositions where Chinese has a verb. All that 'prepositional verb' means is 'Chinese verbs used in a secondary clause where English would use a preposition'. From a purely Chinese perspective these are no different from any other verbs and do not form a separate class, since they can also be used as main verbs, unlike English prepositions. My hope is that you will soon come to see them as ordinary verbs used in series with other verbs.

For the moment we are concerned with six verbs. For each I shall give two examples, the first example having one of these verbs as the main verb of a clause, corresponding to an English verb, and the second example having it as the main verb of a secondary clause in position 2, corresponding to an English preposition. The structure of the first type is /v n = V O/ and that of the second is /vn v = (VO) V/.

依 *yī* X 'rest on X, rely on X': 依人 *yī rén* 'rely on other people'
依 *yī* X V 'V resting on X, V on X': 依石啼 *yī shí tí* '(of bird) sing (perched) on a rock'

隨 *suí* X 'follow X': 隨師 *suí shī* 'follow one's teacher, go with one's teacher'
隨 *suí* X V 'V with X': 隨水流 *suí shuǐ liú* 'drift with the stream'

臨 *lín* X 'look down over X': 臨海 *lín hǎi* 'look down over the sea'
臨 *lín* X V 'V on the edge of X': 臨別泣 *lín bié qì* 'weep on the verge of parting'

傍 *bàng* X 'be beside X': 傍我 *bàng wǒ* 'stand beside me, keep close to me'
傍 *bàng* X V 'V beside X': 傍林飛 *bàng lín fēi* 'fly along the edge of the wood'

同 *tóng* X 'share X, have the same X': 同師 *tóng shī* 'have the same teacher'
同 *tóng* X V 'V in (etc) the same X': 同舟行 *tóng zhōu xíng* 'travel in the same boat'

在 *zài* X 'be at X': 在此 *zài cǐ* 'is here'
在 *zài* X V 'V at X': 在此眠 *zài cǐ mián* 'sleeps here'

Exercise

The following exercise also contains a few non-prepositional examples!

(1)上山臨長江 (2)傍海行幾時 (3)孤鳥依沙宿 (4)落花隨流水 (5)何不同舟返 (6)臨海看行舟 (7)傍河來去步 (8)臨風看雨來 (9)一翁釣秋水 (10)別時客長泣 (11)傍林步到此 (12)童子隨翁歸 (13)白雲依高山 (14)木影依青苔 (15)隨水到青海 (16)舟客相傍坐 (17)孤月臨人白 (18)臨去見客來 (19)師蹤今何在 (20)曉出採山藥 (21)依人能幾時 (22)傍湖依石釣 (23)久在海外今初歸 (24)秋山明月隨人歸 (25)沙間河鳥相傍宿 (26)在外思君何年見 (27)河鳥來宿寒水邊 (28)同鄉居此未相會 (29)今日在此幾時去 (30)秋葉隨風浮空林 (31)曉出看木春色明 (32)一翁依石坐看春 (33)日日臨湖何所看 (34)江鳥宿處今夜寒 (35)月照孤舟依白沙 (36)多少遊人在外宿 (37)松下獨坐看山鳥 (38)故人出外今何在 (39)同日來此同日去 (40)今居深山傍孤松 (41)初覺海鳥隨我舟 (42)夜來亦宿寒海水 (43)今返故鄉幾人在 (44)遊子久在天邊行 (45)天上但見孤鳥飛

9.2 Verbs taking predicates as objects

These verbs, sometimes known as 'modal verbs', correspond to verbs which in English are usually followed by 'to' plus another verb, e.g. 'want to go', 'be unable to see'; with some English modal verbs the 'to' may be absent, e.g. 'can go', 'dare say'. By 'predicate' I mean a clause without a subject, i.e. just /…AVOA/ at the most, /…V/ at the least.

We have already met 能 *néng* 'can, be able to'; now we add to this some of the verbs corresponding to the English for 'want to', 'dare to' and 'ought to'. In my notation a colon is used to separate a verb from its object if the latter is a predicate or clause. Cf. next section.

Note that 應 *yīng* can be used in two senses of the English 'should', referring either to duty (e.g 'You really should go') or to probability (e.g. 'He should be there by now', meaning 'He's probably there by now').

Some of these verbs can also take a noun object, e.g. 欲此 *yù cǐ* /v n = V O/ 'want this', but 欲落 *yù luò* /v v = V:V/ 'is about to fall'.

Exercise

(46) 風大不敢坐舟渡 (47) 雪深應見行人蹤 (48) 小童未能語 (49) 春色豈能久 (50) 夜深天欲明 (51) 君來何所欲 (52) 山高雪深豈敢上 (53) 故人別去我欲泣 (54) 應上山去採此藥 (55) 應知師所居 (56) 人問何泣言悲秋

9.3 Verbs taking clauses as objects

Apart from verbs of perception such as 見 *jiàn* and 聞 *wén*, verbs taking complete clauses (i.e. /ASAVOA/ at the most, /SV/ at the least) as their objects include those of knowledge, emotion and speech. In English the equivalents of these verbs are usually followed by 'that' plus a clause. The 'that' is often omitted in English, so that both 'I know THAT he is here' and 'I know he is here' are equally possible.

We have already met 知 *zhī* 'know that' followed by a clause object; now we meet in addition the words for 'ask', 'say that', 'fear that' and 'be sad that'. There are, of course, many others. A reminder: when these verbs take a noun object, the object will be notated as an ordinary /O/ , i.e. /v n = V O/, but when they take a clause as object there will be a colon between the verb and its object /nv nvn = SV: SVO/. An example of the notation of a verb having as its object a clause which in turn contains a verb with a predicate as its object: 但

恐舟子不敢渡 *dàn kǒng zhōu zǐ bù gǎn dù* 'I'm only afraid that the boatman will not dare cross over', /av n2av v = AV:SAV:V/.

Exercise

(57) 不敢問師何所欲 (58) 不知何在應問人 (59) 翁言不知幾時返 (60) 但恐水深不敢渡 (61) 但悲春花不能久 (62) 誰言今年雪不下 (63) 年年秋來悲木落 (64) 長恐別後久不返

UNIT 10

This unit is concerned with (a) verbs of possession/existence, (b) quantity, and (c) two-line sentences.

Vocabulary

百 百   *bǎi* /q/ hundred 106.1 (W: merging of 一 'one' and 白 'hundred' < S *bái*)

層 層   *céng* /m/ layer; storey; (as qualifier of noun) piled up in layers, extending one behind the other into the distance (of mountains or clouds) 44.12 (M 尸 'sit still', perhaps corruption of 广 'house')

戴 戴   *dài* /v/ wear on the head 62.14 (S)

更 更   *gèng* /a/ further, more, in addition 73.3 (X)

黃 黃   *huáng* /v/ be yellow or brown 201.0 (X)

黃 鳥   *huáng niǎo* /n2/ golden oriole

里 里   *lǐ* /m/ about one-third of a mile 166.0 (X)

笠 笠   *lì* /n/ wide bamboo hat (against sun or rain) 118.5 (M 竹 'bamboo')

樓 樓   *lóu* /n/ storeyed building, tower 75.11 (M 木 'wood')

目 目   *mù* /n/ eye 109.0 (W)

披 披   *pī* /v/ wear draped around the shoulders 64.5 (M 扌 'hand')

千 千   *qiān* /q/ thousand 24.1 (intersection of 一 'one' and 人 'thousand' < S *rén*)

情 情   *qíng* /n/ feelings, emotions. 別情 *bié qíng* /n2/ the sadness of parting 61.8 (M 忄 'heart')

蓑 蓑   *suō* /n/ rush rain-cape (also written 簑) 140.10 (M 艹 'plant')

萬 萬   *wàn* /q/ ten thousand, myriad. 萬物 *wàn wù* /n2/ the myriad creatures, Nature 140.9 (S)

87

無 無 *wú* /v/ there is/are not; not have; be without 86.8 (S)

物 物 *wù* /n/ thing, creature, person. 物外 *wù wài* /np/ beyond this world 93.4 (S)

有 有 *yǒu* /v/ there is/are; have. 有時 *yǒu shí* /a2/ sometimes 74.2 (MX, S 又 *yòu*)

只 只 *zhǐ* /a/ only 30.2 (X)

10.1 Verbs of possession and existence

The basic meaning of 有 *yǒu* seems to be 'have' or 'possess', as in 我有一小舟 *wǒ yǒu yī xiǎo zhōu* /n v qvn = S V O/ 'I have a little boat', but it has also come to mean 'there is'. The negative of 有 *yǒu* is usually 無 *wú* not 不有 *bù yǒu*; it means 'not have' or 'there is not'. In English 'have' is sometimes used in a similar way, as in 'Earth has many a noble city', meaning 'There are many noble cities on earth'. In French 'Il y a un X', literally 'He has an X there', means 'There is an X', though it is not obvious who 'he' originally was. The Chinese equivalent 有 *yǒu* X 'Has X', i.e. 'There is an X', does not even have a 'he'. It may help to think in terms of '[The universe] has X' in such cases.

有 *yǒu* is often preceded by an expression of place, e.g. 河外有高山 *hé wài yǒu gāo shān* /np v vn = A V O/ 'Beyond the river there are high mountains'.

In Classical Chinese prose 有之 *yǒu zhī* /v n = V O/ occurs, literally 'Has it', meaning 'It exists' or 'It happened', but the object-pronoun 之 *zhī* 'it' is not much used in verse, so you can expect to see 有 *yǒu* or 無 *wú* without an object in the sense of 'It exists' or 'It does not exist' respectively. The simplest use I can quote from verse is the last word of the line 青靄入看無[8] *qīng ǎi rù kān wú* 'When I enter the blue mists and look at them, they do not exist', which may be considered as shorthand for *入青靄, 看青靄, 無青靄 *rù qīng ǎi, kān qīng ǎi, wú qīng ǎi*, i.e. where 'there are no blue mists' /v vn = V O/ is reduced to 'there are none' /v = V[O]/, like the prose 無之 *wú zhī*. (靄 *ǎi* 'mist' consists of 雨言曷)

But very often the object of 有 *yǒu* will be followed by other statements to create a structure corresponding in function (but not in structure) to an English relative clause (either specifying or non-specifying). Yet we cannot treat the following statements as qualifiers, for these always precede the head in Chinese.

---

[8] 王維 終南山 唐3

What we have here is a fundamental stylistic difference between Chinese and English: where English would say 'I met an old man wearing a rain-cape', Classical Chinese could only say the equivalent of 'I met an old man; he was wearing a rain-cape'. In other words, where English tends to incorporate its statements into complex sentences consisting of a marked hierarchy of main and secondary clauses, Classical Chinese prefers a series of simple statements with few marked relationships and no hierarchical structure of main and secondary components.

We may call such a statement following / 有 *yǒu* O .../ an 'added description' For convenience of notation I shall treat an added description as if it were an object-clause, separating it from the preceding clause with a colon; this should cause no confusion with the other uses of the colon since this use occurs only in conjunction with the verbs 有 *yǒu* and 無 *wú*.

Here are some examples, all from poems by Du Fu:

(a) 有柏生崇岡 [9] *yǒu bǎi shēng chóng gāng* 'There is a cypress WHICH grows on a lofty ridge' /v n v vn = V O: V O/.

(b) 有徑金沙軟 [10] *yǒu jìng jīn shā ruǎn* 'There is a path WHERE the golden sand is soft' or 'There is a path WHOSE golden sand is soft' /v n nn v = V O: S V/.

(c) 有田種穀今流血 [11] *yǒu tián zhòng gǔ jīn liú xuè* 'There are fields WHERE they planted millet but WHERE now flows blood' /v n v n n v n = V O: {V O, A V S}/. (The comma separates two equal (non-object) clauses, both of which refer to the fields, hence the curly brackets. The final /VS/ word-order is a construction to be dealt with in Unit 14.)

(d) 英雄有時亦如此 [12] *yīng xióng yǒu shí yì rú cǐ* 'Heroes have times WHEN [they] also are like this', i.e. 'Even heroes sometimes do this', literally /n2 v n a v n = S V O: A V O/. I personally prefer to treat 有時 *yǒu shí* as a set phrase (adverbial of time) meaning 'sometimes' /a2/, giving /n2 a2 a v n = S A A V O/ here, which would certainly be a simpler solution.

(e) 中有高唐天下無 [13] *zhōng yǒu gāo táng tiān xià wú* 'In the midst is the Gaotang [Prospect-tower], WHICH under Heaven there is not [the equal of]' or ' ... whose equal does not exist in the world' /p v n2 n2 v = A V O: A V/.

A variation on this structure is when 有 *yǒu* corresponds to the English 'something' as the object of a verb, an abbreviated form of '有所 *yǒu suǒ* Verb', meaning literally 'have that which one Verbs'. In view of my simplified

---

[9] 杜甫　病柏　杜10

[10] 杜甫　陪王使君晦日泛江…，其二　杜13

[11] 杜甫　憶昔二首，其二　杜13

[12] 杜甫　今夕行　杜1

[13] 杜甫　夔州歌十絕句，其十　杜15

treatment of 所 *suǒ* above I shall go for a simple solution here and treat 有所 *yǒu suǒ* or 有 *yǒu* 'something', 無所 *wú suǒ* or 無 *wú* 'nothing' and 何所 *hé suǒ* or 何 *hé* 'what' as preverbal object-pronouns /n v = O V/; for instance 有 所問 *yǒu suǒ wèn* literally 'have THAT WHICH one asks', will be treated as 'something ask', i.e. 'ask something' or 'ask a question'.

Most Chinese verbs form their negative by prefixing 不 *bù*, but the verb 有 *yǒu* is an exception in that 不有 *bù yǒu* rarely occurs, usually in conditional clauses meaning 'if there is not'; otherwise the negative of 有 *yǒu* is 無 *wú* /v/ (or 無有 *wú yǒu* /av/ if the metre requires it), meaning 'there is not' or 'have not' or 'without'.

無 *wú* is used in all the ways mentioned above for 有 *yǒu*, e.g. 無人知 *wú rén zhī* /v n v = V O: V/ 'There is nobody who knows, nobody knows'; 無所 知 *wú suǒ zhī* /n2 v = O V/ or 無知 *wú zhī* /n v = O V/ 'knows nothing'; 無 時 *wú shí* /a2/ 'never'.

Another common use of 無 *wú* is in the structure 無 *wú* X Y /vn n = (VO) N/ meaning 'X-less Y, a Y where there are no Xs, Y without X, Y devoid of X', e.g. 無人境 *wú rén jìng* 'a region where there are no people, an uninhabited region'.

A common use of this structure is 無數 *wú shù* X 'Xs without number, countless Xs, very many Xs'.

10.2 Quantity

The basic Chinese numerals are: 一 *yī* 'one', 二 *èr* 'two', 三 *sān* 'three', 四 *sì* 'four', 五 *wǔ* 'five', 六 *liù* 'six', 七 *qī* 'seven', 八 *bā* 'eight', 九 *jiǔ* 'nine', 十 *shí* 'ten', 百 *bǎi* 'hundred', 千 *qiān* 'thousand', 萬 *wàn* 'ten thousand, myriad'.

Compound numerals are formed by combining these on the following pattern: 三百六十五 *sān bǎi liù shí wǔ* 'three hundred, six tens, and five, 365'. Those between ten and twenty are, for instance, 十三 *shí sān*, not *一 十三 *yī shí sān*.

The higher numerals 百 *bǎi*, 千 *qiān* and 萬 *wàn* are usually not to be taken literally in verse but mean 'many' or 'countless' or 'all the', e.g. long distances are often referred to as 千里 *qiān lǐ* or 萬里 *wàn lǐ*. The other numerals above 'two' are mainly used in verse for referring to standard sets of things, e.g. 五嶽 *wǔ yuè* 'the Five Sacred Mountains'.

Other quantifiers are: 兩 *liǎng* 'a pair', 雙 *shuāng* 'a pair', both sometimes used for 'two' or prefixed to things that go in pairs but where the number is not necessarily mentioned in English or where English would use 'both', e.g. 雙手 *shuāng shǒu* 'hands (one pair), both hands'; 半 *bàn* 'half, half-way'; 幾 *jǐ* 'how many?, several'; 數 *shù* 'several'; 多少 *duō shǎo* 'how many?'

Ordinals are the same as cardinals, e.g. 三月 *sān yuè* 'three months' or 'the third month'. 'First' is an exception: 'the first month' is 正月 *zhēng yuè*, otherwise 'first' is usually 初 *chū* or 首 *shǒu*, e.g. 初日 *chū rì* 'the first rays of the sun'.

Frequency: 一 *yī* before a verb means 'once' or 'by one single action' or 'as soon as'. 'Twice' is expressed as 再 *zài*. Otherwise 度 *dù* or 回 *huí* or 遍 *biàn* 'times' is used, e.g. 三度 *sān dù* 'three times, thrice'.

Quantifiers usually combine directly with a countable noun, as we have seen with 一人 *yī rén* /qn = N/ 'one person', or else with a measure followed by a noun, e.g. 一片月 *yī piàn yuè* /qmn = N/ 'a patch (or expanse) of moonlight'. In the latter case the numeral 一 in the sense of 'a' is often omitted, e.g. 杯酒 *bēi jiǔ* /mn = N/ 'a cup(ful) of wine'. Do not confuse this with 酒杯 *jiǔ bēi* /nn/ 'wine-cup' (not necessarily containing any wine). A numeral plus a quantifier may also follow a noun, e.g. 酒百杯 *jiǔ bǎi bēi* /nqm = N/ 'of wine a hundred cupfuls'. Some measures are usually used without any following noun, such as measures of duration and distance, e.g. 行三日 *xíng sān rì* /v qm = V A/ 'travel for three days' or 行千里 *xíng qiān lǐ* /v qm = V A/ 'travel a thousand (Chinese) miles'. I am treating expressions of duration and distance as adverbials, though you might prefer to see them as objects.

10.3 Two-line sentences

The basic unit of most Chinese verse is not the line but the couplet, i.e. an odd-numbered line together with the even-numbered line following it.

Couplets are in general of two kinds: parallel and free (unstructured, non-parallel). In Tang dynasty eight-line 'regulated verse' the usual pattern was for the first and last couplets to be free, while the middle two couplets were of parallel structure. Parallel lines sometimes ran on to form a single sentence, but in general they did not; free couplets, by contrast, usually did form a single sentence. In the second poem in Unit 12 we shall see this difference illustrated in a quatrain of which the first couplet is parallel, while the second is a free two-line sentence. Some critics would regard such a quatrain as resembling the second half of an eight-line poem with the pattern we have mentioned above (except that the tonal pattern is 'unregulated'). In the poem in question the third line is the subject of a clause while the next line is the predicate.

The usual 'free, parallel, parallel, free' pattern of eight-line regulated verse produces a clear aesthetic effect: the free couplets will feel more prosy and natural while the parallel ones will feel more artificial and hence elevated above everyday language into the poetic realm, so that the overall effect is to capture our attention in an ordinary frame of mind, then to raise us to a higher artistic level where we are given an insight into the poet's inner world in terms of parallel patterns and unusual word-orders, and finally to return us to everyday consciousness before releasing us. In fact, a final couplet will often deliberately bring us down to earth with a bump by means of a very 'unpoetic' sentiment or form of expression. Let me illustrate this with a poem that will go beyond the vocabulary we have met but where an English translation should suffice to illustrate the principle involved:

Example text[14]

Sikong Shu (eighth century): 'Wandering and looking afar in early spring'

> East wind, but not yet the fullness of spring;
> I turn my heart to the Great Wall's folds.
> Green grass reminds me of winter haulms,
> bright flowers of autumn chrysanthemums.
> Youth and joy have departed together,
> age and grief come in company.
>
> I think I'll become a temple-tramp,
> going at dusk to stay with Dong Jing.

But this feature of 'coming down to earth' can be seen well before the Tang-dynasty heyday of Chinese poetry, as the following poem of five centuries earlier shows. The detailed structure is different but the overall effect is similar:

Example text[15]

Zhang Xie (third century): 'Miscellaneous poems, No. 4'

> Glowing clouds welcomed the white morning sun,
> red mists hung over Sunrise Vale;
> now gathering clouds blot out the sky,
> trailing heavy swathes of rain.
>
> Light breezes snap the stiffening grasses,
> hoar-frost makes the tall trees quake.
> Dense leaves grow sparser night and day,
> the close woods cluster faggot-tight.

---

[14] 司空曙　早春游望　全292

[15] 張協　雜詩十首，其四　古A4

> In youth I sighed at laggard time,
> in age I mourn the pressing years.
> Worries haunt my twilight days:
> I think I'll have my fortune told.

But other combinations of free and parallel couplets are quite common, both in regulated and unregulated ('ancient-style') verse.

We shall discuss parallelism further in Unit 12, but for the moment let us look at a few examples of single-sentence, free couplets, typically the first or last couplets of a poem. This will involve unfamiliar vocabulary, but equivalents will be given where necessary.

The sentence may be shared between the two lines in various ways, of which three are exemplified below.

(1) The first line is the subject; the second line is the predicate:

寒禽與衰草　處處伴愁顏[16] *hán qín yǔ shuāi cǎo / chù chù bàn chóu yán* 'Chilly birds and withered grasses / everywhere accompany my sad countenance'. (禽 *qín* bird; 與 *yǔ* and; 衰 *shuāi* wither, fade; 草 *cǎo* grass, herbaceous plants; 伴 *bàn* accompany; 愁 *chóu* sad; 顏 *yán* face, facial expression.)

年年越溪女　相憶採芙蓉[17] *nián nián yuè xī nǚ / xiāng yì cǎi fú róng* 'Every year the women [laundering] by the [Ruoye] stream in Yue / remember when she gathered water-lilies'. (越 *yuè* an ancient state in eastern China; 溪 *xī* stream; 女 *nǚ* woman; 憶 *yì* remember; 芙蓉 *fú róng* water-lily, lotus.)

(2) The first line consists of adverbials of time, place, manner etc.; the second line consists of a predicate, with or without a subject:

明日巴陵道　秋山又幾重[18] *míng rì bā líng dào / qiū shān yòu jǐ chóng* 'Tomorrow on the road to Baling / the autumn hills further [will have] how many ranges?' i.e. 'How many more ranges of autumn hills will you encounter on your journey to Baling [beginning] tomorrow?' (巴陵 *bā líng* a place in present-day Hunan; 道 *dào* road, way; 又 *yòu* again, further; 重 *chóng* layer, range.)

明朝望鄉處　應見隴頭梅[19] *míng zhāo wàng xiāng chù / yīng jiàn lǒng tóu méi* 'At (or 'from') the place where I gaze towards my home town tomorrow morning / I should see the plum-blossom at the end of the field-path'. (朝 *zhāo* morning; 望 *wàng* gaze into the distance at; 隴 *lǒng* a raised

[16] 司空曙　賊平後送人北歸　唐3

[17] 杜荀鶴　春宮怨　唐3

[18] 李益　喜見外弟又言別　唐3

[19] 宋之問　題大庾嶺北驛　唐3

path between paddy-fields; 頭 *tóu* head, end (of long object); 梅 *méi* prunus-blossom, 'plum-blossom', first sign of spring.) It has been suggested by commentators that when the poet goes up to a prospect point he will see local plum-blossom that he could send home to the north as an earlier character in literature did, but I have a suspicion that it may mean '… I should be able to imagine that I see the plum-blossom next to the fields at home'. Who can tell for sure? Whatever the implication of the couplet, the structure is clear: the first line contains a time and a place, while the second contains a predicate, the subject ('I') being understood.

(3) The first line begins with a verbal phrase whose object occupies the rest of the line and the whole of the second line. I have used curly brackets in the notation to enclose and emphasize this overlapping object-clause. An introductory phrase of this kind can alert one to the possibility of the couplet being closely linked into a single sentence.

聞道黃龍戍　頻年不解兵[20] *wén dào huáng lóng shù / pín nián bù jiě bīng* (first couplet) 'I hear tell that the Yellow Dragon garrison / year after year do not remove their weapons'. (道 *dào* say; 龍 *lóng* dragon; 戍 *shù* garrison; 頻 *pín* repeated(ly); 解 *jiě* take off (clothes etc.); 兵 *bīng* weapon. The 'Yellow Dragon garrison' means the Chinese troops defending the frontier near the Hun capital of Dragon City, also known as the Yellow Dragon, presumably after the yellow desert sand.) /V: {S A AVO}/.

誰能將旗鼓　一爲取龍城[21] *shuí néng jiàng qí gǔ / yī wèi qǔ lóng chéng* (last couplet) 'Who can lead the banners and drums / once-and-for-all for [us] to capture Dragon City?', i.e. 'Where is the general who can capture the Hun capital once and for all for us at the head of his troops with their banners and drums?' (將 *jiàng* lead (troops); 旗 *qí* banner; 鼓 *gǔ* drum; 爲 *wèi* act on behalf of; 取 *qǔ* take, capture; 城 *chéng* walled city.) /SV: {(VO) A (V) VO}/.

仍憐故鄉水　萬里送行舟[22] *réng lián gù xiāng shuǐ / wàn lǐ sòng xíng zhōu* (last couplet) 'At least you will feel touched that your homeland river / for a myriad miles will be accompanying your travelling boat'. (仍 *réng* still, in spite of everything (here: travelling far from home); 憐 *lián* to be moved to love or pity that …; 送 *sòng* to see someone off by travelling part-way with them.) /AV: {S A VO}/.

誰見汀洲上　相思愁白蘋[23] *shuí jiàn tīng zhōu shàng / xiāng sī chóu bái pín* 'Who sees me here on this sandbank , missing you, sad for the white

---

[20] 沈期　雜詩三首，其三　唐3

[21] 沈期　雜詩三首，其三　唐3

[22] 李白　渡荊門送別　唐3

[23] 劉長卿　餞別王十一南游　唐3

water-flower?' (汀洲 *tīng zhōu* sandbank, islet; 愁 *chóu* be sad, pity; 蘋 *pín* floating water-plant, symbol of separation.) /SV:{AV,VO}/.

In the next example the introductory verbal phrase (傳聞 *chuán wén*) has been shifted to the second line to make room for other elements taking up the whole of the first line, but it still retains its binding function:

陽月南飛雁 傳聞至此回[24] *yáng yuè nán fēi yàn / chuán wén zhì cǐ huí* (first couplet) literally 'The geese flying south in the *yang* moon, / from legend I hear that when [they] reach here [they] turn back', i.e. 'According to legend, when the geese migrating south in the tenth moon reach this spot they return'. (陽 *yáng* the *yang* principle; 南 *nán* south; 雁 *yàn* wild goose; 傳 *chuán* transmit, pass on (a legend); 至 *zhì* reach, arrive at; 回 *huí* turn, return.) The 'normal' underlying order of this couplet could be thought of as *傳聞 陽月南飛雁至此回 *chuán wén yáng yuè nán fēi yàn zhì cǐ huí* /V: {(AAV)S (VO) V}/. But here the subject of the object-clause has been exposed before the first clause and occupies the whole of the first line, squeezing out the first clause into the second line, followed by the rest of the object-clause. This kind of rearrangement is dealt with more fully in Unit 14.

Exercise

(1) 傍江有高樓 (2) 千山萬木黃葉下 (3) 入谷更步到河邊 只見一翁戴笠坐 (4) 今日別情無人知 (5) 層雲千里一入 目 (6) 林中黃花誰來採 (7) 萬物無情人獨有 (8) 春來百鳥 啼 (9) 河外一孤翁 披蓑雨中行 (10) 但恐山外更有山 (11) 悲君長遊萬里外 (12) 寒風大湖小舟翁 戴笠披蓑雪 中釣 (13) 黃鳥啼聲我獨聞 (14) 昨日在此今無蹤 (15) 前 有雲山更幾層 (16) 故鄉百年後 無人知我情 (17) 空谷百 層無人居 (18) 層層上高樓 (19) 今夜高樓中 悲泣何人知 (20) 情深不能言 (21) 海鳥有時依水宿 (22) 黃鳥一聲知 春到 (23) 誰悲林居人 幽徑久無蹤 (24) 只恐風大無人渡 (25) 臨江遊目千里外 (26) 去鄉居深山 只欲物外遊 (27) 前有小河後有山 (28) 未眠但聞一夜雨 (29) 河里秋水大 無舟豈能渡 (30) 只悲樓上更無層 (31) 篁中只聞萬竹響

(32) 在外一年事　何能一日言 (33) 不覺千山上　夜來雪
已深

---

[24] 宋之問　題大庾嶺北驛　唐 3

UNIT 11

This unit is concerned with five verbs connected with 'ending'.

Vocabulary

岸 岸 *àn* /n/ river-bank, shore 46.5 (M 山 'hill')

壁 壁 *bì* /n/ wall; cliff 32.13 (M 土 'earth')

腸 腸 *cháng* /n/ bowels, intestines as seat of emotions (cf. English 'bowels of mercy') 130.9 (M 肉 'flesh')

燈 燈 *déng* /n/ lamp 86.12 (M 火 'fire')

頂 頂 *dǐng* /n/ top, summit 181.2 (M 頁 'head')

斷 斷 *duàn* /v/ sever, cut off; isolated, lone 69.14 (M 斤 'axe')

光 光 *guāng* /n/ light 10.4 (X)

胡 胡 *hú* /n/ Hu, a general term for peoples to the north and west of China (Altaic, Turkish, Tibetan etc.) with whom China contested her borders 130.5 (S)

盡 盡 *jìn* /v/ use up, reach the end of; /n/ end, edge 108.9 (W: brush cleaning bowl)

酒 酒 *jiǔ* /n/ wine, spirits 164.3 (M 氵 'water')

絕 絕 *jué* /v/ sever, cut off; blocking further progress, impassable 120.6 (M 糸 'silk')

力 力 *lì* /n/ strength, effort 19.0 (W)

路 路 *lù* /n/ road 157.6 (M 足 'foot')

滅 滅 *miè* /v/ extinguish; destroy 85.10 (M 氵 'water')

窮 窮 *qióng* /v/ reach the end of; remote; poor; /n/ end 116.10 (S)

雁 雁 *yàn* /n/ wild goose, esp. migrating 172.4 (M 隹 'bird')

97

11.1 Vocabulary notes on the five verbs

Just in case the reader has gained the idea from the translation exercises so far that there is a one-to-one correspondence between Chinese and English vocabulary, we shall be looking in depth in this unit at the range of meanings of the five new verbs. To do this through real examples we have to go beyond the range of the vocabulary met so far, but since the examples are very short the meaning of any such one-off vocabulary items should be obvious.

Some written Chinese words have more than one (unconnected) meaning because of character-borrowing, but all the meanings of each of these five verbs are extensions of the basic meaning, so you should not be misled by the way each word's range of uses has been divided up: this has more to do with the English equivalents than with the Chinese originals! Try to think of the different 'meanings' of a word as sampling-points from a multidimensional continuous spectrum of meaning, for you will often encounter in texts other shades of meaning that fall between any meanings given in a dictionary. This phenomenon is not limited to Chinese, but can be found in any language, since language is never static, but is always growing and changing and dying, like any other aspect of human culture.

If you go well beyond this course to the stage where you are using Chinese–Chinese dictionaries you will encounter the same problem of adequate definition; for instance the largest of them, the 中文大辭典 *zhōng wén dà cí diǎn*, subdivides the meaning-range of a word according to the different glosses that commentators have made on the word in particular texts in the past. There is room for improvement here, but a perfect solution is impossible because any attempt to represent a multidimensional field of meaning in a one-dimensional text will be even more imperfect than the representation of an analogue signal in digital form. The following is the best I can do within the current constraints.

The first two verbs overlap to a large extent but are by no means completely interchangeable.

11.2 Meanings of the five verbs (1) *jìn*

(a) 'Use up the whole of, exhaust'. Examples: 盡酒 *jìn jiǔ* 'finish up the wine; 盡力 *jìn lì* 'use all one's strength, make the maximum effort'.
(b) 'Cover the whole of, get to the end of': 盡妝 *jìn zhuāng* 'complete one's toilette'; 盡土 *jìn tǔ* 'cover the whole ground'; 盡日 *jìn rì* 'to the end of the day, all day long'; 盡夕 *jìn xī* 'all night long'.
(c) 'Make the most of (something enjoyable)': 盡歡 *jìn huān* ('joy, enjoyment') or 盡興 *jìn xìng* ('happy mood, high spirits') 'enjoy oneself to the full'; 盡美 *jìn měi* 'enjoy its beauty to the full'.

(d) 'Come to an end (in space)': 山盡 *shān jìn* 'the mountains end' (at such-and-such a place); 雲盡 *yún jìn* 'the clouds come to an end' (no more pass over); 路盡 *lù jìn* 'the road ends'; 鳥盡 *niǎo jìn* 'the birds are all gone'.

(e) 'Come to an end (in time)': 曲盡 *qǔ jìn* 'the song is ended'; 色盡 *sè jìn* 'the colour is gone'; 春盡 *chūn jìn* 'spring has ended'; 金盡 *jīn jìn* 'the money's all gone, all spent'; 業盡 *yè jìn* 'his career is over'; 寒盡 *hán jìn* 'the cold weather is over'; 兵戈盡 *bīng gē jìn* 'the fighting is over'; 夢盡 *mèng jìn* 'the dream has ended'.

(f) (as a noun) 'end, edge': 橋盡 *qiáo jìn* 'the end of a bridge'; 崖盡 *yá jìn* 'the edge of a cliff'.

11.3 Meanings of the five verbs (2) *qióng*

窮 *qióng* is a less common equivalent of 盡 *jìn* but with extra meanings of its own.

(a) 'Cover the whole of, get to the end of': 窮山 *qióng shān* 'travel over the whole of the mountains'; 窮絕頂 *qióng jué dǐng* 'get right up to the utmost summit' (see 絕 *jué* below); 窮冬 *qióng dōng* 'to the end of winter, all winter long'; 窮年 *qióng nián* 'all the year long'.

(b) 'Enjoy to the full': 窮壯觀 *qióng zhuàng guān* 'enjoy magnificent views (scenery) to the full'.

(c) 'Come to an end': 水窮 *shuǐ qióng* 'where the river begins' (in the context of tracing it to its source); 力窮 *lì qióng* 'my strength is all used up'.

(d) 'Come to the end of one's resources, be forced into a corner, be in financial straits, have nobody to turn to': 途窮 *tú qióng* 'my road has come to an end, I'm at the end of my resources, I'm done for'; 窮途 *qióng tú* 'get to the end of one's road / tether / resources'.

(e) 'Be remote, off the beaten track, in the back-streets; (hence) shabby, poor (both rural and urban remoteness and poverty)'. This area of meaning is interesting because it seems to represent the convergence of two separate lines of development, viz. getting to the geographical limits of travel away from the wealthy metropolitan centre and simultaneously reaching the limits of one's financial resources. Examples: 窮巷 *qióng xiàng* 'a remote lane (rural), a shabby back-street (urban)'; 窮邊 *qióng biān* 'the extreme frontier' (where no one would choose to be); 窮山 *qióng shān* 'a remote mountain-area' (where it is difficult to scrape a living); 窮人 *qióng rén* 'the poor'. But the meaning is not necessarily negative: if the poet has retired to a humble environment as an escape, his 窮巷 *qióng xiàng* will have overtones of 'a secluded haven' or 'a noble, simple life'.

(f) (As a noun) 'End, ending': 無窮 *wú qióng* 'has no end, is unending', e.g. 愁無窮 *chóu wú qióng* 'my sadness knows no end'.

The next two verbs overlap to a large extent, but, as in the case of the two verbs we have just looked at, they are by no means always interchangeable. They are sometimes combined into one compound word, 斷絕 *duàn jué* 'to sever (communications etc.)'. Whereas the words 盡 *jìn* and 窮 *qióng* imply 'a natural end, a completion', the next two words imply 'ending before completion, being cut off before one's time, being brought to a sudden, unexpected or unwished-for end'.

11.4 Meanings of the five verbs (3) *duàn*

(a) 'Cut off, sever (physical severing)': 斷頭 *duàn tóu* 'decapitate'.
(b) 'Be cut off, severed, interrupted' (of routes, communications, social contacts and links): 信斷 *xìn duàn* 'no more letters come'; 斷消息 *duàn xiāo xī* 'no news gets through any more'; 夢斷 *mèng duàn* 'my dream (of my beloved) has been interrupted'; 弦斷 *xián duàn* 'the lute-string has snapped' (I've lost my mate); 恩斷 *ēn duàn* 'his favours have ceased'; 斷腸 *duàn cháng* ('it severs one's bowels') or 腸斷 *cháng duàn* ('one's bowels are severed') 'be heartbroken'.
(c) 'Cease, be interrupted, disappear': 聲斷 *shēng duàn* 'the sound has stopped'; 雁斷 *yàn duàn* 'the migrant geese have vanished'; 雲斷 *yún duàn* 'the clouds have gone' (after rain).
(d) (Attributive) 'Isolated, lone (applied to natural objects as symbols of being cut off from family or friends)': 斷雲 *duàn yún* 'a lonely cloud'; 斷雁 *duàn yàn* 'a migrant goose which has become separated from its companions'; 斷蓬 *duàn péng* 'a single piece of tumbleweed blown along by the wind'.

11.5 Meanings of the five verbs (4) *jué*

絕 *jué* is a less common equivalent of 斷 *duàn*.
(a) 'Cut off, sever': 路絕 *lù jué* 'the road is blocked' (e.g. by a landslide); 望絕 *wàng jué* 'my hopes are cut off' (I have no longer any hope of seeing the person I was looking forward to seeing returning); 自絕 *zì jué* ('cut oneself off') 'commit suicide'.
(b) 'Cease': 百蟲絕 *bǎi chóng jué* 'all the insects have ceased' (their sounds); 恨絕 *hèn jué* 'resentment has ceased'; 音書絕 *yīn shū jué* 'letters no longer get through'; 愁絕 *chóu jué* 'sadness fades'; 車馬絕 *chē mǎ jué* ('carriages and horses have ceased') 'visitors no longer come to the house'.
(c) (Attributive) 'Blocking further progress, impassable': 絕壁 *jué bì* 'a sheer cliff'; 絕岸 *jué àn* 'a sheer river-bank'; 絕頂 *jué dǐng* 'the extreme summit'.

11.6 Meanings of the five verbs (5) *miè*

(a) 'Extinguish': 滅火 *miè huǒ* 'extinguish a fire'; 滅光 *miè guāng* 'extinguish a light'; 滅燈 *miè dēng* 'extinguish a lamp'; 滅燭 *miè zhú* 'extinguish a candle'.

(b) 'Destroy' (an enemy): 滅胡 *miè hú* 'exterminate the Hu'; 滅蜂蠆 *miè fēng chài* 'destroy wasps and scorpions' (evil people); 宮滅 *gōng miè* 'the palace has been destroyed'.

(c) 'Hide, cover up': 滅跡 *miè jī* 'hide the tracks'; 蹤滅 *zōng miè* 'the tracks have been covered up'.

(d) 'Disappear': 暮光滅 *mù guāng miè* 'the evening light disappears' (from the sky); 雁滅 *yàn miè* 'the wild geese have vanished'; 名滅 *míng miè* 'his name (reputation) has been forgotten'.

11.7 Grammar of the five verbs (1) Followed by a noun

Be careful with this combination, since it may be either a main verb followed by its object /VO/, e.g. 絕路 *jué lù* 'they blocked the road', or else a verb qualifying a noun /(V)N/, e.g. 絕路 *jué lù* 'a blocked road, a dead end'. /VO/ is less common than the /SV/ arrangement that we shall see in the next section, and /(V)N/ is mainly restricted to set phrases, so the possible ambiguity is not so great as might at first sight appear, especially when the context and common sense offer help.

Exercise

Here are some examples for practice. The key will indicate the contextual clues.

(1) 前有絕壁不能上 (2) 斷雁高飛來 (3) 何事去鄉居窮山 (4) 君應盡力窮絕頂 (5) 天邊窮江湖 (6) 斷雲出高林 (7) 今夜何不盡此酒

11.8 Grammar of the five verbs (2) Preceded by a noun

This represents /SV/. A transitive verb without an object often corresponds to an intransitive or passive verb in English. Compare the following English equivalents.

	Followed by object; transitive in English	Not followed by object; passive in English	Not followed by object; intransitive in English
盡 窮	bring to an end use up	be ended be used up	come to an end be over
斷 絕	cut off sever snap	be cut off be severed be snapped	not get through snap vanish
滅	extinguish destroy cover up	be extinguished be destroyed be covered up	go out disappear

There are two specifically marked quasi-passive structures in Chinese verse corresponding to the English 'the subject is verbed by the agent'.

The first of these is the use of a verb meaning 'undergo' followed by an object-clause /SV:SV/, meaning 'the subject undergoes verbing at the hands of the agent'. There are two verbs used in this way: 被 *bèi* 'to undergo, suffer', literally 'to be covered by (a garment)' and 遭 *zāo* 'to encounter'. Both refer to an unpleasant experience. In both cases the agent may be omitted /SV:V/. Here are a couple of examples of each, first with the agent mentioned and then without it:

縱被微雲掩 [25] 'even if it (= the Milky Way) is obscured by light cloud' (縱 *zòng* even if; 微 *wēi* slight, faint; 掩 *yǎn* cover, hide)

聞道松州已被圍 [26] 'I hear tell that Songzhou has been surrounded (by Tibetan invaders)' (道 *dào* say, tell; 松州 *sōng zhōu* a border town in present-day Sichuan; 圍 *wéi* surround, besiege)

---

[25] 杜甫 天河 杜7

[26] 杜甫 黃草 杜15

頗遭官長罵 [27] 'he was soundly berated by his superior (for returning drunk)' (頗 *pō* very, quite a bit; 官長 *guān zhǎng* boss, superior; 罵 *mà* to curse, abuse)

兄弟遭殺戮 [28] 'her brothers were massacred' (兄弟 *xiōng dì* brothers; 殺戮 *shā lù* massacre, slaughter)

The second is a structure meaning literally 'the subject is that which the agent verbs': 'subject 爲 *wéi* agent 所 *suǒ* verb'. The 所 *suǒ* is more often omitted than included, giving 'subject 爲 *wéi* agent verb'. The experience is not necessarily an unpleasant one as it is in the case of the preceding structure, but in practice it often is, as we might expect from the predominance of complaint in Chinese verse. Here are a couple of examples, first with the 所 *suǒ* and then without it:

曾爲人所憐 [29] 'he was once pitied by people' (曾 *céng* once, in the past; 憐 *lián* to pity)

永爲高人嗤 [30] 'I shall forever be laughed at by those in high office' (永 *yǒng* always, for ever; 嗤 *chī* mock, laugh contemptuously at).

But neither of these forms is as common as /SV/ alone, where I treat objectless Chinese verbs merely as 'intransitive', not as 'passive', since they are not overtly marked as passive in Chinese, no matter how we choose to render them in English, which, as the table above shows, often offers a choice of active or passive voice in translation.

Exercise

(8) 歸時春欲盡 (9) 流水無盡時 (10) 夜來鳥語絕 (11) 初覺春光滅 (12) 久行力欲盡 (13) 天寒歸雁斷 (14) 腸斷返故鄉 (15) 胡知幾時滅 (16) 酒盡天欲明 (17) 人力有窮時 (18) 人去蹤未絕

---

[27] 杜甫　戲簡鄭廣文⋯　杜3

[28] 杜甫　佳人　唐1

[29] 杜甫　奉送蘇州李二十五⋯　杜21

[30] 杜甫　赤谷　杜8

11.9 Grammar of the five verbs (3) As part of a postverbal adverbial

Like verbs of direction, these five verbs not infrequently occur in conjunction with preceding verbs to indicate EXTENT or MODE of disappearance, completion or interruption. Here are some examples:

(a) 去盡 *qù jìn* ('have gone TO THE EXTENT THAT they have all gone') 'have all disappeared, none left'. /v v = V(V) = VA/.
(b) 飛滅 *fēi miè* ('have flown UNTIL they have vanished') 'have flown away out of sight'. /v v = V(V) = VA/.
(c) 行盡山林 *xíng jìn shān lín* ('have travelled SO FAR THAT they have covered all the mountain forests') 'have travelled all over the mountain forests; have travelled right through the mountain forest to the other side'. /v v nn = V(VO) = VA/.
(d) 看盡落花 *kàn jìn luò huā* ('have looked TO THE EXTENT THAT they have covered all the fallen blossom') 'have looked at all the fallen blossom'. /ditto/.

The second component here is a secondary predicate and so can include other components, e.g. adverbs such as 已 *yǐ* 'already', 不 *bù* 'not', 未 *wèi* 'not yet', 初 *chū* 'for the first time, only now', 更 *gèng* 'further', or modal verbs such as 應 *yīng* 'ought', 能 *néng* 'can' or 欲 *yù* 'going to, almost'. Examples:

(e) 白日落欲盡 *bái rì luò yù jìn* ('the white sun has sunk UNTIL it is almost all gone') 'the sun has almost completely set; the sun is about to vanish'. /vn v v v = SV(V:V) = SVA/.
(f) 黃鳥飛已斷 *huáng niǎo fēi yǐ duàn* ('the yellow birds have flown SO FAR THAT they have already disappeared') 'the orioles have already flown away out of sight'. /vn v av = SV(AV) = SVA/.

Note that for metrical reasons this does not happen when an object follows, because the three syllables of /vav = V(AV)/ or /vvv = V(V:V)/ fill the final part of a line, whether the line is of five or seven syllables; in such a case any object will be placed in the first part of the line, e.g.

(g) 別淚揮不盡 *bié lèi huī bù jìn* ('parting tears I brush BUT they do not all go away') 'I cannot brush away all the tears of parting' /vn vav = O V(AV)/. The /OV/ word-order will be gone into more fully in Unit 14.

Exercise

(19) 落花隨水流已滅 (20) 林鳥歸去盡 (21) 夜深燈滅絕
(22) 此燈風大吹不滅 (23) 行盡河邊路 (24) 明燈照盡壁

上物 (25) 今年邊上胡滅盡 (26) 寒天歸雁渡欲盡 (27) 雪落人蹤滅已盡

Exercise

Mixed exercise on this unit and earlier units:

(28) 舟傍絕岸行 (29) 秋雁落白沙 (30) 但恐歸路行不盡 (31) 盡日思鄉悲春窮 (32) 故人去絕不復返 (33) 大水入林竹徑絕 (34) 山頂木葉吹欲盡 (35) 雪雲窮天月光滅 (36) 今日雨大應披蓑 (37) 童子坐舟釣秋水 (38) 傍林來去看春花 (39) 高樓獨泣長相思 (40) 白日照盡石上苔 (41) 前有雲山知幾層 (42) 曉出戴笠採山藥 (43) 問翁我師今何在 (44) 水上落花流未斷 (45) 入林盡日步黃葉 (46) 孤雁飛去千里外 (47) 夜深未眠聞琴響 (48) 此別同泣腸欲斷 (49) 但悲百年客中度 (50) 此情何日滅 (51) 松間日影落欲滅 (52) 海上風大豈敢遊 (53) 別後何年復相會

UNIT 12

Translate the following three poems, check your translations against the key, and study the commentary.

Text 1[31]

Wang Zhihuan (early eighth century): 'Ascending Stork Tower'

白日依山盡 *bái rì yī shān jìn*

黃河入海流 *huáng hé rù hǎi liú*

欲窮千里目 *yù qióng qiān lǐ mù*

更上一層樓 *gèng shàng yī céng lóu*

Text 2[32]

Liu Zongyuan (773–819): 'River snow'

千山鳥飛絕 *qiān shān niǎo fēi jué*

萬徑人蹤滅 *wàn jìng rén zōng miè*

孤舟蓑笠翁 *gū zhōu suō lì wēng*

獨釣寒江雪 *dú diào hán jiāng xuě*

---

[31] 王之渙 登鸛雀樓 唐5
[32] 柳宗元 江雪 唐5

Text 3[33]

Jia Dao (early ninth century): 'Visiting a recluse and not finding him at home'

松下問童子 *sōng xià wèn tóng zǐ*

言師採藥去 *yán shī cǎi yào qù*

只在此山中 *zhǐ zài cǐ shān zhōng*

雲深不知處 *yún shēn bù zhī chù*

Discussion of Text 1

The form of this poem illustrates an important feature of Chinese verse: couplet parallelism.

In Chinese prose, parallelism can be multidimensional (i.e. statement A can be parallel to statement B, while A and B in turn can be parallel to statements C and D, and so on). Prose parallelism also matches identical words as structural markers. Verse parallelism does neither of these things apart from occasional identity-matching in unregulated ('ancient-style') verse. In verse, parallelism is restricted to the couplet, the first line of the couplet being odd-numbered (first, third etc.) while the second is the even-numbered line following it.

By parallelism we mean that the nth word in the second line of a couplet matches the nth word of the first line, and this most often applies to all the words of a matching couplet. Matching words will have something in common: they may just belong to the same word-class (part of speech), e.g. a verb will be matched by a verb, an adverb by an adverb, a quantifier by a quantifier etc. In the case of nouns there is a tendency for them to belong to the same semantic subdivision, e.g. they may both be place-names, geographical features, meteorological phenomena, etc.[34] Apart from this kind of textbook matching there are more subtle or ingenious free matchings created by the poet.

---

[33] 賈島　尋隱者不遇　唐5

[34] A detailed treatment of these categories and subcategories is to be found in 王力　漢語詩律學，節14

What is perhaps more important than this one-to-one word-matching is the unspoken world created by the two halves of the couplet as a whole, literally a world 'between the lines'. Just as two nouns can be combined to mean the whole class of which they are members, e.g. 草木 *căo mù* ('herbaceous plants and trees') meaning the whole vegetable kingdom, so two parallel statements can stand for some or all of the other statements of a similar kind: you are expected to use your imagination to conjure these up.

So far we have been thinking in terms of similarity, but now we meet another difference between prose and verse parallelism: whereas in prose parallelism the same idea may be repeated in different words, in the advertiser's hope that repetition will aid persuasion, the essence of parallelism in verse is that the two halves of the couplet should contrast in meaning. So what we should look for here is CONTRAST WITHIN SIMILARITY.

Let us look in detail at the parallelism in this first poem as an example of all this. Both couplets are parallel throughout.

In the first couplet:

白 *bái* 'white' and 黃 *huáng* 'yellow' are both colours;
日 *rì* 'sun' and 河 *hé* 'river' are both natural objects in motion;
依 *yī* 'rest on' and 入 *rù* 'enter' are both verbs involving location;
山 *shān* 'mountain' and 海 *hăi* 'sea' are both geographical features;
盡 *jìn* 'come to an end' and 流 *liú* 'flow' are both verbs.

In the second couplet:

欲 *yù* 'wish to' and 更 *gèng* 'further' are both 'adverbs' (the former is a modal verb, but these are classed by poets with adverbs);
窮 *qióng* 'go to the limits of' and 上 *shàng* 'ascend' are both verbs;
千 *qiān* 'thousand' and 一 *yī* 'one' are both quantifiers;
里 *lĭ* 'mile' and 層 *céng* 'storey' are both measures;
目 *mù* 'eye' and 樓 *lóu* 'tower' are both nouns; these last two are not in the same subcategory (body-part and building respectively) but we shall see below that this is a free and very meaningful match.

There is also strict parallelism of grammatical relationships throughout; this is the general rule, though it is not infrequently broken, giving only word-matching.

Apart from the last word, this poem is an example of what we may call 'formal parallelism'; its features were a strict requirement in poems written in civil service examinations. But what is more important is the 'informal parallelism' that may go beyond these requirements and are of greater artistic importance. The discovery and enjoyment of these informal matches, perhaps better called 'couplet resonances', are a task for you, the reader.

Although both couplets are formally parallel at the word level, there is an important grammatical difference between them: the first two lines are additive, implying an 'and' between them, whereas the third and fourth lines are conditional, linked by an unspoken 'if A then B'. As we shall see in Unit 10, the final couplet of a poem is often one continuous sentence, so even though these two lines are parallel (and hence more characteristic of middle couplets in eight-line poems) this continuity gives them a feeling of finality.

Hitherto in the exercises and examples we have played about with isolated lines simply in order to become familiar with words and the basic grammatical relationships, but what we have to do now with real poems is to begin to see lines first in pairs (couplets), then as parts of whole unitary poems, and that is where wider resonances will come in to create the atmosphere beyond the mere words.

What have 白日 *bái rì* 'the white sun' and 黃河 *huáng hé* 'the Yellow River' in common? They both go on for ever like 'Old Man River' and 'Old Father Thames', unlike human beings, who are born and die in a comparatively short space of time. The sun is part, and hence representative, of 天 *tiān* 'Heaven', and the river is part of 地 *dì* 'Earth', so they represent time and space respectively. 天 *tiān* and 地 *dì* between them represent the whole 天地 *tiān dì*, the whole human universe, so behind these simple words for 'sun' and 'river' lurks a whole cosmic statement about the frailty and impermanence of mankind against the background of the rest of Nature. (These overtones are of course not always present, but are brought out by the parallelism as well as by resonance with the rest of the poem.) The sadness of the human condition seen in this light can be illustrated by another poem:

Example text[35]

Chen Zi'ang (late seventh century): 'A song upon Youzhou Tower'

前不見古人 *qián bù jiàn gǔ rén*

後不見來者 *hòu bù jiàn lái zhě*

念天地之悠悠 *niàn tiān dì zhī yōu yōu*

獨愴然而涕下 *dú chuàng rán ér tì xià*

Before me I have not seen the people of ancient times;
after me I shall not see those who will come.
When I think of the vastness of heaven and earth
I grieve alone and my tears fall.

(古 *gǔ* antiquity; 念 *niàn* think about; A 之 *zhī* B = B of A; 悠悠 *yōu yōu* vast; 愴然 *chuàng rán* grieving; 而 *ér* and; 涕 *tì* tears.)

---

[35] 陳子昂　登幽州台歌　唐2

This poem of Chen Zi'ang's was inspired by part of another one of eight hundred years earlier expressing the same sentiments through the same imagery. It is from the anonymous poem 'Distant wandering' [36]

惟天地之無窮兮 *wéi tiān dì zhī wú qióng xī*

哀人生之長勤 *āi rén shéng zhī cháng qín*

往者余弗及兮 *wǎng zhě yú fú jí xī*

來者吾不聞 *lái zhě wú bù wén*

> … When I think of the endlessness of heaven and earth
> I grieve over the long toil of human life;
> those who have gone I have not been in time to see,
> those yet to come I shall not hear of…

(惟 *wéi* think; 兮 *xī* eh! (line-divider); 哀 *āi* grieve; 生 *shēng* life; 勤 *qín* toil; 往 *wǎng* go; 余 *tú* I; 弗 *fú* not; 及 *jí* reach, catch up with; 吾 *wú* I.)

Vocabulary note on this example: 兮 *xī* was then pronounced 'eh', like the English 'e' in 'men', with smooth vocalic ingress, i.e. not preceded by a glottal stop, but this could only be written with a character pronounced with an initial voiced 'h', which in due course came to be pronounced *xī* in a reading pronunciation. But since 'eh' was extra-phonological, like other prepausal particles and interjections, its pronunciation has remained unchanged to the present day and this sound is used in exactly the same way (viz. to break a sung line into two parts) in modern folksong.

This has been a never-ending tale through the three thousand years of Chinese poetry. Man's vulnerability amid the vastness of heaven and earth has been expressed in Du Fu's striking image:

…飄飄何所似　天地一沙鷗 [37] *piāo piāo hé suǒ sì / tiān dì yī shā ōu* '… Drifting helplessly, what am I like? / A solitary gull [between] earth and sky'. (似 *sì* resemble; 沙鷗 *shā ōu* 'sand-gull' = gull)

We see the shortness of human life in another couplet of his, written in a high place when old and sick:

…無邊落木蕭蕭下　不盡長江滾滾來 [38] *wú biān liò mù xiāo xiāo xià / bù jìn cháng jiāng gǔn gǔn lái* 'Unbounded, [the leaves from] the shedding trees whisper down, / unceasing, the Yangtse comes rolling on'. (蕭蕭 *xiāo xiāo* sadly rustling, sighing etc.; 滾滾 *gǔn gǔn* rolling, tumbling)

---

[36] 無名氏　遠游　楚5

[37] 杜甫　旅夜書懷　唐3

[38] 杜甫　登高　唐4

So much for heaven and earth as a universal theme. Let us now get back to the first couplet of our original poem. 山 *shān* 'mountain' and 海 *hǎi* 'sea' are another formally contrasting *yang-yin* pair representing masculine solidity versus feminine fluidity, even at a crudely anatomical level: the hard, upstanding mountain versus the water-filled depression of the sea. More importantly, they, together with the sun and the river, represent the static versus the dynamic: the setting sun seemingly motionless, at rest on the solid mountain, while the river is constantly in flux, moving unceasingly to the sea. But all these superficial contrasts of the first couplet are overshadowed by the contrast between the permanence of all these four natural features and the impermanence of the poet's own life. The *yang-yin* contrasts provide a formal framework that says 'everything between earth and sky, whether static or moving', and then we see the poet against this overwhelming background, so that his insignificance is made the more striking by being implicit rather than explicit.

It may be that the words 盡 *jìn* 'come to an end' and 流 *liú* 'flow' will also give echoes of human impermanence in this context, for our lives are doomed to flow away as unstoppably as the river and will inevitably be brought to their own sunset and darkness.

While the first couplet is sad in general human terms, the second is sad at the personal level. Why does 目 *mù* 'eye' match 樓 *lóu* 'tower'? Here we come to a constant symbol of Chinese verse since the Han dynasty: the wife who ascends a tower or hill to gaze into the distance, hoping to see her absent husband returning, but never of course actually seeing him. This has become a symbol of yearning by men away on service for the family and friends at home. The 目 *mù* are the woman's eyes straining to see into the distance as she leans on a balustrade high in the 樓 *lóu*.

千里目 *qiān lǐ mù* are keen eyes that can see a thousand miles, far enough (hopefully) to spot the absent man. Climbing up a further storey is a futile gesture, and the poet knows it, for no amount of gazing, however high, will bring the absent husband into view.

The word for gazing hopefully (and despairingly) into the distance is 望 *wàng*. When combined with two of the verbs in the previous unit it gives 望斷 *wàng duàn* or 望絕 *wàng jué*. The original meaning of these expressions was presumably 'to gaze after a departing person until they are lost to sight' but in actual practice they mean 'to gaze into the distance (either physically or mentally) hoping to see the absent person or one's distant home but not seeing them'. A similar expression is 悵望 *chàng wàng* 'to gaze disappointedly or hopelessly'.

We may now go back and see the first couplet in a more personal light. It is not there for mere decoration but to underline the sadness of the second couplet. For the symbolic woman in the tower, the shortness of human life, combined with her despair of ever seeing her husband alive again (he may be dead on a battlefield in the north or in a malarial swamp in the south) means that her life is not only short but also purposeless, since she may die without ever seeing him again.

Although the poem is presented as being in the persona of a woman, as is traditionally done with this theme, it is of course written by a man to or about an absent friend or family, though that in no way diminishes the feelings expressed in it.

Discussion of Text 2

In this poem the first couplet is parallel:

千 *qiān* 'thousand' and 萬 *wàn* 'myriad' are quantifiers;

山 *shān* 'mountain' and 徑 *jìng* 'path' are topographical features;

鳥 *niǎo* 'birds' and 人 *rén* 'people' are living beings;

飛 *fēi* 'fly' and 蹤 *zōng* 'tracks' are verb and noun respectively so not strictly parallel, though both imply movement across the countryside;

絕 *jué* and 滅 *miè* are both verbs of disappearance.

The second couplet is a two-line sentence, as is often the case in final couplets, the first line being the subject and the second the predicate. As such it is not formally parallel, yet it has a few parallel features:

孤 *gū* 'lonely, isolated' and 獨 *dú* 'alone' are close in meaning and in fact can form a compound meaning 'orphans and childless old people', hence 'alone and vulnerable';

舟 *zhōu* 'boat' and 釣 *diào* 'to angle' are connected in meaning;

蓑笠翁 *suō lì wēng* and 寒江雪 *hán jiāng xuě* are structurally similar, consisting of a noun-phrase qualifying a noun. Although none of these features is parallel in textbook terms, they do give a patterned feeling to the couplet without interfering with the continuity of the sentence. This quasi-parallelism may encourage us to look for some sort of resonance between 翁 *wēng* 'old man' and 雪 *xuě* 'snow', e.g. snowy hair and cold extremities from poor circulation; I say 'may' because such things cannot be legislated for but depend on what you, the individual reader, bring to the poem from your own inner world.

Like the two poems by Wang Wei that we read earlier, this poem encapsulates the paradox of isolation. An old man fishing in a rain-cape and bamboo hat is a common image associated with retirement and escape from the world. The retired civil servant sought out the company of 漁樵 *yú qiáo* 'fishermen and woodcutters', at least in his poems, and the poet himself taking up angling became one of the main images of peaceful retirement.

But the angler's solitude ('alone' in his 'lonely' boat) is here set against a background not of the more clement seasons of the year, as in many other poems, but of a vast empty landscape shrouded in snow. His solitude is not relieved by a background of birdsong, since all the birds have vanished. Wang

Wei was glad to hear human voices in the distance and other poets, e.g. Tao Yuanming in Units 29 and 31, were reassured by spirals of kitchen-smoke from distant villages or the far-off crowing of cockerels and barking of dogs; but here there are not even footprints to show that there have been people in this great white silent wilderness.

In the light of this background I feel that, beneath the surface image of peaceful retirement and escape into solitude, a deeper voice is crying out that one can have too much of a good thing, that at the deepest level isolation is not the best option for a biologically social creature.

Discussion of Text 3

Here is a poem with no parallelism; in fact, seemingly artless and uncontrived in its colloquial simplicity.

In terms of semantic structure it is the opposite of Meng Haoran's 'Spring Dawn' that we read in Unit 7. Whereas that poem presented four stages of awakening consciousness, this one does the reverse: it presents four stages of increasing unknowingness. In the first line we have a solid servant-boy under solid pine-trees; in the second, his absent master presented only as hearsay; in the third, we have a location so imprecise as to be quite useless to the visitor; and finally even this vagueness is wrapped in impenetrable cloud. The recluse has escaped completely, untraceable and untrappable.

What are these herbs that he is gathering? And why pine-trees? Here we enter another symbolic world, that of the post-Han neo-Taoist hermit. The seemingly innocent 松 *sōng* and 藥 *yào* are unmistakable code on this point, as also is the artless simplicity of the poem, which takes us back several centuries BC to the regressive simplicity cultivated by the Warring States Taoists, which is where we must begin.

The two earliest Taoist works, *Laozi* (*Laotzu*), later also known as the *Daodejing* (*Taoteching*), and *Zhuangzi* (*Chuangtzu*), include the idea of 'the higher ignorance', where one progresses beyond adult worldly knowledge and wisdom to what is essentially a second infancy, a regression to the 樸 *pǔ*, the rough, uncarved block of wood, a kind of primal innocence devoid of cunning and deception and competition and even of simple technology. This poem shows, if not an uncarved block, at least the skilful removal of the chisel-marks, an artistic substitute for simplicity. So our recluse has opted out of the hurly-burly of political infighting and now seeks a simple life, though naturally not without servants and other conveniences.

Several centuries later the term 'Taoism' came to be applied to ideas which have little in common with early Taoism except the wish to escape. The wished-for escape was now not from politics but from death. Whereas Zhuangzi had argued for treating birth and death equally as being simply part of the 道 *dào* 'the Way' in the sense of 'Nature's way', the later Taoists were obsessed with extending their natural life-span to become 仙 *xiān* 'immortals', and for them 'the Way' meant 仙道 *xiān dào* 'the Way to immortality'. They sought to achieve this by consuming magical herbs, poisonous chemicals (especially 丹 *dān* 'cinnabar, mercuric sulphide' and sulphides of arsenic, both still used in some Chinese herbal remedies!), Tantric-type sexual practices, unusual diets (e.g. cereal-free), yogic breathing etc. The mythical Taoist immortal often went off to live in the mountains, where he became a 羽人 *yǔ rén* 'feathered person' and floated through the air like a bird and lived on (among other things) pine-resin. The pine-tree was, and still is, a symbol of prolonged life, its rugged, twisted roots clinging grimly to rocks and cliff-faces.

I am not suggesting that the poet was visiting someone who was actually practising any of these allegedly life-prolonging techniques. The Taoist hermit, like the old fisherman in the previous poem, was a literary symbol for someone who has retired to a country villa and potters about the hills amusing himself.

What I have hoped to show through the poems we have read so far is that even when you have passed the hurdle of language you will still need to exercise your imagination and common sense and whatever Chinese cultural background you can acquire.

UNIT 13

This unit is concerned with the meanings and grammar of twin-words (reduplicative binomes), using an overlapping group of five as examples.

Vocabulary

冥冥冥冥 *míng míng* /v/ be hidden or obscured by darkness, mist, distance, mystery or secrecy; be dark, with no light penetrating 14.8 (X)

杳杳杳杳 *yǎo yǎo* /v/ = 冥冥 75.4 (X)

濛濛濛濛 *méng méng* /v/ be misty, hazy, blurring, obscuring (also written 蒙蒙) 85.14 (M 氵 'water')

茫茫茫茫 *máng máng* /v/ be vast, unbounded, obscured by distance 140.6 (S)

蒼蒼蒼蒼 *cāng cāng* /v/ = 茫茫 *máng máng*; misty, grey, bleak 140.10 (S)

Note: other new vocabulary is given *in situ* with the examples.

13.1 Introduction to five twin-words

An important fact about China that needs to be borne in mind when reading verse about men serving far from home is that China is physically enormous. A soldier serving in Kashgar was eight thousand miles from the capital as the wild goose flies; a magistrate sent by his emperor to serve in what is now Vietnam was four thousand miles from the capital; and even Liu Zongyuan serving in Liuzhou in one of our examples below was getting on for three thousand miles from home. So when a poet serving in an outpost of empire talks of being vast distances from home he is not referring to a few miles and exaggerating under poetic licence.

The road system was primitive. Travel was slow and arduous, by boat or horse. The northern frontier consisted of steppe and desert, the west of mountains, the south of jungle and malarial swamps. And not only the frontiers offered such obstacles: since rivers and mountain-ranges in China tend to run from west to east, north–south travel meant crossing mountains and rivers, by horse and boat respectively.

115

The poet's frequent question 'When shall we ever meet again?' was no idle one. The image of the wife waiting hopelessly for a distant husband to return home alive runs through Chinese poetry from its earliest surviving works onwards; it is not just a literary conceit, but an image based on an unpleasant reality.

In this unit we look at five twin-words that have to do with distance and separation.

All the examples are from poems covering the period from the Han to the Sung dynasties, showing the continuity of these images through a thousand years of history. Since they are real examples, not made-up exercise material, extra vocabulary is inevitably involved (almost 120 new words, in fact). Any words not met so far in the vocabularies are glossed after each example so that you can understand each example in detail. If you wish to memorize any of these new words, so much the better, but this is not necessary for what follows in the course.

A twin-word is a doubled syllable like *ting-ting* in English. These we may call 'identical twin-words'. A further-developed form involves a high–low vowel alternation, like *ding-dong*, *tick-tock* or *zig-zag* in English, or else a different initial consonant, like the English *heebie-jeebies*. These, of course, will be 'non-identical twin-words'. Words formed in this way are widespread in the languages of the world. In Chinese they have always been used far more in verse than in prose, for a very good reason: they commonly involve sensory or emotional impressions rather than precise prosaic description. They may, as onomatopes, represent a repeated sound such as the twittering of birds, or they may represent light-phenomena such as glittering, or movements such as fluttering, or emotional states. They are often difficult to define simply and precisely, and Chinese commentators on older poetry are often in violent disagreement about their meaning. In fact, dictionaries often give up the attempt to define them at all and simply record that they are descriptive (貌 *mào* 'appearance') of mountains or water flowing or whatever, which is not terribly useful if we are trying to understand something like 'the water flows X-X', and a dictionary tells us that it means 'the water flows with the appearance of water flowing'!

I suggest that you go through the examples for the first time concentrating on the MEANINGS of the twin-words so far as they can be grasped from the English versions, and ignoring the grammar for the time being. The grammatical status and relationships of twin-words will be dealt with in the next section of this unit, after the examples.

As you will see below, they do overlap in meaning, like the five verbs in Unit 11; but, unlike those words, it is not easy to subdivide the meanings of these words into narrower areas of meaning, if only because of their vagueness in intellectual terms. The equivalents which I give in my translations of the examples are more precise than their originals and should be taken not as clearly defined areas of meaning but rather as samples of the whole range of meaning of each of the five words. Try to grasp the FEELING behind these five words rather than trying to pin down a precise, intellectual definition. Remember this is poetry, not physics!

13.2 Examples of twin-words (1) *míng míng*

'Hidden or obscured by darkness, mist, distance, mystery or secrecy; dark, with no light penetrating' (cf. 深林 *shēn lín* 'deep in the woods').

(1) 鴻飛冥冥日月白 [39] *hóng fēi míng míng rì yuè bái* 'The wild geese fly over, **indiscernible** (because of distance, only sensed by their cries), while sun and moon are white (in the clear autumn air)'. They are travelling between the poet and someone far away but he cannot go with them or even give them a message to take. Their distance and faintness also symbolize the distance between the two people. (鴻 *hóng* strictly 'swan-goose' but commonly used for wild geese in general.)

(2) 今我遊冥冥　弋者何所慕 [40] *jīn wǒ yóu míng míng / yì zhě hé suǒ mù* (The poet is speaking as a lone wild goose) 'But now I am wandering **too high to be seen clearly**, so how can the fowler be after me?' He means that he is beyond the reach of his political enemies. (弋 *yì* shoot (birds); 慕 *mù* set one's heart on.)

(3) 冥冥孤高多烈風 [41] *míng míng gū gāo duō liè fēng* (Referring to the top of a tall memorial pine-tree) '**Faintly seen**, lonely and high, where there are many fierce winds' (symbolizing the vulnerability of anyone in a high political position). (烈 *liè* fierce, violent.)

(4) 冥冥花正開 [42] *míng míng huā zhèng kāi* '**Secretly** (i.e. imperceptibly) the flowers are just opening'. (正 *zhèng* just now; 開 *kāi* open, bloom.)

(5) 紅塵蔽天地　白日何冥冥 [43] *hóng chén bì tiān dì / bái rì hé míng míng* (Speaking of a desert dust-storm) 'The red dust blots out sky and earth, / how **dimly seen** is the white sun!' (紅 *hóng* red; 塵 *chén* dust; 蔽 *bì* cover, screen, blot out.)
(6) 清水揚波兮冒冥冥 [44] *qīng shǐ yáng bō xī mào míng míng* 'The limpid water lifts its waves (eh!) shrouded **to faintness**'. (清 *qīng* pure, clear;

---

[39] 杜甫　寄韓諫議注　唐2

[40] 張九齡　感遇十二首，其四　唐1

[41] 杜甫　古柏行　唐2

[42] 韋應物　長安遇馮著　唐1

[43] 無名氏　擬蘇李詩二首，其二　古A1

[44] 無名氏　河激歌，其三　古B1

揚 *yáng* raise; 波 *bō* waves; 兮 *xī* eh! (interjection used as line-splitter in songs and ancient verse); 冒 *mào* cover over.)

(7) 浩浩風起波　冥冥日沉夕 [45] *hào hào fēng qǐ bō / míng míng rì chén xī* 'Wide-flooding, the wind raises the waves; / **dimly-seen**, the sun drowns in dusk'. (浩浩 *hào hào* vast, sweeping; 起 *qǐ* raise; 沉 *chén* sink, drown; 夕 *xī* evening, dusk, night.)

(8) 淮南皓月冷千山　冥冥歸去無人管 [46] *huái nán hào yuè lěng qiān shān / míng míng guī qù wú rén guǎn* 'South of the River Huai the resplendent moon chills a thousand hills; / **lost in the mists** [of my thoughts of you] I go back home with no one to heed me'. (淮 *huái* R. Huai; 南 *nán* south; 皓 *hào* brilliantly white; 冷 *lěng* cold; 管 *guǎn* heed, take care of, attend to.)

(9) 兒今日冥冥　令母在後單 [47] *ér jīn rì míng míng / lìng mǔ zài hòu dān* 'Her son is now daily more **distant and unreachable**, causing his mother [left] behind [at home] to be lonely' (and vulnerable to pressure from her in-laws). (兒 *ér* son; 母 *mǔ* mother; 單 *dān* single, alone, lonely.)

(10) 長夜何冥冥　一往不復還 [48] *cháng yè hé míng míng / yī wǎng bù fù huán* 'How **remote and inaccessible** is the long night [of death]: once you go there you do not return again'(還 *huán* return.). 冥 is often applied to the dark underworld, where the souls of the dead go. It is distant in that there is no reliable communication between the *yin* ('dark') world of the dead and this *yang* ('sunlit') world of light, just as it is difficult to communicate between home and exile.

(11) 神女去已久　雲雨空冥冥 [49] *shén nǚ qù yǐ jiǔ / yún yǔ kōng míng míng* 'The spirit-woman (i.e. the goddess of Witch Mountain) is gone long ago, / and the clouds and rain (i.e. love-making with her) are sadly **lost in the mists of time**'. (神 *shén* god, nature-spirit; 女 *nǚ* woman; 空 *kōng* in vain, uselessly.)

(12) 冥冥子規叫　微徑不敢取 (Unit 33) *míng míng zǐ guī jiào / wēi jìng bù gǎn qǔ* '**Faint in the distance** a cuckoo calls; / this narrow path I dare not take'. Du Fu is tempted to retire into a Buddhist monastery that he comes across in his travels, but the cuckoo calls him home. The word for 'cuckoo' sounds like 子歸 'You should go home!' It is faint in the distance because he

---

[45] 韋應物　夕次盱眙縣　唐1

[46] 姜夔　踏莎行　宋

[47] 無名氏　古詩爲焦仲卿妻作　古A1

[48] 曹植　三良詩　古A2

[49] 張九齡　巫山高　古A16

is far from home in the wilds of Sichuan. (子規 *zǐ guī* cuckoo; 叫 *jiào* cry, shout; 微 *wēi* faintly-visible, minute; 取 *qǔ* take, choose.)

This selection should have given you some idea of the difficulty of defining the literal meaning of a twin-word, let alone its emotional overtones, which in poetry are of course even more important.

13.3 Examples of twin-words (2) *yǎo yǎo*

This is essentially the same as 冥冥. It is written with 日 'the sun' under 木 'a tree', and the traditional interpretation is that it represents the coming of darkness when the sun sinks below the trees on the horizon, though another possibility is that the 木 is the sound-element.

(13) 日照天正綠　杳杳歸鴻吟 [50] *rì zhào tiān zhèng lù / yǎo yǎo guī hóng yín* 'The sun lights up the sky to a vivid green; / **faint and high** the returning geese cry plaintively'. (綠 *lù* green; 鴻 *hóng* (swan-) goose; 吟 *yín* chant, moan.)

(14) 下有陳死人　杳杳即長暮 [51] *xià yǒu chén sǐ rén / yǎo yǎo jí cháng mù* 'Below are people who are past and dead, / **lost beyond recall**, gone to the long twilight'. (陳 *chén* old, worn-out, obsolete; 死 *sǐ* die, dead; 即 *jí* go to; 暮 *mù* dusk, evening.)

(15) 凝淚眼　杳杳神京路　斷鴻聲遠長天暮 [52] *níng lèi yǎn / yǎo yǎo shén jīng lù / duàn hóng shēng yuǎn cháng tiān mù* 'Through tear-filled eyes / the road to the sacred capital **is faint and far** / as a solitary goose's cry goes far across the long sky's dusk'. (凝 *níng* congeal, gather; 淚 *lèi* tears; 眼 *yǎn* eyes; 神 *shén* of a god, holy, imperial; 京 *jīng* capital city; 路 *lù* road; 遠 *yuǎn* far.)

(16) 回首經年　杳杳音塵都絕 [53] *huí shǒu jīng nián / yǎo yǎo yīn chén dōu jué* 'When I look back across the years, / **obscured by distance**, all news of you has been cut off'. (回 *huí* turn round; 首 *shǒu* head; 經 *jīng* go through; 音 *yīn* sound, news; 音塵 *yīn chén* news; 都 *dōu* all.)

(17) 杳杳星出雲 [54] *yǎo yǎo xīng chū yún* '**Faintly seen**, the stars emerge from the clouds'. (星 *xīng* star.)

---

[50] 柳宗元　覺衰　古A17

[51] 無名氏　古詩十九首，其十三　古A1

[52] 柳永　夜半樂　宋

[53] 賀鑄　石州慢　宋

[54] 何遜　野夕答孫郎擢　古A10

(18) 杳杳深谷攢青楓 [55] *yǎo yǎo shēn gǔ cuán qīng fēng* **'Faintly seen in the distance**, green maples cluster in the deep valley'. (攢 *cuán* gather, cluster; 楓 *fēng* maple-tree.)

13.4 Examples of twin-words (3) *méng méng*

This is usually not so much 'obscured' as 'obscuring', and is used of rain and mist and the white haze of floating willow-down.

(19) 濛濛殘雨籠晴 [56] *méng méng cán yǔ lǒng qíng* **'With its haze** the last of the rain mantles the clear sky'. (殘 *cán* remnant; 籠 *lǒng* envelop; 晴 *qíng* cloudless sky, sunny weather.)

(20) 濛濛秋雨駛 [57] *méng méng qiū yǔ shǐ* **'Blindingly** the autumn rain drives'. (駛 *shǐ* drive.)

(21) 濛濛夕煙起 [58] *méng méng xī yān qǐ* **'Shrouding the distance**, the evening mists rise'. (煙 *yān* mist.)

(22) 碧窗宿霧濛濛濕 [59] *bì chuāng sù wù méng méng shī* 'At my green-gauze window the overnight fog is **blurringly** wet'. (碧 *bì* green, blue; 窗 *chuāng* window; 霧 *wù* mist, fog; 濕 *shī* wet.)

(23) 飛絮濛濛 [60,61] *fēi xù méng méng* 'The floating willow-down **forms a haze**'. (絮 *xù* floss-silk; the white 'thistle-down' of pussy-willow that floats on the breeze in May.)

(24) 五陵北原上 萬古青濛濛 [62] *wǔ líng běi yuán shàng / wàn gǔ qīng méng méng* 'The Five Royal Tombs on the northern plain / [stand] **hazy-green** through a myriad ages'. (五 *wǔ* five; 陵 *líng* tumulus, tomb-mound; 北 *běi* north; 原 *yuán* a plain.)

---

[55] 韓愈 杏花 古B37

[56] 宋秦觀 八六子 宋

[57] 何遜 從主移西州… 古A10

[58] 沈約 長歌行二首，其一 古A10

[59] 杜甫 江陵節度使… 杜21

[60] 張先 一叢花 宋

[61] 歐陽修 采桑子 宋

[62] 岑參 與高適薛據登慈恩寺浮圖 唐1

13.5 Examples of twin-words (4) *máng máng*

Whereas 冥冥 and 杳杳 are concerned with obscured vision, and 濛濛 with haziness, 茫茫 is often more concerned with vast distances, though misty obscurity is also an element, as with the other words in this group. Etymologically, 茫 is no doubt related to 盲 *máng* 'blind' and 亡 *wáng* (from Old Chinese **miang*) 'disappear, be lost, die', and perhaps also to 荒 *huāng* (from **hmang*) 'desolate, wild' and to 喪 *sāng* (from **smang*) 'connected with death', and even to 望 *wàng* (from **miangs*) 'gaze into the distance' (these characters share a common sound-element 亡, which may indicate that the script-makers felt that they were related, whether they were or not). The actual value of 茫茫 in poetry is to give a feeling of vast distances that separate people and prevent their keeping in touch, as well as the future uncertainties that one faces in life, particularly during the foreign and civil wars to which China has been prone throughout her history.

(25) 風吹花片片 春動水茫茫[63] *fēng chuī huā piàn piàn / chūn dòng shuǐ máng máng* (Seen from the wall of a city from which the inhabitants have fled to avoid the fighting) 'The wind blows the blossom down, petal by petal; / springtime moves the waters **as far as the eye can see**'. (片 *piàn* piece, fragment; 動 *dòng* move.) The shattered blossom symbolizes the refugees; the uncontrollable force of the flood-waters represents the tide of war, and their uncertain extent represents the refugees' uncertain future. And through these human tragedies the spring goes blithely on its way, as it does in another of Du Fu's poems:

國破山河在 城春草木深[64] *guó pò shān hé zài / chéng chūn cǎo mù shēn* 'The State is broken but the mountains and rivers remain; / the city wall is bright with spring where the flowers and trees grow deep' (the city wall is ruined and overgrown with vegetation). (國 *guó* country, State; 破 *pò* break; 城 *chéng* city wall; 春 *chūn* (as a verb) be bright with spring light and colours.) The 深 here has something in common with the 茫茫 of the other poem: both represent Nature out of human control and hence threatening to human vulnerability.

This relationship is even seen in landscape painting, where a tiny human figure will be seen against a vast expanse of mountains. The best-known manual of painting advises against making such human figures too detailed or clear. Although Chinese poetry (like all poetry?) is ultimately human-centred, my own feeling is that both in poetry and in painting the Chinese artist is not asserting himself as a Westerner might do, but is acknowledging his weakness in the face of an all-powerful Nature and fate (both 天), which has its social

---

[63] 杜甫 城上 杜13

[64] 杜甫 春望 唐3

parallel (especially in Confucianism under the empire) in the individual's submission first to his parents and then to the imperial hierarchy.

(26) 登高壯觀天地間 大江茫茫去不還 [65] *dēng gāo zhuàng guān tiān dì jiān / dà jiāng máng máng qù bù huán* 'Ascending to a high place, I have a magnificent view between sky and earth; / the Great River goes **on and on into the hazy distance** and [once gone] it does not return'. (登 *dēng* ascend; 壯 *zhuàng* strong, virile, magnificent; 觀 *guān* view; 地 *dì* earth; 還 *huán* return.) Li Bai is glorying in Nature's power and magnificence, enjoying the scenery and inviting a distant friend to join him in his enjoyment; but why does he say 不還? Because time cannot be reversed, old age cannot be stayed. The very power and permanence of the river hint at the vulnerability and ephemeral life of the tiny figure of the poet on the mountain, whose future life and links with his friends are as unknown as the fate of the flooding waters. This is true whether the 去不還 was written consciously or unconsciously.

(27) 別時茫茫江浸月 [66] *bié shí máng máng jiāng jìn yuè* (Bai Juyi is saying goodbye to a friend who is leaving on a river-boat) 'As we say goodbye, **boundlessly flowing**, the river immerses the moon'. (浸 *jìn* immerse, soak.) The moon, a symbol of togetherness and its loss at parting, is drowned (or at least its reflection is) in the river representing the flood of time that carries all away to unknown destinations.

(28) 明日隔山岳 世事兩茫茫 [67] *míng rì gé shān yuè / shì shì liǎng máng máng* (Du Fu is having a brief reunion with an old friend) 'Tomorrow we shall be separated by the mountains, / and neither of us will know what the other is doing in his life' (literally: '[information about] our affairs in the world for both of us **will be cut off by a vast expanse**'). (隔 *gé* be separated by, be on the other side of; 山岳 *shān yuè* mountains; 世 *shì* world; 兩 *liǎng* both.)

(29) 茫茫江漢上 日暮復何之 [68] *máng máng jiāng hàn shàng / rì mù fù hé zhī* (Liu Changqing is saying goodbye to an old friend, a general, who is going home into retirement) 'On the **vast and boundless** Yangtse and Han, / as the sun sets, where will you go next?' (漢 *hàn* R. Han, which flows into the Yangtse at Wuhan; 暮 *mù* evening, (of the sun) begin to set; 之 *zhī* go.) The question is not about his geographical destination but what he is going to do in retirement after an outstanding military career. His sun is setting but the

---

[65] 李白　廬山謠寄盧侍御虛舟　唐2

[66] 白居易　琵琶行　唐2

[67] 杜甫　贈衛八處士　唐1

[68] 劉長卿　送李中丞歸漢陽別業　唐3

evening of his life is vague and unpredictable. The 茫茫 ostensibly refers to the rivers but actually it refers to his future.

(30) 城上高樓接大荒　海天愁思正茫茫 [69] *chéng shàng gāo lóu jiē dà huāng / hǎi tiān chóu sì zhèng máng máng* 'The high tower on the city wall touches a great wilderness; / sad thoughts like the sea and the sky now **flood unbounded**'. (城 *chéng* city wall; 接 *jiē* be connected with, be in immediate contact with; 荒 *huāng* wild, uncultivated land; 正 *zhèng* just at this moment.) Liu Zongyuan is at the back of beyond, in Guangxi, as the magistrate of Liuzhou; his poem is addressed to friends posted to other far-off corners of the empire. The vastness of the distances between them is now compared to the largest measure available: the height of the sky and the breadth of the ocean. The 荒 *huāng* of the first line is not just a decorative statement about the wild landscape that comes right up to the city wall, but is a symbol of the lack of cultured company and friends of his own background in this southern backwater.

(31) 雲渺渺　水茫茫　征人歸路許多長 [70] *yún miǎo miǎo / shuǐ máng máng / zhēng rén guī lù xǔ duō cháng* 'The clouds are vast, / the waters **are unbounded**; / how long is the soldier's journey home!' (渺渺 *miǎo miǎo* = 茫茫; 征 *zhēng* military campaign (also applied to long journeys for non-military purposes); 許多 *xǔ duō* how much!)

(32) 十年生死兩茫茫 [71] *shí nián shēng sǐ liǎng máng máng* (On the tenth anniversary of his wife's death) 'For ten years the living and the dead have both been **boundlessly separated**'. (十 *shí* ten; 生 *shēng* alive; 死 *sǐ* dead; 兩 *liǎng* both, in both directions.)

(33) 四顧何茫茫　東風搖百草 [72] *sì gù hé máng máng / dōng fēng yáo bǎi cǎo* 'Wherever I look, how **vast and hopeless**! / The east wind blasts every herb'. (四 *sì* four, in all four directions; 顧 *gù* look around; 東 *dōng* east; 搖 *yáo* shake, blow the leaves off, cause to wither; 草 *cǎo* grass, herbaceous plant.) The unknown poet is bewailing the brevity of human life in this case, not separation from someone else. Every herb, every man, must come to death, and in all this vast wilderness there is no hope of reprieve from Nature's doom.

---

[69] 柳宗元　登柳州城樓…　唐4

[70] 晏幾道　鷓鴣天　宋

[71] 蘇軾　江城子　宋

[72] 無名氏　古詩十九首，其十一　古A1

13.6 Examples of twin-words (5) *cāng cāng*

There are complications with this word, for in addition to having the range of
meaning of 茫茫 (it is sometimes, in fact, combined with it to form the
compound 蒼茫, meaning 茫茫), it is also used as a colour word.

As a colour 蒼 (a single syllable) means 'blue' or 'green' (like 青) or 'grey'
(e.g. grey fur, grey hair, grey beard). It also means 'old, decaying, fading'. My
own feeling is that even when meaning 'blue' or 'green' it refers to a pale,
washed-out, greyish or misty version of those colours, not a deep or vivid
version as some dictionaries suggest.

When doubled as 蒼蒼 it is still sometimes used as a colour-word, though
in my view the important aspect of the word is not so much its colour
component (spectral wavelength) as its other visual content and emotional
overtones. Like 茫茫 it refers visually to a vast expanse fading into a misty
distance where eyesight fails, while emotionally it has overtones of
uncertainty, hopelessness and vulnerability, in other words an emotional
greyness or weakness.

(34) 寒陰籠白日 大谷晦蒼蒼[73] *hán yīn lǒng bái rì / dà gǔ huì cāng
cāng* 'A chill overcast shrouds the white sun; / the Great Valley is obscured by
misty greyness'. (陰 *yīn* overcast; 籠 *lǒng* enfold; 晦 *huì* the dark of the
moon, dark, obscure.)

(35) 萬里蒼蒼煙水暮[74] *wàn lǐ cāng cāng yān shuǐ mù* 'For a myriad
miles **there stretches grey before me** the dusk on misted waters'. (煙 *yān*
mist; 暮 *mù* evening, dusk.)

(36) 古戍蒼蒼烽火寒 大荒沉沉飛雪白[75] *gǔ shù cāng cāng fēng
huǒ hán / dà huāng chén chén fēi xuě bái* 'The ancient garrison **is bleak and
grey**, and the beacon-fires are chill; / the great wilderness is sunk in gloom,
and the flying snow is white'. (戍 *shù* garrison; 烽 *fēng* beacon; 火 *huǒ* fire;
荒 *huāng* wilderness; 沉沉 *chén chén* gloomy, depressing.)

(37) 蒼蒼丁零塞 今古緬荒途[76] *cāng cāng dīng líng sài / jīn gǔ
miǎn huāng tú* '**Vast and bleak is** the Dingling frontier; / down the ages
unceasing the wilderness road'. (丁零 *dīng líng* a country west of the Altai
Mountains, to the extreme north-west of China; 塞 *sài* frontier; 古 *gǔ*
antiquity; 緬 *miǎn* stretch unbroken into the distance; 荒 *huāng* wilderness;
途 *tú* road.) The road stretching unbroken down the ages means that frontier
wars have never ceased and men go on forever marching and dying in this

---

[73]江淹 鮑參軍照戎行 古A11

[74]韓愈 桃源圖 古B6

[75]李頎 聽董大彈胡笳聲⋯ 唐2

[76]陳子昂 感遇詩，其三 古A16

vast, hopeless wilderness. Space and time combine in one eternal vista of despair.

(38) 江水蒼蒼　望倦柳愁荷　共感秋色 [77] *jiāng shuǐ cāng cāng / wàng juàn liǔ chóu hé / gòng gǎn qiū sè* 'The waters of the river **stretch far and grey**; / as I gaze afar at the weary willows and sad water-lilies, / I, like them, am saddened by autumn's aspect'.(望 *wàng* look at in the distance; 倦 *juàn* weary; 柳 *liǔ* willow; 愁 *chóu* sad; 荷 *hé* water-lily; 共 *gòng* together (with them); 感 *gǎn* be moved by, feel emotion at, be saddened by.)

13.7 Grammar of twin-words: introduction

Grammatically twin-words are quality-verbs, though in parallel couplets they tend to match other twin-words, not other kinds of quality-verbs, and in this sense they tend to be felt as belonging to a different subclass of quality-verbs. This is no doubt helped by their emotional overtones and the impression that by being doubled they are exaggerating or intensifying the feelings they convey. We shall see under the second section below that they have been used throughout Chinese poetry in initial position whereas non-twin quality-verbs have not often been so used; this difference in distribution also contributes to this feeling that they belong to a different class.

Twin-words have five major uses:

(1) as the main verb /v2 = V/ preceded by the subject /SV/;
(2) as the main verb followed by the subject /VS/;
(3) as an adverbial /v2 = A/ in position 1 /(V)SV = ASV/;
(4) as an adverbial in position 2 /S(V)V = SAV/;
(5) as an adverbial in position 3 /SV(V) = SVA/.

The adverbial uses have various possible meanings: result, cause, degree, manner etc. — in fact, any of the relationships that secondary verbs may have with main verbs. We shall illustrate these five categories with the examples given above. To some extent my classification is necessarily subjective and other analyses are possible, particularly in seven-syllable lines.

13.8 Twin-word as main verb preceded by subject

Examples from those above:

(5) 白日何冥冥 *bái rì hé míng míng* 'How dimly-seen is the white sun!' /n a v2 = S A V/.

---

[77] 史達祖　秋霽　宋

(9) 兒今日冥冥 *ér jīn rì míng míng* 'Her son is now daily more distant and unreachable' /n n n v2 = S A A V/.

(10) 長夜何冥冥 *cháng yè hé míng míng* 'How remote and inaccessible is the long night [of death]!' /vn a v2 = S A V/.

(11) 雲雨空冥冥 *yún yǔ kōng míng míng* 'The clouds and rain are sadly lost in the mists of time' /nn a v2 = S A V/.

(23) 飛絮濛濛 *fēi xù méng méng* 'The floating willow-down forms a haze' /vn v2 = S V/.

(28) 世事兩茫茫 *shì shì liǎng máng máng* 'Our affairs in the world for both of us will be cut off by a vast expanse' /nn a v2 = S A V/.

(30) 海天愁思正茫茫 *hǎi tiān chóu sì zhèng máng máng* 'Sad thoughts like the sea and the sky now flood unbounded' /nnvn a v2 = S A V/.

(31) 水茫茫 *shuǐ máng máng* 'The waters are unbounded' /n v2 = S V/.

(32) 十年生死兩茫茫 *shí nián shēng sǐ liǎng máng máng* 'For ten years the living and the dead have both been boundlessly separated' /qn nn a v2 = A S A V/.

(33) 四顧何茫茫 *sì gù hé máng máng* 'Wherever I look, how vast and hopeless!' /av a v2 = A A V/.

(36) 古戍蒼蒼 *gǔ shù cāng cāng* 'The ancient garrison is bleak and grey' /vn v2 = S V/.

(38) 江水蒼蒼 *jiāng shuǐ cāng cāng* 'The waters of the river stretch far and grey' /nn v2 = S V/.

13.9 Twin-word as main verb followed by subject

This is one of the oldest occurrences of twin-words in Chinese verse. We may compare it with the prose structure exemplified in 大哉堯之爲君也 [78] *dà zāi yáo zhī wéi jūn yě* 'Great indeed was Yao's rule!' (Literally: 'Was great *final exclamation-particle* Yao's being a ruler *topic-particle*!' /vf dnf = VF SF/.) In the light of this comparison we might be tempted to see the twin-word in this function as an exclamatory predicate followed by an 'afterthought' subject.

The trouble with this idea is that, even if this was the original prose use of the initial twin-word, in verse (for me at least) a twin-word in position 1 does not seem to be any more exclamatory than one in the usual V position; in fact,

---

[78] 論 9

the marked exclamations among the examples above are those in (1) above, where the twin-words are in the normal V position after the exclamatory adverb 何.

This can be seen even in the earliest poetry, the *Shijing*, dating from perhaps the eleventh to seventh centuries BC, where twin-words occur freely in initial and normal V position with no apparent difference in emphasis between the two; an example is a poem [79] about a peach-tree which contains the line 灼灼其華 *zhuó zhuó qí huá* 'Bright is its blossom' /v2 nn = VS/ and also the line 其葉蓁蓁 *qí yè zhēn zhēn* 'Its leaves are luxuriant' /nn v2 = SV/.

My own feeling is that this inversion in five-syllable verse from the Han onwards is either for metrical reasons (a twin-word fits conveniently into the first part of a line with a three-syllable subject to follow /xx xxx/) or else to echo the practice of more ancient poetry.

Examples from those above:

(15) 杳杳神京路 *yǎo yǎo shén jīng lù* 'Faint and far is the road to the sacred capital' /v2 nnn = V S/.

(35) 萬里蒼蒼煙水暮 *wàn lǐ cāng cāng yān shuǐ mù* 'For a myriad miles there stretches grey before me the dusk on misted waters' /qm v2 nnn = A V S/.

(37) 蒼蒼丁零塞 *cāng cāng dīng líng sài* 'Vast and bleak is the Dingling frontier' /v2 n2n = V S/.

13.10 Twin-word as adverbial in position 1

Structure: /(V)SV = ASV/. The notation /(V)S.../ is of course ambiguous, since it is not clear whether the /(V)/ is qualifying the /S/ or the main verb /V/. I have made the notation deliberately ambiguous because there is sometimes no way of proving that it is one or the other. My own feeling about it is that it began as an adverbial and perhaps always remained one in five-syllable verse, whereas in the first two syllables of a seven-syllable line it has often come to be felt by modern Chinese readers (and perhaps also by earlier ones) as a subject-qualifier. As the first two syllables of a four-syllable phrase it is felt to be closely connected to the following subject, whereas when it stands alone before the so-called caesura in five-syllable verse it is felt to be less intimately connected with the subject and hence still free to qualify the main verb.

Examples from those above:

(4) 冥冥花正開 *míng míng huā zhèng kāi* 'Secretly (= imperceptibly) the flowers are just opening'. /v2 n a v = (V) S A V/.

---

[79] 無名氏 桃夭 詩6

(7) 冥冥日沉夕 *míng míng rì chén xī* 'Dimly seen, the sun drowns in dusk'. /v2 n v n = (V) S V O/.

(12) 冥冥子規叫 *míng míng zǐ guī jiào* 'Faint in the distance a cuckoo calls'. /v2 n2 v = (V) S V/.

(13) 杳杳歸鴻吟 *yǎo yǎo guī hóng yín* 'Faint and high the returning geese mourn' /v2 vn v = (V) S V/.

(16) 杳杳音塵都絕 *yǎo yǎo yīn chén dōu jué* 'Obscured by distance, all news of you has been cut off' /v2 n2 a v = (V) S A V/.

(17) 杳杳星出雲 *yǎo yǎo xīng chū yún* 'Faintly seen, the stars emerge from the clouds' /v2 n v n = (V) S V P/.

(18) 杳杳深谷攢青楓 *yǎo yǎo shēn gǔ cuán qīng fēng* 'Faintly seen in the distance, the green maples cluster in the deep valley' /v2 vn v vn = (V) A V S/. This /VS/ word-order will be dealt with in the next unit.

(19) 濛濛殘雨籠晴 *méng méng cán yǔ lǒng qíng* 'With its haze the last of the rain mantles the clear sky' /v2 vn v n = (V) S V O/.

(20) 濛濛秋雨駛 *méng méng qiū yǔ shǐ* 'Blindingly the autumn rain drives' /v2 nn v = (V) S V/.

(21) 濛濛夕煙起 *méng méng xī yān qǐ* 'Shrouding the distance, the evening mists rise' /v2 nn v = (V) S V/.

(27) 別時茫茫江浸月 *bié shí máng máng jiāng jìn yuè* 'When we part, boundlessly flowing, the river immerses the moon' /vn v2 n v n = A (V) S V O/.

(29) 茫茫江漢上　日暮復何之 *máng máng jiāng hàn shàng / rì mù fù hé zhī* 'Across the boundless Yangtse and Han / as the sun sets, where will you go next?' if we take the (V) as qualifying the rivers. Or: 'Into a boundless, uncertain future, on the Yangtse and Han, …' if we take it as adverbial. But the total effect will be the same. /v2 nnp nv aav = (V) A A AAV/.

13.11 Twin-word as adverbial in position 2

Structure: /S(V)V = SAV/.

   Examples from those above:

(3) 冥冥孤高多烈風 *míng míng gū gāo duō liè fēng* 'Faintly seen, lonely and high …' /v2v2 v vn = (V)(V) VS/.

(8) 冥冥歸去無人管 *míng míng guī qù wú rén guǎn* 'Lost in the mists [of my thoughts of you], I go back home with no one to heed me' /v2vv vnv = (V)V-V, VO:V/.

(14) 杳杳即長暮 *yǎo yǎo jí cháng mù* 'Lost beyond recall, gone to the long twilight' /v2 vvn = (V) VO/.

(22) 碧窗宿霧濛濛濕 *bì chuāng sù wù méng méng shī* 'At my green-gauze window the overnight mist is blurringly wet' /vnvn v2v = AS AV/.

(26) 大江茫茫去不還 *dà jiāng máng máng qù bù huán* 'The Great River goes on and on into the hazy distance and [once gone] does not return' /vnv2 vav = S(V) V-AV/.

13.12 Twin-word as adverbial in position 3

Structure: /SV(V) = SVA/.

Examples from those above:

(1) 鴻飛冥冥 *hóng fēi míng míng* 'The geese fly over, indiscernible' (because of distance) /n v v2 = S V (V)/.

(2) 今我遊冥冥 *jīn wǒ yóu míng míng* 'But now I am wandering too high to be seen clearly' /n n v vv = A S V (V)/.

(6) 清水揚波兮冒冥冥 *qīng shuǐ yáng bō xī mào míng míng* 'The limpid water lifts its waves (eh!), shrouded to faintness' /vn v n f v vv = S V O F V (V)/.

(24) 萬古青濛濛 *wàn gǔ qīng míng míng* '[Stand] hazy-green through a myriad ages' /qn v vv = A V (V)/.

(25) 春動水茫茫 *chūn dòng shuǐ máng máng* 'Springtime moves the waters as far as the eye can see' /n v n vv = S V O (V)/.

(34) 大谷晦蒼蒼 *dà gǔ huì cāng cāng* 'The Great Valley is obscured by misty greyness' /n2 v vv = S V (V)/.

This /V(V)/ structure with a twin-word at /(V)/ has an exact counterpart in modern Chinese intensive compounds such as 熱騰騰 *rè tēng tēng* 'steaming hot' and 黑漆漆 *hēi qī qī* 'pitch-black', but whereas the modern compounds are set phrases the poet is creating free ('nonce') compounds that can be difficult to translate, e.g. Yuan Zhen's 風動落花紅簌簌 [80] *fēng dòng luò huā hóng sù sù* 'The wind stirs the fallen [peach-] blossom, crowdedly pink', meaning that in this neglected, overgrown old palace garden an excessive amount of peach-blossom has accumulated, creating a condensed mass of colour that is cloyingly overwhelming. /n v vn v vv = S V O (V (V))/, where the final /V(V)/ has itself become an adverbial. (簌簌 in close profusion.)

---

[80] 元稹 連昌宮詞 全419

Twin-words occur frequently in the earliest extant poetry and have been used ever since as part of a continuous tradition stemming from that early poetry. As such they are a reminder that Chinese poetry should not be regarded as a form of crippled prose but as part of a three-thousand-year tradition that owes far more to its earlier self and to the folk-song tradition than to current prose styles.

I felt this unit was heavy enough without adding an exercise!

UNIT 14

This unit is concerned with (a) verbless statements, (b) post-verbal subjects, and (c) exposure.

Vocabulary

床 床 *chuáng* /n/ bed 53.4 (M 木 'wood')

帶 帶 *dài* /v/ carry, bear 50.8 (X)

低 低 *dī* /v/ be low 9.5 (M 人 'person')

地 地 *dì* /n/ earth, ground 32.3 (M 土 'earth')

對 對 *duì* /v/ face towards; (noun-qualifier) facing, opposite 41.11 (S)

荷 荷 *hè* /v/ carry on back or shoulder 140.7 (S)

還 還 *huán* /v/ return 162.13 (M 辶 'go')

舉 舉 *jǔ* /v/ raise, lift 134.10 (X)

瞑 瞑 *mìng* /n/ darkness, night (cf 冥冥 *míng míng*) 72.10 (M 日 'sun')

起 起 *qǐ* /v/ rise; stand up 156.3 (M 走 'run')

是 是 *shì* /v/ be 72.5 (M 日 'sun')

霜 霜 *shuāng* /n/ hoarfrost 173.9 (M 雨 'rain')

寺 寺 *sì* /n/ Buddhist temple (with monastery attached) 41.3 (S)

頭 頭 *tóu* /n/ head; /p/ end (extremity) 181.7 (M 頁 'head')

晚 晚 *wǎn* /v/ be late; /n/ evening 72.7 (M 日 'sun')

望 望 *wàng* /v/ gaze afar at; long for 74.7 (S)

溪 溪 *xī* /n/ stream, brook 85.10 (M 氵 'water')

稀 稀 *xī* /v/ be few, sparse, rare 115.7 (S)

斜 斜 *xié* /v/ slant, be oblique, be at an angle 68.7 (S)

陽 陽 *yáng* /n/ sunlight; the south (sunny) side of a hill or north side of a river; the *yang* (male, positive) principle; the sun. The opposite of all these is 陰 *yīn* /n/ overcast; the *yin* principle; the moon 170.9 (M 阝 'hills')

衣 衣 *yī* /n/ clothes 145.0 (W)

疑 疑 *yí* /v/ suspect; think (wrongly) that 103.9 (X)

盈 盈 *yíng* /v/ fill 108.4 (M 皿 'bowl')

遠 遠 *yuǎn* /v/ be far; be long (of road or journey) 162.10 (M 辶 'go')

鐘 鐘 *zhōng* /n/ (temple) bell 167.12 (M 金 'metal')

醉 醉 *zuì* /v/ be drunk; get drunk on, be enthralled by 164.8 (M 酉 'wine')

Exercise on new vocabulary

(1) 長暝無歸路 (2) 月明霜盈天 (3) 披衣坐望月 (4) 舉燈照白壁 (5) 對岸霜地白 (6) 寒床獨宿久 (7) 隨溪還山寺 (8) 雨斜晚鳥稀 (9) 風帶溪響遠 (10) 童子荷琴還 (11) 黃花對春陽 (12) 疑是故人聲 (13) 低雲滅斜陽 (14) 冥冥聞寺鐘 (15) 春風吹來盈我衣 (16) 盡日隨溪醉春花 (17) 上樓望鄉不覺暝 (18) 雪地鳥蹤日日稀 (19) 醉翁在地不能起 (20) 童年去鄉白頭還 (21) 地低水高不見岸 (22) 斜雨濛濛寒木遠 (23) 斜陽照明床後壁 (24) 前望遠岸水茫茫 (25) 暝中燈光杳杳見 (26) 晚來鐘聲江邊聞 (27) 翁荷長物出林來 (28) 頭戴大笠衣帶雨 (29) 君我同是江湖客 (30) 落花疑是夜來雪 (31) 舉目遠望雁冥冥 (32) 坐望明月鄉思起

14.1 Verse and prose

So far in this course (except for some one-off quoted examples) we have kept largely within the area common to prose and verse grammar, apart from some unproselike locations of some adverbials. In this unit we meet three constructions that are fairly common in verse but not met in these forms in prose.

All three are derived from prose constructions but have been extended in a way that would not be acceptable in prose. To some extent all three of them involve changes in word-order that seriously disrupt the prose principle of 'topic before comment', so reducing the expressive power of word-order. It is my belief that these disruptions of word-order began for prosodic reasons, viz. to fit in with metrical, tonal and rhyming patterns, but were then exploited deliberately, especially in parallel couplets, to create 驚句 *jīng jù* 'startling lines' and generally to produce an artificial effect that is felt to be more elevated and hence appropriate to verse, like the rituals and language that in all cultures distinguish the sacred from the profane. While this sort of juggling conveys the message 'You are now reading verse', it is difficult to see how it can contribute to the spontaneity and sincerity that we in the West expect from lyrical poetry. But I shall say no more on this subject here, since it would take us outside our remit into the wider realms of psychology and comparative cultural anthropology. Here I am only concerned to help you read the texts, not to investigate why Chinese poetry was written in the first place.

14.2 The verbless statement

In both verse and prose two things can be equated with the verbs 是 *shì*, 爲 *wéi*, (negative 非 *fēi*), 當 *dāng*, 屬 *shǔ* or 作 *zuò*, all meaning 'is/are'; a thing can be linked to a following place with 在 *zài* 'is at'; and a place can be linked to a following thing with 有 *yǒu* 'there is' (negative 無 *wú*). In prose two things can be equated without a verb but such a statement usually takes the form /N₁ 者 *zhě* N₂ 也 *yě*/, meaning 'N₁ is N₂', using two particles to mark off the subject and the 'object' of the non-existent verb, neither of which two particles is normally used in verse.

In verse we often find things or places linked without a verb of any kind between them, and our first impulse may be to assume that one of the above verbs has been omitted. In fact, I'm not sure that we should be thinking in terms of 'omission' at all, but rather of the static presentation of two images as in a painting, leaving the reader to combine them as seems appropriate.

Let us take an example: the poet is going up a hill to visit a friend without prior notice on the off-chance that he may be at home (a custom still to be observed among some Chinese today), and as he gets to the top of the hill he says 絕頂一茅茨 (Unit 35) *jué dǐng yī máo cí* 'The very top, a single thatched cottage'. If we think in terms of omitted verbs, what verb are we to supply? 'At the very top THERE IS a cottage'? Or 'At the very top I SEE (FIND, ENCOUNTER etc) a cottage'? Or 'At the very top a cottage STANDS (or IS SEEN, APPEARS etc.)'? We cannot even decide whether the cottage is the subject or the object of any hypothetical 'omitted' verb. All we have is the juxtaposition of two images, a hilltop and a cottage — and our own imaginations, free to choose among the possibilities, or preferably not to choose a left-brain linguistic connection at all but to be content instead with a right-brain spatial visualization, for, whatever else Chinese poetry may be, it is certainly strongly visual rather than cerebral.

What about notation? Since, in the absence of a main verb, our two noun-phrases cannot be assigned to subject or object or adverbial, we cannot adopt our old notation for them; so I propose to mark them as /N/, denoting a noun-phrase of indeterminate (uncommitted) status. So our example is notated /vn qnn = N N/.

Here are some more examples. In some a noun-phrase is part of a line, in others it constitutes a whole line or perhaps the whole couplet. The grouping implicit in my versions is not the only possible interpretation, since the absence of overt markers means that we can only make subjective judgments about the structure of these lines and couplets.

(a) 慈母手中線 遊子身上衣[81] *cí mǔ shǒu zhōng xiàn / yóu zǐ shēn shàng yī* 'The thread in the loving mother's hand, / the clothes on her travelling son's back'. (慈 *cí* loving, maternal; 母 *mǔ* mother; 手 *shǒu* hand; 線 *xiàn* thread; 身 *shēn* body.)

(b) 妾心井中水[82] *qiè xīn jǐng zhōng shuǐ* 'My heart, water in a well'. (妾 *qiè* concubine, I (said by wife in self-deprecation); 心 *xīn* heart; 井 *jǐng* a well.) Water is a sign of purity, here faithfulness to her absent husband.

(c) 少婦今春意 良人昨夜情[83] *shào fù jīn chūn yì / liáng rén zuó yè qíng* 'The young wife's state of mind this spring, / her [absent] husband's feelings last night'. (少 *shào* young; 婦 *fù* woman, wife; 意 *yì* state of mind; 良 *liáng* good; 良人 *liáng rén* 'the goodman', dear husband.)

(d) 浮雲遊子意 落日故人情[84] *fú yún yóu zǐ yì / luò rì gù rén qíng* (In a farewell poem) 'Floating clouds, the wanderer's state of mind; / the setting sun, old friends' feelings'. (意 *yì* state of mind.) Clouds symbolize travellers; the departing friend cannot be held back any more than the setting sun can.

---

[81] 孟郊 游子吟 唐1

[82] 孟郊 烈女操 唐1

[83] 沈期 雜詩 唐3

[84] 李白 送友人 唐3

(e) 雨中黃葉樹　燭下白頭人 [85] *yǔ zhōng huáng yè shù / zhú xià bái tóu rén* 'Yellow-leaved trees in the rain, / a white-haired person in the candle-light'. (樹 *shù* tree; 燭 *zhú* candle.)

(f) 古臺搖落後　秋日望鄉心 [86] *gǔ tái yáo luò hòu / qiū rì wàng xiāng xīn* 'The ancient tower, after leaf-fall, / an autumn day, a heart yearning for home'. (古 *gǔ* ancient; 臺 *tái* tower; 搖 *yáo* shake (wind shaking trees); 心 *xīn* heart.)

(g) 長安一片月　萬戶擣衣聲 [87] *cháng ān yī piàn yuè / wàn hù dǎo yī shēng* 'Chang'an, a stretch of moonlight, / a myriad households, the sound of pounding clothes'. (安 *ān* peace, tranquillity; 長安 *cháng ān* an ancient capital near present-day Xi'an; 片 *piàn* slice, flat fragment, patch of; 戶 *hù* door, household; 擣 *dǎo* to pound.) The sound of women fulling clothes for winter wear is a standard feature of autumn in Chinese verse (see Unit 16).

(h) 山中一夜雨　樹杪百重泉 [88] *shān zhōng yī yè yǔ / shù miǎo bǎi chóng quán* 'A night of rain in the hills, / hundredfold streams on the tips of the branches'. (樹 *shù* tree; 杪 *miǎo* tip of branch or twig; 重 *chóng* -fold; 泉 *quán* spring, lively brook near a spring.)

(i) 長亭酒一瓢 [89] *cháng tíng jiǔ yī piáo* 'The long summer-house, a ladleful of wine'. (亭 *tíng* summerhouse, pavilion; 瓢 *piáo* half-gourd ladle.)

(j) 草色新雨中　松聲晚窗裏 (Unit 35) *cǎo sè xīn yǔ zhōng / sōng shēng wǎn chuāng lǐ* 'The colour of grass in the new rain, / the voice of pines at the twilight window'. (草 *cǎo* grass, herbs; 新 *xīn* new, fresh, recent; 窗 *chuāng* window.)

(k) 高風漢陽渡　初日郢門山 [90] *gāo fēng hàn yáng dù / chū rì yǐng mén shān* 'A high wind, Hanyang ferry; / the first sun, Mount Yingmen'. (漢 *hàn* R. Han; 漢陽 *hàn yáng* Hanyang, city at confluence of Han and Yangtse, part of present-day Wuhan; 渡 *dù* ferry; 郢 *yǐng* ancient capital of state of Chu; 門 *mén* gate.) 郢門山 is present-day 荊門山 Jingmenshan, 150 miles to west of Hanyang.)

[85] 司空曙　喜外弟盧綸見宿　唐3

[86] 劉長卿　秋日登吳公台上寺遠眺　唐3

[87] 李白　子夜四時歌，秋歌　唐1

[88] 王維　送梓州李使君　唐3

[89] 許渾　秋日赴闕…　唐3

[90] 溫庭筠　送人東游　唐3

(l) 江流天地外　山色有無中[91] *jiāng liú tiān dì wài / shān sè yǒu wú zhōng* 'The river's flow, beyond earth and sky; / the mountains' colour, between existent and non-existent'.

(m) 鳴箏金粟柱　素手玉房前[92] *míng zhēng jīn sù zhù / sù shǒu yù fáng qián* 'The singing zither, gold-patterned pegs, / white-silk hands, at the front (here implying 'window') of the jade chamber'. (鳴 *míng* sing (of birds); 箏 *zhēng* zither; 金 *jīn* gold; 粟 *sù* millet (here a pattern); 柱 *zhù* pillar, tuning-peg; 素 *sù* plain silk; 手 *shǒu* hand; 素手 *sù shǒu* the white hands of a beautiful woman; 玉 *yù* jade; 房 *fáng* room; 玉房 *yù fáng* a beautifully-appointed boudoir.)

(n) 客路青山外　行舟綠水前[93] *kè lù qīng shān wài / xíng zhōu lù shuǐ qián* 'The exile's way, beyond the blue mountains, / my travelling boat, in front of (facing into) green waters'.

(o) 落葉他鄉樹　寒燈獨夜人[94] *luò yè tā xiāng shù / hán dēng dú yè rén* 'Fallen leaves, another district's trees; / a chilly lamp, someone in the lone night'. (他 *tā* other.)

To these we may add the two examples from Unit 6, where I deferred comment on the overall structure until this unit:

(p) 古木無人徑　深山何處鐘 (Unit 24) *gǔ mù wú rén jìng / shēn shān hé chù zhōng* 'Ancient trees, a path without people; deep in the mountains, a bell somewhere'.

(q) 月下飛天鏡　雲生結海樓[95] *yuè xià fēi tiān jìng / yún shēng jié hǎi lóu* 'The moon descends, a mirror floating in the sky; clouds are born, towers building on the sea'.

14.3 The post-verbal subject

So far we have seen subjects preceding their predicates and have treated this as the 'normal' order, but not infrequently in Chinese verse (and also to a lesser extent in modern Chinese) we find subjects following their predicates when

[91] 王維　漢江臨泛　唐3
[92] 李端　聽箏　唐5
[93] 王灣　次北固山下　唐3
[94] 馬戴　灞上秋居　唐3
[95] 李白　渡荊門送別　唐3

the verb is not a twin-word. This is not to be regarded purely as poetic licence but (in principle at least) a normal feature of Chinese grammar.

In modern Chinese this structure is limited to verbs of existence, posture, appearance and disappearance. In Chinese verse this range has been extended to include verbs of movement and, it would seem, any intransitive verb with an indefinite subject, and even with a definite subject such as 'the moon'. Let us look as some examples, first where the main verb follows an adverbial of place:

(a) 漠漠水田飛白鷺　陰陰夏木囀黃鸝[96] *mò mò shuǐ tián fēi bái lù / yīn yīn xià mù zhuàn huáng lí* 'Vast paddy-fields fly egrets;/ shady summer trees sing orioles', i.e. 'Egrets fly across the vast expanse of paddy-fields;/ orioles sing in the shady summer trees'. (漠漠 *mò mò* be spread out widely; 田 *tián* arable field; 鷺 *lù* egret; 陰陰 *yīn yīn* be shady; 夏 *xià* summer; 囀 *zhuàn* sing (of birds); 鸝 *lí* oriole.)

(b) 渡頭餘落日　墟里上孤煙[97] *dù tóu yú luò rì / xū lǐ shàng gū yān* 'Ferry head linger setting sun; / market village rise solitary smoke', i.e. 'The setting sun's last rays linger on the ferry-landing;/ solitary spirals of kitchen-smoke rise from the market-village'. (渡 *dù* ferry; 餘 *yú* be in its final stages, peter out; 墟 *xū* market; 里 *lǐ* village; 煙 *yān* smoke.)

(c) 蕩胸生層雲　決眥入歸鳥[98] *dàng xiōng shēng céng yún / jué zì rù guī niǎo* 'Cleansed breast be born layered clouds;/ burst eye-sockets enter home-going birds', i.e. 'Piled-up clouds arise from my clean-swept breast;/ homegoing birds enter my breached eyes' (Du Fu is gazing at a vast mountain). (蕩 *dàng* cleanse, sweep clean of worldly cares as if with a huge gush of water; 胸 *xiōng* chest, bosom, heart, mind; 決 *jué* burst, be breached, as a dyke under the pressure of a flood (here continuing the water image, cf (e) below); 眥 *zì* eye-sockets.)

(d) 茅亭宿花影　藥院滋苔紋[99] *máo tíng sù huā yǐng / yào yuàn zī tái wén* Literally 'Thatched summer-house spend the night flower-gleams;/ herb-yard increase moss pattern', i.e. 'The gleam of the flowers lasts into the night against the thatched summer-house;/ the patterns of the moss grow deeper in the herb-garden'. (茅 *máo* thatch; 亭 *tíng* summer-house, pavilion; 院 *yuàn* courtyard; 滋 *zī* increase; 紋 *wén* pattern.)

Instead of an expression of place before the main verb we may find a direct object:

---

[96] 王維　積雨輞川莊作　唐4

[97] 王維　輞川閑居贈裴秀才迪　唐3

[98] 杜甫　望岳　唐1

[99] 常建　宿王昌齡隱居　唐1

(e) 客心洗流水　餘響入霜鐘 (Unit 15) *kè xīn xǐ liú shuǐ / yú xiǎng rù shuāng zhōng* (A description of lute-music played by a visiting monk) Literally 'Guest heart wash flowing water; / remnant echo enter frost bell', i.e. 'Flowing water washes my heart;/ a frosty bell enters the dying notes' (meaning that the music has refreshed my heart like cool water, and the notes of the angelus from the monk's monastery up on the mountainside come clear through the chill evening air and combine with the dying notes of the lute). (洗 *xǐ* wash; 餘 *yú* remnant.)

Or we may even find a clause of result:

(f) 竹喧歸浣女　蓮動下漁舟 [100] *zhú xuān guī huàn nǚ / lián dòng xià yú zhōu* Literally 'Bamboos rustle, go home laundering women; / water-lilies move, descend fishing-boat', i.e. 'Bamboos rustle, women go home from washing clothes [in the river];/ water-lilies move, a fishing-boat comes down [the river]'. (喧 *xuān* make a din, sound; 浣 *huàn* launder; 女 *nǚ* woman; 蓮 *lián* water-lily; 動 *dòng* move; 漁 *yú* fishing.) In each line the action in the initial clause (rustling, moving) is the result of the action in the second clause (women or boat passing through)

14.4 Exposure

In prose we meet the phenomenon of 'exposure', where some element of a clause which may also occur in medial or final position, such as expressions of time or place, or the object of the main verb, occurs instead in initial position. This may be done for either of two reasons:

(1) Rhetorical, to distinguish the essence of the message from a preliminary orientation. The exposed element becomes the 'topic' of the clause; the rest of the clause will be the point of the message, the 'comment'. An English parallel would be, instead of saying 'I went to see my brother Jim last week', to say 'You know my brother Jim? Well, I went to see him last week'. Jim, the object of my visit, has been exposed as the topic of my news of a visit and the hearer's attention is now focused on him as the point of departure; then follows the actual news of my visit to him. This arrangement may be compared to setting the scene on a stage as a starting-point or background to the action that takes place there.

(2) Stylistic, to create an aesthetically more pleasant rhythm and flow. An important principle in Chinese literary style, both in verse and in prose, is that one should endeavour to avoid long, clumsy sentences, and in particular complicated objects; these should be got out of the way by exposure purely for aesthetic reasons. Long qualifiers are also avoided and replaced with predication. The distance between intimately connected components should

[100] 王維　山居秋暝　唐3

also be kept to a minimum. The preferred Chinese style has always been to break one's discourse down into short, self-contained chunks.

Similar rearrangements are used in verse, but not necessarily for the same purposes. We must be careful of mechanically projecting prose structures on to verse simply because of a superficial resemblance. Just as with twin-words, initial position does not necessarily mean topicalization, either for de-emphasis or for rhythmical reasons, nor does final position necessarily mean something new. The arrangement of words in a line of Chinese verse is subject to very different constraints from those operating in prose: the poet has to fit in with the requirements of metre and rhyme and also, in regulated verse, of tonality (discussed in a future unit) and of parallelism. His dancing-chains are indeed quite heavy. The rearrangement of words to fit in with prosodic demands is a widespread phenomenon in other languages; we should not expect the Chinese poet alone to go scot-free of this universal tax.

This does not mean, however, that the considerations affecting prose word-order did not apply to verse; what it does mean is that in addition to these the poet was also subject to prosodic considerations, so each case must be judged on its merits. Sometimes initial position indubitably represents topicalization; in other cases it undoubtedly results from rhythmical or prosodic considerations. What is the value of such a dubious correspondence for actually understanding the meaning or emphasis of a line? None that I can see, for since we shall have to judge the topic–comment relationship in terms of the context and common sense, it is only after deciding this that we can say either 'Ah, yes, it's there because it's a topic' or else 'Ah, yes, a clear case of word-juggling'.

Of course, for academic purposes, the study of 'word-juggling' in the works of a particular poet or within a particular historical period could well be of interest, and might even eventually deliver a statistical probability of its having occurred in any particular case. But this is not of concern to us in this course since such statistics are not yet available, so far as I know.

In classical Greek and Latin verse the poet enjoyed considerable freedom of word-order since grammatical terminations, in concert with prepositions and conjunctions, marked the class and function of most words, but Chinese is a language that has always depended heavily upon word-order to indicate functional relationships since it lacks the Greek and Latin marking-apparatus, so any modification of word-order entails risks of ambiguity.

Once again we are thrown back upon common sense and cultural knowledge to eke out the reduced reliability of a word-order that is subject to subversion by prosodic limitations. In the final analysis what we are often confronted with is a series of words that will yield sense only if we begin with the situation on the ground as suggested by the vocabulary and background information, and work backwards to the grammar.

For the moment we are concerned with components that are moved back from their expected position to the beginning of a statement. I shall be dealing here only with objects and other normally post-verbal components.

(a) 今夜鄜州月　閨中只獨看[101] *jīn yè fū zhōu yuè / guī zhōng zhǐ dú kān* 'Tonight Fuzhou moon / in her boudoir only alone look at', i.e. 'She will be looking at the moon all alone in her boudoir in Fuzhou tonight' (Du Fu is imprisoned in Chang'an while his wife is taking refuge in Fuzhou). /nn n2n np aav = O A AAV/. (鄜州 *fū zhōu* a town 140 miles away; 閨 *guī* women's quarters.) It would sound so impossibly clumsy to swap the two lines over, so as to put the object in its 'proper' position, that this is in fact the only acceptable order.

(b) 幽林歸獨臥　滯慮洗孤清[102] *yōu lín guī dú wò / zhì lù xǐ gū qīng* 'Secluded woods return alone lie / clogging cares wash isolated pure', i.e. 'I have returned to the secluded woods to rest alone;/ my clogging cares are being washed away to leave me free and clean'. /vn vav twice = O V(AV) twice/. (臥 *wò* lie; 滯 *zhì* accumulate and clog; 慮 *lù* worry; 洗 *xǐ* wash.) The 獨臥 *dú wò* is an adverbial of purpose, while 孤清 *gū qīng* is an adverbial of result. Although this is unregulated verse, this couplet shows a regulated-verse tonal pattern: oooxx,xxxoo (which, incidentally, excludes the reading 虛 *xū* for the seventh character; I have followed the 全唐詩 reading here). But I don't think the exposure was to 'get the tone' here, for how else could these words have been arranged? *歸幽林獨臥　洗滯慮孤清 **guī yōu lín dú wò / xǐ zhì lù gū qīng* /v vn v2 = V O: V/ would have given a metre of 1-2-2 instead of the usual 2-3, for the object would then be split across the metrical divide between syllables 2 and 3. At the end of Unit 24 we meet 雨洗平沙淨 *yǔ xǐ píng shā jìng* 'The rain has washed the level sands clean' /n v vn v = S V O: V/. Although this line presents verb, object and result in the same order as our hypothetical version just given, the object is not split across the divide and the metre is the usual 2-3. My own feeling is that it was to get this 2-3 metre that the object was exposed in initial position in this example.

(c) 古調雖自愛　今人多不彈[103] *gǔ diào suī zì ài / jīn rén duō bù tán* Literally 'Ancient tunes, although [I] myself love, / people today mostly do not play', i.e. 'Although I myself love these ancient tunes, most people nowadays do not play them'. /vn aav nn aav = O AAV, S AAV/. (調 *diào* tune; 雖 *suī* although; 愛 *ài* love.)

Notice that although this couplet is formally parallel (i.e. in terms of word-classes) it is not parallel in terms of functions: the first line has no subject (the 'I' is understood) and the second shares the object 'ancient tunes' with the first line. The placement of the object in initial position enables these two statements to be made about it without repeating it or using a pronoun

---

[101] 杜甫　月夜　唐3

[102] 張九齡　感遇，其三　唐1

[103] 劉長卿　彈琴　唐5

substitute as English does. The effect of the Chinese word-order is 'These ancient tunes: although I personally am very fond of THEM, most people nowadays don't play THEM'. In prose the 'them' in such cases is optionally expressed as 之 *zhī* (third-person object-pronoun), but this is rarely used in verse, perhaps never in regulated verse.

(d) 鴻雁不堪愁裏聽　雲山況是客中過[104] *hóng yàn bù kān chóu lǐ tīng / yún shān kuàng shì kè zhōng guō* 'Wild geese I cannot bear in my sadness to listen to,/ clouded mountains especially when in exile I cross', i.e. 'I cannot bear to listen to wild geese in my sadness, / especially when crossing clouded mountains far from home'. /nnaa npv twice = OAA AV twice/. (鴻 *hóng* swan-goose; 鴻雁 *hóng yàn* wild geese in general; 堪 *kān* can bear to; 愁 *chóu* sadness; 聽 *tìng* listen to; 況是 *kuàng shì* especially when, all the more so as.)

There can be little doubt that the rearrangement was made either to meet the prosodic requirements of regulated verse or else to produce a strange effect, since the word-order sounds odd, especially that of the second line, for 況是 *kuàng shì* and its synonyms normally come at the beginning of the second line of a couplet; also, if the purpose was topicalization, it has produced an absurd emphasis on the relatively unimportant verbs 聽 *tìng* and 過 *guō* instead of on the significant 'geese' and 'mountains' that would normally be in final position.

Finally, a half-way exposure, where the removed objects don't quite make it to the beginning of the lines:

(e) 幾時杯重把　昨夜月同行[105] *jǐ shí bēi zhòng bǎ / zuó yè yuè tóng xing* 'When wine-cup again hold?/ Last night moonlight together walked', i.e. 'When shall we raise our glasses together again?/ Last night we walked together in the moonlight'. (重 *zhòng* again; 把 *bǎ* hold.) 行月 *xíng yuè* is like 步月 *bù yuè* (see the first poem in the next unit), where the 月 *yuè* is an object of place, viz. 'IN the moonlight', after an intransitive verb. /qn nav nn nav = A OAV, A OAV/.

Why the exposure? Not for topicalization and not for metrical reasons, obviously. Since this is from a poem in regulated verse, it is almost certainly for tonal reasons (tones: xooxx,xxxoo) or else to produce a bizarre effect.

---

[104]李頎　送魏萬之京　唐4

[105]杜甫　奉濟驛重送嚴公四韻　唐3

UNIT 15

Translate these three poems and check your translation against the key:

Text 1[106]

Li Bai (701–762): 'Self-consolation'

對 酒 不 覺 暝 *duì jiǔ bù jué mìng*

落 花 盈 我 衣 *luò huā yíng wǒ yī*

醉 起 步 溪 月 *zuì qǐ bù xī yuè*

鳥 還 人 亦 稀 *niǎo huán rén yì xī*

Text 2[107]

Li Bai (701–762): 'Night yearning'

床 前 明 月 光 *chuáng qián míng yuè guāng*

疑 是 地 上 霜 *yí shì dì shàng shuāng*

舉 頭 望 明 月 *jǔ tóu wàng míng yuè*

低 頭 思 故 鄉 *dī tóu sī gù xiāng*

---

[106] 李白 自遣 李23
[107] 李白 夜思 唐5

Text 3[108]

Liu Changqing (eighth century): 'Seeing off [the Rev.] Lingche'

蒼蒼竹林寺 *cāng cāng zhú lín sì*

杳杳鐘聲晚 *yǎo yǎo zhōng shēng wǎn*

荷笠帶斜陽 *hè lì dài xié yáng*

青山獨歸遠 *qīng shān dú guī yuǎn*

Discussion of Text 1

Chinese poets often mention wine and drunkenness, and Li Bai (Li Po) is perhaps more closely associated with rice-alcohol in the popular mind than any other poet. It may be no accident that he is also regarded as the doyen of free spirits (no pun, of course, intended) and the chief exponent of the carefree imagination that can become intoxicated with Nature herself. As for his long-suffering wife, he addresses her thus in a poem:

Example text[109]

Li Bai: 'For Her Indoors'

三百六十日 *sān bǎi liù shí rì*

日日醉如泥 *rì rì zuì rú ní*

雖爲李白婦 *suī wéi lǐ bái fù*

何異太常妻 *hé yì tài cháng qī*

Three hundred and sixty days,
every day I'm as drunk as mud (= floppy).
Although you are Li Bai's woman,

---

[108]劉長卿　送靈澈　唐5

[109]李白　贈內　李25

how are you different from the archbishop's wife?

(三 *sān* three; 六 *liù* six; 十 *shí* ten; 如 *rú* like, as; 泥 *ní* mud; 雖 *suī* although; 爲 *wéi* be; 婦 *fù* woman, wife; 異 *yì* be different from; 太 *tài* great; 常 *cháng* constant; 太 常 *tài cháng* minister responsible for religion and ceremonial; 妻 *qī* wife.)

The 'archbishop' referred to was 周 澤 *zhōu zé* of the Latter Han dynasty (AD 25–220). His wife was anxious that he was ruining his health by fasting and abstaining from sex (as he was required to do before conducting a ceremony), so she disturbed him in his fasting-room to ask him about it. He was furious at having his purification-process intruded upon (a breach of taboo), and imprisoned her as a punishment. A popular song at the time described Zhou Ze as follows (*loc. cit.*, commentary):

一歲三百六十日 *yī suì sān bǎi liù shí rì*

三百五十九日齋 *sān bǎi wǔ shí jiǔ rì zhāi*

一日不齋醉如泥 *yī rì bù zhāi zuì rú ní*

There are three hundred and sixty days in the year;
for three hundred and fifty-nine days he fasts;
for one day he breaks his fast and is as drunk as mud.

(歲 *suì* year; 五 *wǔ* five; 九 *jiǔ* nine; 齋 *zhāi* to fast.)

We shall see other poems on drinking by Li Bai.

Discussion of Text 2

This very simple poem is still a universal favourite with the Chinese. I think this is not because it has anything new or startling to say or that it says something in a new way, but precisely because it doesn't. It encapsulates in the smallest possible compass the whole 'exile' experience: the longing for home, and the full moon as a symbol of separation from one's family and friends. We shall see this image in more detail in the next unit.

We may see the same sentiment defined in a poem written almost three hundred years earlier:

Example text[110]

Zhang Rong (444–497): 'A poem of parting'

白雲山上盡 *bái yún shān shàng jìn*

清風松下歇 *qīng fēng sōng xià xiē*

欲識離人悲 *yù shì lí rén bēi*

孤臺見明月 *gū tái jiàn míng yuè*

The white clouds are gone from the hills;
the pure breeze pauses beneath the pines.
If you wish to taste the grief of parting,
see the bright moon from a lonely tower.

(清 *qīng* pure, clear, cool; 歇 *xiē* pause for a rest; 識 *shì* know, get acquainted with; 離 *lí* leave, be separated; 離人 *lí rén* someone parted from loved ones; 臺 *tái* tower.)

Discussion of Text 3

For me this has something of the feeling of a poem by Li Bai about a visit from a musical monk (a couplet from it was quoted in Unit 14 to illustrate non-SVO word-order):

Example text[111]

Li Bai: 'Listening to the Sichuan monk Jun playing the lute'

蜀僧抱綠綺 *shǔ sēng bào lǜ qǐ*

西下峨眉峰 *xī xià é méi fēng*

爲我一揮手 *wèi wǒ yī huī shǒu*

如聽萬壑松 *rú tīng wàn hè sōng*

客心洗流水 *kè xīn xǐ liú shuǐ*

---

[110]張融 別詩 古A9

[111]李白 聽蜀僧 彈琴 唐3

餘響入霜鐘 *yú xiǎng rù shuāng zhōng*

不覺碧山暮 *bù jué bì shān mù*

秋雲暗幾重 *qiū yún àn jǐ chóng*

A Sichuan monk, cradling a 'Green Silk' lute,
westward descends Mt Emei's peak.
A single brush of his hand for me
is like listening to pines in a myriad valleys.
Flowing water washes over my heart;
the frost-chilled sound of his temple-bell enters the dying notes (of
the lute).
I had not been aware that in the green hills' dusk
the autumn clouds had darkened severalfold.

(聽 *téng* listen; 蜀 *shǔ* present-day Sichuan in south-west China, Li Bai's birthplace; 僧 *sēng* Buddhist monk; 抱 *bào* cradle in the arms; 綠 *lǜ* green; 綺 *qǐ* silk; 綠綺 *lǜ qǐ* a superior make of lute, a 'Strad'; 西 *xī* west; 峨眉 *é méi* a mountain in Sichuan; 峰 *fēng* peak; 爲 *wèi* for, on behalf of; 揮 *huī* to wave; 手 *shǒu* hand; 如 *rú* be like; 壑 *hè* valley, ravine; 心 *xīn* heart; 洗 *xǐ* wash; 餘 *yú* remnant; 碧 *bì* green, blue; 暮 *mù* evening, dusk; 暗 *àn* be dark; 幾 *jǐ* several; 重 *chóng* -fold.)

UNIT 16

By this point we have broken the back of Chinese verse grammar but have not of course gone into all the details. Although there will be more discussion of some areas of grammar in future units, from this point onward the emphasis will shift from grammar to literary symbols associated with particular topics. The range of topics will be limited to avoid an excessive burden of vocabulary in an elementary course of this kind.

The next seven units will be devoted to poems using the moon as a symbol of separation, loneliness and the impermanence of human life. At the same time we shall also be looking at some technical areas such as tonal patterning, standardized epithets and the role of tradition.

I suggest you try translating the poem in this unit with the help of the vocabulary below. You will already know the words constituting three-quarters of the text, and perhaps more, so do not be deterred by the length of the poem. The language is deceptively simple, almost naive, and this gives an impression of sincerity and deeply-felt emotion. I am not alone in considering it one of the most evocative of Chinese poems of separation. As usual, I give an English prose version in the key so that you can check your translation, but if you have battled through the course so far it should not give you too much trouble. And when you are satisfied that you understand it, why not try making a literary translation of your own? That is always a good exercise for concentrating one's attention on the details of a text!

Note on prosody: each verse is marked by a change of rhyme and has the rhyme-scheme 'aaba.'

Vocabulary

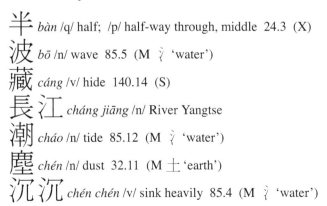

半 *bàn* /q/ half; /p/ half-way through, middle 24.3 (X)

波 *bō* /n/ wave 85.5 (M 氵 'water')

藏 *cáng* /v/ hide 140.14 (S)

長江 *cháng jiāng* /n/ River Yangtse

潮 *cháo* /n/ tide 85.12 (M 氵 'water')

塵 *chén* /n/ dust 32.11 (M 土 'earth')

沉沉 *chén chén* /v/ sink heavily 85.4 (M 氵 'water')

成 *chéng* /v/ become, form 62.2 (S)

乘 *chéng* /v/ avail oneself of (here: /prep/ by the light of) 4.9 (X)

愁 *chóu* /n/ sadness 61.9 (M 心 'heart')

代 *dài* /n/ generation; epoch, age; dynasty 9.3 (M 人 'person')

待 *dài* /v/ wait for 60.6 (M 彳 'go')

擣 *dǎo* /v/ pound in a mortar or on a block, esp. fulling clothes on a block 64.14 (M 扌 'hand')

擣衣砧 *dǎo yī zhēn* /n/ stone fulling-block

甸 *diàn* /n/ meadow 102.2 (M 勹 'enclose')

度 = 渡 *dù* /v/ cross, pass over 53.6 (S)

芳 *fāng* /v/ be fragrant; /n/ fragrance, flower 140.4 (M 艹 'plant')

楓 *fēng* /n/ maple-tree 75.9 (M 木 'tree')

拂 *fú* /v/ brush off, brush against 64.5 (M 扌 'hand')

共 *gòng* /v/ be together with 12.4 (W)

鴻 *hóng* /n/ swan-goose, large wild goose 196.6 (M 鳥 'bird')

鴻雁 *hóng yàn* /n/ wild geese in general (symbolic messengers)

戶 *hù* /n/ door, window 63.0 (W)

華 *huá* /n/ splendour, glory 140.8 (X)

還 *huán* /a/ still, yet, again

家 *jiā* /n/ home, family 40.7 (M 宀 'house')

皎皎 *jiǎo jiǎo* /v/ be brilliant 106.6 (M 白 'white')

皆 *jiē* /a/ all (X)

碣石 *jié shí* /n/ 'standing stone', name of a mountain in Hebei province, symbolic of North China (where his wife is) 112.9 (M 石 'stone')

鏡 *jìng* /n/ mirror 167.11 (M 金 'metal')

卷 *juǎn* /v/ roll up 26.6 (X)

可 *kě* /a/ may, can, -able 30.2 (S)

可憐 *kě lián* /v/ be delightful; be pitiable

空 *kōng* /n/ the void, the air, the sky

離 *lí* /v/ depart, leave, be away 172.11 (S)

離人 /n/ someone separated from another, e.g. husband away or wife at home

連 *lián* /v/ connect with 162.7 (X)

憐 *lián* /v/ have tender feelings for, be moved by; love; pity 61.12 (M 忄 'heart')

簾 *lián* /n/ curtain, bamboo-slat blind 118.13 (M 竹 'bamboo')

龍 *lóng* /n/ dragon (a water creature) 212.0 (W)

輪 *lún* /n/ wheel 159.8 (M 車 'vehicle')

滿 *mǎn* /v/ be full; fill 85.11 (M 氵 'water')

夢 *mèng* /n/ /v/ dream 36.11 (M 夕 'night')

畔 *pàn* /n/ side 102.5 (M 田 'field')

裴回 *péi huí* = 徘徊 *pái huái* /v/ linger, hesitate (see Unit 19)

片舟 *piān zhōu* /n/ small boat

片 *piàn* /n/ piece, fragment 91.0 (W)

平 *píng* /v/ be level 51.2 (X)

浦 *pǔ* /n/ river-bank 85.7 (M 氵 'water')

潛 *qián* /v/ dive, lurk out of sight under water 85.12 (M 氵 'water')

窮已 *qióng yǐ* /n/ end

遶 *rào* /v/ go round, wind round 162.12 (M 辶 'go')

生 *shēng* /v/ be born, emerge, come into being; /n/ life 100.0 (W)

勝 *shèng* /v/ be able to bear 19.10 (M 力 'strength')

樹 *shù* /n/ tree 75.12 (M 木 'tree')

似 *sì* /v/ resemble, be like, be as if 9.5 (M 亻 'person')

送 *sòng* /v/ see off, accompany departure of 162.6 (M 辶 'go')

臺 *tái* /n/ table, stand　133.8　(X)　(consists of 吉 plus 室 without the top dot)

潭 *tán* /n/ pool (deep part of river etc.)　85.12　(M 氵 'water')

汀 *tīng* /n/ islet in river, ait　85.2　(M 氵 'water')

宛轉 *wǎn zhuǎn* /v/ be winding, sinuous　(1) 40.5　(M 宀 'house'); (2) 159.11　(M 車 'vehicle')

文 *wén* /n/ writing; ripples (here a pun on both meanings)　67.0　(W)

無限 *wú xiàn* /v/ have no end, be unending

霧 *wù* /n/ mist, fog　173.11　(M 雨 'rain')

西 *xī* /n/ west　146.0　(W)

纖 *xiān* /n/ speck of　120.17　(M 糸 'silk')

閒 *xián* /v/ be quiet, undisturbed (also written 閑)　169.4　(X)

霰 *xiàn* /n/ frozen rain, sleet　173.12　(M 雨 'rain')

限 *xiàn* /n/ limit　170.6　(M 阝 'hills')

瀟湘 *xiāo xiāng* /n/ two rivers in Hunan, symbols of South China (where the husband is)　(1) 85.16　(M 氵 'water'); (2) 85.9　(M 氵 'water')

灩灩 *yàn yàn* /v/ flood, come in a flood　85.28　(M 氵 'water')

搖 *yáo* /v/ shake, agitate, disturb　64.10　(M 扌 'hand')

已 *yǐ* /v/ finish, end

悠悠 *yōu yōu* /v/ be far off　61.7　(M 心 'heart')

魚 *yú* /n/ fish (symbolic messenger)　195.0　(W)

玉 *yù* /n/ jade; a woman's ...　96.0　(W)

玉戶 *yù hù* /n/ boudoir window

願 *yuàn* /a/ wish; I wish I could　181.10　(S)

躍 *yuè* /v/ leap　157.14　(M 足 'foot')

砧 *zhēn* /n/ block for beating on (esp. fulling-block or anvil)　112.5　(M 石 'stone')

衹 = 只 *zhǐ* /a/ only 113.4 (S)

逐 *zhú* /v/ pursue, follow 162.7 (M 辶 'go')

妝 *zhuāng* /n/ toilette, make-up 38.4 (M 女 'woman')

妝鏡臺 *zhuāng jìng tái* /n/ dressing-table

Text for translation[112]

Zhang Ruoxu (seventh to eighth centuries): 'A night of blossom and moonlight on the Yangtse in springtime'

01 春江潮水連海平 *chūn jiāng cháo shuǐ lián hǎi píng*

02 海上明月共潮生 *hǎi shàng míng yuè gòng cháo shēng*

03 灧灧隨波千萬里 *yàn yàn suí bō qiān wàn lǐ*

04 何處春江無月明 *hé chù chūn jiāng wú yuè míng*

05 江流宛轉遶芳甸 *jiāng liú wǎn zhuǎn rào fāng diàn*

06 月照花林皆似霰 *yuè zhào huā lín jiē sì xiàn*

07 空裏流霜不覺飛 *kōng lǐ liú shuāng bù jué fēi*

08 汀上白沙看不見 *tīng shàng bái shā kàn bù jiàn*

09 江天一色無纖塵 *jiāng tiān yī sè wú xiān chén*

10 皎皎空中孤月輪 *jiǎo jiǎo kōng zhōng gū yuè lún*

11 江畔何人初見月 *jiāng pàn hé rén chū jiàn yuè*

12 江月何年初照人 *jiāng yuè hé nián chū zhào rén*

13 人生代代無窮已 *rén shēng dài dài wú qióng yǐ*

14 江月年年衹相似 *jiāng yuè nián nián zhǐ xiāng sì*

15 不知江月待何人 *bù zhī jiāng yuè dài hé rén*

---

[112]張若虛 春江花月夜 全117

16 旦見長江送流水 *dàn jiàn cháng jiāng sòng liú shuǐ*

17 白雲一片去悠悠 *bái yún yī piàn qù yōu yōu*
18 青楓浦上不勝愁 *qīng fēng pǔ shàng bù shèng chóu*
19 誰家今夜片舟子 *shuí jiā jīn yè piān zhōu zǐ*
20 何處相思明月樓 *hé chù xiāng sī míng yuè lóu*

21 可憐樓上月裴回 *kě lián lóu shàng yuè péi huí*
22 應照離人妝鏡臺 *yīng zhào lí rén zhuāng jìng tái*
23 玉戶簾中卷不去 *yù hù lián zhōng juǎn bù qù*
24 擣衣砧上拂還來 *dǎo yī zhēn shàng fú huán lái*

25 此時相望不相聞 *cǐ shí xiāng wàng bù xiāng wén*
26 願逐月華流照君 *yuàn zhú yuè huá liú zhào jūn*
27 鴻雁長飛光不度 *hóng yàn cháng fēi guāng bù dù*
28 魚龍潛躍水成文 *yú lóng qián yuè shuǐ chéng wén*

29 昨夜閒潭夢落花 *zuó yè xián tán mèng luò huā*
30 可憐春半不還家 *kě lián chūn bàn bù huán jiā*
31 江水流春去欲盡 *jiāng shuǐ liú chūn qù yù jìn*
32 江潭落月復西斜 *jiāng tán luò yuè fù xī xié*

33 斜月沉沉藏海霧 *xié yuè chén chén cáng hǎi wù*
34 碣石瀟湘無限路 *jié shí xiāo xiāng wú xiàn lù*
35 不知乘月幾人歸 *bù zhī chéng yuè jǐ rén guī*
36 落月搖情滿江樹 *luò yuè yáo qíng mǎn jiāng shù*

Notes on the vocabulary

擣衣砧 *dǎo yī zhēn* 'fulling-block'. A stone block on which cloth for winter clothes was beaten with a wooden beetle (杵 *chǔ*) to make the cloth more dense and weather-proof. Though the technique was different, the purpose was the same as the 'waulking' of tweed in the Western Isles of Scotland. The sound of the fulling-block was a standard image for autumn throughout Chinese poetry, like the full moon and red maple-leaves and southward-flying wild geese, all of which are mentioned in this poem.

鴻 雁 *hóng yàn* 'wild geese'. Though two different kinds of geese are involved in this expression, my own feeling is that Chinese poets used the words indiscriminately, which was quite understandable. Unless one is an ornithologist living on the migration-route of wild geese and just happens to be on the look-out with binoculars when they pass over, it seems unlikely that one would spot the difference.

This may be a convenient place to point out that Chinese poetic images were based more on literary tradition than on immediate personal observation of Nature. The same tendency is to be observed in traditional Chinese landscape painting, which was not usually done at first hand in the open air, but was a combination of remembered impressions and conventions of composition and technique (for instance, drawing people with short legs and expressionless faces and subordinating human figures to landscape features). Poets also worked with conventional forms such as metres and used conventional images to express conventional sentiments. But more of this anon in a later unit.

For the moment suffice it to say that the image of wild geese has two conventional uses: (a) as envied travellers and (b) as messengers.

(a) Just as in other parts of the Northern hemisphere, wild geese breed in the Arctic during the summer, fly to the south in autumn for a warmer climate, and return northwards in the spring. They are free to travel between north and south China, unlike the civil servant or soldier far from home. Their cries as they pass over are considered sad and lonely.

(b) The goose as messenger is based on the story of Su Wu, sent as an envoy to the Hunnish (匈 奴 *xiōng nú*) court by the Han dynasty emperor Wudi (reigned 141–87 BC). The Hunnish king (the 單 于 *chán yú*) imprisoned him, then sent him to be a shepherd in an isolated place. Nineteen years later the Chinese concluded a treaty with the Huns and sent an envoy; the Huns pretended that Su Wu was dead, but another envoy who had accompanied Su Wu managed to see the new envoy secretly by night and told him the whole story, suggesting that the new envoy tell the Hunnish king that the Chinese emperor had shot a migrant goose in the imperial park, with a letter from Su Wu attached to its foot, giving his present location. When the Hunnish king heard this he allowed Su Wu to return to China, not because he believed this highly improbable story but because he realised it was a coded message that the Chinese had somehow got this information at the Hunnish court. The 雁

足書 *yàn zú shū* 'goose foot letter' then became a metaphor for a message from someone far from home.

卷簾 *juǎn lián* 'roll up the blind' to make 虛窗 *xū chuāng* 'an empty window' or 虛幌 *xū huǎng* 'an empty curtain' through which to view the full moon either for pleasure or to think of an absent husband or friend. The window would not be made of glass but would be of wooden lattice-work or covered with green silk gauze and shuttered when necessary.

可憐 *kě lián*, although in modern Chinese meaning only 'pitiable', had a wider range of meaning in poetry, including that of the modern 可愛 *kě ài* 'delightful, charming, dear'. Basically it means some thing or person that touches one deeply, but the exact feelings involved have to be deduced from the context.

度 = 渡.

魚龍 *yú lóng* 'fish and dragons'. The Chinese dragon is a water-dwelling creature inhabiting deep pools and the sea, as well as underground watercourses known as 龍脈 *lóng mài* 'dragon-veins', an important feature of Chinese geomancy (風水 *fēng shuǐ*). It does however emerge at the spring equinox to fly in the sky, floating on a cloud of its own breath, then at the autumnal equinox it descends to lurk in deep water again. Its earliest appearance seems to be on the Shang-dynasty oracle-bones (the earliest Chinese inscriptions), where a rainbow, depicted as a dragon with a head at each end, drinks from the Yellow River (this belief survives among the present-day Hakka of south China). The dragon is the rain-bringer, so it was natural that the emperor was referred to as the dragon, since the main function of the ruler of a semi-arid country heavily dependent on rain for its crops was to ensure adequate rainfall. The dragon itself is also a ruler, the king of all scaly creatures.

In this poem 'fish and dragons' just means 'water-creatures'. Since the Yangtse was at one time the habitat of both crocodiles and alligators, it may be that poets had these water-creatures in mind when they referred to dragons.

The fish as a messenger is first encountered in an ancient poem [113] that contains the lines: 客從遠方來　遺我雙鯉魚　呼童烹鯉魚　中有尺素書 *kè cóng yuǎn fāng lái / wèi wǒ shuāng lǐ yú / hū tóng pēng lǐ yú / zhōng yǒu chǐ sù shū* 'A visitor came from far away, / gave me a pair of carp; / I called the servant-boy to cook the carp: / inside was a foot-long silk letter'.

Geese and fish are sometimes mentioned together as messengers, as in the expression 魚雁 *yú yàn*.

---

[113] 無名氏　飲馬長城窟行　樂38

片舟 *piān zhōu* 'little boat' is not just any small boat, or indeed a *small* boat at all, but the fragile craft of the traveller far from home, exposed to all the dangers of river travel.

送 *sòng* 'see off'. The Chinese custom was to accompany a departing friend several stages (i.e. inns) on his journey, not just to say goodbye on the doorstep. This gave the opportunity for composing poems of farewell as well as drowning the sorrows of parting.

玉 *yù* 'jade' is, properly speaking, nephrite, especially the white 'mutton-fat' variety (羊脂美玉 *yáng zhī měi yù* 'sheep fat beautiful jade'), though the word has also been applied to a wide range of hard minerals of all the colours of the rainbow. Because of its hardness (above that of steel) any worked jade has a high intrinsic value in labour terms, and in ancient China it had something of the status-value of gold elsewhere. Yet it was prized not just for its economic value but also for its symbolism and its beauty. As the inscription on the tea-cups in your local Chinese restaurant may well tell you, 美人如玉 *měi rén rú yù* 'A beautiful woman is like jade' (i.e. pleasant to look at, pleasant to listen to and pleasant to touch). As a colour-word it means 'white', e.g. when applied to a woman's skin. From this its meaning has been extended to mean 'beautiful', here applied to a lady's boudoir.

UNIT 17

Vocabulary

澄 *chéng* /v/ be limpid, clear 85.12 (M 氵 'water')

更 *gēng* /n/ night-watch (5 watches of 2 hours each from 7 p.m. to 5 a.m.)

耿 *gěng* /v/ be bright, brilliant 128.4 (M 火 'fire')

金 *jīn* /n/ gold; bronze (older meaning); metal 167.0 (W)

況乃 *kuàng nǎi* /a/ all the more since, especially when (1) 85.5 (S); (2) 4.1 (X)

連 *lián* /v/ connect, be connected

漏 *lòu* /v/ drip; /n/ water-clock, clepsydra 85.11 (M 氵 'water')

露 *lù* /n/ dew 173.13 (M 雨 'rain')

凝 *níng* /v/ condense, congeal, concentrate 15.14 (M 冫 'ice')

清 *qīng* /v/ be pure, clear 85.8 (M 氵 'water')

升 *shēng* /v/ rise, ascend 24.2 (S)

天河 *tiān hé* /n/ the Milky Way

向 *xiàng* /a/ hitherto 30.3 (S)

向來 *xiàng lái* /a/ hitherto, all this time

隱 *yǐn* /v/ hide, be obscured 170.14 (M 阝 'hills')

映 *yìng* /v/ reflect, be reflected in 72.5 (M 日 'sun')

餘 *yú* /v/ be left over, remnant, fading 184.7 (M 食 'food')

玉 *yù* /n/ jade, jewel

玉繩 *yù shéng* /n/ 'jewel-strings' of stars forming constellations (see note)

元 *yuán* /a/ originally, all along 10.2 (X)

緣 *yuán* /v/ climb; /prep/ along 120.9 (S)

驟 *zhòu* /v/ be sudden 187.14 (M 馬 'horse')

珠 *zhū* /n/ pearl; bead (e.g. of Buddhist rosary) 96.6 (M 玉 'jade')

自 *zì* /a/ by itself, with no help from outside, naturally 132.0 (S)

Text for translation[114]

Du Fu (712–770): 'Stars and moon by the Yangtse'

1 驟雨清秋夜 *zhòu yǔ qīng qiū yè*	x x o o x
2 金波耿玉繩 *jīn bō gěng yù shéng*	o o x x o
3 天河元自白 *tiān hé yuán zì bái**	o o o x x
4 江浦向來澄 *jiāng pǔ xiàng lái chéng*	O x x o o
5 映物連珠斷 *yìng wù lián zhū duàn*	x x o o x
6 緣空一鏡升 *yuán kōng yī* jìng shēng*	o o x x o
7 餘光隱更漏 *yú guāng yǐn gēng lòu*	o o X O x
8 況乃露華凝 *kuàng nǎi lù huá níng*	x x x o o

Language notes on the text

(1) Lines 1 and 2: the middle word of each line is a quality-verb used causatively, i.e. 'cause to be X'.

(2) Line 2: 玉繩 *yù shéng* is usually understood to be a particular pair of small stars, but I feel that Du Fu intends the expression more generally here, with the same sense as the 'connected beads (or pearls)' in line 5.

(3) Line 6: the moon was not infrequently compared to a mirror, i.e. a circular mirror of polished bronze.

(4) Line 7: reversed word-order /OVS/, cf. 客心洗流水 *kè xīn xǐ liú shuǐ* 'Flowing water washes over my heart' in Unit 15.

---

[114]杜甫 江邊星月 杜21

17.1 The four tones

During the Tang dynasty (618–907) a form of tonally-patterned verse called 'regulated verse' (律詩 *lǜ shī*) was developed. It was also known as 'modern-style verse' (近體詩 *jìn tǐ shī* or 今體詩 *jīn tǐ shī*) to distinguish it from 'ancient-style verse' (古體詩 *gǔ tǐ shī*), which tended to use ancient expressions and themes and tried to avoid the tonal patterns of regulated verse. 'Ancient-STYLE verse' should be distinguished from pre-Tang verse, which was known as 'ancient verse' (古詩 *gǔ shī*).

I shall discuss the pronunciation of Tang verse in a later unit, when we deal with rhyme, but for the moment I shall confine myself to the tones. Four tonal categories were distinguished in the Tang and have been preserved in modern Cantonese, a dialect mainly based on the court language of north China during the Tang and hence of purer descent than the Mandarin *lingua franca*, which has suffered in various ways as a result of its wide usage by speakers of different dialects and even languages. If you are fortunate enough to know Cantonese you should have no trouble with Tang tonal patterns, but, for those who do not, here is how they correspond to Mandarin tones:

> (1) Level tone (平聲 *píng shēng*), corresponding to Mandarin first and second tones (e.g. *yī* and *yí*) except as mentioned below;
>
> (2) Rising tone (上聲 *shǎng shēng*), corresponding to Mandarin third and sometimes fourth (e.g. *yǐ*);
>
> (3) Departing tone (去聲 *qù shēng*), corresponding to Mandarin fourth (e.g. *yì*);
>
> (4) Entering tone (入聲 *rù shēng*), redistributed among all four tones of Mandarin.

These four tones were for prosodic purposes grouped into two categories:

> (1) Level tone (平聲 *píng shēng*), consisting of level-tone words only. I shall use the symbol 'o' (suggestive of zero rise or fall) for these.
>
> (2) Oblique tone (仄聲 *zè shēng*), consisting of the other three tones. I shall use the symbol 'x' (suggestive of both upward and downward movement in pitch) for these.

How can we distinguish these two categories from a Mandarin transcription? Mandarin third and fourth correspond to Tang oblique ('x'), so there is no problem there. Mandarin first and second ending in a consonant (-*n*, -*ng* or -*r*) are Tang level ('o'). The problem is with Mandarin first and second ending in a vowel, which can be either Tang level or Tang oblique. In my notation I shall from now on mark the latter with an asterisk in poem texts. Mathews' *Chinese-English Dictionary* marks them as '5' in addition to the Mandarin tone. These awkward words all end in -*p*, -*k* or -*t* in Cantonese. Briefly, then:

Mandarin first (*yī*) and second (*yí*) without an asterisk are level ('o');

Mandarin third (*yǐ*) and fourth (*yì*) and any with an asterisk (*yī** or *yí**) are oblique ('x').

17.2 Tonal patterns

Let us begin with the two tonal patterns of the couplet in five-syllable regulated verse (五律 *wǔ lǜ*):

(a) Oblique-start (仄起 *zè*) couplet. The 'starting' syllable is the second syllable in the first line, not the first syllable (the first was variable, so not a reliable guide). Couplet pattern: xx oox / oo xxo.

(b) Level-start (平起 *píng qǐ*) couplet. Pattern: oo oxx / xx xoo.

There are two possible patterns for a four-couplet poem:

(a) Oblique-start poem: the four couplets are oblique, level, oblique, level, viz.

x x o o x / o o x x o
o o o x x / x x x o o
x x o o x / o o x x o
o o o x x / x x x o o

(b) Level-start poem: the four couplets are level, oblique, level, oblique, viz.

o o o x x / x x x o o
x x o o x / o o x x o
o o o x x / x x x o o
x x o o x / o o x x o

There are several things to be noticed about these patterns:

(1) A couplet always ends in 'o'. Since this is where the rhyme comes, rhymes are always level-tone (I am ignoring here the minority of cases where regulated verse uses oblique-tone rhymes).

(2) Except at the end of a line, an isolated level tone (孤平 *gū píng*) is avoided (or, as we shall see below, compensated for). The basic pattern on the whole consists of groups of two or three identical tones.

(3) Every tone in the second line of a couplet is the opposite of the corresponding tone in the preceding line.

There are (inevitably!) further complications:

(a) If the first line of the poem is allowed into the rhyme-scheme its tonal pattern will be replaced with that of the fourth line.

(b) The tones in positions 1 and 3 of the line are often allowed to vary, i.e. 'o' can be replaced with 'x' and vice versa. This can be seen, for example, in the first syllable of line 4 of the poem above (my capitals mark a departure from the theoretical basic pattern).

(c) But if this leads to an isolated level-tone and/or to four oblique tones in the first line of a couplet, this imbalance (拗 *ào* 'awkwardness') has to be compensated for (救 *jiù* 'rescued') either in the same line or in the second line. This imbalance-plus-compensation is often used deliberately in line 7 of an 8-line poem; an example is in line 7 of the above poem, where 'oo oxx' has become 'oo XOx'.

17.3 Other patterns in this poem

Apart from the tonal patterning and the parallelism of the first three couplets, Du Fu has created patterns that I find quite unusual: (a) of eye-movement, (b) of light-phenomena and (c) of relationship polarities between couplet halves. The numbers are line-numbers.

1	Downward	Increasing light	
2	Upward	Increasing light	Equality with preceding line
3	'River' above	Realisation of light	
4	River below	Realisation of light	Equality with preceding line
5	Downward	Dispersion of light	
6	Upward	Unity of light	Contrast with preceding line
7	Stars above	Fading light	
8	'Stars' below	Growing light	Contrast with preceding line

Strangely enough (or perhaps not so strangely), these patterns are reminiscent of tonal patterns. The tonal contrasts between the two lines of each couplet are matched by the contrasts in sense: upward movement versus downward movement of the eye, metaphor versus literalness, dispersion versus unity of light, fading versus growing of light. And between the two halves of the poem we have equality versus contrast. The overall eye-movement pattern is the most striking of all: 'down, up, up, down, down, up, up, down' matches the pattern of the tones at positions 2 and 4: o,x,x,o,o,x,x,o, where 'down' matches 'o' and 'up' matches 'x'. This tone-pattern is generated by the rule of alternating contrast (對 *duì* 'opposition') and equality (黏 *nián* 'adhesion') of the tones between successive lines at these positions.

What is the poem about? The 清 *qīng* 'pure, clean, clear, cool, free' of the first line sets the tone and the whole poem is, for me at least, pervaded by a feeling of tranquillity and wonder. I feel Du Fu has escaped from his constant anxieties in a contemplation of the cosmos that leaves no room for any mention of himself. Yet the images of moon and Yangtse silently remind us that this is a poem of exile, and we remember that 清 *qīng* can also have overtones of chilly isolation and that even the voluntary exile or recluse can only have freedom at the cost of loneliness.

UNIT 18

Vocabulary

杯 *bēi* /n/ cup 75.4 (M 木 'wood')

曾 *céng* /a/ previously 73.8 (X)

曾經 *céng jīng* /a/ previously, once in the past

嫦娥 *cháng é* /n/ Chang'e (see note below) (1) 38.11; (2) 38.7 (M 女 'woman')

從 *cóng* /v/ from 60.8 (M 辵 'go')

丹 *dān* /n/ cinnabar, vermilion 3.3 (W)

當 *dāng* /v/ be in front of, in the presence of, facing, at 102.8 (S)

得 *dé* /v/ get, achieve; find 60.8 (S)

發 *fā* /v/ emit, shoot out 105.7 (M 弓 'bow')

歌 *gē* /v/ sing; /n/ singing, song 76.10 (M 欠 'gape')

共 *gòng* /a/ together

古 *gǔ* /n/ antiquity, ancient times 30.2 (X)

輝 *huī* /n/ radiance 159.8 (M 光 'light')

經 *jīng* /a/ already 120.7 (M 糸 'silk')

鄰 *lín* /n/ neighbour; /v/ be a neighbour 163.12 (M 阝 'town')

綠 *lǜ* /v/ be green 120.8 (M 糸 'silk')

沒 *mò* /v/ drown, sink out of sight 85.4 (M 氵 'water')

寧 *nìng* /a/ how could? 40.11 (X)

攀 *pān* /v/ pull down (e.g. a branch) 64.15 (M 手 'hand')

棲 *qī* /v/ roost (of birds), dwell (of people) 75.8 (M 木 'tree')

卻 *què* /a/ nevertheless, though 26.7 (X)

162

闕 *què* /n/ palace gateway 169.10 (M 門 'gate')

如 *rú* /v/ be like; like, as 38.3 (M 口 'mouth')

若 *ruò* /v/ be like; like, as 140.5 (S)

停 *tíng* /v/ stop, pause 9.9 (M 亻 'person')

兔 *tù* /n/ hare, rabbit 10.6 (W)

唯 *wéi* /a/ only 30.8 (M 口 'mouth')

向 *xiàng* /v/ face towards, towards

宵 *xiāo* /n/ night 40.7 (S)

煙 *yān* /n/ mist; smoke 86.9 (M 火 'fire')

一 *yī* /a/ once, just

與 *yǔ* /v/ with; /c/ and 134.7 (X)

之 *zhī* /n/ it, him, her, them 4.3 (S)

樽 *zūn* /n/ wine-kettle 75.12 (M 木 'wood')

Note on the vocabulary

Chang'e was a lady who stole the elixir of immortality and ran off to the moon, where she lives forever in cold and loneliness, an object of pity. Her name was originally 恆 娥 *héng é*, but was later changed to avoid the taboo on the personal name (恆 *héng* 'constant') of Emperor Xiaowen (reigned 180–147 BC). The first character was changed to 常 *cháng*, also meaning 'constant', and the meaning-element 女 'woman' was added to match that of the second character.

Her original name is interesting: 恆 was originally 亘 , with the moon standing between heaven and earth, and said to mean 'the waxing moon', but I suspect this interpretation was based on a guess about the meaning of the ancient couplet 如 月 之 恆   如 日 之 升 [115] *rú yuè zhī héng / rú rì zhī shēng* 'like the regularity of the moon, like the rising of the sun', referring to the constancy of Heaven in supporting the king's virtuous endeavours and comparing it to the regularity of the moon's phases and of the daily rising of the sun. So 恆 *héng* seems an appropriate part of a moon-goddess's name.

---

[115] 無名氏 天保 詩166

Text for translation[116]

Li Bai (701–762): 'Questioning the moon with a cup of wine in my hand'

01 青天有月來幾時 *qīng tiān yǒu yuè lái jǐ shí*

02 我今停杯一問之 *wǒ jīn tíng bēi yī* wèn zhī*

03 人攀明月不可得 *rén pān míng yuè bù kě dé**

04 月行卻與人相隨 *yuè xíng què yǔ rén xiāng suí*

05 皎如飛鏡臨丹闕 *jiǎo rú fēi jìng lín dān què*

06 綠煙滅盡清輝發 *lù yān miè jìn qīng huī fā**

07 但見宵從海上來 *dàn jiàn xiāo cóng hǎi shàng lái*

08 寧知曉向雲間沒 *nìng zhī xiǎo xiàng yún jiān mò*

09 白兔擣藥秋復春 *bái* tù dǎo yào qiū fù chūn*

10 嫦娥孤棲與誰鄰 *cháng é gū qī yǔ shuí lín*

11 今人不見古時月 *jīn rén bù jiàn gǔ shí yuè*

12 今月曾經照古人 *jīn yuè céng jīng zhào gǔ rén*

13 古人今人若流水 *gǔ rén jīn rén ruò liú shuǐ*

14 共看明月皆如此 *gòng kàn míng yuè jiē rú cǐ*

15 唯願當歌對酒時 *wéi yuàn dāng gē duì jiǔ shí*

16 月光長照金樽裏 *yuè guāng cháng zhào jīn zūn lǐ*

18.1 More prepositional verbs

We have met subordinate verbs such as 在 *zài*, 隨 *suí* and 傍 *bàng* used like the English prepositions 'at', 'with' and 'beside' respectively. In this unit we meet four more: 從 *cóng* 'follow, following' somehow comes to mean 'from', though I personally cannot see how; 向 *xiàng* 'face towards, facing, towards'

---

[116]李白 把酒問月 李20

is rather like 對 *duì*; 與 *yǔ* 'be with, with' can also mean 'and' when connecting two nouns; and 如 *rú* 'resemble, be like, like, as' is used AFTER the main verb as part of a position-3 adverbial. Here are some examples:

> 從 林 出 *cóng lín chū* 'from woods emerge' = 'emerge from the woods' (the same as 出 林 *chū lín*)
>
> 向 我 來 *xiàng wǒ lái* 'towards me come' = 'come towards me'
>
> 與 誰 去 *yǔ shuí qù* 'with who go' = 'who are you going with?'
>
> 白 如 雪 *bái rú xuě* 'white like snow' = 'it is as white as snow'

18.2 Comments on the contents of the poem

This poem is in four verses marked by a change of rhyme.

We have seen the moon as a symbol of parting, but here it is used as a contrast to the ephemeral nature of human life.

1-2: In the first couplet the moon is treated as a visitor who has dropped in on the party, whereas the poet, of course, with his brief life, is a visitor dropping in on the moon's everlasting party.

3-4: In the second couplet we cannot control the moon, i.e. the passing of time, and the moon mocks us by following us home while staying forever out of reach.

5-6: In the second verse the moon (and also, of course, time and death) looks as pitilessly and mockingly upon the emperor as it does upon the poet; when the mist of our brief lives has melted away the moon will blaze as bright as ever.

7-8: In the second half of this verse the moon has become a symbol not of permanence but of human transience: we come to life like the moon from the sea but try to forget that we too shall one day sink from sight.

9-10: In the third verse we meet two inhabitants of the moon (the others are a three-legged toad and a man trying to fell a tree which heals up after each stroke of the axe, a kind of Sisyphus). The white hare is preparing an elixir of immortality that will change old age to youth again; my guess is that the succession of the seasons is also a wry reminder that time cannot be turned back even with elixirs but runs inexorably on. Chang'e is a figure of pity in her icy palace, neighbourless and paying the only possible price for immortality, viz. loneliness as our kith and kin die off. We shall meet her again in future poems.

11-12: In the second couplet of the third verse we are reminded again that the moon links all generations of short-lived mortals. Chang'e has seen us all come and go, but can be close to none of us.

13-14: In the last verse we are reminded that our lives, like the river, are forever flowing away. We may enjoy the light of the full moon with family and friends but this sharing will also be swept away by the river of time.

15-16: The final couplet offers Li Bai's usual suggested solution: let's be happy while we may; *gaudeamus igitur*; eat, drink and be merry. We shall meet this sentiment of his again.

UNIT 19

Vocabulary

伴 *bàn* /n/ companion; /v/ have as companions 9.5 (M 人 'person')

分 *fēn* /v/ to separate, part 18.2 (M 刀 'knife')

各 *gè* /a/ each, variously 30.3 (S)

漢 *hàn* /n/ R. Han 85.11 (M 氵 'water')

壺 *hú* /n/ wine-kettle, 'jug' 33.9 (X)

歡 *huān* /v/ joy, happiness 76.18 (M 欠 'gape')

及 *jí* /v/ catch up with, make the most of 29.2 (X)

旣 *jì* /a/ both ... and (no 'and' here) 71.7 (W)

將 *jiāng* /c/ and 41.8 (M 寽 'take')

交 *jiāo* /v/ exchange, share 8.4 (X)

交歡 *jiāo huān* /v/ get along together as friends

結 *jié* /v/ contract, tie oneself to 120.6 (M 糸 'silk')

解 *jiě* /v/ understand; /a/ know how to, can 148.6 (W)

樂 *lè* /n/ pleasure, enjoyment 75.11 (S)

零亂 *líng luàn* /v/ be in disorder, in confusion (1) 173.5 (M 雨 'rain'); (2) 5.12 (W)

邈 *miǎo* /v/ be distant, far off 162.14 (M 辶 'go')

徘徊 *pái huái* /v/ walk up and down (1) 60.8 (M 彳 'go'); (2) 60.6 (M 彳 'go')

期 *qī* /v/ make a date, fix a time 74.8 (M 月 'moon')

親 *qīn* /v/ be intimate, close 147.9 (M 見 'see')

三 *sān* /q/ three 1.2 (W)

167

散 *sàn* /v/ scatter 66.8 (M 攴 'hit')

身 *shēn* /n/ body 158.0 (W)

徒 *tú* /a/ in vain, uselessly 60.7 (M 辵 'go')

舞 *wǔ* /v/ dance 136.8 (M 舛 'go opposite ways')

相親 *xiāng qīn* /av/ be close to me; /n/ close friend

行 *xíng* /v/ do, engage in

醒 *xǐng* /v/ be awake, sober 164.9 (M 酉 'wine')

須 *xū* /a/ must, ought 181.3 (S)

邀 *yāo* /v/ invite 162.13 (M 辶 'go')

飲 *yǐn* /v/ drink 184.4 (X)

永 *yǒng* /a/ forever, eternally 85.1 (S)

遊 *yóu* /n/ friendship

雲漢 *yún hàn* /n/ the Milky Way

暫 *zàn* /a/ for now 72.11 (M 日 'sun')

酌 *zhuó* /v/ pour /wine/, drink 164.3 (M 酉 'wine')

Text for translation[117]

Li Bai (701–762): 'Drinking alone in the moonlight'

01 花間一壺酒 *huā jiān yī* hú jiǔ*

02 獨酌無相親 *dú* zhuó* wú xiāng qīn*

03 舉杯邀明月 *jǔ bēi yāo míng yuè*

04 對影成三人 *duì yǐng chéng sān rén*

05 月既不解飲 *yuè jì bù jiě yǐn*

06 影徒隨我身 *yǐng tú suí wǒ shēn*

---

[117]李白 月下獨酌 唐1

07 暫伴月將影 *zàn bàn yuè jiāng yǐng*

08 行樂須及春 *xíng lè xū jí* chūn*

09 我歌月徘徊 *wǒ gē yuè pái huái*

10 我舞影零亂 *wǒ wǔ yǐng líng luàn*

11 醒時同交歡 *xǐng shí tóng jiāo huān*

12 醉後各分散 *zuì hòu gè fēn sàn*

13 永結無情遊 *yǒng jié* wú qíng yóu*

14 相期邈雲漢 *xiāng qī miǎo yún hàn*

Exercise (no key)

(a) Regulated verse does not as a rule allow the same word to be used twice in the same poem. Do you notice any repetitions?

(b) Parallelism is used in both regulated and ancient-style verse. Look at the pattern of parallel and free couplets in this poem by marking the pattern of nouns, verbs, adverbs etc. (e.g. Line 1 is /nnqmn/). Would you agree that the parallelism coincides with high-points of emotion?

(c) In view of the distribution of free and parallel couplets, why do you think Li Bai broke the poem into two verses by means of a rhyme-change? What is the effect of this structure?

(d) Mark the tonal patterning using 'o' and 'x' as in Unit 17. Does the pattern tell you whether this poem is ancient-style or regulated?

(e) Why 無情 in line 13?

UNIT 20

Vocabulary

北 *běi* /p/ north 21.3 (S)

草 *cǎo* /n/ grass 140.6 (M ⁺⁺ 'plant')

蟲 *chóng* /n/ insect 142.12 (W)

村 *cūn* /n/ village 75.3 (M 木 'wood')

定 *dìng* /v/ be steady, fixed, settled 40.5 (S)

動 *dòng* /v/ move 19.9 (M 力 'strength')

發 *fā* /v/ flourish (of vegetation)

扉 *fēi* /n/ casement 63.8 (M 戶 'door')

共 *gòng* /v/ share

桂 *guì* /n/ 'cassia-tree' (*Osmanthus fragrans*) 75.6 (M 木 'tree')

靜 *jìng* /v/ be quiet, peaceful, inactive 174.8 (M 爭 'fight')

冷 *lěng* /v/ be cold 15.5 (M 冫 'ice')

列 *liè* /n/ rank, row; /v/ set in a row 18.4 (S)

麥 *mài* /n/ wheat, barley 199.0 (S)

綺 *qǐ* /n/ bright pattern (originally damask silk pattern) 120.8 (M 糸 'silk')

蕎麥 *qiáo mài* /n/ buckwheat 140.12 (M ⁺⁺ 'plant')

切切 *qiè qiè* /v/ make a low agitated chirping (associated with autumn and sadness) 18.2 (S)

缺 *quē* /v/ be chipped (of plate); waning (of moon) 121.4 (M 缶 'pot')

田 *tián* /n/ arable fields 102.0 (W)

庭 *tíng* /n/ courtyard 53.7 (M 广 'house')

委 *wěi* /v/ throw down (on to) 38.5 (S)

170

席 *xí* /n/ over-mat, cover placed over 筵 *yán* 'under-mat' as floor seat 50.7
    (M 巾 'cloth')

宿 *xiù* /n/ constellation 40.8 (W)

懸 *xuán* /v/ hang 61.16 (M 心 'heart')

鴉 *yā* /n/ crow, rook 196.4 (M 鳥 'bird')

野 *yě* /n/ far countryside 166.4 (M 里 'village')

依 *yī* /v/ remain, be the same as ever, cling, not go away

逾 *yú* /a/ even more 162.9 (M 辶 'go')

園 *yuán* /n/ garden 31.10 (M 囗 'enclosure')

圓 *yuán* /v/ be round, full (of moon) 31.10 (M 囗 'enclosure')

Text 1[118]

Du Fu (712–770): 'Full moon'

孤月當樓滿 *gū yuè dāng lóu mǎn*

寒江動夜扉 *hán jiāng dòng yè fēi*

委波金不定 *wěi bō jīn bù dìng*

照席綺逾依 *zhào xí* qǐ yú yī*

未缺空山靜 *wèi quē* kōng shān jìng*

高懸列宿稀 *gāo xuán liè xiù xī*

故園松桂發 *gù yuán sōng guì fā**

萬里共清輝 *wàn lǐ gòng qīng huī*

Note: Line 2: Moonlight reflected from the waves dances through the window,
making it seem to move.

---

[118]杜甫　月圓　杜17

Text 2[119]

Wang Jian (eighth to ninth centuries): 'Gazing at the moon on the fifteenth night, [a poem] for Departmental Director Du'

中庭地白樹棲鴉 *zhōng tíng dì bái* shù qī yā*

冷露無聲濕桂花 *lěng lù wú shēng shī* guì huā*

今夜月明人盡望 *jīn yè yuè míng rén jìn wàng*

不知秋思在何家 *bù zhī qiū sì zài hé jiā*

Text 3[120]

Bai Juyi (772–846): 'Village night'

霜草蒼蒼蟲切切 *shuāng cǎo cāng cāng chóng qiè qiè*

村南村北行人絕 *cūn nán cūn běi xíng rén jué**

獨出門前望夜田 *dú* chū* mén qián wàng yè tián*

月明蕎麥花如雪 *yuè míng qiáo mài huā rú xuě*

20.1 The lunar calendar.

The lunar Festival Year or *yin*-calendar (陰曆 *yīn lì*) year consisted of twelve moons, each of twenty-nine or thirty days; since these did not add up to an exact year, but left 11¼ days over, an extra 'intercalary moon' (閏月 *rùn yuè*) was inserted in some years to adjust the cumulative discrepancy. The first three moons constituted spring, beginning with Lunar New Year (元旦 *yuán dàn* 'the first dawn'), which fell upon the second new moon after the winter solstice, i.e. between January 21st and February 20th, with a mean average date of February 5th. The mean dates for the beginning of the lunar seasons and lunar months are given below:

---

[119] 王建 十五夜望月寄杜郎中 全301

[120] 白居易 村夜 全437

Spring (春 *chūn*)	1st moon	February 5th
	2nd moon	March 6th
	3rd moon	April 4th
Summer (夏 *xià*)	4th moon	May 4th
	5th moon	June 2nd
	6th moon	July 2nd
Autumn (秋 *qiū*)	7th moon	July 31st
	8th moon	August 30th
	9th moon	September 28th
Winter (冬 *dōng*)	10th moon	October 28th
	11th moon	November 26th
	12th moon	December 26th

Remember that these dates are all plus or minus up to a fortnight, and that the beginning date of those following an intercalary month will be shifted by a whole month in addition to this.

This irregularity of dates (rather like that of Easter and the movable feasts dependent upon it) was the reason why the lunar calendar could not be used for agriculture but had to be supplemented by a parallel Farmers' Calendar or *yang*-calendar (陽曆 *yáng lì*) that was based on the positions of the sun (solstices and equinoxes), which determined temperature and rainfall, not on the phases of the moon; it begins on February 5th, the mean date of Lunar New Year, and consists of twenty-four Solar Periods (二十四節氣 *èr shí sì jié qì*) of about a fortnight each. A convenient table of these is to be found in Mathews' *Chinese-English Dictionary*, p. 1178 ('The Twenty-four Solar Terms').

In the first poem we meet the word 宿 *xiù* 'constellation'. Although in this poem it refers to the stars in general, its technical use is to mean one of the 二十八宿 *èr shí bā xiù* '28 lunar mansions' along the ecliptic. It is written with the same character as 宿 *sù* 'spend the night', and is in fact derived from it, for each lunar mansion is one of the 28 constellations of the Chinese zodiac, i.e. the part of the sky where the moon spends one night of the lunar month. Again, a list of these is to be found in Mathews, p. 1177 (Table V).

Since each lunar month began with a new moon, the fifteenth day of a moon was 望 *wàng* 'full moon', the same word as 'gaze longingly', appropriately enough! A Han dynasty poem [121] has the couplet 三五明月滿　四五蟾兔缺 *sān wǔ míng yuè mǎn / sì wǔ chán tù quē* 'Three fives and the bright moon is full,/ four fives and the toad and hare [in the moon] are waning'.

The three months of autumn were referred to as the 三秋 *sān qiū* 'three autumns', and the eighth moon was 中秋 *zhōng qiū* 'the middle autumn [moon]', but since an ancient grammatical construction in poetry allowed the word 中 to precede a noun instead of following it in the sense of 'in the

---

[121] 無名氏　古詩十九首，其十七　古1

middle of' (as in the first line of the second poem), 中秋 *zhōng qiū* could also be taken as 'the middle of autumn', i.e. the fifteenth day of the eighth moon. This was a special day known as the 八月節 *bā yuè jié* 'eighth moon festival' or 中秋節 *zhōng qiū jié* 'mid-autumn festival' or as 月夕 *yuè xī* 'the moon-night' because it was believed that on this night the moon was twice as bright as at other times, like our own 'harvest moon'. It was a time for giving 月餅 *yuè bǐng* circular 'moon-cakes' decorated with the toad and the hare and symbolizing 團圓 *tuán yuán* 'the family circle complete', and for having expeditions and picnics in the moonlight to enjoy its unusual radiance. One writer even attributes the origination of the festival to Du Fu, the author of the first poem in this unit. The festival is still celebrated today.

20.2 Cassia

The cassia (specifically *Osmanthus fragrans*, not the other plants known as 'cassia') is a handsome evergeen shrub or tree producing fragrant flowers in autumn; 桂月 *guì yuè* 'the cassia moon' and 桂秋 *guì qiū* 'cassia autumn' are names for the eighth moon (roughly September). The five-thousand-foot tree on the moon that 吳剛 *wú gāng* is vainly trying to fell is a cassia, so the 月宮 *yuè gōng* 'moon palace' of Chang'e is also called the 桂宮 *guì gōng* 'cassia palace' and the moon itself is sometimes called the 桂魄 *guì pò* 'cassia *yin*-soul'. The *yin*-soul or earth-soul is the one most closely connected with the body (as distinct from the 魂 *hūn* '*yang*-soul' or sky-soul that goes a-wandering in sleep or after death), and in the case of the moon it refers to the dark part of the moon's surface that 'dies' at full moon; from this meaning 桂魄 *guì pò* has shifted to mean 'the moon' in general.

Exercises (no key)

(a) Analyse the tonal patterns; can the tonality of the second and third poems, seven-syllable quatrains, be regarded as an extension or modification of that of five-syllable regulated verse? (The first lines of both are part of the rhyme-scheme.)

(b) Analyse the parallelism of the first poem. What is the effect of the lack of parallelism in the second and third poems?

UNIT 21

Vocabulary

臂 *bì* /n/ arm 130.13 (M 肉 'flesh')

變 *biàn* /v/ change 149.16 (M 攵 'hit')

長安 *cháng ān* /n/ Chang'an, the Tang western capital, near Xi'an

窗 *chuāng* /n/ window 116.7 (M 穴 'hole')

窗戶 *chuāng hù* /n/ window

淡 *dàn* /v/ be weak, faint (of colour); tinge 85.8 (M 氵 'water')

杜 *dù* = 杜若 *dù ruò* /n/ *Pollia japonica*, a fragrant plant 75.3 (M 木 'tree')

兒 *ér* /n/ son 10.6 (W)

兒女 *ér nǚ* /n/ children, offspring

鄜州 *fū zhōu* /n/ present-day 富縣 *fù xiàn*, 140 miles north of Chang'an on the R. Luo 163.11 (M 阝 'town')

乾 *gān* /v/ be dry 5.10 (X)

高臥 *gāo wò* /v/ take one's ease

閨 *guī* /n/ women's quarters, boudoir 169.6 (M 門 'door')

痕 *hén* /n/ traces; scars 104.6 (M 疒 'illness')

還寢 *huán qǐn* /v/ go back to bed

鬟 *huán* /n/ hair done up in a bun 190.13 (M 髟 'hair', S 睘)

幌 *huǎng* /n/ curtain, bamboo-slat blind 50.10 (M 巾 'cloth')

幾 *jǐ* /a/ how many times

佳 *jiā* /v/ be good, fine 9.6 (M 亻 'person')

佳期 *jiā qī* /n/ happy reunion

175

竟 *jìng* /n/ end; /v/ last until the end of (cf. 盡) 117.6 (X)

竟夕 *jìng xī* /a2/ all night long

開 *kāi* /v/ open 169.4 (W)

堪 *kān*/a/ can, may 32.9 (S)

苦 *kǔ* /v/ be bitter, painful, hard to bear 140.5 (M ⁺⁺ 'plant')

蘭 *lán* /n/ orchid 140.17 (M ⁺⁺ 'plant')

淚 *lèi* /n/ tears 85.8 (M 氵 'water')

美 *měi* /v/ be beautiful, fine (here of character) 123.3 (X)

南 *nán* /n/ south 24.7 (X)

女 *nǚ* /n/ daughter 38.0 (W)

其 *qí* /n/ it (padding-syllable) 12.6 (S)

起 *qǐ* /v/ arise, come to the surface

寢 *qǐn* /v/ sleep 40.11 (M 宀 'bedroom')

情 *qíng* /n/ emotion, esp. feelings of friendship and love

情人 *qíng rén* /n/ close friends, lovers, esp. when parted

苒苒 *rǎn rǎn* /v/ be gradual, imperceptible 140.5 (M ⁺⁺ 'plant')

濕 *shī*/v/ be damp, wet 85.14 (M 氵 'water')

是 *shì* /d/ this

手 *shǒu* /n/ hand 64.0 (W)

雙 *shuāng* /q/ couple, pair 172.10 (W: two birds in the hand)

天涯 *tiān yá* /n/ the edge of the sky, horizon, the ends of the earth

吐 *tǔ* /v/ emit, come out 30.3 (M 口 'mouth')

微 *wēi* /v/ be slight, subtle 60.10 (X)

帷 *wéi* /n/ curtain 50.8 (M 巾 'cloth')

臥 *wò* /v/ lie 131.2 (X)

夕 *xī* /n/ night 36.0 (W)

香 *xiāng* v/ be fragrant, perfumed 186.0 (X)

虛 *xū* /v/ be empty 141.6 (X)

虛幌 *xū huǎng* /n/ window with blind up or curtain drawn aside

涯 *yá* /n/ edge, shore 85.8 (M 氵 'water')

演漾 *yǎn yàng* /v/ ripple, dance 85.11, 85.11 (M 氵 'water')

遙 *yáo* /v/ be distant, (of night) long; /a/ in the distance 162.10 (M 辶 'go')

倚 *yǐ* /v/ lean against, lean on 9.8 (M 亻 'person')

憶 *yì* /v/ remember 61.13 (M 忄 'heart')

吟 *yín* /v/ chant; /n/ song 30.4 (M 口 'mouth')

怨 *yuàn* /v/ grieve resentfully 61.5 (M 心 'heart')

越 *yuè* /n/ an ancient state on the coast south of the Yangtse 156.5 (S)

雲鬟 *yún huán* /n/ cloud-shaped coiffure

贈 *zèng* /v/ make a present of, give respectfully 154.12 (M 貝 'money')

齋 *zhāi* /n/ studio, study 210.3 (S)

州 *zhōu* /n/ prefecture 47.3 (S)

燭 *zhú* /n/ candle 86.13 (M 火 'fire')

滋 *zī* /v/ increase 85.9 (M 氵 'water')

Notes on the vocabulary

蘭杜 *lán dù* 'orchid and pollia': these two fragrant plants were an old symbol of men of noble character.

越 *yuè* is where Mr Cui is now. Although he is not a native of Yue, 越吟 *yuè yín* 'Yue songs' means songs of home that one sings when feeling homesick, based on an ancient story of a homesick native of Yue.

Text 1[122]

Wang Changling (early eighth century): 'Enjoying the moonlight in the South Study with my cousin Xiao and remembering Mr Cui, Assistant Prefect of Shaoxing'

高臥南齋時 *gāo wò nán zhāi shí*

開帷月初吐 *kāi wéi yuè chū tǔ*

清輝淡水木 *qīng huī dàn shuǐ mù*

演漾在窗戶 *yǎn yàng zài chuāng hù*

苒苒幾盈虛 *rǎn rǎn jǐ yíng xū*

澄澄變今古 *chéng chéng biàn jīn gǔ*

美人清江畔 *měi rén qīng jiāng pàn*

是夜越吟苦 *shì yè yuè yín kǔ*

千里其如何 *qiān lǐ qí rú hé*

微風吹蘭杜 *wēi fēng chuī lán dù*

Text 2[123]

Zhang Jiuling (678–740): 'Gazing at the moon and thinking of someone afar'

海上生明月 *hǎi shàng shēng míng yuè*

天涯共此時 *tiān yá gòng cǐ shí*

情人怨遙夜 *qíng rén yuàn yáo yè*

竟夕起相思 *jìng xī* qǐ xiāng sī*

滅燭憐光滿 *miè zhú* lián guāng mǎn*

披衣覺露滋 *pī yī jué* lù zī*

---

[122] 王昌齡 同從弟銷南齋玩月憶山陰崔少府 唐1

[123] 張九齡 望月懷遠 唐3

不堪盈手贈 *bù kān yíng shǒu zèng*

還寢夢佳期 *huán qǐn mèng jiā qī*

Text 3[124]

Du Fu (712–770): 'Moonlit night'

今夜鄜州月 *jīn yè fū zhōu yuè*

閨中只獨看 *guī zhōng zhǐ dú* kān*

遙憐小兒女 *yáo lián xiǎo ér nǚ*

未解憶長安 *wèi jiě yì cháng ān*

香霧雲鬢濕 *xiāng wù yún huán shī**

清輝玉臂寒 *qīng huī yù bì hán*

何時倚虛幌 *hé shí yǐ xū huǎng*

雙照淚痕乾 *shuāng zhào lèi hén gān*

Note: Du Fu is imprisoned by the An Lushan rebels in Chang'an while his family are staying during the fighting at Fuzhou, 140 miles to the north.

21.1 Quality-verbs as adverbials of distance, duration and frequency

(a) Distance: 遠 *yuǎn* far; 迥 *jiǒng* far; 遙 *yáo* far; 僻 *pì* far off the beaten track; 高 *gāo* high; 低 *dī* low; 深 *shēn* deep; 闊 *kuò* wide, extensive; 遍 *biàn* everywhere;
(b) Duration and relative time: 久 *jiǔ* for a long time; 早 *zǎo* early; 遲 *chí* late;
(c) Frequency: 頻 *pín* often; 多 *duō* often; 稀 *xī* rarely; 少 *shǎo* rarely.

These quality-verbs are used adverbially both in position 2 and in position 3 without any apparent difference in meaning or emphasis.

Examples of position 2:

茲山亦深登 [125] *zī shān yì shēn dēng* 'These mountains, too, I deeply ascend', 'I also go deep into these mountains'. (茲 *zī* this; 登 *dēng* ascend.)

---

[124]杜甫 月夜 唐3

遠謁雲端僧 (*ibid.*) *yuǎn yè yún duān sēng* 'I visit afar a monk at the end of the clouds'. (謁 *yè* visit a superior, pay one's respects to; 端 *duān* end, edge; 僧 *sēng* Buddhist monk.)

樓高月迥明 [126] *lóu gāo yuè jiǒng míng* 'The tower is high and the moon is bright in the distance'.

遙憐小兒女 (Unit 21) *yáo lián xiǎ ér nǚ* 'From afar I pity my little children'. (兒女 *ér nǚ* sons and daughters, children.)

山雲低度牆 [127] *shān yún dī dù qiáng* 'The mountain clouds pass low over the wall'. (牆 *qiáng* wall.)

頻遊任履穿 [128] *pín yóu rèn lǚ chuān* 'Frequently wandering, I let my shoes become holed'. (任 *rèn* let, allow; 履 *lǚ* shoe; 穿 *chuān* make a hole in.)

遊子久在外 [129] *yóu zǐ jiǔ zài wài* 'The wanderer has been long away from home'.

春來常早起 [130] *chūn lái cháng zǎo qǐ* 'When spring comes I regularly get up early'. (常 *cháng* regularly.)

方外酒徒稀醉眠 [131] *fāng wài jiǔ tú xī zuì mián* 'The drinker far from home rarely goes to bed drunk'. (方外 *fāng wài* beyond the (civilised) world; 酒徒 *jiǔ tú* drinker.)

Examples of position 3:

枕簟入林僻　茶瓜留客遲 [132] *zhěn diàn rù lín pì / chá guā liú kè chí* (枕 *zhěn* neck-rest, pillow; 簟 *diàn* bed-mat; 茶 *chá* tea; 瓜 *guā* melon; 留 *liú* detain.) 'With pillow and bed-mat he has gone far off the beaten track into the woods; / with tea and melon he keeps his visitors late'.

以我獨沉久　愧君相見頻 [133] *yǐ wǒ dú chén jiǔ / kuì jūn xiāng jiàn pín* 'Because I have been alone and fallen on hard times for so long, / I am embarrassed that you should come and see me so often'. (以 *yǐ* because; 愧 *kuì* be ashamed, embarrassed that.)

---

[125] 杜甫　陪章留後惠義寺⋯　杜12

[126] 杜甫　季秋蘇五弟纓江樓⋯　杜20

[127] 杜甫　秦州雜詩二十首，其十七　杜7

[128] 杜甫　春日江村五首，其二　杜14

[129] 杜甫　水檻　杜13

[130] 杜甫　早起　杜10

[131] 杜甫　逼側星贈畢四曜　杜6

[132] 杜甫　巳上人茅齋　杜1

[133] 司空曙　喜外弟盧綸見宿　唐3

蜀星陰見少　江雨夜聞多 [134] *shǔ xīng yīn jiàn shǎo / jiāng yǔ yè wén duō* 'The Sichuan stars are rarely seen through the overcast; / the Yangtse rain is often heard in the night'. (蜀 *shǔ* Shu, Sichuan; 星 *xīng* star; 陰 *yīn* overcast.)

鶴巢松樹遍　人訪篳門稀 [135] *hè cháo sōng shù biàn / rén fǎng bì mén xī* 'The cranes nest everywhere in the pinetrees; / people rarely visit my rustic gate'. (鶴 *hè* crane; 巢 *cháo* to nest; 訪 *fǎng* visit; 篳 *bì* bamboo lattice; 門 *mén* gate, door.)

樹色隨山迴　河聲入海遙 [136] *shù sè suí shān jiǒng / hé shēng rù hǎi yáo* 'The colour of the trees follows the hills into the distance; / the sound of the river enters the sea far off'.

無食起我早 [137] *wú shí qǐ wǒ zǎo* 'Lack of food gets me up early'. (食 *shí* food.)

晚見雁行頻 [138] *wǎn jiàn yàn háng pín*) 'In the evening I often see the goose-skeins'. (行 *háng* row, skein (of geese).

一路見人稀 [139] *yī lù jiàn rén xī* 'All the way I see people rarely', 'I see few people along the way'.

---

[134] 杜甫　散愁二首，其一　杜9

[135] 王維　山居即事　王7

[136] 許渾　秋日赴闕…　唐3

[137] 杜甫　雨過蘇端　杜4

[138] 馬戴　灞上秋居　唐3

[139] 戴叔倫　山行　全273

UNIT 22

I have chosen two rather light-hearted and two gloomier poems about the insomnia of lonely wives as a finale to the moon-poems.

Vocabulary

碧 *bì* /v/ be blue, green 112.9 (M 石 'stone')

冰 *bīng* /n/ ice 15.4 (M 冫 'ice')

長河 *cháng hé* /n/ Milky Way

打 *dǎ* /v/ strike, chase 64.3 (M 扌 'hand')

打起 *dǎ qǐ* /v/ chase away upwards

得 *dé* /v/ be able to, manage to, have a chance to

簟 *diàn* /n/ mat (for sleeping on) 118.12 (M 竹 'bamboo')

兒 *ér* in 黃鳥兒 diminutive suffix

二 *èr* /q/ two 7.0 (W)

忿 *fèn* /v/ be angry, indignant 61.4 (M 心 'heart')

過 *guò* /v/ pass over 162.9 (M 辶 'go')

悔 *huǐ* /v/ regret 61.7 (M 忄 'heart')

漸 *jiàn* /a/ gradually 85.11 (M 氵 'water')

教 *jiào* /v/ let, allow, cause (cf. German *lassen*) 66.7 (M 攴 'hit')

驚 *jīng* /v/ startle, shock 187.13 (M 馬 'horse')

遼西 *liáo xī* /n/ an ancient county near where the Great Wall meets the sea, on the north-east frontier with the Koreans and Khitans 162.12 (S)

靈 *líng* /v/ be magical; efficacious 173.16 (M 巫 'shaman')

門 *mén* /n/ door, gate 169.0 (W)

莫 *mò* /a/ don't! 140.7 (S)

難 *nán* /v/ be difficult (to), cannot be …ed 172.11 (S)

屏 *píng* /n/ screen 44.6 (S)

屏風 *píng fēng* /n/ screen (風 here = 'draught')

妾 *qiè* /n/ concubine; I (self-reference by a woman) 38.5 (M 女 'woman')

輕 *qīng* /v/ be light (not heavy) 159.7 (M 車 'vehicle')

鵲 *què* /n/ magpie (symbol of parted lovers being reunited) 196.8 (M 鳥 'bird')

十 *shí* /q/ ten 24.0 (S)

偷 *tōu* /v/ steal 9.9 (M 亻 'person')

喜 *xǐ* /n/ joy 30.9 (M 口 'mouth')

心 *xīn* /n/ heart, mind 61.0 (W)

星 *xīng* /n/ star 72.5 (M 日 'sun')

銀 *yín* /n/ silver 167.6 (M 金 'metal')

雲母 *yún mǔ* /n/ mica (lit. 'cloud-mother', cf. English 'mother of pearl')

朝 *zhāo* /n/ morning 74.8 (X)

枝 *zhī* /n/ branch, twig 75.4 (M 木 'tree')

Text 1[140]

Jin Changxu (Tang, no dates): 'Spring resentment'

> 打起黃鳥兒 *dǎ qǐ huáng niǎo ér*
>
> 莫教枝上啼 *mò jiào zhī shàng tí*
>
> 啼時驚妾夢 *tí shí jīng qiè mèng*
>
> 不得到遼西 *bù dé* dào liáo xī*

---

[140]金昌緒　春怨　唐5

Text 2[141]

Li Duan (late eighth century): 'Boudoir feelings'
月落星稀天欲明 *yuè luò xīng xī tiān yù míng*
孤燈未滅夢難成 *gū dēng wèi miè mèng nán chéng*
披衣更向門前望 *pī yī gèng xiàng mén qián wàng*
不忿朝來鵲喜聲 *bù fèn zhāo lái què xǐ shēng*

Text 3[142]

Wen Tingyun (early ninth century): 'Jewelled zither grief'
冰簟銀床夢不成 *bīng diàn tín chuáng mèng bù chéng*
碧天如水夜雲輕 *bì tiān rú shuǐ yè yún qīng*
雁聲遠過瀟湘去 *yàn shēng yuǎn guò xiāo xiāng qù*
十二樓中月自明 *shí* èr lóu zhōng yuè zì míng*

Text 4[143]

Li Shangyin (early ninth century): 'Chang'e'
雲母屏風燭影深 *yún mǔ píng fēng zhú* yǐng shēn*
長河漸落曉星沉 *cháng hé jiàn luò xiǎo xīng chén*
嫦娥應悔偷靈藥 *cháng é yīng huǐ tōu líng yào*
碧海青天夜夜心 *bì hǎi qīng tiān yè yè xīn*

---

[141]李端　閨情　全286
[142]溫庭筠　瑤瑟怨　唐6
[143]李商隱　嫦娥　唐6

22.1 Some colour-words

The last two poems contain words for 'green' or 'blue', one of which may have been puzzling you since Unit 1. To add to your possible puzzlement, we encountered 'green mists' in Unit 18 and earlier we had 'a green sky' in Unit 13.

Let us begin by looking at the five emblematic colours corresponding to the other ancient sets of five comprehended in the term 五 行 *wǔ xíng* the 'five movements' or 'five processes', commonly (but I think misleadingly) translated as the 'five elements'. These were five stages of birth, development and destruction to be found in Nature. They were symbolized by five substances, five colours, five directions, five seasons and a multitude of other fivefold categories that flourished from the Han dynasty onwards. Here are some of these that are germane to our present purpose:

木 *mù* wood	春 *chūn* spring	東 *dōng* east	青 *qīng* green/blue
火 *huǒ* fire	夏 *xià* summer	南 *nán* south	赤 *chì* red
土 *tǔ* earth	大暑 *dà shǔ*	中 *zhōng* centre	黃 *huáng* yellow
金 *jīn* metal	秋 *qiū* autumn	西 *xī* west	白 *bái* white
水 *shuǐ* water	冬 *dōng* winter	北 *běi* north	黑 *hēi* black

The centre two columns are the four seasons and the four directions. In order to fit these in with the Five Processes, an extra season (大暑 *dà shǔ* 'great heat', the last fortnight of summer) and an extra direction (中 zero-direction) were inserted: the facts must be made to fit the theory, not vice versa!

The two rows that concern us most are the first and the fourth:

木 wood　春 spring　東 east　青 green/blue

金 metal　秋 autumn　西 west　白 white

The reason for this is that Chinese poetry is about change, not about stasis, and the two seasons of change are spring, the season of birth and growth, and autumn, the season of decline and death. These are reflected in the other columns. In spring the constellation 青 龍 *qīng lóng* 'the green dragon' rises in the east and the trees become green. The symbols of autumn are not so obvious: metal is autumn's sword that cuts down the leaves, the west is where the sun sets hence where the year declines, and white is the colour of mourning in China. These two seasons are sometimes called 青 春 *qīng chūn* 'green spring' and 素 秋 *sù qiū* 'white autumn' (素 is 'plain white silk' and 素 衣 *sù yī* 'white-silk clothes' means 'mourning attire'). In human terms, of course, spring and autumn mean youth and old age respectively, and it is in this connection that we meet them in Chinese poetry.

There are five main words in Chinese verse that mean both 'green' and 'blue', and in addition some of them mean 'black', 'grey' or 'pale'. They are 青 *qīng*, 綠 *lǜ*, 蒼 *cāng*, 碧 *bì* and 翠 *cuì* (I am ignoring 藍 *lán* 'indigo, blue' since it is not much used in verse).

This colour-range of a single word is not restricted to Chinese, for Japanese has *aoi* 'be blue, green, pale' and Korean has *p'urŭda* 'be blue, green'. It is not even restricted to the Far East, for the Far West of the Eurasian continent knows the same phenomenon. Gaelic has distinct words for 'blue' (*gorm*), 'green' (*uaine*) and 'grey' (*liath*), but it also has *glas* covering all three plus 'pale'. One anthology [144] translates *glas* variously, when referring to eyes, as 'grey', 'green' and 'blue', so clearly the translators have had as much difficulty with finding an English equivalent for *glas* as we have with its Chinese counterparts. The Welsh *glas* has the same range: 'blue', 'green', 'grey' and 'pale'.

Both 青 *qīng* and 蒼 *cāng* have been applied to the colour of blood; this switching of the two ends of the light-spectrum is reminiscent of Homer's *oinops* 'wine-faced, wine-coloured', applied both to deep-red oxen and to the sea, which seems even more inappropriate than the 'red, red gold' of the Border ballads.

When referring to hair, 綠 *lǜ*, 翠 *cuì* and 青 *qīng* mean 'glossy black, raven-black' and 蒼 *cāng* means 'grey'. This is in addition to their existing range of 'blue' and 'green'!

What on earth is happening here? The professional Homeric bards may well have been blind, but I refuse to believe that Chinese poets down the ages have been colour-blind, for they knew quite well that 青 *qīng* 'blue' was a primary colour (正 色 *zhèng sè* 'proper colour') whereas 綠 *lǜ* 'green' was an intermediate colour (間 色 *jiàn sè* 'in-between colour'), a mixture of 青 *qīng* 'blue' and 黃 *huáng* 'yellow'. In poetry we are clearly not in the realm of physics, of colour purely as a wavelength of light.

The use of 綠 *lǜ* 'green' for the glossy, raven-black hair of youth as distinct from the 白 *bái* 'white, grey' hair of old age may give us a clue, for 青 年 *qīng nián* 'the green years' are the years of youth, the salad-days. 青 *qīng* is the colour of spring and vegetation, while 白 *bái* is the colour of autumn and death, as we saw when we looked at the five emblematic colours. The Gaelic *glas* also means 'young and fresh, unripe' and this is a range of meaning parallel to that of the Chinese equivalents. It may be no coincidence that the sound-element of the character 青 *qīng* is 生 *shēng* (originally a picture of a plant growing from the ground), meaning 'unripe' and 'young man' as well as 'be born' and 'grow'. This suggests that the underlying words may have been felt by the prehistoric script-makers to be related or of similar meaning.

One quality of youth is vitality, so it may be that our 'blue/green' words were sometimes chosen to express vividness, brightness and glossiness, irrespective of the wavelength. But this cannot be taken as a general rule: we have already seen in Unit 13 that 蒼 *cāng* is the reverse of this and is associated with misty distances and old age.

---

[144] Seán Mac Réamoinn ed. The Pleasures of Gaelic Poetry. Allen Lane, London, 1982

This brings us to 'green mists'. It seems that this usually means a green background (leaves, hillsides, the sea) seen through a mist and so seeming to colour it, so it would then be a poetic reversal of the prosaic 'misted green'. One word for 'misted mountain-sides' is 翠微 *cuì wēi* 'blue/green faintness' as in a poem by Li Bai: 卻顧所來徑　蒼蒼橫翠微 [145] *què gù suǒ lái jìng / cāng cāng héng cuì wēi* 'When we look back along the path we have come along,/ mistily-distant lies crosswise the mist-shrouded green of the hillsides'. One problem here is that green mountains can look blue or grey in the distance, which does not help us choose an English equivalent.

Incidentally, this poem just quoted contains three other words for 'green' in its eight lines: 碧山 *bì shān* 'green hill', 綠竹 *lǜ zhú* 'green bamboos', and 青蘿 *qīng luó* 'green creepers'. I do not believe that Li Bai was trying to distinguish different shades of green; even if he were, he could not rely on his readers' distinguishing them since the words concerned are interchangeable, as we shall see below.

The third and fourth poems in this unit both have colour-words for a moonlit night sky: the third has 碧天 *bì tiān* and the fourth has 青天 *qīng tiān*, but also 碧海 *bì hǎi* for the sea. In the latter case the 碧海青天 *bì hǎi qīng tiān* gives a perfect tonal pattern of 'xxoo'; interchanging the colour-words would have given 'oxxo', which, while permitted by the rules of prosody, would obviously not give the smooth tonality appropriate to the stillness of the scene.

What I am suggesting on the evidence of these three poems is that the choice of word for 'green' or 'blue' may be influenced by two considerations among others: variety ('elegant variation') and tonality.

Does the etymology of the five words help us distinguish them? Let us look at their origins and actual usage.

(1) 青 *qīng*. The meaning-element of the character is 丹 *dān* 'cinnabar, vermilion', with which this word forms the compound 丹青 *dān qīng* meaning 'painting'. An excavated Han dynasty banner depicts two dragons, one red and one blue, which suggests that 青 *qīng* is what we should call 'blue' when referring to a pigment.

(2) 綠 *lǜ*. Like some other colour-words, it has the meaning-element 糸 'silk', so may have been a green vegetable dye for fabrics. In use it mostly meant 'green' and its occasional use for 'blue' and 'black' will be poetic licence.

(3) 蒼 *cāng*. The meaning-element is ⺾ 'grass', suggesting a basic meaning of 'green', but already in the earliest poetry it was applied to the sky, which suggests that it had as wide a range as 青 *qīng*.

(4) 碧 *bì*. The meaning-element is 石 'stone', added to a presumably earlier meaning-element 玉 'jade'. Both point to a mineral, though it has not been

---

[145] 李白　下終南山⋯ 唐1

identified, so we cannot say whether the primary meaning was 'blue' or 'green'.

(5) 翠 *cuì*. The meaning-element is 羽 'feathers' or 'wings' and the compound 翡 翠 *fěi cuì* means 'kingfisher' (kingfisher-feathers were used for ornamentation), so it would seem that the primary meaning was 'kingfisher blue' or 'turquoise', especially as the mineral turquoise was also called 翡 翠 *fěi cuì*.

It may be useful at this point to tabulate the various uses of our five words so that you may see the areas of overlap. A cross means that the word is applied to the area of meaning in the left-hand column.

	青	綠	蒼	碧	翠
The sky	x	x	x	x	x
Clouds, mist	x	x	x	x	x
Vegetation	x	x	x	x	x
Hills, mountains	x	x	x	x	x
Rivers, ponds	x	x	x	x	x
The sea	x		x	x	x
Foreigners' blue eyes	x	x		x	
Dew	x				x
Rain		x			x
Snow, sleet			x		
Lamp, flame	x	x			
Dragons	x		x		x
Horses	x	x	x		x
Black hair, eyebrows, fur	x	x			x
Grey hair, fur	x		x		
Blood	x		x		

This table is not necessarily complete and you may find that some of the gaps can be filled. The only striking thing that I notice about the above distribution is that 碧 *bì* is used only for 'blue' or 'green', not for 'grey' or 'black'.

青 雲 *qīng yún* 'blue clouds' refers to the top of the ladder of success; I suspect it really means 'blue sky' or perhaps 'the clouded blue'.

We now come to the question of why these vague colour-words were used at all. The sun was often called 白 日 *bái rì* 'the white sun', just as the moon was often called 明 月 *míng yuè* 'the bright moon'. We seem to be dealing here with conventional epithets that added nothing to the meaning since they were often absent without the meaning being affected. One possible explanation would be metrical padding to fill out the line; another would be that the purpose was to convey the message 'This is poetry, so don't read it as if it were prose'; a third would be conscious or unconscious adherence to ancient phraseology; a fourth would be that vivid epithets enhance the poetic mood, the childlike awareness of colours and bright objects that becomes dulled by the prosaic concerns of adult life. I myself guess that the motivation was multifactorial, combining these reasons in various ways. But here we are entering the realm of guesswork, and your guess, dear reader, is as good as mine.

UNIT 23

Four poems about one aspect of spring.

Vocabulary

殘 *cán* /v/ be left over, the last remaining 78.8 (M 歹 'death')

城 *chéng* /n/ city, city wall 32.6 (土 'earth')

春 *chūn* /v/ be bright with spring, show evidence of spring's arrival

催 *cuī* /v/ stimulate, encourage 9.11 (M 亻 'person')

笛 *dí* /n/ flute 118.5 (M 竹 'bamboo')

調 *diào* /n/ tune 149.8 (M 言 'speak')

關 *guān* /n/ gateway in the Great Wall 169.11 (M 門 'door')

候 *hòu* /n/ signs, symptoms 9.8 (M 亻 'person')

忽 *hū* /a/ suddenly 61.4 (M 心 'heart')

懷 *huái* /v/ harbour thoughts of 61.16 (M 忄 'heart')

宦 *huàn* /v/ be an official 40.6 (S)

宦遊 *huàn yóu* /v/ travel on official business

巾 *jīn* /n/ cloth, handkerchief 50.0 (W)

柳 *liǔ* /n/ willow 75.5 (M 木 'tree')

羅 *luó* /n/ silk gauze 122.14 (M 糸 'silk')

洛 *luò* /n/ River Luo 85.6 (M 氵 'water')

洛城 *luò chéng* /n/ 'Luo City', i.e. Luoyang, the Tang eastern capital

梅 *méi* /n/ prunus, ornamental plum (flowers the earliest, even in snow) 75.7 (M 木 'tree')

偏 *piān* /a/ particularly, unlike others 9.9 (M 亻 'person')

蘋 *pín* /n/ a white-flowered water-weed 140.16 (M ⁺⁺ 'plant')

氣 *qì* /n/ air, breath 84.6 (X)

羌 *qiāng* /n/ a nation to the west of China, probably Tibetans 123.2 (M 儿 'person')

秦 *qín* /n/ present-day Shaanxi, the area of Chang'an, the Tang western capital 115.5 (S)

晴 *qíng* /v/ be fine, unclouded (of sky) 72.8 (M 日 'sun')

仞 *rèn* /m/ fathom (about 2 metres, mainly used for heights of mountains) 9.3 (S)

桑 *sāng* /n/ mulberry-tree 75.6 (W)

識 *shì* /v/ know, be acquainted with 149.12 (M 言 'speak')

淑 *shú* /v/ be mild, gentle 85.8 (S)

曙 *shù* /n/ dawn; /v/ be bright with dawn-light 72.14 (M 日 'sun')

絲 *sī* /n/ silk, silk threads 120.6 (W)

幃 *wéi* /n/ curtain 50.9 (M 巾 'cloth')

物候 *wù hòu* /n/ Nature's signs of the change of seasons

細 *xì* /v/ be slender, thin, slight 120.5 (M 糸 'silk')

霞 *xiá* /n/ coloured clouds or mists at sunrise or sunset 173.9 (M 雨 'rain', S 叚)

新 *xīn* /v/ be new 69.9 (S)

燕 *yān* /n/ the region around present-day Peking 86.12 (S)

楊 *yáng* /n/ poplar 75.9 (M 木 'tree')

楊柳 *yáng liǔ* /n/ 'poplars and willows', willows in general

陰陰 *yīn yīn* /v/ be shady, in full leaf 170.8 (M 阝 'hills')

鶯 *yīng* /n/ golden oriole 196.10 (M 鳥 'bird')

玉門關 *yù mén guān* /n/ 'Jade Gate Pass', a gateway in the Great Wall near Dunhuang; beyond it were the Eastern Turks

霑 *zhān* /v/ soak (usually with tears) 173.8 (M 雨 'rain')

轉 *zhuǎn* /v/ turn, swing round 159.11 (M 車 'vehicle')

Notes on the vocabulary

Nouns used as verbs (here 春 *chūn* and 曙 *shù*): some other nouns of time are also used in this way, e.g. 秋 *qiū* and 夜 *yè*.

催 *cuī*: cf. Chaucer's 'Then smale fowles maken melodye … so *priketh* hem nature in hir corages'.

Liangzhou was a north-west frontier town.

Text 1[146]

Du Shenyan (late seventh century): 'In reply to a poem from Mr Lu, assistant magistrate of Jinling county, entitled "Wandering and looking afar in early spring"'

獨有宦遊人 *dú yǒu huàn yóu rén*

偏驚候物新 *piān jīng wù hòu xīn*

雲霞出海曙 *yún xiá chū* hǎi shù*

梅柳渡江春 *méi liǔ dù jiāng chūn*

淑氣催黃鳥 *shú* qì cuī huáng niǎo*

晴光轉綠蘋 *qíng guāng zhuǎn lǜ pín*

忽聞歌古調 *hū* wén gē gǔ diào*

歸思欲霑巾 *guī sì yù zhān jīn*

---

[146]杜審言　和晉陵陸丞早春游望　唐3

Text 2[147]

Wu Yuanheng (late eighth century): 'Springtime arousal'

楊柳陰陰細雨晴 *yáng liǔ yīn yīn xì yǔ qíng*

殘花落盡見流鶯 *cán huā luò jìn jiàn liú yīng*

春風一夜吹香夢 *chūn fēng yī* yè chuī xiāng mèng*

夢逐春風到洛城 *mèng zhú* chūn fēng dào luò chéng*

Text 3[148]

Wang Zhihuan (early eighth century): 'Liangzhou song'

黃河遠上白雲間 *huáng hé yuǎn shàng bái yún jiān*

一片孤城萬仞山 *yī* piàn gū chéng wàn rèn shān*

羌笛何須怨楊柳 *qiāng dí* hé xū yuàn yáng liǔ*

春風不度玉門關 *chūn fēng bù dù yù mén guān*

Text 4[149]

Li Bai (701–762): 'Missing him in springtime'

燕草如碧絲 *yān cǎo rú bì sī*

秦桑低綠枝 *qín sāng dī lǜ zhī*

當君懷歸日 *dāng jūn huái guī rì*

是妾斷腸時 *shì qiè duàn cháng shí*

春風不相識 *chūn fēng bù xiāng shì*

---

[147] 武元衡 春興 全317

[148] 王之渙 涼州詞 全253 （出塞 唐6）

[149] 李白 春思 唐1

何事入羅幃 *hé shì rù luó wéi*

Note: She is at home in Qin, the area of the capital, while he is away fighting in the Yan region of the north-east frontier.

Grammar note: the 當 *dāng* 'on' is to be ignored in translation; the couplet is an example of anacolouthon, viz. a conflation of 'On the day when A, B' and 'The day when A is the time when B', giving literally 'On the day when A is the day when B'.

23.1 Willow

柳 *liǔ* or 楊柳 *yáng liǔ* 'willow-trees', like 梅 *méi* 'prunus', are symbolic of early spring. Whereas 楊 *yáng* is strictly a poplar, or a willow that lifts its leaves skyward, the 柳 *liǔ* is a drooping 'weeping willow'. Chinese poets were not botanists and seem not to have distinguished the poplar, the pussy-willow and the weeping willow, using the words 楊 *yáng*, 柳 *liǔ* and 楊柳 *yáng liǔ* indiscriminately. The yellow flowers and early leaves of the weeping willow are often mentioned in verse, as also are the seeds of the goat-willow (pussy-willow, sallow) floating away on the breeze in the form of 柳絮 *liǔ xù* 'willow-down'.

Bai Juyi (772–846) describes the weeping willow (referred to in the title as 楊柳 *yáng liǔ*) in this couplet: 一樹春風千萬枝　嫩於金色軟於 絲 [150] *yī shù chūn fēng qiān wàn zhī / nèn yú jīn sè ruǎn yú sī* 'A treeful of spring breezes, a thousand myriad fronds, / more tender than the colour of gold, softer than silk threads'. (於 *yú* '...er than')

As well as being a symbol of spring, the willow is associated with parting by a pun on 柳 *liǔ* and 留 *liú* 'stay, detain a departing guest': snapping off a willow-twig and giving it to someone departing meant 'I wish you could stay'.

The drooping fronds of the willow were called 柳絲 *liǔ sī* 'willow silk threads', and as we saw in the last unit tears are sometimes compared to silk threads, and this provides a link via silk with the weeping willow. Thin rain is called 雨絲 *yǔ sī* 'rain silk threads', and again we have seen that tears are sometimes compared to rain. This whole network of associations is reinforced by a pun on 絲 *sī* 'silk threads' and 思 *sì* 'yearning for the absent beloved'. This is the kind of thing that makes translation impossible!

A four-line song, which I quote for the sake of its content rather than for its lyrical qualities, makes an overt connection between willows and sadness:

---

[150] 白居易　楊柳枝詞　全460

Example text[151]

Bai Juyi: 'Eight songs about willow-fronds, No. 8'

人言柳葉似愁眉 *rén yán liǔ yè sì chóu méi*

更有愁腸似柳絲 *gèng yǒu chóu cháng sì liǔ sī*

柳絲挽斷腸牽斷 *liǔ sī wǎn duàn cháng qiān duàn*

彼此應無續得期 *bǐ cǐ yīng wú xù dé* qī*

People say that willow-leaves are like sad eyebrows,
but, more than this, a sorrowing heart is like a willow-frond:
a willow-frond can be snapped and a heart can be tugged till it breaks,
but neither the one nor the other can ever be whole again.

Exercise (no key)

What have these four poems in common in imagery and mood?

23.2 Terminal tears and other echoes

The last line of the first poem contains a conventional image of sadness: the soaked handkerchief. A constant feature of Chinese poetry from the Han onwards is the mention of weeping in the final couplet, most often in the last line. This is variously expressed as 垂淚 *chuí lèi* 'have tears hanging down'; 流涕 *liú tì* 'have tears flowing'; 下淚 *xià lèi* and 落淚 *luò lèi*, both 'let tears fall'; 淚下 *lèi xià*, 泣下 *qì xià*, 涕下 *tì xià* and 淚落 *lèi luò*, all four meaning 'tears fall'. Sometimes it is not tears from the eyes but 泗 *sì* 'a sinus overflow from the nose': 涕泗流 *tì sì liú* 'eyes and nose streaming'. The tears are sometimes doubled to mean 'on both sides': 雙淚 *shuāng lèi*, 雙涕 *shuāng tì* or 兩行淚 *liǎng háng lèi* 'a double row of tears'.

The tears soak the front of the clothes: 霑懷抱 *zhān huái bào* 'soak the bosom', 霑襟 *zhān jīn* 'soak the front of the clothes' or 滿襟 *mǎn jīn* 'fill (= cover) the front of the clothes'; or a handkerchief: 霑巾 *zhān jīn* or else they run down the hat-strings: 緣纓流 *yuán yīng liú* literally 'along hat-strings flow' (hat-strings tie under the chin to keep the hat on). Or else they soak the

---

clothing in general: 霑裳衣 *zhān cháng yī*, 霑裳 *zhān cháng*, 霑衣 *zhān yī*, 霑我衣 *zhān wǒ yī*, 霑人衣 *zhān rén yī*.

Sometimes the tears are compared to other things: 如雨 *rú yǔ* 'like rain', 如霑露 *rú zhān lù* 'like soaking dew', 如流霰 *rú liú xiàn* 'like drifting sleet', 如連絲 *rú lián sī* 'like connected silk threads', 比散絲 *bǐ sàn sī* 'like scattered silk threads'.

Or else the tears are unstoppable: 誰能禁 *shuí néng jìn* 'who can prevent them?' or 應無已 *yīng wú yǐ* 'will probably have no end'.

I am using this image as an example of the strength of tradition in Chinese verse. In the West we have in recent times come to view the poet's art not as a traditional craft, the skilful manipulation of words to conjure up familiar emotions in forms that are new enough to be interesting without departing too far from a known code, but rather as an area for innovation of technique and (supposedly) of ideas. This is a very different approach from that of classical Chinese verse.

Where we admire novelty at whatever cost, China has traditionally cherished stability and slowness to change.

When a Tang poet incorporates a phrase or even a whole line by an earlier poet he is not plagiarizing in the sense of stealing someone else's intellectual property and passing it off as his own: he is consolidating a tradition that is well-known public property, for no one is seen to be owning the Chinese language or the way it has been used. His re-use of a phrase is a deliberate echo that will be appreciated as such by his contemporaries and successors. The treasure-house of imagery and phraseology is open to all to re-use, modify and add to. It is not unusual for every line of an eight-line poem to contain an echo of an older poem; the skill of the craftsman is in combining these echoes to create something new while staying firmly within the discipline of the tradition. In fact, one might say that Arthur Koestler's definition of the act of creation as the recombination of existing elements fits Chinese poetic creation perfectly, provided that we are prepared to see whole phrases and metaphors as primary elements.

The last-line weeping-images do ring the changes on words, but the process of echoing is also taken farther by extending the original image or finding parallels to it. An example of the former is to have a candle weeping tears of molten wax in the poet's stead; [152] and of the latter, to end a poem with the sad cries of gibbons or the neighing of departing horses or the quasi-weeping of rain. Putting such indirect images into the final line, the place of soaking tears, tells the reader unmistakably what their function is.

Echoing can be even more subtle: the atmosphere created by one poem may be echoed in another without any direct connection in wording or imagery. This is difficult to exemplify briefly, and in any case I feel it is better left to you, the reader, to be prepared for this technique and to notice and enjoy it

---

[152] 杜牧 贈別，其二 唐6

when you encounter it, as you undoubtedly will, even within the narrow confines of this course.

All this means that the perfect translation of Chinese poetry is well-nigh impossible. Without a detailed commentary giving the sources and contexts of echoes and allusions, the reader is going to miss a great deal, perhaps even the essentials of a poem; but who in the West wants to plough through commentaries? We feel that a poem should speak directly heart to heart within our own shared codes, but if we are going to explore Chinese poetry seriously we must be prepared to immerse ourselves in the great sea of words that extends over the last three thousand years, ever discovering new echoes and resonances. In the course of such an exploration we should not expect to find startlingly new ideas, just subtle and surprising variations on age-old themes, a more rarefied pleasure than being yelled at or mystified in modern European languages.

UNIT 24

For the next five units we shall be looking at poems about Buddhist temples as places of retreat.

Vocabulary

安 *ān* /v/ be calm, peaceful 40.3 (S)

薄 *bó* /v/ approach, be close to 140.13 (S)

禪 *chán* /n/ meditation (from Sanskrit *dhyāna*, gave Japanese *zen*) 113.12 (M 示 'revelation')

禪房 *chán fáng* /n/ monks' quarters behind temple

晨 *chén* /n/ morning 72.7 (M 日 'sun')

毒 *dú* /n/ poison; /v/ be poisonous, vicious 80.4 (X)

房 *fáng* /n/ room 63.4 (M 戶 'door')

峰 *fēng* /n/ peak 46.7 (M 山 'mountain')

積 *jī* /v/ accumulate 115.11 (M 禾 'grain')

寂 *jì* /v/ be silent, still 40.8 (S)

俱 *jū* /a/ all 9.8 (M 亻 'person')

籟 *lài* /n/ sounds (of Nature) 118.16 (M 竹 'bamboo')

暮 *mù* /n/ evening, dusk 72.11 (M 日 'sun')

磬 *qìng* /n/ chiming-bowl, a bowl-shaped bell used in Buddhist services (originally meant 'stone chimes') 112.11 (M 石 'stone')

曲 *qū* /n/ curve, bend (of river etc) 73.2 (X)

泉 *quán* /n/ spring (of water), stream near source, upland burn 85.5 (W)

數 *shù* /n/ number; /q/ a number of, several 66.11 (S)

通 *tōng* /v/ lead to, give access to 162.7 (M 辶 'go')

198

萬籟 *wàn lài* /n/ all the sounds of Nature

危 *wēi* /v/ precipitous 26.4 (X)

惟 *wéi* /a/ only 61.8 (S)

性 *xìng* /n/ (inborn) nature 61.5 (M 忄 'heart')

咽 *yè* /v/ sob, choke with sobs 30.6 (M 口 'mouth')

音 *yīn* /n/ sound 180.0 (X)

悅 *yuè* /v/ delight, make happy 61.7 (M 忄 'heart')

制 *zhì* /v/ control, restrain 18.6 (S)

Text 1[153]

Wang Wei (early eighth century): 'Visiting the Temple of Accumulated Incense-smoke'

不知香積寺 *bù zhī xiāng jī* sì*

數里入雲峰 *shù lǐ rù yún fēng*

古木無人徑 *gǔ mù wú rén jìng*

深山何處鐘 *shēn shān hé chù zhōng*

泉聲咽危石 *quán shēng yè wēi shí**

日色冷青松 *rì sè lěng qīng sōng*

薄暮空潭曲 *bó* mù kōng tán qū**

安禪制毒龍 *ān chán zhì dú* lóng*

---

[153] 王維　過香積寺　唐3

Text 2[154]

Chang Jian (early eighth century): 'Inscribed in the monks' quarters behind Broken Hill Temple'

清晨入古寺 *qīng chén rù gǔ sì*

初日照高林 *chū rì zhào gāo lín*

竹徑通幽處 *zhú* jìng tōng yōu chù*

禪房花木深 *chán fáng huā mù shēn*

山光悅鳥性 *shān guāng yuè niǎo xìng*

潭影空人心 *tán yǐng kōng rén xīn*

萬籟此俱寂 *wàn lài cǐ jū jì*

惟餘鐘磬音 *wéi yú zhōng qìng yīn*

Notes on the poems

In the first poem 無人徑 *wú rén jìng* looks at first sight as if it could mean 'there are no paths for people' (i.e. only for wild animals or birds), but if we take into account the parallelism of this phrase with 'a bell somewhere' in the following line we shall have to understand it as 'a path without people'. But parallelism is more reliable for determining word-classes than for solving structural ambiguities, so we cannot be absolutely sure of either interpretation here. The situation would suggest that there would be a path or road of some kind to any temple, for these were tourist-attractions, at least for poets. Not meeting anyone else on the path would have enhanced Wang Wei's sense of solitude, and in the context of this poem this escape from people is more important than the underfoot state of the path.

The opening line of the second poem contains another ambiguity: 清晨入 *qīng chén rù* can mean either 'clear dawn enters' or 'at clear dawn I enter'. The parallel phrase in the second line 初日照 *chū rì zhào* 'the first sun shines on' suggests the former interpretation. Line 9 of the poem in Unit 26 has 洩雲蒙清晨 *xiè yún méng qīng chén* 'disintegrating clouds obscure the pure morning', showing that 清晨 *qīng chén* can be treated as a thing as well as a time; this provides further support. The situation is a third factor we have to consider: has the poet been staying at the monastery overnight, as was often

---

154常建 題破山寺後禪院 唐3

done, or had he travelled through the hills overnight to reach the monastery at dawn? To me personally the former seems the more likely.

I have spent some time on these two ambiguities to focus attention on the need for intelligent thought and imagination as well as a consideration of parallelism when dealing with any Chinese poem.

Central-couplet parallelism contrasts with the tendency of the first and last couplets to run on and form two-line sentences, as in the first poem here. The effect of this contrast is to create an overall poem structure that begins and ends informally, sometimes prosaically, while the centre constitutes the high-point of formal artistry. We are led gently, as it were, from the everyday world into a higher realm of deeper insights into the underlying patterns and contrasts in the structure of the world, for instance time and distance in 古 *gǔ* and 深 *shēn* in the second couplet, and hearing and vision in 聲 *shēng* and 色 *sè* in the third couplet, before being brought back to earth again.

As I have said before, Wang Wei was attracted to Buddhism, and this is spelled out explicitly in the final couplet of the first poem. In the key I have translated 空 *kōng* as 'silent' rather than 'deserted', since the 'emptiness' that Wang Wei is seeking is the absence of noise and turmoil and conflict; he wants the pool of his mind to be still, with an unruffled surface, not a rushing, turbid river.

Traditionally, deep pools, like Loch Ness, are the abode of dragons, as we saw in Unit 16. In China they are beneficent, rain-bringing creatures, not the fiery monsters of European legend. But Buddhism seems to have brought with it the concept of the poisonous dragon, perhaps originating in the Indian *naga*. There is a legend about Shakyamuni Buddha transforming himself into a poisonous dragon which sacrifices itself to others, and if Wang Wei has this legend in mind, he may here be not so much trying to subdue his biological self as to transform it into something altruistic.

24.1 Quality-verbs as adverbials of manner or result

These seem less common than in Western verse. They correspond to English adverbs ending in '-ly'. Like the quality-verbs of distance, duration and frequency that we looked at in Unit 21, these may occur either in position 2 or in position 3. In parallelism those of distance etc. may match those of manner. In the following examples we meet 暗 *àn* darkly, obscurely; 悲 *bēi* sadly; 慘 *cǎn* miserably, distressingly, cruelly; 寒 *hán* coldly, with a chilly light; 疾 *jí* urgently; 急 *jí* hurriedly; 淨 *jìng* clean; 狂 *kuáng* madly, wildly; 懶 *lǎn* lazily; 亂 *luàn* in confusion; 明 *míng* clearly; 輕 *qīng* lightly 清 *qīng* clearly; 速 *sù* swiftly; 閑 *xián* unoccupied, not busy; 斜 *xié* obliquely, aslant 徐 *xú* slowly; 易 *yì* easily, all too soon; 幽 *yōu* in seclusion; 迂 *yū* cramped, narrow and bent.

Examples of position 2:

狂歌五柳前 [155] *kuáng gē wǔ liǔ qián* 'Wildly singing in front of my "five willows" (=house)'.

孤燈寒照雨　深竹暗浮煙 [156] *gū dēng hán zhào yǔ / shēn zhú àn fú yān* 'A lonely lamp coldly shines on the rain; / deep in the bamboos mist floats obscurely'.

小園花亂飛 [157] *xiǎo yuán huā luàn fēi* 'In my little garden the blossom swirls in confusion'.

永夜角聲悲自語 [158] *yǒng yè jué shēng bēi zì yǔ* 'In the long night the sound of the bugle sadly talks to itself'. (角 bugle.)

密雨斜侵薜荔牆 [159] *mì yǔ xié qīn bì lì qiáng* 'The dense rain, blown aslant, invades the wall with its climbing fig'. (密 dense; 侵 invade; 薜荔 climbing fig; 牆 wall.)

閑坐悲君亦自悲 [160] *xián zuò bēi jūn yì zì bēi* 'Sitting unoccupied, I am sad for you, and also sad for myself'.

清聞樹杪磬 [161] *qīng wén shù miǎo qìng* 'I clearly hear a chiming-bowl through the tips of the branches'. (杪 tips of branches.)

此事恍惚難明論 [162] *cǐ shì huǎng hū nán míng lún* 'This matter is vague and difficult to explain clearly'. (恍惚 vague; 論 *lún* (usually *lùn*) discuss, explain.)

赤汗微生白雪毛 [163] *chì hàn wēi shēng bái xuě máo* (Of a 'blood-sweating' Ferghanan horse) 'The red sweat faintly appears on its snow-white hide'. (赤 red; 汗 sweat; 毛 hair, fur.)

---

[155]王維　輞川閑居贈裴秀才迪　唐3

[156]司空曙　雲陽館與韓紳宿別　唐3

[157]李商隱　落花　唐3

[158]杜甫　宿府　唐4

[159]柳宗元　登柳州城樓…　唐4

[160]元稹　遣悲懷，其三　唐4

[161]杜甫　陪章留後惠義寺…　杜12

[162]杜甫　石筍行　杜10

徐行得自娛 [164] *xú xíng dé zì yú* 'Walking slowly, I can enjoy myself'. (娛 give pleasure to.)

戰骨當速朽 [165] *zhàn gǔ dāng sù xiǔ* 'Battlefield bones will quickly rot'. (戰 battle; 骨 bone; 當 will; 朽 rot, decay.)

輕霑鳥獸群 [166] *qīng zhān niǎo shòu qún* (Of morning rain) 'It lightly wets the flocks of birds and beasts'. (獸 beast, animal; 群 flock, herd, crowd.)

幽棲身懶動 [167] *yōu qī shēn lǎn dòng* 'Dwelling in seclusion, my body moves lazily'. (懶 lazy.)

兩株慘裂苔蘚皮 [168] *liǎng zhū cǎn liè tái xiǎn pí* (Of a painting of ancient pine-trees) 'On their twin trunks the mossy bark is cruelly split'. (兩 pair of; 株 trunk; 慘 tragic, harsh; 裂 split; 蘚 moss; 皮 skin, bark.)

青春易盡急還鄉 [169] *qīng chūn yì jìn jí huán xiāng* (Of migrant geese) 'The green springtime ends all too soon, and you return **in haste** to your home country'.

安得壯士挽天河　淨洗甲兵長不用 [170] *ān dé zhuàng shì wǎn tiān hé / jìng xǐ jiǎ bīng cháng bù yòng* 'Where shall we find a heroic warrior to harness the sky-river / and wash clean away the armour and weapons so that they will for a long time not be used?' (安 where; 壯 heroic; 士 warrior; 挽 pull down; 甲 armour; 兵 weapon; 用 use.)

---

[163] 杜甫　驄馬行　杜4

[164] 杜甫　陪李金吾花下飲　杜3

[165] 杜甫　前出塞九首，其三　杜2

[166] 杜甫　晨雨　杜18

[167] 杜甫　絕句六首，其二　杜13

[168] 杜甫　戲爲韋偃雙松圖歌　杜9

[169] 杜甫　官池春雁二首，其二　杜12

[170] 杜甫　洗兵行　杜6

Examples of position 3:

雲裏相呼疾 [171] *yún lǐ xiāng hū jí* 'In the clouds they call to one another urgently'.

眼尾淚侵寒 [172] *yǎn wěi lèi qīn hán* 'In the corner of her eye a tear coldly invades'. (尾 tail)

月冷猿啼慘　天高雁去遲 [173] *yuè lěng yuán tí cǎn / tiān gāo yàn qù chí* 'The moon is cold and the gibbons cry miserably; / the skies are high and the geese are leaving late'. (猿 gibbon)

翻然出地速 [174] *fān rán chū dì sù* (Of lettuces growing) 'Before you know it they are out of the ground in a flash'. (翻然 suddenly (of a change).)

胡行速如鬼 [175] *hú xíng sù rú guǐ* 'The Hu move as swiftly as ghosts'. (鬼 ghost, demon.)

寒日出霧遲　清江轉山急 [176] *hán rì chū wù chí / qīng jiāng zhuǎn shān jí* 'A cold sun emerges late from the mist; / the clear river twists hurriedly through the hills'.

Result in position 3

In position 3 a quality-verb will sometimes indicate not the *manner* of the action, but its *result*, as in the following examples:

寒食東風御柳斜 [177] *hán shí dōng fēng yù liǔ xié* 'At the Cold Food Festival the east wind drives the willow[-frond]s aslant'. (食 food; 御 drive.)

---

[171] 杜甫　歸雁二首，其一　杜23

[172] 李賀　謝秀才有妾⋯四首，其二　全392

[173] 戴叔倫　冬日有懷李賀長吉　全273

[174] 杜甫　種萵苣　杜15

[175] 杜甫　塞蘆子　杜4

[176] 杜甫　早發射洪縣⋯　杜11

[177] 韓翃　寒食　唐6

峽雲籠樹小　湖日蕩船明[178] *xiá yún lǒng shù xiǎo / hú rì dàng chuán míng* 'The clouds in the gorge shroud the trees so that they appear small; / the sunlight over the lake floods the boat so that it is bright'. (峽 gorge, especially the Yangtse Gorges; 籠 enfold, shroud; 蕩 to flood, cleanse with a surge of water; 船 boat.)

雨洗平沙淨　天銜闊岸迂[179] *yǔ xǐ píng shā jìng / tiān xián kuò àn yū* 'The rain has washed the level sands clean; / the sky engulfs the broad banks so that they look cramped'. (銜 hold in the mouth; 闊 broad; 迂 cramped.)

---

[178] 杜甫　送段功曹歸廣州　杜 11
[179] 杜甫　舟出江陵南浦⋯　杜 22

UNIT 25

Vocabulary

貝葉 *bèi yè* /n/ palm-leaf 154.0 (S)

貝葉書 *bèi yè shū* /n/ Buddhist text written in palm-leaf book

禪經 *chán jīng* /n/ Buddhist scriptures

超 *chāo* /v/ go beyond, transcend, transcendental 156.5 (M 走 'run')

持 *chí* /v/ hold 64.6 (M 扌 'hand')

齒 *chǐ* /n/ teeth 211.0 (S 止 *zhǐ*+ M (OB) 🔲 'teeth')

澹然 *dàn rán* /v/ be calm, tranquil 85.13 (M 氵 'water')

道 *dào* /n/ way; (Taoist) the Tao, the way reality works; (Buddhist) doctrine

道人 *dào rén* /n/ one who has achieved enlightenment, either Taoist or
   Buddhist (here refers to the 'transcendental master' of the title)

東 *dōng* /n/ east 75.4 (W)

讀 *dú* /v/ read 149.15 (M 言 'speak')

服 *fú* /n/ clothes 74.4 (S)

膏 *gāo* /n/ ointment, hair-oil; /v/ anoint 130.10 (S 高 + M 月 'flesh')

何由 *hé yóu* /a/ by what means? how?

跡 *jī* /n/ tracks; achievement, miracle, wonder 157.6 (M 足 'foot')

汲 *jí* /v/ draw water (from well or stream) 85.4 (M 氵 'water')

冀 *jì* /v/ hope 12.14 (X) (北田共)

井 *jǐng* /n/ a well, cistern (often relatively shallow like OT *bĕ'ēr*) 7.2 (W)

了 *liǎo* /a/ at all (plus negative) 6.1 (X)

冥 *míng* /v/ understand without explicit words, intuit

沐 *mù* /v/ wash the hair 85.4 (M 氵 'water')

取 *qǔ* /v/ take, draw upon 29.6 (X)

然 *rán* /a/ thus, so; adjectival or adverbial ending ('-ly') 86.8 (S)

繕 *shàn* /v/ mend 120.12 (M 糸 'silk')

世 *shì* /n/ the world, the unenlightened 1.4 (S)

書 *shū* /n/ writing; book; letter 73.6 (M 聿 'pen')

熟 *shú* /v/ be ripe, mature, perfect 86.11 (M 灬 'fire')

漱 *shù* /v/ rinse 85.11 (M 氵 'water')

說 *shuō* /n/ theory 149.7 (M 言 'speak')

庭宇 *tíng yǔ* /n/ courtyards and buildings, outdoors and in

妄 *wàng* /v/ be vain, useless 38.3 (M 女 'woman')

無 *wú* /n/ (here =) nobody

悟 *wù* /v/ wake up, become aware, achieve *satori* 61.7 (M 忄 'heart')

言說 *yán shuō* /n/ talk, philosophizing, theorizing

遺 *yí* /v/ bequeath, hand down 162.12 (M 辶 'go')

遺言 *yí yán* /n/ sayings handed down from ancient sages

詣 *yì* /v/ visit (someone one respects) 149.6 (M 言 'speak')

由 *yóu* /prep/ by means of 102.0 (X)

宇 *yǔ* /n/ building 40.3   (M 宀 'house')

源 *yuán* /n/ source, spring 85.10 (M 氵 'water')

院 *yuàn* /n/ (here) monastery 170.7 (S)

眞 *zhēn* /v/ be true; /n/ one's own inner truth, self-realisation 109.5 (X)

足 *zú* /v/ be sufficient; be content 157.0 (S)

Notes on the vocabulary

超師 *chāo shī* 'transcendental master' may be the monk's name or it may be Liu Zongyuan's respectful way of referring to his guru; I just don't know.

禪 經 *chán jīng*: not 'Zen scriptures', but a general term for Buddhist scriptures (*sūtras*). A variant reading is 蓮 經 *lián jīng* 'Lotus Sutra', an abbreviation of 妙法蓮花經 *miào fǎ lián huā jīng* 'The Sutra of the Lotus Flower of the Marvellous Dharma'.

Text[180]

Liu Zongyuan (773–819): 'Visiting the Transcendental Master's monastery at dawn to read Buddhist scriptures'

01 汲井漱寒齒 *jí* jǐng shù hán chǐ*

02 清心拂塵服 *qīng xīn fú* chén fú**

03 閒持貝葉書 *xián chí bèi yè shū*

04 步出東齋讀 *bù chū* dōng zhāi dú**

05 眞源了無取 *zhēn yuán liào wú qǔ*

06 妄跡世所逐 *wàng jī* shì suǒ zhú**

07 遺言冀可冥 *yí yán jì kě míng*

08 繕性何由熟 *shàn xìng hé yóu shú**

09 道人庭宇靜 *dào rén tíng yǔ jìng*

10 苔色連深竹 *tái sè lián shēn zhú**

11 日出霧露餘 *rì chū* wù lù yú*

12 青松如膏沐 *qīng sōng rú gāo mù*

13 澹然離言說 *dàn rán lí yán shuō**

14 悟悅心自足 *wù yuè xīn zì zú**

---

[180]柳宗元　晨詣超師院讀禪經　唐1

25.1 Rhyme

Chinese verse normally rhymes on the even-numbered lines, with the first line being optionally included in the rhyme-scheme. In short poems there is normally one rhyme throughout, but long poems are often broken into verses by a change of rhyme. This ancient-style poem has one rhyme throughout, but it is broken into verses by another device that may not have been noticed before: the tonal pattern of the last couplet of each verse except the last one. While the other lines have no pattern that I can detect (this is normal with ancient-style verse), the couplets in question have a complementary pattern where the tone of each syllable of the second line is the opposite of that of the corresponding syllable in the first line (in capitals below), as if it were regulated verse:

> Verse 1: x x x o x / o o x o x / O O X X O / X X O O X
> Verse 2: o o x o x / x x x x x / O O X X O / X X O O X
> Verse 3: x o o x x / o x o o x / X X X X O / O O O O X
> Verse 4: x o o o x / x x o x x

The resulting 4+4+4+2-line structure is reminiscent of a Shakespearian sonnet or the three stanzas plus an *envoi* that one meets in medieval French ballades. Does this structure perhaps have a universal aesthetic appeal?

You may have noticed that classical Chinese verse does not always rhyme in a modern transcription any more than Chaucer does if given a modern English pronunciation. If you examine pre-Han verse you will find that it often does not rhyme if read in a Tang pronunciation. The reason of course is that major sound-shifts have taken place between these three stages. Up to the Han most extant verse and rhymed prose rhymed fairly consistently: this was the period of the Old Chinese sound-system. Between the Han and the Tang dynasties Chinese pronunciation underwent a massive change to give Middle Chinese. Since the Tang, and especially during the Sung dynasty, even more drastic changes have taken place, especially in the northern dialects on which modern Mandarin (Standard Chinese) is based.

We saw that the entering-tone words (those ending in *-p*, *-k* or *-t*) were redistributed among the four tones of Mandarin; at the same time the vowels preceding *-p*, *-k* or *t* underwent drastic changes, e.g. *-auk* became *-ue*, *-uo*, *-ao* or *-u*. While final *-m* and *-n* both became *-n*, and final *-ng* remained unchanged, the vowels preceding them often changed under the influence of preceding medial semivowels, so that *-in* became *-in*, *-en* or *-un*.

In this poem the last words in lines 3, 5 and 11 end in *-u* in Mandarin, but they are not of course part of the rhyme-scheme since they are at the end of odd-numbered lines. These three words ended in open vowels in the Tang, whereas all the rhyming words (except one, see below) ended in *-uk*.

The rhymes of regulated verse had to adhere strictly to standard categories usually known as the 平水 *píng shuǐ* rhymes or simply as the 詩韻 *shī yùn* 'verse rhymes', which were mainly formed by continuing or combining the rhyme-categories of the *Qieyun*, a rhyme-dictionary of AD 601; this probably reflected changes in standard (court) Chinese literary pronunciation during the seventh century. But ancient-style verse allowed itself a certain latitude in using hedge-rhymes, i.e. imperfect rhymes, perhaps influenced by mistaken ideas about ancient rhyming practice. We see an example in the poem in this unit, where the final word of the poem rhymes *-ôk* while all the other rhymes are *-uk*, something that would not have been allowed in a regulated poem except in an optionally-rhyming first line. Another ancient-style poem by Liu Zongyuan [181]alternates two hedge-rhymes in what looks like a deliberate pattern: *-iek*, *-iak*, *-iek*, *-iak*, *-iek*, *-iak* (寂跡壁夕滴積).

It would not be appropriate to go more deeply into Tang phonology in an elementary course like this one. 'But isn't the sound of Chinese verse important?' you may ask. Outside of tones and rhymes, I don't think so. I know of nothing in Chinese verse like Gaelic vowel-patterns or Welsh consonantal patterns, only the rhyme and tonal patterns of Tang (and later) regulated verse and Sung dynasty song-style verse. And I think there is a good reason for it, for Chinese verse depended so heavily on traditional vocabulary and phraseology that expressions that might have had an onomatopoeic or psychophonic value in pre-Han verse would have been known to Tang poets only in written form, and hence pronounced in a very different way from their ancient pronunciation. Add to this the great variation in the dialect pronunciations of the same written words throughout Chinese history, and there is little common ground for sound-values that would remain valid over space and time. So the main medium of Chinese verse is visual imagery, not suggestive sound-values.

---

[181]柳宗元　贈江華長老　全351

UNIT 26

Vocabulary

粲 *càn* /v/ be bright, gleaming, brilliant 119.7 (S)

策 *cè* /n/ staff 118.6 (M 竹 'bamboo')

嬋娟 *chán juān* /v/ be elegant, charming, lovely (of woman) 38.12, 38.7 (M 女 'woman')

法 *fǎ* /n/ law, dharma 85.5 (S)

根 *gēn* /n/ root, bottom 75.6 (M 木 'tree')

回回 *huí huí* /v/ be winding 31.3 (W < ⊡)

叫 *jiào* /v/ shout, call 30.2 (M 口 'mouth')

淨 *jìng* /v/ be clean, pure 85.8 (M 氵 'water')

炯 *jiǒng* /v/ be bright, glowing 86.5 (M 火 'fire')

聚 *jù* /v/ assemble, gather, cluster 128.8 (M 卝 'crowd')

可數 *kě shǔ* /v/ be countable, distinct

勞 *láo* /n/ labour, toil, exhaustion 19.10 (M 力 'strength')

勞苦 *láo kǔ* /n/ hard work, exhausting toil

蒙 *méng* /v/ cover, obscure 140.10 (M 艹 'plant')

甍 *méng* /n/ ridge of roof, ridge-tiles 98.11 (M 瓦 'tile')

勉強 *miǎn qiǎng* /v/ do one's best 19.7 (M 力 'strength'), 57.8 (M 弓 'bow')

破 *pò* /v/ break 112.5 (M 石 'stone')

冉冉 *rǎn rǎn* /v/ droop, hang limply 13.3 (X)

傷 *shāng* /v/ wound 9.11 (S)

神 *shén* /n/ spirit 113.5 (M 示 'revelation')

211

適 *shì* /v/ go to 162.11 (M 辶 'go')

數 *shǔ* /v/ count 66.11 (S)

他 *tā* /d/ other 9.3 (M 亻 'person')

亭午 *tíng wǔ* /n/ high noon 8.7 (S)

籜 *tuò* /n/ sheaths of bamboo-shoots 118.16 (M 竹 'bamboo')

忘 *wàng* /v/ forget 61.3 (M 心 'heart')

危 *wēi* /v/ be in danger

午 *wǔ* /n/ noon 24.2 (X)

蘚 *xiǎn* /n/ moss 140.17 (M 艹 'plant')

蕭索 *xiāo suǒ* /v/ be lonely and chilly, vulnerable 140.12, 120.4 (S, S)

泄 *xiè* /v/ disintegrate 85.5 (M 氵 'water')

崖 *yá* /n/ cliff 46.8 (M 山 'mountain')

翳 *yì* /v/ be obscured 124.11 (S)

牖 *yǒu* /n/ window 91.10 (X)

終 *zhōng* /n/ end; /a/ in the end 120.5 (M 糸 'silk')

朱 *zhū* /v/ be red, vermilion 75.2 (X)

拄 *zhǔ* /v/ lean on (a staff) 64.5 (M 扌 'hand')

子規 *zǐ guī* /n/ cuckoo 39.0, 147.4 (S, S)

Text[182]

Du Fu (712–770): 'Mirror-of-the-Law Temple'

身危適他州 *shēn wēi shì tā zhōu*

勉強終勞苦 *miǎn qiǎng zhōng láo kǔ*

神傷山行深 *shén shāng shān xíng shēn*

---

[182] 杜甫 法鏡寺 杜8

愁破崖寺古 *chóu pò yá sì gǔ*

嬋娟碧蘚淨 *chán juān bì xiǎn jìng*
蕭索寒籜聚 *xiāo suǒ hán tuò jù*
回回山根水 *huí huí shān gēn shuǐ*
冉冉松上雨 *rǎn rǎn sōng shàng yǔ*

泄雲蒙清晨 *xiè yún méng qīng chén*
初日翳復吐 *chū rì yì fù tǔ*
朱甍半光炯 *zhū méng bàn guāng jiǒng*
戶牖粲可數 *hù yǒu càn kě shǔ*

拄策忘前期 *zhǔ cè wàng qián qī*
出夢已亭午 *chu* mèng yǐ tíng wǔ*
冥冥子規叫 *míng míng zǐ guī jiào*
微徑不敢取 *wēi jìng bù gǎn qǔ*

Notes on the poem

子規 *zǐ guī* 'cuckoo' is a pun on 子歸 *zǐ guī* 'You return home!' The cuckoo (*Cuculus poliocephalus*) contained the spirit of 杜宇 *dù yǔ*, one of the ancient kings of Shu (now Sichuan province) with the title 望帝 *wàng dì*, who seduced the wife of one of his ministers, then in a fit of remorse abdicated his throne and went away without trace. Mention in this poem of a cuckoo heard faintly in the distance may suggest that Du Fu had already crossed into Sichuan, or it may only indicate his intended objective (see below).

I have divided this poem into four stanzas not because there is any division by rhyme or tone-pattern, but because (a) this is an ancient-style poem and real ancient poems often divide naturally into four-line stanzas, and (b) it seems to fall into four parts: an introduction, the surroundings of the temple, the temple itself in the sunlight, and a conclusion. As in regulated verse, the parallelism occurs mainly in the central half, elevating the description of the temple and its surroundings to a higher, dream-like plane as a break from the unpleasant reality that precedes and follows it.

The exact occasion and place of this poem is not known, but it can be dated within six months and located within 300 miles!

At the beginning of autumn in the year 759, Du Fu resigned from his
government post at Huazhou (east of the capital Chang'an) during the An
Lushan rebellion and went west to Qinzhou (now Tianshui) in what is now
Gansu province to stay with a nephew, taking his family with him. After a
couple of months he moved south to Tonggu (now Chengxian, also in Gansu)
and at the beginning of the twelfth moon he travelled south to Chengdu in
what is now Sichuan province, arriving at the end of the month.

Stated as baldly as this, his two journeys southwards do not seem
remarkable. But let us consider what they meant in terms of experience. It was
winter; the journeys totalled three hundred miles across mountains; he was
accompanied by his family, plus a deer and a monkey (pets); he had little
money and was trying to live off the land (wild plants, roots etc.), so that the
children cried with hunger; their transport was a white horse that became grey
with mud; he was not a peasant accustomed to rural hardship but a senior civil
servant, scion of an ancient family of office-holders and grandson of the poet
Du Shenyan (one of whose poems we read in Unit 23). Not surprisingly, he
found the experience mentally and physically exhausting.

Remarkably, or perhaps not so remarkably, he wrote a great deal of poetry
on these epic journeys, and this is one of these poems. The location of the
temple is not known.

My guess is that the last line implies that he wishes he could enter the
monastery attached to the temple and retire there away from the troubles of the
world, but, with a family to get to Chengdu and a new home, the call of duty
symbolized by the Sichuanese cuckoo is louder than the temptation.

26.1 Ambiguity of vocabulary

In Unit 16 we met two words for 'wild goose', in Unit 22 some rather
confusing colour-words, and in Unit 23 two words for 'willow'. In each case
we had not a one-to-one mapping between word and meaning but a many-to-
many mapping. Let me now add a further example of this:

木 *mù*	tree	wood (material)	
樹 *shù*	tree		to plant
種 *zhòng*			to plant

Not only do the first two rows show more than one meaning for each word
(polysemy), but the first and third columns show more than one word for each
meaning (synonymy).

Compare this with modern spoken Chinese, where we have a one-to-one
mapping in this area:

木頭 *mùtou*	wood (material)
樹 *shù*	tree
種 *zhòng*	to plant

What are the implications for classical Chinese verse? There are both gains and losses. The columns show the gains: more synonyms, allowing elegant variation, i.e. the avoidance of dull repetition and the maintenance of aesthetic stimulus by using a wider vocabulary for a narrow range of meanings, for instance by the preservation or resuscitation of senescent or obsolete words, a familiar phenomenon in other languages as well. The danger, of course, is that semantic drift will lead to some words acquiring new meanings, so that their continued literary use in an old sense could lead to ambiguity or at least hindrances to comprehension, as has happened with the language of the King James Bible, for instance.

In literary Chinese this situation was exacerbated by a very special development, that of prose parallelism. In the West we tend to think of parallelism in terms of Old Testament poetry, but in China it was more akin to euphuistic prose in that it involved repeating the same thing (or something very similar) in different words, as a literary fashion. But what happened when one could not find an appropriate synonym? One roped in a near-synonym, a word with a similar but not identical meaning. A trivial example from 賦 *fù*, a genre halfway between verse and prose, is having two words for 'and' between clauses. The traditional prose word was 而 *ér*; to avoid repeating it in the parallel line the word 以 *yǐ* was used, even though it did not originally mean 'and' at all, but 'in order to'. From now on it meant either. This process of blunting of meaning meant the devaluation of the words concerned and a consequent increase in vagueness and ambiguity, an opposite development to that of semantic precision in the West (the Jesuit '*distinguo*', for instance).

Although this development was most noticeable in prose it inevitably affected verse as well. We have seen an example similar to that of the '而 *ér* and 以 *yǐ*' matching in the matching of 中 *zhōng* with 裏 *lǐ*, both in the sense of 'in', but since euphuistic parallelism was frowned upon in verse it was not this that had an adverse effect, but a consequent semantic devaluation of individual vocabulary items in the literary language as a whole, both prose and verse. The result of this process is a literary language with lots of words but a limited number of meanings; the overall gain is infinite variety and the loss is the dilution of precision and a headache for the student who wants to know exactly and with certainty what a line of verse means. I personally prefer to see it as a never-ending challenge to my intellect and imagination.

UNIT 27

Two poems by the same writer visiting two different temples.

Vocabulary

靄 *ǎi* /n/ haze, light mist 173.16 (M 雨 'rain', S 謁)

遍 *biàn* /m/ times, occasions (= 度, 回) 162.9 (M 辶 'go')

波濤 *bō táo* /n/ waves 85.5, 85.14 (M 氵 'water')

垂 *chuí* /v/ hang 32.5 (S)

垂淚 *chuí lèi* /v/ 'have tears hanging down', weep

殿 *diàn* /n/ worship-hall of a temple 79.9 (S)

逢 *féng* /v/ meet 162.7 (M 辶 'go')

隔 *gé* /prep/ on the other side of, through, across 170.10 (M 阝 'hills')

好 *hào* /v/ like, admire 38.3 (M 女 'woman')

鶴 *hè* /n/ crane 196.10 (M 鳥 'bird')

壑 *hè* /n/ valley, ravine 32.14 (M 土 'earth')

回 *huí* /v/ look back

昏 *hūn* /n/ dusk, twilight 72.4 (M 日 'sun')

界 *jiè* /n/ boundary, area within a boundary 102.4 (M 田 'field')

鏡湖 *jìng hú* /n/ Mirror Lake, in a beauty spot just south of Shaoxing

苦海 *kǔ hǎi* /n/ sea of troubles or suffering

老 *lǎo* /v/ be old, aged 125.0 (W)

平 *píng* /v/ be calm, still

容 *róng* /v/ allow, be allowed to 40.7 (X)

僧 *sēng* /n/ Buddhist monk (from Sanskrit *sangha*) 9.12 (M 亻 'person')

216

蛇 *shé* /n/ snake 142.5 (M 虫 'reptile or insect')

世界 *shì jiè* /n/ world (originally a Buddhist term)

曙 *shù* /n/ dawn

莎 *suō* /n/ sedge 140.7 (M ⁺⁺ 'plant')

濤 *táo* /n/ wave 85.14 (M 氵 'water')

王 *wáng* /n/ king 96.0 (S)

王城 *wáng chéng* /n/ the royal city, the capital

霞 *xiá* /n/ coloured clouds or mists at sunrise or sunset

星漢 *xīng hàn* /n/ Milky Way

依止 *yī zhǐ* /v/ find a refuge, stay somewhere depending on others

因 *yīn* /a/ then, next 31.3 (W)

螢 *yíng* /n/ firefly 142.10 (M 虫 'reptile, insect')

瞻 *zhān* /v/ gaze into the distance 109.13 (M 目 'eye')

蜇 *zhé* /v/ hibernate, lie hidden 142.7 (M 虫 'reptile, insect')

止 *zhǐ* /v/ stop 77.0 (S)

Text 1[183]

Lu Lun (late eighth century): 'Inscribed at the pond behind the Temple of Promoting Goodness'

隔窗棲白鶴 *gé* chuāng qī bái* hè*

似與鏡湖鄰 *sì yǔ jìng hú lín*

月照何年樹 *yuè zhào hé nián shù*

花逢幾遍人 *huā féng jǐ biàn rén*

岸莎青有路 *àn suō qīng yǒu lù*

---

[183]盧綸 題興善寺後池 全279

苔徑綠無塵 *tái jìng lǜ wú chén*

永願容依止 *yǒng yuàn róng yī zhǐ*

僧中老此身 *sēng zhōng lǎo cǐ shēn*

Text 2[184]

Lu Lun (late eighth century): 'Staying the night at Stone Jar Temple'

殿有寒燈草有螢 *diàn yǒu hán dēng cǎo yǒu yíng*

千林萬壑寂無聲 *qiān lín wàn hè jì wú shēng*

煙凝積水龍蛇蜇 *yān níng jī* shuǐ lóng shé zhé**

露濕空山星漢明 *lù shī* kōng shān xīng hàn míng*

昏靄霧中悲世界 *hūn ǎi wù zhōng bēi shì jiè*

曙霞光裏見王城 *shù xiá guāng lǐ jiàn wáng chéng*

回瞻相好因垂淚 *huí zhān xiāng hào yīn chuí lèi*

苦海波濤何日平 *kǔ hǎi bō táo hé rì píng*

27.1 Ambiguity of function: final quality-verbs

In earlier units we have seen some of the structures that can be represented by /vnv/. In this unit we shall be looking at the ambiguity that can arise when the first /v/ is a verb of movement or posture, while the second /v/ is a quality-verb that is not functioning as an adverbial (like those in Units 21 and 24) but as the object (destination or place) of the first verb.

First, let us exclude a structure that is easily confused with this. In Unit 9 we looked at 'prepositional verbs', subordinate verbs corresponding in translation to English prepositions. These verbs, together with their objects, form adverbials in position 2 /vnv = (VO)V/. In addition to those that correspond to English prepositions, any transitive verb may in principle be used in this way. Here is an example; Wang Wei is warning a monk of the perils he will be facing at sea as he sails home to Japan: 鰲身映天黑　魚眼射波紅 [185]

[184] 盧綸　宿石甕寺　全279

[185] 王維　送祕書晁監還日本國　王12

áo shēn yìng tiān hēi / yú yǎn shè bō hóng. Word-for-word: 'The giant turtle's body will stand out against the sky black; / the fish's eyes will shine on the waves red'. (鰲 *áo* mythical giant turtle; 黑 *hēi* black; 眼 *yǎn* eye; 射 *shè* shoot, project (light) on to; 紅 *hóng* red.) 'Black' clearly refers to the monster's vast bulk and 'red' refers to the glaring eyes of a monstrous fish. This indicates that what we have here is /nn vn v = S (VO) V/ 'The giant turtle's body will be black against the sky; / the fish's eyes will be red, casting beams on the waves'.

What we are concerned with in this section is not this familiar structure but something that looks superficially like it in terms of verbs and nouns but which actually has a different deep structure in terms of functions, viz. /n v nnv = SVO/, where the second verb has been substantivized (made into a noun). Let us look at a couple of examples and see how these two structures may be distinguished from one another.

人歸山郭暗 雁下蘆洲白[186] *rén guī shān guō àn / yàn xià lú zhōu bái* A word-for-word translation: 'People return hill village dark / geese descend reed sandbank white'. (郭 *guō* village; 暗 *àn* dark; 蘆 *lú* reeds; 洲 *zhōu* sandbank in river.) If we take this as /n v nn v = S (V O) V/ the translation will be 'People, returning to their hill-village, are dark; / wild geese, descending on the reed-grown sandbanks, are white'. If we take it as /n v nnv = S V O/ the translation will be 'People return to the darkness of their hill-village; / wild geese descend upon the whiteness of the reed-grown sandbanks'. Since grammatical analysis cannot help us to choose, we apply our usual non-grammatical application of common sense and Chinese poetic custom.

What is dark, the people or the village? Obviously the village or the whole environment. And what is white, the geese or the sandbanks? Theoretically, either, but the sandbank is more probable on three grounds: (a) 'white' is not an epithet commonly applied to wild geese in Chinese verse; (b) 'white' is commonly applied to sand in Chinese verse; and (c) this is a parallel couplet contrasting the people going home in the evening to their dark hill-village with the geese seeking refuge for the night among the reeds on the white sandbanks. These considerations will lead us to choose the second interpretation.

Instead of making 暗 *àn* and 白 *bái* into nouns ('darkness' and 'whiteness'), could the poet not have used these words as attributes ('dark' and 'white') as the third word of each line? No, because that would have given a different meaning. In Unit 1, Section (5), we saw that three nouns tend to be grouped logically as /{nn}n/, not as /n{nn}/. This grouping-principle would apply also here, though we are dealing not with three nouns, but with a quality-verb and two nouns: *暗山郭 *àn shān guō* would mean 'a village in the dark hills', not 'a dark village in the hills' and *白蘆洲 *bai lú zhōu* would mean

---

[186]韋應物 夕次盱眙縣 唐1

'sandbanks grown with white reeds', not 'white sandbanks grown with reeds'. The former is a minor difference, since both the hills and the village are in darkness, but the latter is a major difference, since the reeds do not share the sandbanks' whiteness.

Could the poet not have written *蘆白洲 *lú bái zhōu? Unfortunately, no: this would have given 'sandbanks where the reeds are white' /{nv}n/ according to the grouping-rule, not /n{vn}/. So what we are seeing here is the only way that Chinese five-syllable verse can express 'People return to their dark hill-village; / wild geese descend upon the white, reed-grown sandbanks'. The substantivization of the two quality-verbs is not a freely-chosen 'poetical' device but is actually imposed by the restraints of line-length and the grouping-rule.

Here is another example of the same structure: 紅入桃花嫩 青歸柳葉新 [187] hóng rù táo huā nèn / qīng guī liǔ yè xīn Word-for-word: 'Pink enters peach blossom tender; / green returns willow leaves new'. (紅 hóng pink, red; 桃 táo peach; 嫩 nèn tender; 柳 liǔ willow; 新 xīn new.) In other words: 'Pinkness enters the tenderness of the peach-blossom;/ greenness returns to the newness of the willow-leaves', corresponding to the English 'A pink blush comes into the tender peach-blossom;/ green returns to the new willow-leaves'. Here again, though, we have a solution of how to express in Chinese five-syllable verse what in English would be an adjective qualifying the second noun of a noun-phrase rather than the first one.

A third example: 星垂平野闊 月湧大江流 [188] xīng chuí píng yě kuò / yuè yǒng dà jiāng liú 'Stars hang level counyside vast; / moon surge great river flow'. (闊 kuò wide, vast; 湧 yǒng surge, well up.) That is: 'The stars hang down [over] the vastness of the level plain;/ [the reflection of]the moon wells up in the Yangtse's flow'. Here the 'flow' is not a quality-verb but an action-verb, one that is quite commonly used as a noun in any case, in the sense of 'current'. This helps us decide that the matching 'vast' is probably also a noun here, rather than being the main verb in *'The stars are vast as they hang down over the level plain'. This second possibility is also excluded by the context: the poet is far from home, so it is the vastness of the earth, not of the sky, that increases his loneliness.

If we now look back at the first example we shall see that this, too, represents a way of getting around the restrictions imposed by the metre on the use of qualifying quality-verbs, for we could equally translate it into English as 'The giant turtle's black body will loom against the sky;/ the fish's red eyes will cast a glow on the waves'. The only difference is that in that example we are dealing with the subject of a verb whereas in the following three examples we were dealing with an object. This, in fact, will be the question you will have to ask: does the final quality-verb refer to the subject or to the object?

---

[187] 杜甫 奉酬李都督表丈早春作 杜9

[188] 杜甫 旅夜書懷 唐3

Each case will have to be judged individually. Grammatical analysis cannot help you, only semantic analysis, i.e. weighing the probabilities of meaning. I can offer no other general rules, only warn you of the possible ambiguity.

UNIT 28

Two light-hearted temple-poems by Bai Juyi.

Vocabulary

參差 *cēn cī* /v/ be uneven (in height) 28.9, 48.7 (S, S)

場 *cháng* /n/ site, place, ceremonial site 32.9 (M 土 'earth')

澹蕩 *dàn dàng* /v/ be relaxed, calm, free and easy

島 *dǎo* /n/ island 46.7 (M 山 'mountain')

道場 *dào cháng* /n/ Buddhist temple

芳菲 *fāng fēi* /v/ be fragrant; /n/ fragrant blossoms 140.4, 140.8 (M ⁺⁺ 'plant')

宮 *gōng* /n/ palace 40.7 (M 宀 'house')

恨 *hèn* /v/ be sad and annoyed, regret 61.6 (M 忄 'heart')

回 *huí* /v/ turn round

開 *kāi* /v/ open, bloom 169.4 (W hands lifting door-bar)

空碧 *kōng bì* /n/ the azure void, the sky

蓮 *lián* /n/ water-lily, lotus 140.11 (M ⁺⁺ 'plant')

涼 *liáng* /v/ be cool 85.8 (M 氵 'water')

盧橘 *lú jú* /n/ cumquat 108.11 (S), 75.12 (M 木 'tree')

覓 *mì* /v/ seek 147.4 (W)

橈 *náo* /n/ oar; often used in verse to mean 'boat' by metonymy 75.12 (M 木 'tree, wood')

蓬萊 *péng lái* /n/ Penglai, Isle of the Immortals in the Eastern Sea 140.11, 140.8 (M ⁺⁺ 'plant')

請 *qǐng* /v/ request, ask 149.8 (M 言 'speak')

222

人間 *rén jiān* /a/ among people, in the (ordinary) world

盛 *shèng* /a/ fully, luxuriantly 108.6 (M 皿 'bowl')

始 *shǐ* /a/ for the first time, only then 38.5 (M 女 'woman')

首 *shǒu* /n/ head 185.0 (W)

四 *sì* /q/ four 31.2 (X)

桃 *táo* /n/ peach 75.6 (M 木 'tree')

戰 *zhàn* /v/ tremble 62.12 (M 戈 'halberd')

中央 *zhōng yāng* /n/ centre, middle 2.3, 37.2 (X)

重 *zhòng* /v/ be heavy 166.2 (W)

轉 *zhuǎn* /v/ transfer, shift

子 *zǐ* /n/ (here) fruit

棕櫚 *zōng lǘ* /n/ palm-tree 75.8, 75.15 (M 木 'tree')

Text 1[189]

Bai Juyi (772–846): The peach-blossom at Great Forest Temple

人間四月芳菲盡 *rén jiān sì yuè fāng fēi jìn*

山寺桃花始盛開 *shān sì táo huā shǐ shèng kāi*

長恨春歸無覓處 *cháng hèn chūn guī wú mì chù*

不知轉入此中來 *bù zhī zhuǎn rù cǐ zhōng lái*

---

[189] 白居易　大林寺桃花　全439

Text 2[190]

Bai Juyi (772–846): For my guests when returning home in the evening at West Lake and looking back at the temple on Lonely Hill [Island]

柳湖松島蓮花寺 *liǔ hú sōng dǎo lián huā sì*

晚動歸橈出道場 *wǎn dòng guī náo chū dào cháng*

盧橘子低山雨重 *lú jú zǐ dī shān yǔ zhòng*

棕櫚葉戰水風涼 *zōng lǘ yè zhàn shuǐ fēng liáng*

煙波澹蕩搖空碧 *yān bō dàn dàng yáo kōng bì*

樓殿參差倚夕陽 *lóu diàn cēn cī yǐ xī yáng*

到岸請君回首望 *dào àn qǐng jūn huí shǒu wàng*

蓬萊宮在海中央 *péng lái gōng zài hǎi zhōng yāng*

28.1 Ambiguity of function: initial noun-phrase

In Unit 2 we saw an example of this kind of ambiguity in the couplet:
    [From] the walls of the capital [we] look down over the Three Qin;
    [through] wind and mist [we] gaze afar towards the Five Fords.

In Unit 24 we saw that 清晨入 *qīng chén rù* could mean either 'clear dawn enters' (cf. the first example below) or '[at] clear dawn [I] enter'.

In the former case the potential ambiguity arises from a noun-phrase of place; in the latter, a noun-phrase of time. In both cases the ambiguity is caused by the possibility that a noun-phrase of time or place may be used either as the performer of the action /nv... = SV.../or else adverbially (to indicate where or when something occurred) /nv... = AV.../ . The problem is here made worse by the absence of prepositions or pronouns, or of equivalent indicators of relationship, to help us choose between the two alternatives. In the former case the ambiguity was resolved by recourse to 'common sense'; in the latter it remained unresolved, since either interpretation seemed reasonable. Here are examples of the various types.

(1) Time-phrase as subject. This is less common than the adverbial use.

白露團甘子　清晨散馬蹄[191] *bái lù tuán gān zǐ / qīng chén sàn mǎ tí* 'White dew pearls the mandarin oranges; / the clear dawn (scatters =) frees

---

[190] 白居易　西湖晚歸回望孤山寺贈諸客　全443

[191] 杜甫　白露　杜19

my horse's hooves'. (團 *tuán* be globular; 甘子 *gān zǐ* mandarin orange; 馬 *mǎ* horse; 蹄 *tí* hoof.)

春動水茫茫 [192] *chūn dòng shuǐ máng máng* 'Springtime moves the waters as far as the eye can see'

春歸客未還 [193] *chūn guī kè wèi huán* 'Spring has returned but the exile has not gone home'

春深秦山香　葉墜清渭朗 [194] *chūn shēn qín shān xiāng / yè zhuì qīng wèi lǎng* 'When spring was (deep =) well-advanced, the hills of Qin were fragrant; / when the leaves fell, the clear River Wei was bright'. (墜 *zhuì* fall; 渭 *wèi* R. Wei; 朗 *lǎng* bright, clear.)

年侵腰腳衰 [195] *nián qīn yāo jiǎo shuāi* 'As the years encroach, back and feet grow weak'. (侵 *qīn* invade; 腰 *yāo* waist, lower back; 腳 *jiǎo* foot; 衰 *shuāi* fade, grow weak.)

百年已過半　秋至轉飢寒 [196] *bǎi nián yǐ guò bàn / qiū zhì zhuǎn jī hán* 'My hundred years (= my life) have already passed the halfway mark; / as autumn arrives they change to hunger and cold'. (至 *zhì* arrive; 飢 *jī* famine, hunger.)

(2) Time-phrase as adverbial. This is the most common function of an initial time-phrase.

晚年惟好靜 [197] *wǎn nián wéi hào jìng* '[In] my twilight years [I] only like quietude'.

晚見雁行頻 [198] *wǎn jiàn yàn háng pín* '[In] the evening [I] see goose-skeins frequently'. (頻 *pín* frequently.)

(3) Place-phrase as subject. This occurs quite frequently, since topographical features (e.g. mountains and rivers), buildings, settlements and so on, can function as either things or places.

山隨平野盡　江入大荒流 [199] *shān suí píng yě jìn / jiāng rù dà huāng liú* 'The mountains come to an end with the level plain; / the Yangtse flows into the great wilderness'.

---

[192] 杜甫　城上　杜13

[193] 杜甫　入宅三首，其二　杜18

[194] 杜甫　故著作郎貶台州司戶…　杜16

[195] 杜甫　寄贊上人　杜7

[196] 杜甫　因崔五侍御寄高彭州一絕　杜9

[197] 王維　酬張少府　唐3

[198] 馬戴　灞上秋居　唐3

[199] 李白　渡荊門送別　唐3

荒城臨古渡　落日滿秋山 [200] *huāng chéng lín gǔ dù / luò rì mǎn qiū shān* 'The ruined city-wall looks down over the ancient ferry;/ the [light of the] setting sun fills the autumn hills'. (The poet is not himself looking down from the walls.)

郡邑浮前浦 [201] *jùn yì fú qián pǔ* 'The [reflection of the] prefectural seat floats in the shallows before us'. (郡 *jùn* prefecture; 邑 *yì* city; 浦 *pǔ* shallows near riverbank.)

(4) Place-phrase as adverbial.

莓苔見履痕 [202] *méi tái jiàn lǚ hén* '[On] the moss [I] see your shoe-prints'. (莓苔 *méi tái* moss; 履 *lǚ* shoe.)

茅屋訪孤僧 [203] *máo wū fǎng gū sēng* '[In] his thatched cottage [I] visit the lonely monk'. (訪 *fǎng* visit.)

寒塘獨下遲 [204] *hán táng dú xià chí* (Of a migrant goose) '[On] the cold pond [you] descend alone, belatedly'. (塘 *táng* pond; 遲 *chí* late, delayed.)

How are such ambiguities to be resolved? The use of time- and place-phrases as subjects of verbs often involves metaphor, for instance in the examples above we have the dawn scattering something, springtime moving something or being deep or returning, years encroaching on something or passing something, mountains coming to an end, a wall looking down over something, and a city floating on water. Such metaphors are commonplace in Western literature ('The mountains look on Marathon, and Marathon looks on the sea', for instance).

But what about the adverbial phrases? Could these not also be seen as metaphorical subjects? After all, we could say such things in English as 'My twilight years are in love with quietude', 'The evening sees the return of the geese', 'Only the moss sees me as I pass by', 'His thatched cottage visits my dreams', or 'The cold pond descends to the depths of despair'. The answer is

---

[200] 王維　歸嵩山作　唐3

[201] 王維　漢江臨汎　唐3

[202] 劉長卿　尋南溪常山道人隱居　唐3

[203] 李商隱　北青蘿　唐3

[204] 崔塗　孤雁　唐3

that the usual range of metaphorical combinations of subjects and verbs in traditional Chinese verse is more limited than that encountered in Western literature. But we are now entering a vast domain that would take us beyond the scope of this book and will have to await a separate study. For now I can only urge caution in supposing that an initial phrase and its verb constitute a metaphor; only experience and the intelligent use of evidence from parallelism and semantic context can guide you here.

UNIT 29

Vocabulary

愛 *ài* /v/ love 61.9 (M 心 'heart')

曖曖 *ài ài* /v/ be dim in the distance 72.13 (M 日 'sun')

八 *bā* /q/ eight 12.0 (S)

本 *běn* /a/ originally, basically 75.1 (W)

辯 *biàn* /v/ explain, argue a case 160.14 (M 言 'speak')

草屋 *cǎo wū* /n/ thatched cottage

塵 *chén* /n/ dust, the the conventional world

塵網 *chén wǎng* /n/ the worldly trap, the rat race

池 *chí* /n/ pond 85.3 (M 氵 'water')

巔 *diān* /n/ top 46.19 (M 山 'mountain')

而 *ér* /n/ but 126.0 (S)

爾 *ěr* /v/ be thus, do this 89.10 (X)

樊 *fán* /n/ fence, cage 75.11 (S)

樊籠 *fán lóng* /n/ cage

方 *fāng* /v/ be square 70.0 (X)

吠 *fèi* /v/ bark 30.4 (W mouth + dog)

狗 *gǒu* /n/ dog 94.5 (M 犭 'dog')

戶 *hù* /n/ door; household

戶庭 *hù tíng* /n/ indoors and out

荒 *huāng* /n/ waste land, wilderness 140.6 (M ⁺⁺ 'plant')

羈 *jī* /v/ be trapped, caged, under restraint 122.19 (M 罒 'net')

228

雞 *jī* /n/ cock 172.10 (M 隹 'bird')

間 *jiān* /m/ space between two pillars as measure of size of house

境 *jìng* /n/ area, district 32.11 (M 土 'earth')

九 *jiǔ* /q/ nine 5.1 (S)

舊 *jiù* /v/ be old, original (= 故) 134.12 (S)

菊 *jú* /n/ chrysanthemum 140.8 (M ⁺⁺ 'plant')

開 *kāi* /v/ open up, cultivate for the first time

籬 *lí* /n/ fence 118.19 (M 竹 'bamboo')

李 *lǐ* /n/ plum 75.3 (X)

里 *lǐ* /n/ village 166.0 (X)

戀 *liàn* /v/ yearn for 61.19 (M 心 'heart')

籠 *lóng* /n/ cage 118.16 (M 竹 'bamboo')

廬 *lú* /n/ hut, cottage 53.16 (M 广 'house')

羅 *luó* /v/ spread over or across

馬 *mǎ* /n/ horse 187.0 (W)

畝 *mǔ* /m/ mu, one-sixth of an acre 102.5 (X)

偏 *piān* /v/ be out-of-the-way, off the beaten track, quiet 9.9 (M 亻 'person')

氣 *qì* /n/ breath, air, (here) mist, vapour breathed out by the ground

丘 *qiū* /n/ hill, mound 1.4 (X)

桑 *sāng* /n/ mulberry

少 *shào* /v/ be young

適 *shì* /v/ fit in with

室 *shì* /n/ room 40.6 (M 宀 'house')

守 *shǒu* /v/ keep, preserve 40.3 (M 宀 'house')

俗 *sú* /n/ the common herd, conventional people 9.7 (M 亻 'person')

堂 *táng* /n/ main reception-room opening on to steps down to courtyard 32.8 (M 土 'earth')

庭 *tíng* /n/ courtyard, garden

網 *wǎng* /n/ net 120.8 (M 糸 'silk')

屋 *wū* /n/ house 44.6 (X)

誤 *wù* /a/ by mistake 149.7 (M 言 'speak')

巷 *xiàng* /n/ lane 49.6 (S)

墟 *xū* /n/ market 32.12 (M 土 'earth')

墟 里 *xū lǐ* /n/ market-village

喧 *xuān* /n/ din 30.9 (M 口 'mouth')

煙 *yān* /n/ smoke

簷 *yán* /n/ eaves 118.13 (M 竹 'bamboo')

依 依 *yī yī* /v/ be clinging, rise slowly and lazily (of smoke)

蔭 *yīn* /v/ to shade 140.11 (M 艹 'plant')

悠 然 *yōu rán* /v/ be far off, in the distance

有 餘 *yǒu yú* /v/ there is plenty of, more than enough

餘 *yú* /q/ (after numeral) -odd, -plus, and more

榆 *yú* /n/ elm 75.9 (M 木 'tree')

淵 *yuān* /n/ deep pool (in river) 85.8 (M 氵 'water')

韻 *yùn* /n/ taste for 180.10 (M 音 'sound')

雜 *zá* /n/ din 172.10 (M 衣 'clothes', S 集, rearranged)

宅 *zhái* /n/ smallholding, property (house and land) 40.3 (M 宀 'house')

拙 *zhuó* /n/ simplicity, lack of sophistication 64.5 (S)

自 然 *zì rán* /n/ naturalness

Text 1[205]

Tao Yuanming (365–427): 'Back to the land, No. 1'

少無適俗韻 *shào wú shì sú* yùn*

性本愛丘山 *xìng běn ài qiū shān*

誤落塵網中 *wù luò chén wǎng zhōng*

一去十三年 *yī* qù shí* sān nián*

羈鳥戀舊林 *jī niǎo liàn jiù lín*

池魚思故淵 *chí yú sī gù yuān*

開荒南野際 *kāi huāng nán yě jì*

守拙歸園田 *shǒu zhuō* guī yuán tián*

方宅十餘畝 *fāng zhái* shí* yú mǔ*

草屋八九間 *cǎo wū* bā* jiǔ jiān*

榆柳蔭後簷 *yú liǔ yīn hòu yán*

桃李羅堂前 *táo lǐ luó táng qián*

曖曖遠人村 *ài ài yuǎn rén cūn*

依依墟里煙 *yī yī xū lǐ yān*

狗吠深巷中 *gǒu fèi shēn xiàng zhōng*

雞鳴桑樹巔 *jī míng sāng shù diān*

戶庭無塵雜 *hù tíng wú chén zá**

虛室有餘閑 *xū shì yǒu yú xián*

久在樊籠裏 *jiǔ zài fán lóng lǐ*

復得返自然 *fù dé* fǎn zì rán*

---

[205] 陶淵明　歸田園居五首，其一　漢6

Text 2[206]

Tao Yuanming (365–427): Drinking wine, No. 5

結廬在人境 *jié* lú zài rén jìng*
而無車馬喧 *ér wú chē mǎ xuān*
問君何能爾 *wèn jūn hé néng ěr*
心遠地自偏 *xīn yuǎn dì zì piān*

採菊東籬下 *cǎi jú* dōng lí xià*
悠然見南山 *yōu rán jiàn nán shān*
山氣日夕佳 *shān qì rì xī* jiā*
飛鳥相與還 *fēi niǎo xiāng yǔ huán*

此中有眞意 *cǐ zhōng yǒu zhēn yì*
欲辯已忘言 *yù biàn yǐ wàng yán*

Notes on the texts

These two poems by Tao Yuanming (also known as 陶潛 *táo qián*) are immortal favourites and the phrase 'chrysanthemums under the eastern fence' has passed into the language as a symbol of escape from public life to a peaceful rural retreat. We are not dealing here with escape into a monastery or hermitage in the mountains, but simply to a country cottage not too far from other human habitations. Poems on the same topic by later poets often contrive to convey the impression of complete isolation from the human race but this is of course a poetic convention. Here we have the ideal of escape firmly anchored in the real world, within reach of neighbours and markets.

The not-uncommon image of distant crowing cocks and barking dogs as a symbol of utopian contentment seems to originate with Chapter 80 of the Taoist work *Laozi* (*Laotzu, Taoteching*), where the inhabitants of two well-governed neighbouring states can hear each others' cocks crowing and dogs barking without evincing the slightest desire to visit the other state. Tao uses this image also in the preface to his poem on the Peach-blossom Source (see Unit 31).

---

[206]陶淵明 飲酒，其五 漢6

29.1 Ambiguity of function: noun-phrase after intransitive verb

As with initial noun-phrases in the preceding unit, there are the two possibilities here of noun-phrases following intransitive verbs being either the subject of the verb /...VS/ or an adverbial of place /...VA/. There are in addition two further possibilities: (a) that the verb is being used causatively and that the following noun is its object /...VO/, and (b) that the final noun-phrase is an adverbial of comparison.

(1) As the subject of the verb. This was dealt with and exemplified in Unit 14 under 'Post-verbal subject'.

(2) As an adverbial of place /SVA/.

泉聲咽危石　日色冷青松[207] *quán shēng yè wēi shí / rì sè lěng qīng sōng* 'A brook's voice sobs [between] precipitous rocks; / the sunlight is cold [on] the blue pines'.

日月低秦樹　乾坤繞漢宮[208] *rì yuè dī qín shù / qián kūn rào hàn gōng* 'Sun and moon are low [over] the trees of Qin; / celestial and chthonic powers surround the Han palace' (i.e. the Emperor's restored power is being acknowledged by the cosmic authorities). (乾 *qián* the power of Heaven; *kūn* 坤 the power of Earth; *rào* 繞 = 遶 .)

綠草垂石井[209] *lǜ cǎo chuí shí jǐng* 'Green grasses hang [over] the stone well'.

小樹開朝徑　長茸濕夜煙[210] *xiǎo shù kāi zhāo jìng / cháng róng shī yè yān* 'Little trees blossom [over] the morning paths; / long grasses are wet [in] the night mists'. (茸 *róng* grass.)

暮靄生深樹　斜陽下小樓[211] *mù ǎi shēng shēn shù / xié yáng xià xiǎo lóu* 'Evening mists grow [in] the deep trees; / the slanting sun descends [upon] the little towers'.

(3) As the object of a causative verb /SVO/.

驟雨清秋夜　金波耿玉繩[212] *zhòu yǔ qīng qiū yè / jīn bō gěng yù shéng* 'A sudden shower [makes] pure this autumn night; / the gilded waves [make] bright the jewel-strings (of stars)'.

---

[207] 王維　過香積寺　唐3

[208] 杜甫　投贈哥舒開府翰二十韻　杜3

[209] 李賀　泳懷二首，其一　全390

[210] 李賀　南園十三首，其十三　全390

[211] 杜牧　題揚州禪智寺　全522

[212] 杜甫　江邊星月二首，其一　杜21

威鳳高其翔[213] *wēi fèng gāo qí xiáng* 'The mighty phoenix [makes] high her soaring'. (威 *wēi* imposing, possessing authority; 鳳 *fèng* 'phoenix', the queen of the birds; 翔 *xiáng* soar.)

今日明人眼[214] *jīn rì míng rén yǎn* 'This day [makes] keen-sighted one's eyes'. (眼 *yǎn* eye.)

滄江急夜流[215] *cāng jiāng jí yè liú* 'The misty-blue river [makes] hurried its night flow' (i.e. speeds up its flow in the darkness) (滄 *cāng* = 蒼 when referring to water; 急 *jí* hurried, swift.)

(4) As an adverbial of comparison /SVA/.

徐關深水府　碣石小秋毫[216] *xú guān shēn shuǐ fǔ / jié shí xiǎo qiū háo* (Describing a flood) 'The Xu Pass is [as] deep [as] the water gods' palace; / Standing Stone Mountain is [as] small [as] an autumn hair'. (徐 *xú* an ancient state in east China; 府 *fǔ* palace; 毫 *háo* fine hair on an animal.)

When a qualitative verb is both preceded and followed by a noun-phrase /NvN/, it may be difficult to choose between these three possibilities. For instance, could the first example under (2) not mean 'A brook's voice makes the precipitous rocks sob; / the sunlight chills the blue pines'? No, because the causation clearly works in the opposite direction: the rocks confining the stream create the sobbing and the dark pines make the sunlight seem chill. The functional ambiguity can only be resolved by the usual means: a combination of semantic context, parallelism and experience of the kind of things that are said in Chinese verse. We shall look at this problem further in the next unit, in combination with ambiguity of vocabulary, by studying one particular quality-verb.

---

[213]杜甫　晦日尋崔戢李封　杜4

[214]杜甫　秦州雜逝二十首，其九　杜7

[215]孟浩然　宿桐廬江寄廣陵舊遊　全160

[216]杜甫　臨邑舍弟書至⋯　杜1

UNIT 30

Vocabulary

帶 *dài* /v/ to girdle

斷續 *duàn xù* /v/ (cease and continue =) be intermittent

覆 *fù* /v/ to cover 146.12 (M 襾 'cover')

梗 *gěng* /v/ to block 75.7 (M 木 'tree, wood')

故 *gù* /a/ since antiquity, all the time

荒 *huāng* /v/ be wild, tangled; abandoned and overgrown

皇 *huáng* /n/ emperor, ruler 106.4 (X)

機 *jī* /n/ machine, mechanical device 75.12 (M 木 'tree, wood')

機心 *jī xīn* /n/ a calculating mind, worldly cunning (see notes)

寂歷 *jì lì* /v/ be forlorn, desolate

踐 *jiàn* /v/ tread on 157.8 (M 足 'foot')

津 *jīn* /n/ cliff 85.6 (M 氵 'water')

驚 *jīng* /v/ to alarm, startle

鹿 *lù* /n/ deer 198.0 (W)

麋鹿 *mí lù* /n/ Père David's deer, *milu* 198.6 (M 鹿 'deer', S 米)

杪 *miǎo* /n/ tip of a branch 75.4 (M 木 'tree, wood')

杪秋 *miǎo qiū* /n/ late autumn, the end of autumn

民 *mín* /n/ people, subjects 83.1 (X)

平津 *píng jīn* /n/ steep-sided plateau

上皇 *shàng huáng* /n/ (legendary) earliest rulers

疏 *shū* /v/ be sparse 103.7 (X)

235

修 *xiū* /v/ be tall 9.8 (M 彡 'stripes', S 攸, rearranged)

續 *xù* /v/ continue 120.15 (M 糸 'silk')

榛 *zhēn* /n/ thicket 75.10 (M 木 'tree, wood')

Text 1[217]

Bo Daoyou (fifth century): 'A poem inspired by gathering herbs in the mountains'

連峰數千里 *lián fēng shù qiān lǐ*

修林帶平津 *xiū lín dài píng jīn*

雲過遠山翳 *yún guò yuǎn shān yì*

風至梗荒榛 *fēng zhì gěng huāng zhēn*

茅茨隱不見 *máo cí yǐn bù jiàn*

雞鳴知有人 *jī míng zhī yǒu rén*

閒步踐其徑 *xián bù jiàn qí jìng*

處處見遺薪 *chù chù jiàn yí xīn*

始知百代下 *shǐ zhī bǎi dài xià*

故有上皇民 *gù yǒu shàng huáng mín*

Text 2[218]

Liu Zongyuan (773–819): 'Walking through an abandoned village in South Gorge on an autumn morning'

杪秋霜露重 *miǎo qiū shuāng lù zhòng*

---

[217] 帛道猷 陵峰采藥觸興爲詩 古A5

[218] 柳宗元 秋曉行南谷經荒村 全352

晨起行幽谷 *chén qǐ xíng yōu gǔ*

黃葉覆溪橋 *huáng yè fù xī qiáo*

荒村唯古木 *huāng cūn wéi gǔ mù*

寒花疏寂歷 *hán huā shū jì lì*

幽泉微斷續 *yōu quán wēi duàn xù*

機心久已忘 *jī xīn jiǔ yǐ wàng*

何事驚麋鹿 *hé shì jīng mí lù*

Note on Text 2

The expression 機心 *jī xīn* comes from the mainly-Taoist anthology *Zhuangzi* (*Chuangtzu*), Chapter 12, where the use of a well-sweep instead of human power for drawing water from a cistern is condemned because it is a mechanical contraption, an artificial replacement of natural human effort, a degrading attempt to cheat Nature for a cheap advantage. Liu supposes that his leaving worldly designs behind and reverting to a natural innocence would be sensed by wild animals, who would trust him because they knew they had nothing to fear from him, like St Francis of Assisi's birds.

30.1 Ambiguity of function: noun-phrases with the verb *yìng*

The sections on ambiguity in the last four units have been leading up to this unit, where we shall see all these ambiguities of meaning and function combined in the varied behaviour of the quality-verb 映 *yìng*.

We have already met the noun 影 *yǐng*, meaning a light or dark contrasting image and also a reflection; 映 is the corresponding verb and no doubt etymologically related to it.

(1) The simplest meaning is 'be bright, shine, gleam'.

渭水天邊映[219] *wèi shuǐ tiān biān yìng* 'The River Wei gleams on the edge of the sky'. (渭 *wèi* R. Wei.)

Used adverbially, it means 'brightly'.

妓堂花映發[220] *jì táng huā yìng fā* 'Around the entertainments-room the blossom flourishes brightly'. (妓 *jì* female entertainers, i.e. musicians, singers, dancers.)

---

[219] 王維　奉和聖製登降聖觀… 　王 11

[220] 孟浩然　宴張記室宅　全 160

It seems likely that 英 *yīng* 'flower' is derived from this use, meaning 'the bright one', just as peach-blossom is sometimes referred to simply as 紅 *hóng* 'the red one'.

(2) It can be combined with a verb of opposite meaning in the phrases 隱映 *yǐn yìng*, 掩映 *yǎn yìng* and 杳映 *yǎo yìng* (literally 'now hidden, now visible') to mean 'half-seen, showing intermittently'. (Note that some modern dictionaries understand 掩映 *yǎn yìng* as 映 *yìng* alone in the sense of 'to contrast with'.)

滄江大如綖　隱映入遠天 [221] *cāng jiāng dà rú yán / yǐn yìng rù yuǎn tiān* 'The misty-blue river is as big as a ribbon(?), / glimpsed here and there as it enters the distant sky'. (綖 *yán* is the flat black top of the mortar-board style ancient official hat, also written 延 . I suspect that the poet supposed it to be a word for 'ribbon' or 'string' since it consists of 延 'extend' plus 糸 'silk'.)

星月揜 (or 掩) 映雲朣朧 [222] *xīng yuè yǎn yìng yún tóng lóng* 'Stars and moon show intermittently through the veiling cloud'. (朣朧 *tóng lóng* (of mist or cloud) to veil or render indistinct.)

赤墀櫻桃枝　隱映銀絲籠 [223] *chì chí yīng táo zhī / yǐn yìng yín sī lǒng* 'Cherry-branches by the red steps (in the imperial palace): / now hiding, now revealing [the steps], the silver fronds enfold them'. (赤 *chì* red; 墀 *chí* steps; 櫻桃 *yīng táo* cherry.)

漸入空濛迷鳥道　寧知掩映有人家 [224] *jiàn rù kōng méng mí niǎo dào / nìng zhī yǎn yìng yǒu rén jiā* (Of a painting of the fisherman discovering the Peach-blossom Source) 'Gradually he entered a path where an isolating haze made [even] the birds lose their bearings; / to his surprise, half-seen [through the haze] there were human dwellings'. (迷 *mí* lose one's way, become confused; 寧知 *nìng zhī* how could he know that …, he could not have foreseen that ….)

山河杳映春雲外　城闕參差曉樹中 [225] *shān hé yǎo yìng chūn yún wài / chéng què cēn cī xiǎo shù zhōng* 'The hills and rivers are glimpsed here and there beyond the spring clouds; / the city walls show unevenly among the dawn trees'.

(3) As a causative verb it means 'to cause to be bright, illuminate, light up'.

---

[221] 獨孤及　初晴抱琴登馬退山　全246

[222] 韓愈　謁衡嶽廟… 全338

[223] 杜甫　往在　杜16

[224] 權德輿　桃源篇　全329

[225] 楊巨源　春日題龍門香山寺　全333

青天白日映樓臺 [226] *qīng tiān bái rì yìng lóu tái* 'A white sun in a blue sky lights up the tower'.

微月映皓鶴 [227] *wēi yuè yìng hào hè* (Of an immortal) 'A faint moon illuminated his gleaming-white crane'. (皓 *hào* brilliantly white.)

晨光映遠岫 [228] *chén guāng yìng yuǎn xiù* 'The dawn light illuminates the distant peaks'. (岫 *xiù* peak.)

殘霞飛丹映江草 [229] *cán xiá fēi dān yìng jiāng cǎo* 'The floating vermilion of the last of the sunset clouds colours the riverside grasses'.

In this use it can also be applied metaphorically to someone's public image:

紫綬映暮年 [230] *zǐ shòu yìng mù nián* 'The purple ribbon (badge of senior military governor) made glorious his twilight years'. (紫 *zǐ* purple; 綬 *shòu* ribbon, cordon.)

(4) In a 'passive' use of this causative sense it means 'be illuminated by, reflect the light of, be bright in the light of'.

衡山碧色映朝陽 [231] *héng shān bì sè yìng zhāo yáng* 'The green colour of Mount Heng is illuminated by (or 'reflects' or 'is bright in') the morning sun'. (衡 *héng* Mt Heng.)

As well as functioning as a main verb in this sense, it often occurs in a subordinate (adverbial) capacity. This may be in position 1:

映日杏花明 [232] *yìng rì xìng huā míng* 'In the sunlight the apricot-blossom is bright'. (杏 *xìng* apricot.)

Or it may be in position 2:

寒山映月在湖中 [233] *hán shān yìng yuè zài hú zhōng* 'The cold hills, illuminated by the moonlight, are [reflected] in the lake'.

A more complex use in this position is where moonlight reflected from snow provides an indirect source of illumination:

映雪讀書徒白首 [234] *yìng xuě dú shū tú bái shǒu* 'Studying by the light from the snow only [leaves one in the end with] a white head'. (This is a reference to the story of the industrious student who studied by snowlight for

[226] 韓愈　同水部張員外⋯　全344

[227] 杜甫　昔遊　杜20

[228] 杜甫　甘林　杜19

[229] 李白　訓殷明佐見贈五雲裘歌　李8

[230] 杜甫　故右僕射相國⋯　杜16

[231] 司空曙　送曲山人之衡州　全292

[232] 權德輿　雜言和常州李員外副使⋯，其一　全328

[233] 嚴維　酬諸公宿鏡水宅　全263

[234] 權德輿　旅館雪晴⋯　全328

lack of money for oil or candles. Whatever we achieve in life through hard work, we end up with the infirmities of old age.)

(5) Followed by an adverbial of place, it may mean 'stand out bright against, be light against a dark background'.

早梅發高樹　迴映楚天碧 [235] *zǎo méi fā gāo shù / jiǒng yìng chǔ tiān bì* 'The early plum-blossom bursts out on the high trees, / distantly bright against the blue of the Chu sky'. (早 *zǎo* early; 迴 *jiǒng* distant; 楚 *chǔ* Chu, ancient state south of Yangtse.)

映階碧草自春色　隔葉黃鸝空好音 [236] *yìng jiē bì cǎo zì chūn sè / gé yè huáng lí kōng hǎo yīn* 'Bright against the steps, the green grasses [create] unaided the colours of spring; / behind the leaves the golden orioles [sing] unheard their lovely songs'. (階 *jiē* steps; 鸝 *lí* oriole.)

閑花滿巖谷　瀑水映杉松 [237] *xián huā mǎn yán gǔ / pù shuǐ yìng shān sōng* 'Untroubled flowers fill the cliff[-sided] valley; / the waters of the cataract are bright against the firs and pines'. (巖 *yán* cliff; 瀑 *pù* waterfall; 杉 *shān* fir.)

映林同落雪　拂水狀翻潮 [238] *yìng lín tóng luò xuě / fú shuǐ zhuàng fān cháo* (Of flying egrets) 'Bright against the woods, they look like falling snow; / skimming the water, they resemble the tumbling (= breaking) tide'. (狀 *zhuàng* resemble; 翻 *fān* turn over.)

(6) This literal meaning is extended to human beings and their achievements: 'be outstanding among / in'. It may be that it was from this use of 映 that 英 *yīng* in the sense of 'outstanding man, hero' was derived.

向來映當時　豈獨勸後世 [239] *xiàng lái yìng dāng shí / qǐ dú quàn hòu shì* 'He was always outstanding in his own times, / not just an encouragement to later generations'. (當時 *dāng shí* the time in question; 勸 *quàn* encourage.)

我志在刪述　垂輝映千春 [240] *wǒ zhì zài shán shù / chuí huī yìng qiān chūn* 'My ambition is confined to editing and transmitting [ancient values], / that their lasting glory may shine through a thousand springtimes'. (志 *zhì* will, ambition; 刪 *shān* delete, edit; 垂 *chuí* to last.)

---

[235] 柳宗元　早梅　全353

[236] 杜甫　蜀相　唐4

[237] 王維　韋侍郎山居　王3

[238] 李端　白鷺詠　全284

[239] 杜甫　贈秘書監江夏李公邕　杜16

[240] 李白　古風五十九首，其一　李2

(7) The opposite kind of contrast is also met, though less commonly: 'stand out dark against a light background, be silhouetted against' (especially sky and clouds).

鼇身映天黑 [241] *áo shēn yìng tiān hēi* 'The giant turtle's body will be black against the sky'. (鼇 *áo* mythical giant turtle; 黑 *hēi* black.)

萬里飛蓬映天過 [242] *wàn lǐ fēi péng yìng tiān guō* 'Tumbleweed passes, flying a myriad miles, silhouetted against the sky'. (蓬 *péng* tumbleweed.)

裊裊枯藤萬丈懸 萬丈懸 拂秋水 映秋天 [243] *niǎo niǎo kū téng wàn zhàng xuán / wàn zhàng xuán / fú qiū shuǐ / yìng qiū tiān* 'Gracefully swaying, the withered vines hang down a myriad fathoms, / hang down a myriad fathoms, / brushing against the autumn floodwater, / silhouetted against the autumn sky'. (裊裊 *niǎo niǎo* graceful and sinuous; 枯 *kū* dried up, withered; 藤 *téng* vine, liana; 丈 *zhàng* three metres.)

(8) Colour-contrasts, whether attractive or not, also use 映. First, some attractive ones:

千里鶯啼綠映紅 [244] *qiān lǐ yīng tí lǜ yìng hóng* 'For a thousand miles the orioles sing, and green [leaves] contrast with pink [blossom]'.

映葉朱唇似花發 [245] *yìng yè zhū chún sì huā fā* 'Bright against the leaves, her red lips look like flowers blooming'. (唇 *chún* lips.)

融融白玉輝 映我青蛾眉 [246] *róng róng bái yù huī / yìng wǒ qīng é méi* 'Harmoniously the splendour of my white jades / sets off my blue[-kohled] moth[-antenna] eyebrows'. (融融 *róng róng* harmoniously; 蛾 *é* moth; 眉 *méi* eyebrow.)

But, equally, the contrast may be unattractive for some reason:

麗服映頹顏 朱燈照華髮 [247] *lì fú yìng tuí yán / zhū dēng zhào huá fà* 'My splendid [official] robes contrast with my haggard face; / the red lamp[-light] shines on my greying hair'. (麗 *lì* splendid; 頹 *tuí* gaunt, haggard, ageing; 顏 *yán* face; 華 *huá* pepper-and-salt, greying; 髮 *fà* hair.)

[241] 王維 送秘書晁堅還日本國 王12

[242] 杜甫 復陰 杜21

[243] 任華 懷素上人草書歌 全261

[244] 杜牧 江南春絕句 全522

[245] 歐陽詹 汝川行 全349

[246] 李白 擬古 李6

[247] 王維 冬夜書懷 王5

多事紅花映白花 [248] *duō shì hóng huā yìng bái huā* 'I can't cope with the contrast between red blossom and white' (the red reminds him of the rosy cheeks of youth and the white of the white hair of approaching old age). (多事 *duō shì* have too much to handle, feel overwhelmed.)

(9) The idea of contrast, particularly in subordinate ('prepositional') use, is often so weakened that 映 actually means little more than 'against' (a background), or even 'by, close to, at'. In such cases it is often parallelled by other 'prepositional' verbs of location or movement such as 連 *lián* 'connected to', 接 *jiē* 'touching', 當 *dāng* 'right in front of, at', 逐 *zhú* 'following, with', 經 *jīng* 'passing through', 過 *guò* 'crossing', 穿 *chuān* 'going through', 鄰 *lín* 'next to', 對 *duì* 'facing' or 垂 *chuí* 'hanging down over'.

映花鶯上下　過水蝶飛揚 [249] *yìng huā yīng shàng xià / guō shuǐ dié fēi yáng* 'Among the blossom the orioles rise and dip; / over the water the butterflies flutter and soar'. (蝶 *dié* butterfly; 揚 *yáng* be lifted on the breeze.)
　紫葛垂苔壁　青菰映柳絲 [250] *zǐ gé chuí tái bì / qīng gū yìng liǔ sī* 'Purplevine hangs down over the mossy cliff; / wild rice grows against the willow-fronds'. (紫葛 *zǐ gé* Vitis coignetiae; 青菰 *qīng gū* Zizania latifolia.)

(10) With water as the subject, it may mean 'reflect something above it'.

明湖映天光　徹底見秋色 [251] *míng hú yìng tiān guāng / chè dǐ jiàn qiū sè* 'The bright lake reflects the light of the sky; / down to the bottom we see the autumn colours'. (徹 *chè* go right down to; 底 *dǐ* bottom.)

　碧水映丹霞 [252] *bì shuǐ yìng dān xiá* 'The green water reflects the vermilion sunset clouds'.
　揚子澄江映晚霞 [253] *yáng zǐ chéng jiāng yìng wǎn xiá* 'The Yangtse's limpid river reflects the evening red clouds'. (揚子 *yáng zǐ* Yangtse.)
　清泉映疏松 [254] *qīng quán yìng shū sōng* 'The pure brook reflects the sparse pines'. (疏 *shū* sparse.)
　寒塘映衰草 [255] *hán táng yìng shuāi cǎo* 'The chill pond reflects the withered grasses'. (塘 *táng* pond; 衰 *shuāi* wither, fade.)

[248]杜甫　江畔獨步尋花七絕句，其三　杜10

[249]李端　與鄭錫遊春　全285

[250]李端　暮春尋終南柳處士　全286

[251]李白　秋登巴陵望洞庭　李21

[252]李端　山下泉　全285

[253]劉商　白沙宿竇常宅觀妓　全304

[254]李白　望月有懷　李23

(11) With water as an adverbial of place in position 3, it may mean 'is reflected in'.

門前月色映橫塘 [256] *mén qián yuè sè yìng héng táng* 'Before my door the moonlit scene is reflected in the crosswise pond'. (橫 *héng* lie crosswise, across the field of vision; 塘 *táng* pond.)

雪映龍潭水更清 [257] *xuě yìng lóng tán shuǐ gèng qīng* 'With the snow reflected in the dragon-pool, the water looks even purer'.

In the following example the 映浦 *yìng pǔ* is adjectival, qualifying 檣 *qiáng*.

天連映浦檣 [258] *tiān lián yìng pǔ qiáng* 'The sky touches our mast reflected in the shallows'. (檣 *qiáng* mast.)

(12) The uses given above cover most of the occurrences of 映. But even these categories are not clearly unambiguous, for example:

一樹紅花映綠波 [259] *yī shù hóng huā yìng lǜ bō*. Is this 'A treeful of red blossom is reflected in the green waves' or '…contrasts with the green waves'? Or does it combine both of these and mean '…is reflected in the green waves, creating a contrast with them'?

The full extent of the combined ambiguities of meaning and structure of /N 映 N/ may be seen in the following summary of the above:

/SVO/
    (3) illuminate
    (10) reflect

/SVA/
    (4) be illuminated by
    (5) be bright against
    (6) be outstanding among

---

[255] 王維　奉寄韋太守陟　王2

[256] 劉方平　烏棲曲二首，其二　全251

[257] 李端　送皎然上人歸山　全286

[258] 耿湋　津亭有懷　全268

[259] 楊巨源　臨水看花　全333

(7) be dark against
(8) contrast in colour with
(9) be against, close to, by, at
(11) be reflected in

As we have so often seen in this course, ambiguities of this kind cannot be solved by grammatical analysis, only by common sense and imagination, and even then there is no guarantee of a solution.

UNIT 31

31.1 The Peach-blossom Source

The peach in China has four symbolic values:

(1) Peach-wood in various forms deters evil spirits and disasters in general; this may be because the Chinese words for 'peach' (桃) and 'flee' (逃) sound identical (*táo*).

(2) The fruit is associated with marriage and consequently with offspring ('fruit of the womb') and brothers, and eventually with disciples as quasi-children; the first literary example of this association with marriage is a poem [260] of perhaps the seventh century BC. Could this be because the pink of the blossom or the red of the fruit suggested the colour of sex-organs?

(3) The peach is associated with the cheeks of young women, the bloom of youth, and, presumably via this, it becomes the fruit of everlasting youth and longevity.

(4) The blossom is one of the signs of spring, the second lunar month (April or May) being the 'peach moon'. Spring, in turn, often symbolizes youth, so reinforcing the association with eternal youth, and also birth, so linking in with the marriage theme.

The legend of the Peach-blossom Source consists of two distinct elements: the lost utopia and the dreamlike journey to it. The utopia is an ordinary, down-to-earth place, a survival of an imaginary prehistoric golden age of peaceful, idyllic village life, with the well-worn image of cocks crowing and dogs barking. The journey is something very different, something from a dream or a vision. The lost land is discovered by accident and cannot be found again intentionally ('no way back'), even though the route has been marked; it is reached, like the womb, through a narrow opening at the source of a stream; and it is approached through a long, pink tunnel of peach-blossom. The journey has no literary antecedents known to me, and it is my feeling that it is inspired by a very personal vision of the quality of Blake's 'Tyger' or Coleridge's 'Ancient Mariner'. This may explain why the longer poems that have been based on it have (in my opinion at least) on the whole a very lack-lustre, pedestrian quality, as if inspiration never strikes the same spot twice.

The heart of the legend is about refugees from tyranny who became cut off from the rest of the world, an unremarkable story in itself; the outer part of the legend is the mysterious, unrepeatable journey replete with symbolism. One would have thought that this in itself would have been enough, but Tao

---

[260] 無名氏 桃夭 詩6

245

Yuanming himself and several later poets felt the need to embroider it in verse in different ways.

First, a translation of the legend as told by Tao Yuanming in his prose preface to his poem:

> In the Taiyuan reign-period (376–397) a fisherman of Wuling followed a stream, losing count of the distance. He suddenly came to a grove of peach-blossom extending several hundred paces along the banks, with no other kinds of trees among them, but with fresh and lovely fragrant herbs and fallen blossom in bright profusion beneath them. The fisherman was struck with wonder, but he went on in order to find the end of the grove. It ended at the source of the stream, and there he encountered a cliff with a small opening in it. He thought he could see daylight through it, so he left his boat and entered the opening; at first it was very narrow and he could barely pass through, but after a few dozen paces he suddenly came out into the open.
>
> He was on a level plain with neat cottages, with fertile fields and fine ponds, with mulberries and bamboo and all such things. Paths criss-crossed between the fields, crowing cocks and barking dogs answered one another. Among these things peasant men and women came and went, all dressed in clothes just like the people outside; old and young alike were happy and contented.
>
> When they saw the fisherman they were astonished and asked him where he had come from; he answered all their questions. Then they invited him home, set out wine, killed a chicken and prepared a meal. When the rest of the villagers heard about the visitor they all came to question him.
>
> They said that their ancestors had fled from the civil war of Chin times (third century BC) and had brought their families and neighbours to this isolated place; they had never left it and so had become cut off from the world outside. They asked him what dynasty now ruled; it turned out that they knew nothing of the Han dynasty, let alone of the Wei and Tsin. The fisherman told them in detail everything he knew, which made them sigh.
>
> The rest of the villagers all invited him to their homes and entertained him with wine and food. After staying a few days he said goodbye; the villagers said there was no need to tell people outside about them. After he had emerged he found his boat and returned the way he had come, marking the route at various points.
>
> When he reached his prefecture he went to see the prefect and told his story. The prefect at once sent people to follow his route, seeking out the signs he had left, but they went astray and could not find the way again.
>
> An unworldly gentleman of Nanyang, named Liu Ziji was excited to hear of it and planned to go there, but his plan was never carried

out, for he soon afterwards fell ill and died. After that no one else tried to find the way there.

Next, a translation of Tao Yuanming's own poem on the legend (I am not including the Chinese text, which would impose unreasonable vocabulary burdens at this stage of the course). This poem has no magical journey, only the bucolic idyll, which is reminiscent of his poems about retirement to the countryside in the previous unit. He provides his lost-landers with no taxes, no calendar, no learning: the complexities of agriculture and social existence look after themselves, as in a child's view of the world. These are not real people, whereas those of the legend might well be. It is hard to believe that Tao himself created the legend since he is either unaware of, or uninterested in, the magical element and its implications. His final couplet is an echo of the *Nineteen Old Poems*, the image of flying away like a swan. Or could it be the image of a flying 'immortal'?

Example text[261]

Tao Yuanming (365–427): 'The Peach-blossom Source'

When Chin disrupted the natural order,
men of ability fled the world;
the Four Greybeards retired to Mount Shang,
these people likewise took their leave.
Their departing footprints gradually faded,
their path was overgrown and lost.

They urged one another to till the soil
and seek their place of rest with the sun.
Bamboo and mulberry gave generous shade,
beans and millet grew in their season.
In spring their silkworms gave long silk,
in autumn their harvests went untaxed.

Sharing secret untrodden ways,
linked by the voices of roosters and dogs,
their rites were those of ancient times,
their dress untouched by fashion's change.
The children sang their carefree songs,

---

[261] 陶淵明　桃花源詩　漢6；古6

the white-haired strolled to visit friends.

Flowering told of warmth to come,
leaf-fall warned of biting winds;
they had no calendar to guide them,
but still the seasons made the year.
Contentment was theirs, and joy abundant:
what need of learning to trouble their heads?

Five hundred years was this marvel hid,
till the day their magical world was bared;
but deep minds and shallow are different streams,
and soon they were safely forgotten once more.

May I ask those people still trapped in this world:
how can they go deep beyond dust and din?
I wish I could tread the gentle breeze,
be lifted high to seek my kind.

The above is intended as a background to the texts of this unit and any other
references you may find to peach-blossom in other poems.

Vocabulary

別 *bié* /a/ separately, elsewhere (but 'say goodbye' in the first poem)

船 *chuán* /n/ boat 137.5 (M 舟 'boat')

答 *dá* /v/ to reply 118.6 (S)

當 時 *dāng shí* /n/ that time (in the past)

蕩 *dàng* /v/ to row 140.12 (S)

洞 *dòng* /n/ cave 85.6 (M 氵 'water')

渡 頭 *dù tóu* /n/ ferry-landing

非 *fēi* /v/ is not, are not 175.0 (X)

老 子 *lǎo zǐ* /n/ Laozi (Laotzu)

吏 *lì* /n/ an official 30.3 (X)

欹 *qī* /v/ to lean 65.8 (M 支 'support')

橋 *qiáo* /n/ bridge 75.12 (M 木 'tree, wood')

曲 *qǔ* /n/ song

三日 *sān rì* /n/ the Shangsi festival

石磯 *shí jī* /n/ crag overhanging a river 112.0, 112.12 (M 石 'stone')

孫 *sūn* /n/ grandchild, descendant 39.7 (M 子 'child')

昔 *xī* /n/ days gone by (anything from yesterday to antiquity!) 72.4 (M 日 'sun')

仙 *xiān* /n/ an immortal 9.3 (M 亻 'person')

笑 *xiào* /v/ laugh, smile 118.4 (S)

歇 *xiē* /v/ to pause for a rest 76.9 (M 欠 'gape')

信 *xìn* /v/ believe 9.7 (M 言 'speak')

尋 *xún* /v/ seek, go to visit (not necessarily successfully!) 41.9 (X)

窅然 *yǎo rán* /a/ mysteriously, into secret depths 116.5 (M 穴 'hole')

意 *yì* /n/ purpose 61.9 (M 心 'heart')

隱隱 *yǐn yǐn* /v/ be dimly seen, faint

永和 *yǒng hé* /n/ 'Everlasting Harmony', the reign-period 345–356 和: 30.5 (M 口 'mouth')

猶 *yóu* /a/ still, yet 94.9 (S)

余 *yú* /n/ I, me 9.5 (S)

園吏 *yuán lì* /n/ superintendent of parks, gardens and orchards

直 *zhí* /a/ all the way 109.3 (X)

株 *zhū* /n/ tree-trunk, measure-word for trees 75.6 (M 木 'tree, wood')

莊 *zhuāng* /n/ estate, villa 140.7 (M ⺾ 'plant')

Text 1[262]

Zhang Jie (late ninth century): 'The Peach[-blossom] Source'

絕壁相攲是洞門 *jué* bì xiāng qī shì dòng mén*

昔人從此入仙源 *xī* rén cóng cǐ rù xiān yuán*

數株花下逢珠翠 *shù zhū huā xià féng zhū cuì*

半曲歌中老子孫 *bàn qǔ gē zhōng lǎo zǐ sūn*

別後自疑園吏夢 *bié* hòu zì yí yuán lì mèng*

歸來誰信釣翁言 *guī lái shuí xìn diào wēng yán*

山前空有無情水 *shān qián kōng yǒu wú qíng shuǐ*

猶遶當時碧樹村 *yóu rào dāng shí bì shù cūn*

Text 2[263]

Chang Jian (early eighth century): 'Going to visit Li the Ninth's estate on the Shangsi festival'

雨歇楊林東渡頭 *yǔ xiē* yáng lín dōng dù tóu*

永和三日蕩輕舟 *yǒng hé sān rì dàng qīng zhōu*

故人家在桃花岸 *gù rén jiā zài táo huā àn*

直到門前溪水流 *zhí* dào mén qián xī shuǐ liú*

---

[262] 章碣　桃源　全 669

[263] 常建　三日尋李九莊　全 144

Text 3[264]

Zhang Xu (seventh to eighth centuries): 'Peach-blossom stream'

隱隱飛橋隔野煙 *yǐn yǐn fēi qiáo gé* yě yān*

石磯西畔問漁船 *shí* jī xī pàn wèn yú chuán*

桃花盡日隨流水 *táo huā jìn rì suí liú shuǐ*

洞在清溪何處邊 *dòng zài qīng xī hé chù biān*

Text 4[265]

Li Bai (701–762): 'An answer from the hills'

問余何意棲碧山 *wèn yú hé yì qī bì shān*

笑而不答心自閑 *xiào ér bù dá* xīn zì xián*

桃花流水窅然去 *táo huā liú shuǐ yǎo rán qù*

別有天地非人間 *bié* yǒu tiān dì fēi rén jiān*

Notes on Text 1

Here the peach-blossom legend is given a Taoist slant in two ways. In the first half the inhabitants of the lost valley are made into descendants of the supposed author of the Taoist work *Laozi*, to whom neo-Taoists centuries later ascribed the status of founder of Taoism, just as Confucius was regarded as the founder of the various later systems of thought called 'Confucianism'. In the second half, reference is made to the best-known dream of Chinese literature, the Butterfly Dream. It comes from the Taoist anthology *Zhuangzi* [266]and recounts how the supposed author, Zhuang Zhou (once a superintendent of gardens) dreamed he was a butterfly. When he awoke he wondered whether he

---

[264]張旭　桃花溪　唐6

[265]李白　山中問答　李19

[266]莊子2

was a man who had just dreamed he was a butterfly or whether he was really a butterfly who was now dreaming he was a man.

What are we to make of this admixture of Taoism in a legend of escape? The early Taoism of *Zhuangzi* was about survival in a dangerous world by avoiding being employed as a minister or other public servant, in other words by using the world to one's own personal advantage. The later *Laozi* is about the art of kingship using unconventional means. Both books use highly imaginative language for symbolic purposes, but from the Han dynasty onwards not-so-imaginative neo-Taoists tried to reinterpret them as guides to mystical or even magical escape from the world. The names of their putative authors and the word 'Taoism' itself acquired very different associations. The Tao (道 *dào* 'way') was no longer the way to survive in the human world or a way of ruling a country 'from below', but the ways to achieve immortality and escape from this world altogether.

In later popular religion things went a stage farther: in the novel *Xiyouji* we find Laozi in Heaven making cinnabar pills, while the gods renew their immortality by eating celestial peaches.

In this poem the author seems to be using 'Laozi's descendants' to mean people who have not just taken refuge in a lost valley but who have escaped into another dimension, another reality, and become 'immortals'. The mention of the Butterfly Dream reinforces this idea if one twists it into an allegory of being transported to another reality in a dreaming state. Why does the poet refer to Zhuangzi as the 園 吏 *yuán lì* 'superintendent of gardens' here? I have a suspicion that it is to suggest that the peach-orchard in the lost valley was producing the same kind of peaches of immortality as those eaten in Heaven and that Zhuangzi, as one of the founders of Taoism and hence supposedly an expert on immortality, was in some sense in charge of the orchard and hence bestowing magical qualities upon the peaches. The 'emerald-trees' are not just beautifully green trees, but are the jewel-trees of the Taoist paradise ruled over by 西王母 Xiwangmu, the Mother-Queen of the West.

Notes on Text 2

Here the peach-blossom theme is combined with another one connected with the same time of year: the 上巳 *shàng sì* festival, celebrated on the third day of the third moon. Its purpose was to dispel evil influences and it is closely linked with water (hence the boat trip). Whatever its unknown original form, whether as lustration or as river-sacrifice, it developed for the literati into a kind of literary picnic where wine-cups were floated along an artificial curved channel, then drunk from, followed by the composition and recitation of poems to celebrate the occasion.

The event referred to in this poem was one which occurred four centuries earlier, the celebration of the Shangsi festival by forty-one eminent literati in the year 353 at Lanting on the north side of Mt Kuaiji in present-day Zhejiang.

The great calligrapher Wang Xizhi was there to brush his most famous piece of calligraphy extolling the distinguished company, the beautiful setting and the glorious weather.

The third and fourth poems speak for themselves.

UNIT 32

Vocabulary

欸 乃 *ǎi nǎi* (onomatope) creak-creak! (sound of oars) 76.7 (M 欠 'gape'); 4.1 (S)

楚 *chǔ* /n/ an ancient state, the Sinicized area south of the Yangtse, centred on present-day Hubei province 75.9 (M 林 'woods')

斗 *dǒu* /n/ peck-measure 68.0 (W)

竿 *gān* /n/ pole, fishing-rod 118.3 (M 竹 'bamboo')

迴 *huí* /v/ turn around 162.6 (M 辶 'go')

際 *jì* /n/ edge; /v/ be on the edge of 170.11 (M 阝 'hills')

口 *kǒu* /n/ mouth 30.0 (W)

瀰 漫 *mí màn* /v/ be hazy, vague, obscure, uncertain 85.17, 85.11 (M 氵 'water')

南 斗 *nán dǒu* /n/ Southern Dipper constellation (part of Sagittarius)

偶 *ǒu* /v/ meet by chance 9.9 (S)

且 *qiě* /a/ in fact 1.4 (S)

燃 *rán* /v/ burn; ignite, to light 86.12 (M 火 'fire')

溶 溶 *róng róng* /v/ swirl and merge 85.10 (M 氵 'water')

叟 *sǒu* /n/ old man 29.8 (M 父 'father')

爲 *wéi* /v/ be, become 87.8 (S)

湘 *xiāng* /n/ the river Xiang in Hunan province 85.9 (M 氵 'water')

銷 *xiāo* /v/ melt away, disperse, vanish 167.7 (M 金 'metal')

巖 *yán* /n/ cliff 46.20 (M 山 'mountain')

漁 *yú* /n/ fishing 85.11 (M 氵 'water')

中流 *zhōng liú* /n/ midstream

轉 *zhuǎn* /v/ turn, turn into

Text 1[267]

Liu Zongyuan (773–819): 'The old fisherman'

漁翁夜傍西巖宿 *yú wēng yè bàng xī yán sù*

曉汲清湘燃楚竹* *xiǎo jí* qīng xiāng rán chǔ zhú**

煙銷日出不見人 *yān xiāo rì chū* bù jiàn rén*

欸乃一聲山水綠 *ǎi nǎi yī* shēng shān shuǐ lǜ*

迴看天際下中流 *huí kān tiān jì xià zhōng liú*

巖上無心雲相逐 *yán shàng wú xīn yún xiāng zhú**

Text 2[268]

Qiwu Qian (early eighth century): 'Drifting on the Ruoye Stream in spring'

幽意無斷絕 *yōu yì wú duàn jué**

此去隨所偶 *cǐ qù suí suǒ ǒu*

晚風吹行舟 *wǎn fēng chuī xíng zhōu*

花路入溪口 *huā lù rù xī kǒu*

際夜轉西壑 *jì yè zhuǎn xī hè*

隔山望南斗 *gé* shān wàng nán dǒu*

潭煙飛溶溶 *tán yān fēi róng róng*

---

[267]柳宗元　漁翁　唐2；柳43

[268]綦毋潛　春泛若耶溪　唐1

林月低向後 *lín yuè dī xiàng hòu*

生事且瀰漫 *shēng shì qiě mí màn*
願爲持竿叟 *yuàn wéi chí gān sǒu*

Notes on Text 1

Here again we have the archetypal lone angler, symbol of the retired gentleman, except that this time he is not sitting hunched miserably amid the snow but is floating carefree in a magical green world in the sunny South.

The first three lines seem straightforward enough, but the fourth suddenly plunges us into another dimension, though I find it impossible to say how. It is as if a single creak of an oar has transported us from the static world of the first three lines into both movement and a sudden awareness of the all-enveloping greenness, a green tunnel, almost.

The poet and critic Su Dongpo (1036–1101), who admired this poem for its novel charm, expressed the opinion (somewhat condescendingly, I feel) that the final couplet was 'unnecessary' but 'nevertheless permissible'.[269] For me it is the key to the whole poem.

As he moves out into midstream the fisherman looks back at the sky above the cliffs and sees the clouds going by. We are suddenly in the world of Man's relationship with Nature. Midstream is where the current is strongest and the fisherman has chosen it so that it will take charge and sweep him along, just as the river of time sweeps us all along to the great sea of death. River or time, what does it matter? We are powerless against either. Matching the river's power below is the indifference of the clouds overhead, symbolizing Nature's indifference to Man. Nature is commonly represented in verse as 無情 *wú qíng* 'having no feelings', meaning having no interest in human affairs; Nature's other creatures, whether birds or flowers or clouds or whatever, act 自 *zì* 'by themselves', requiring no help from human beings. The poet often resents this and speaks of flowers blooming and birds singing 'in vain' (空 *kōng* or 徒 *tú*), meaning that there is no one around to enjoy their colours and scents and songs, like Thomas Gray's flowers wasting their sweetness on the desert air.

Our fisherman seems to have accepted his insignificance in Nature's eyes and is content to enjoy what he sees, even though it is not a show staged for his entertainment.

---

[269] 柳宗元　漁翁　柳 43 commentary

UNIT 33

Vocabulary

遍 *biàn* /v/ be everywhere on, cover

並 *bìng* /v/ stand side by side 1.7 (W)

殘 *cán* /v/ be remnant, dying

叢 *cóng* /n/ clump, cluster 29.16 (X)

分 *fēn* /v/ distinguish

負 *fù* /v/ turn one's back on, betray 154.2 (M 亻 'person')

負言 *fù yán* /VO/ go back on one's word

鄰並 *lín bìng* /n2/ neighbour

鳴 *míng* /v/ cry (of animals and birds), make a sound 30.10 (W)

蓬 *péng* /n/ tumbleweed

敲 *qiāo* /v/ knock (on door) 66.10 (M 攴 'hit')

侵 *qīn* /v/ invade, be immersed in 9.7 (M 亻 'person')

桐 *tóng* /n/ paulownia-tree, lute-tree 75.6 (M 木 'tree, wood')

先 *xiān* /a/ first, in advance 10.4 (M 止 'foot')

移 *yí* /v/ shift, move 115.6 (S)

擁 *yōng* /v/ hug, hold tight 64.13 (M 扌 'hand')

墜 *zhuì* /n/ to fall 32.12 (M 土 'earth')

Text 1[270]

Jia Dao (779–843): 'Inscribed at Li Ning's retreat'

(Note: when not finding him at home)

閒居少鄰並 *xián jū shǎo lín bìng*

草徑入荒園 *cǎo jìng rù huāng yuán*

鳥宿池邊樹 *niǎo sù chí biān shù*

僧敲月下門 *sēng qiāo yuè xià mén*

過橋分野色 *guò qiáo fēn yě sè*

移石動雲根 *yí shí* dòng yún gēn*

暫去還來此 *zàn qù huán lái cǐ*

幽期不負言 *yōu qī bù fù yán*

Text 2[271]

Sikong Shu (eighth century): 'Rock well'

苔色遍春石 *tái sè biàn chūn shí**

桐陰入寒井 *tóng yīn rù hán jǐng*

幽人獨汲時 *yōu rén dú* jí* shí*

先樂殘陽影 *xiān lè cán yáng yǐng*

---

[270]賈島　題李凝幽居　全572

[271]司空曙　石井　全292

Text 3[272]

Lu Lun (late eighth century): 'On an old tree in the mountains'

高木已蕭索 *gāo mù yǐ xiāo suǒ*

夜雨復秋風 *yè yǔ fù qiū fēng*

墜葉鳴叢竹 *zhuì yè míng cóng zhú**

斜根擁斷蓬 *xié gēn yōng duàn péng*

半侵山色裏 *bàn qīn shān sè tǐ*

長在水聲中 *cháng zài shuǐ shēng zhōng*

此地何人到 *cǐ dì hé rén dào*

雲門去亦通 *yún mén qù yì tōng*

---

[272]盧綸　山中詠古木　全280

UNIT 34

Vocabulary

暗 *àn* /v/ be dark 72.9 (M 日 'sun')

白石 *bái shí* /n/ white stones, supposed food of Taoist hermits

閉 *bì* /v/ to close, close off 169.3 (M 門 'door')

底 *dǐ* /n/ bottom 53.5 (M 广 'house')

忽 *hū* /a/ suddenly

急 *jí* /v/ be swift, hurried 61.5 (M 心 'heart')

集 *jí* /v/ assemble 172.4 (W)

澗 *jiàn* /n/ ravine 85.12 (M 氵 'water')

荊 *jīng* /n/ thorn-bush 140.6 (M 艹 'plant', S 刑, rearranged))

經 *jīng* /v/ pass through

郡 *jùn* /n/ prefecture, prefecture office, yamen 170.7 (M 阝 'town')

露 *lòu* /v/ reveal (N.B. same character as for *lù* 'dew')

履 *lǚ* /n/ shoes 44.12 (M 尸 'shoes')

莓苔 *méi tái* /n/ moss 140.7 (M 艹 'plant')

念 *niàn* /v/ think of 61.4 (M 心 'heart')

瓢 *piáo* /n/ ladle; /m/ ladleful 97.11 (M 瓜 'melon, gourd')

樵 *qiáo* /n/ woodcutter 75.12 (M 木 'tree, wood')

樵客 *qiáo kè* /n/ woodcutter

識 *shì* /v/ recognise

束 *shù* /n/ bundle; /v/ to bundle up 75.3 (M 木 'tree, wood')

慰 *wèi* /v/ to comfort, cheer up 61.11 (M 心 'heart')

薪 *xīn* /n/ firewood 140.13 (M ^艹 'plant')

意 *yì* /n/ mind, state of mind, consciousness

煮 *zhǔ* /v/ to cook, boil 86.9 (M 灬 'fire')

渚 *zhǔ* /n/ islet in river 85.9 (M 氵 'water')

主 *zhǔ* /n/ host 3.4 (X)

主人 *zhǔ rén* /n/ host

Text 1²⁷³

Wei Yingwu (late eighth century): 'To the Taoist in the mountains of Quanjiao'

今朝郡齋冷 *jīn zhāo jùn zhāi lěng*

忽念山中客 *hū* niàn shān zhōng kè*

澗底束荆薪 *jiàn dǐ shù jīng xīn*

歸來煮白石 *guī lái zhǔ bái* shí**

欲持一瓢酒 *yù chí yī* piáo jiǔ*

遠慰風雨夕 *yuǎn wèi fēng yǔ xī**

落葉滿空山 *luò yè mǎn kōng shān*

何處尋行跡 *hé chù xún xíng jī**

Text 2²⁷⁴

Liu Changqing (eighth century): 'Visiting the retreat of the Changshan Taoist at Nanxi'

一路經行處 *yī* lù jīng xíng chù*

273韋應物　寄全椒山中道士　唐1

274劉長卿　尋南溪常山道人隱居　唐3

莓苔見履痕 *méi táijiàn lǔ hén*

白雲依靜渚 *bái* yún yī jìng zhǔ*

春草閉閑門 *chūn cǎo bì xián mén*

過雨看松色 *guò yǔ kān sōng sè*

隨山到水源 *suí shān dào shuǐ yuán*

溪花與禪意 *xī huā yǔ chán yì*

相對亦忘言 *xiāng duì yì wáng yán*

Note: the alternative tones of 看 *kàn* (viz. kān) and 忘 *wàng* (viz. *wáng*) are here required by the tonal pattern.

Text 3[275]

Wen Tingyun (early ninth century): 'The mountain dwelling of the recluse Lu Hu'

西溪問樵客 *xī xī wèn qiáo kè*

遙識主人家 *yáo shì zhǔ rén jiā*

古樹老連石 *gǔ shù lǎo lián shí**

急泉清露沙 *jí* quán qīng lòu shā*

千峰隨雨暗 *qiān fēng suí yǔ àn*

一徑入雲斜 *yī* jīng rù yún xié*

日暮飛鴉集 *rì mù fēi yā jí**

滿山蕎麥花 *mǎn shān qiáo mài huā*

---

[275]溫庭筠 處士盧岵山居 全581

UNIT 35

Vocabulary

案 *àn* /n/ table (large, long) 75.6 (M 木 'tree, wood')

必 *bì* /a/ necessarily, must 61.1 (X)

賓 *bīn* /n/ guest 154.7 (X)

差池 *chā chí* /a/ by mistake, through miscalculation

柴 *chái* /n/ firewood, rough timber 75.5 (M 木 'tree, wood')

車 *chē* /n/ vehicle 159.0 (W)

蕩 *dàng* /v/ wash, cleanse

耳 *ěr* /n/ ear 128.0 (W)

非 *fēi* /v/ is not (negative of 是 *shì*)

關 *guān* /n/ barrier, door

何必 *hé bì* /a/ why must? no need to

及 *jí* /v/ reach, arrive at

几 *jǐ* /n/ small table (Modern *jī*) 16.0 (W)

巾 *jīn* /n/ cloth, covering, awning

巾柴車 *jīn chái chē* /n/ a rough cart with an awning (reference to Tao Yuanming in retirement)

空 *kōng* /a/ in vain

叩 *kòu* /v/ knock 30.2 (X)

窺 *kuī* /v/ peep 116.11 (M 穴 'hole')

理 *lǐ* /n/ principle, essence, truth 96.7 (S)

茅茨 *máo cí* /n/ thatch; thatched cottage 140.5, 140.6 (M ⁺⁺ 'plant')

黽勉 *mǐn miǎn* /v/ make strenuous efforts 205.0 (S)

263

頗 *pō* /a/ very much, quite a bit 181.5 (S)

僕 *pú* /n/ servant 9.12 (M 亻 'person')

契 *qì* /v/ feel in tune with, be in harmony with 37.6 (X)

清淨 *qīng jìng* /n/ inner peace

若 *ruò* /a/ if

雖 *suī* /a/ although, even though 172.9 (S)

童僕 *tóng pú* /n/ servant-boy

新 *xīn* /v/ be new

興 *xìng* /n/ interest, heightened mood 134.9 (X)

仰 *yǎng* /v/ look up (to) 9.4 (M 亻 'person')

仰止 *yǎng zhǐ* /v/ pay one's respects to, call on (a superior)

幽絕 *yōu jué* /n/ superbly secluded and peaceful place

之子 *zhī zǐ* /n/ this gentleman (in earliest verse: this lady)

茲 *zī* /n/ this; here 140.6 (S)

Text[276]

Qiu Wei (eighth century): 'Going to visit a recluse in the Western Hills but not finding him at home'

絕頂一茅茨 *jué* dǐng yī* máo cí*

直上三十里 *zhí* shàng sān shí* lǐ*

叩關無童僕 *kòu guān wú tóng pú**

窺室惟案几 *kuī shì wéi àn jǐ*

若非巾柴車 *ruò fēi jīn chái chē*

應是釣秋水 *yīng shì diào qiū shuǐ*

---

[276] 邱爲 尋西山隱者不遇 唐1

差池不相見 *chā chí bù xiāng jiàn*
黽勉空仰止 *mǐn miǎn kōng yǎng zhǐ*

草色新雨中 *cǎo sè xīn yǔ zhōng*
松聲晚窗裏 *sōng shēng wǎn chuāng lǐ*
及茲契幽絕 *jí* zī qì yōu jué**
自足蕩心耳 *zì zú* dàng xīn ěr*

雖無賓主意 *suī wú bīn zhǔ yì*
頗得清淨理 *pō dé* qīng jìng lǐ*
興盡方下山 *xìng jìn fāng xià shān*
何必待之子 *hé bì dài zhī zǐ*

UNIT 36

In the next three units we shall be looking at the connection between flowers and parting in poems from the Han, Tang and Sung dynasties respectively.

Vocabulary

抱 *bào* v/ to embrace; /m/ a double armful 64.5 (M 扌 'hand')

采 *cǎi* /v/ gather, pluck (= 採) 165.1 (W)

悵望 *chàng wàng* /n/ yearning 61.8 (M 忄 'heart')

杜蘅 *dù héng* /n/ wild ginger 蘅: 140.16 (M 艹 'plant')

繁華 *fán huá* /n/ glory (of flowers)

芙蓉 *fú róng* /n/ water-lily, lotus 140.4, 140.10 (M 艹 'plant')

感 *gǎn* /v/ be upset about 61.9 (M 心 'heart')

貢 *gòng* /v/ send as a gift 154.3 (M 貝 'money')

顧 *gù* /v/ look back 181.12 (M 頁 'head')

浩浩 *hào hào* /v/ be without limit 85.7 (M 氵 'water')

何所 *hé suǒ* /a/ how?

何足 *hé zú* = 不足 /a v/ is not worth ...ing

華 *huá* /n/ blossom (= 花)

懷 *huái* /n/ bosom; /v/ hold in one's bosom

懷抱 *huái bào* /n/ a hug, an embrace

還 *huán* /v/ turn the head

會 *huì* /a/ soon

將 *jiāng* /a/ going to, will

經時 *jīng shí* /VO/ to last a long time

266

枯槁 *kū gǎo* /v/ wither, fade 75.5, 75.10 (M 木 'tree, wood')

蘭蕙 *lán huì* /n/ kind of orchid 140.17, 140.12 (M ⁺⁺ 'plant')

慢 *màn* /v/ go on and on, extend 61.11 (S)

莫 *mò* /a/ cannot

葩 *pā* /n/ flower 140.9 (M ⁺⁺ 'plant')

奇 *qí* /v/ be wonderful, outstanding 37.5 (M 大 'great')

其 *qí* /d/ his, her, its, their; the

榮 *róng* /n/ bright blossom, splendour 75.10 (M 木 'tree, wood')

涉 *shè* /v/ wade across 85.7 (W)

樹 *shù* /v/ to plant

送 *sòng* /v/ send

條 *tiáo* /n/ twig, branch 75.7 (M 木 'tree, wood', S 攸, rearranged))

遺 *wèi* /v/ give (same character as *yí*)

新 *xīn* /a/ newly, recently

馨香 *xīn xiāng* /n/ fragrance 186.11 (M 香 'fragrant', S same as S of 聲)

袖 *xiù* /n/ sleeve 145.5 (M 衤 'clothes')

以 *yǐ* /v/ use; /prep/ by means of; sign of direct object (see notes); (in second poem) thus (metrical padding) 9.3 (M 人 'person', S 厶)

易 *yì* /v/ is easy to, will soon 72.4 (S)

用 *yòng* /v/ use 101.0 (X)

憂傷 *yōu shāng* /v/ be grief-stricken 61.11 (M 心 'heart')

雜 *zá* /a/ mixed among them

澤 *zé* /n/ marsh, low-lying land 85.13 (M 氵 'water')

折 *zhé* /v/ snap off 64.4 (M 扌 'hand')

致 *zhì* /v/ cause to arrive, send 133.4 (M 攴 'hit')

終老 *zhōng lǎo* /a/ to the end of old age, all my life long

終朝 *zhōng zhāo* /a/ all day long

滋 *zī* /v/ to overflow, be profuse

Text 1[277]

Anon (Han dynasty): 'Three ancient poems, No. 3'

新樹蘭蕙葩 *xīn shù lán huì pā*

雜用杜蘅草 *zá* yòng dù héng cǎo*

終朝采其花 *zhōng zhāo cǎi qí huā*

日暮不盈抱 *rì mū bù yíng bào*

采之欲遺誰 *cǎi zhī yù wèi shuí*

所思在遠道 *suǒ sī zài yuǎn dào*

馨香易銷歇 *xīn xiāng yì xiāo xiē**

繁華會枯槁 *fán huá huì kū gǎo*

悵望何所言 *chàng wàng hé suǒ yán*

臨風送懷抱 *lín fēng sòng huái bào*

Text 2[278]

Anon (Han dynasty): 'Nineteen ancient poems, No. 6'

涉江採芙蓉 *shè jiāng cǎi fú róng*

蘭澤多芳草 *lán zé* duō fāng cǎo*

采之欲遺誰 *cǎi zhī yù wèi shuí*

---

[277] 無名士　古詩三首，其三　古A1

[278] 無名士　古詩十九首，其六　古A1

所思在遠道 *suǒ sī zài yuǎn dào*

還顧望舊鄉 *huán gù wàng jiù xiāng*
長路慢浩浩 *cháng lù màn hào hào*
同心而離居 *tóng xīn ér lí jū*
憂傷以終老 *yōu shāng yǐ zhōng lǎo*

Text 3[279]

Anon (Han dynasty): 'Nineteen ancient poems, No. 9'

庭中有奇樹 *tíng zhōng yǒu qí shù*
綠葉發華滋 *lǜ yè fā* huā zī*
攀條折其榮 *pán tiáo zhé* qí róng*
將以遺所思 *jiāng yǐ wèi suǒ sī*

馨香盈懷袖 *xīn xiāng yíng huái xiù*
路遠莫致之 *lù yuǎn mò zhì zhī*
此物何足貢 *cǐ wù hé zú* gòng*
但感別經時 *dàn gǎn bié* jīng shí*

Notes on the texts

In this unit flowers are being gathered by the wife to send to her absent husband, but of course she cannot actually send them.

The flowers in the first poem are garden flowers, those in the second are wild flowers, and those in the third are fruit-tree blossom. Of the three the blossom becomes the dominant type in later verse, but then it is no longer gathered but assumes a different role, as we shall see.

It may be worth reminding you at this point that 草 *cǎo* includes both grass and the wild flowers that grow among the grass, while 花 *huā* includes both

---

[279] 無名士 古詩十九首，其九 古A1

these flowers and fruit-tree blossom. In Tang and Sung verse 花 seems to refer mainly to blossom, while wild flowers are called 草.

But botanical distinctions are not very important, since the whole point of mentioning spring flowers or blossom is as a symbol of a woman's youth and beauty. The fading of the flowers in the first poem represents her youth passing and her beauty fading before her husband can return from his tour of duty.

While such poems may originally have been written by women in the style of folksong, they were imitated mainly by men in order to convey greetings to an absent male friend. The reason for this adoption of a female persona was to convey respect, since in Chinese society a woman's social status was inferior to a man's, so by assuming a female voice one was implying that the friend to whom the poem was addressed was of higher status. This is similar to the custom of referring to oneself as 弟 *dì* 'younger brother' in a letter, and to the addressee as 兄 *xiōng* 'elder brother'.

You will have noticed that one couplet was shared by the first and second poems. This is not regarded as plagiarism but as the use of a common public stock of phrases.

UNIT 37

Vocabulary

穿 *chuān* /v/ to burst through, to strain 116.4 (M 穴 'hole')

閣 *gé* /n/ balcony, prospect-place on high building 169.6 (M 門 'door')

黃昏 *huáng hūn* /n/ dusk

暉 *huī* /n/ sunlight 72.9 (M 日 'sun')

火 *huǒ* /n/ fire 86.0 (W)

寂寞 *jì mò* /v/ be lonely 40.8, 40.11 (S)

接 *jiē* /v/ make contact with 64.8 (M 扌 'hand')

竟 *jìng* /a/ finally

枯 *kū* /v/ wither, fade

梨 *lí* /n/ pear 75.7 (M 木 'tree, wood')

離離 *lí lí* /v/ be lush, luxuriant

陌 *mò* /n/ path (raised) 170.6 (M 阝 'hills')

萋萋 *qī qī* /v/ be lush, luxuriant 140.8 (M 艹 'plant')

忍 *rěn* /v/ can bear to 61.3 (M 心 'heart')

仍 *réng* /a/ still, yet 9.2 (M 亻 'person')

榮 *róng* /v/ flourish

掃 *sǎo* /v/ sweep 64.8 (M 扌 'hand')

紗 *shā* /n/ silk gauze 120.4 (M 糸 'silk')

燒 *shāo* /v/ burn 86.12 (M 火 'fire')

歲 *suì* /n/ year 77.9 (S)

迢遞 *tiáo dì* /v/ be distant 162.5, 162.10 (M 辶 'go')

271

王孫 *wáng sūn* /n/ (descendant of kings =) 'my prince'

眼 *yǎn* /n/ eye 109.6 (M 目 'eye')

原 *yuán* /n/ a plain, prairie 27.8 (M 厂 'cliff')

Text 1[280]

Liu Fangping (early eighth century): 'Grieving resentfully in spring'

紗窗日落漸黃昏 *shā chuāng rì luò jiàn huáng hūn*

金屋無人見淚痕 *jīn wū* wú rén jiàn lèi hén*

寂寞空庭春欲晚 *jì mò kōng tíng chūn yù wǎn*

梨花滿地不開門 *lí huā mǎn dì bù kāi mén*

Text 2[281]

Li Shangyin (early ninth century): 'Fallen blossom'

高閣客竟去 *gāo gé* kè jìng qù*

小園花亂飛 *xiǎo yuán huā luàn fēi*

參差連曲陌 *cēn cī lián qū* mò*

迢遞送斜暉 *tiáo dì sòng xié huī*

腸斷未忍掃 *cháng duàn wèi rěn sǎo*

眼穿仍欲歸 *yǎn chuān réng yù guī*

芳心向春盡 *fāng xīn xiàng chūn jìn*

所得是霑衣 *suǒ dé* shì zhān yī*

---

[280]劉方平　春怨　唐6

[281]李商隱　落花　全539

Text 3[282]

Bai Juyi (772–846): 'Saying goodbye amid the grasses of the ancient plain' (written on a given theme)

離離原上草 *lí lí yuán shàng cǎo*

一歲一枯榮 *yī* suì yī* kū róng*

野火燒不盡 *yě huǒ shāo bù jìn*

春風吹又生 *chūn fēng chuī yòu shēng*

遠芳侵古道 *yuǎn fāng qīn gǔ dào*

晴翠接荒城 *qíng cuì jiē* huāng chéng*

又送王孫去 *yòu sòng wáng sūn qù*

萋萋滿別情 *qī qī mǎn bié* qíng*

Notes on the texts

In the first two poems fallen blossom represents the passing of spring, the passing of youth for the woman left alone.

The third poem, written when the poet was sixteen years old, contrasts Nature's powers of renewal with human vulnerability in the face of separation. The flowers are no longer a symbol of youth but of uncaring Nature, flourishing unabated while the poet suffers the pangs of parting.

That is the superficial meaning, but I personally have a suspicion that something else is being said at a deeper, perhaps unconscious, level. The first four lines may be hinting that our love is indestructible, whatever 'wildfire' the world may subject us to. Line 7 may imply 'Your fragrance (= moral qualities) from afar will imbue our long-standing love' and line 8 'Your evergreen love will reach me in my desolation when I remember you'. This is just a guess.

There are two possible puns (puns are respectable in Chinese verse!): in the first line 離離 *lí lí* 'luxuriant' suggests 離 *lí* 'parting'; in the last line 萋萋 *qī qī* 'luxuriant' sounds the same as 淒淒 *qī qī* 'bleak, sad'.

---

[282]白居易　賦得古原草送別　全436

37.1 'My prince'

王孫 *wáng sūn* seems always to be associated with 春草 *chūn cǎo* 'spring flowers and grasses'. Its first recorded occurrence is in the second century BC, in the anonymous poem 'Summoning the recluse' [283] (i.e. to join the galaxy of thinkers at the court of Liu An, Prince of Huainan). The poem describes the mountains as a horrible, dangerous place for the recluse to be. Near the beginning is the couplet 王孫遊兮不歸　春草生兮萋萋 *wáng sūn yóu xī bù guī / chūn cǎo shēng xī qī qī* 'Prince, you are wandering and do not come home;/ the spring grasses are growing luxuriantly'. The poem ends 王孫兮歸來　山中兮不可以久留 *wáng sūn xī guī lái / shān zhōng xī bù kě yǐ jiǔ liú* 'Come home, prince, / you cannot stay long in the mountains'. (可以 *kě yǐ* 'may'; 留 *liú* 'stay'.)

Vocabulary note on this example: 兮 *xī* was then pronounced 'eh', like the English 'e' in 'men', with smooth vocalic ingress, i.e. not preceded by a glottal stop, but this could only be written with a character pronounced with an initial voiced 'h', which in due course came to be pronounced *xī* in a reading pronunciation. But since 'eh' was extra-phonological, like other prepausal particles and interjections, its pronunciation has remained unchanged to the present day and this sound is used in exactly the same way (viz. to break a sung line into two parts) in modern folksong.

Nine hundred years later Wang Wei contradicted this view in the poem 'Autumn twilight at my mountain dwelling' [284] extolling the pleasure of living as a recluse in the mountains: 隨意春芳歇　王孫自可留 *suí yì chūn fāng xiē / wáng sūn zì kě liú* 'Who cares if the spring flowers are over? / Of course you may stay [here in the mountains], my prince'.

In general, though, the 'prince' is the object of complaints about not hurrying home while his wife is yet blooming like the spring vegetation. Here are two quatrains from the fifth century:

Example text 1[285]

Xie Tiao (464–499): 'My prince is wandering'

綠草漫如絲 *lǜ cǎo màn rú sī*

雜樹紅英發 *zá* shù hóng yīng fā**

---

[283] 無名氏　招隱士　楚12

[284] 王維　山居秋暝　唐3

[285] 謝朓　王孫游　樂74

無論君不歸 *wú lùn jūn bù guī*

君歸芳已歇 *jūn guī fāng yǐ xiē**

The green grasses spread like silk threads;
on the various trees pink blossoms burst forth.
Even if you do come home,
when you come the fragrant flowers will be over.

Example text 2[286]

Wang Rong (467–493): 'My prince is wandering'

置酒登廣殿 *zhì jiǔ dēng guǎng diàn*

開襟望所思 *kāi jīn wàng suǒ sī*

春草行已歇 *chūn cǎo xíng yǐ xiē**

何事久佳期 *hé shì jiǔ jiā qī*

I set out the wine when I go up on to [the balcony of] the spacious
palace;
I open the front of my gown and yearn for my dear one.
The spring flowers will soon be over;
why does he keep me waiting so long for a reunion?

A poem with the same title from the Tang:

Example text 3[287]

Cui Guofu (eighth century): 'My prince is wandering'

自與王孫別 *zì yǔ wáng sūn bié**

頻看黃鳥飛 *pín kān huáng niǎo fēi*

應由春草誤 *yīng yóu chūn huā wù*

著處不成歸 *zhù chǔ bù chéng guī*

---

[286]王融　王孫游　樂74

[287]崔國輔　王孫游　樂74

Since I said goodbye to my prince
I have frequently watched the orioles flying.
He must have become entranced by the spring flowers
and be stuck somewhere, unable to complete his journey home.

However, not all 'princes' are absent husbands or friends, even though
mentioned together with spring flowers, as we see in the following poem.

Example text 4[288]

Liu Changqing (eighth century): 'Passing by the old silk-washer's tomb'

昔賢懷一飯 *xī xián huái yī* fàn*

茲事已千秋 *zī shì yǐ qiān qiū*

古墓樵人識 *gǔ mù qiáo rén shì*

前朝楚水流 *qián cháo chǔ shuǐ liú*

渚蘋行客薦 *zhǔ pín xíng kè jiàn*

山木杜鵑愁 *shān mù dù juān chóu*

春草茫茫綠 *chūn cǎo máng máng lù*

王孫舊此遊 *wáng sūn jiù cǐ yóu*

That worthy of long ago never forgot those meals,
but those events are now a thousand autumns past.
Her ancient tomb is known to the wood-cutters,
while the river of the former state of Chu flows on.
The islet's water-weeds are a couch for the exile;
in the mountain trees a cuckoo mourns.
Spring grasses stretch far, misty-green,
here where the prince once wandered.

Han Xin, the 'prince' referred to here, was literally a 王孫, 'a descendant
of kings', being a grandson of the King of Han through a concubine. [289] While
still a commoner without financial resources [290] he was fishing by the River
Huai when an old woman who washed silk there noticed that he was starving

---

[288] 劉長卿　經漂母墓　全147

[289] 史記93

[290] 史記92

and for several weeks she fed him. He said: 'One day I shall be able to reward you handsomely.' She replied angrily: 'You're a man who can't feed himself. I fed you because I was sad for you, a prince (王 孫); I certainly wasn't looking for a reward!' Later, in 198 BC, when he was made Prince of Chu by the founder of the Han dynasty, he summoned the old woman and gave her a thousand ounces of silver.

UNIT 38

Vocabulary

寶 *bǎo* /v/ be precious 40.17 (M 貝 'money')

寸 *cùn* /m/ inch 41.0 (M 寸 'inch' < 'thumb')

寸寸 *cùn cùn* /m/ every inch, inch by inch

帶 *dài* /n/ belt

杜宇 *dù yǔ* /N/ cuckoo

短 *duǎn* /v/ be short 111.7 (S)

斷魂 *duàn hún* /VO/ to break one's heart

翻 *fān* /a/ however, but < turn over 124.12 (M 羽 'wings')

繁 *fán* /v/ bloom profusely

粉 *fěn* /n/ face-powder 119.4 (M 米 'rice')

館 *guǎn* /n/ inn; residence 184.8 (M 食 'eat')

紅 *hóng* /n/ pink blossom 120.3 (M 糸 'silk')

候館 *hòu guǎn* /n/ prospect-tower

胡蝶 *hú dié* /n/ butterfly 142.9 (M 虫 'reptile, insect')

緩 *huǎn* /v/ be slack 120.9 (M 糸 'silk')

魂 *hún* /n/ spirit, sky-soul 194.4 (M 鬼 'ghost')

薺菜 *jì cài* /n/ shepherd's purse 140.14, 140.8 (M 艹 'plant')

近 *jìn* /v/ be close (to) 162.4 (M 辶 'go')

闌 *lán* /n/ balustrade, balcony-rail 169.9 (M 門 'door')

奩 *lián* /n/ (toilet case =) mirror (therein) 37.11 (X)

梅 *méi* /n/ prunus, ornamental plum

278

木蘭 *mù lán* /n/ magnolia

暖 *nuǎn* /v/ be warm 72.9 (M 日 'sun')

轡 *pèi* /n/ bridle 159.15 (X)

平蕪 *píng wú* /n/ a plain, prairie 140.12 (M ⁺⁺ 'plant')

欺 *qī* /v/ deceive 76.8 (M 欠 'gape')

柔 *róu* /v/ be soft, tender 75.5 (M 木 'tree, wood')

試 *shì* /v/ try -ing 149.6 (M 言 'speak')

迢迢 *tiáo tiáo* /v/ be distant

無窮 *wú qióng* /v/ be endless

薰 *xūn* /v/ be fragrant 140.14 (M ⁺⁺ 'plant')

盈盈 *yíng yíng* /v/ be full, brimming over

游 *yóu* /v/ swim, float 85.9 (M 氵 'water')

游絲 *yóu sī* /n/ (floating threads = gossamer =) hair

征 *zhēng* /n/ journey, expedition 60.5 (M 彳 'go')

Text 1[291]

Li Jia (Sung dynasty): '[On the pattern] "Remembering my prince": a spring song'

萋萋芳草憶王孫 *qī qī fāng cǎo yì wáng sūn*

柳外樓高空斷魂 *liǔ wàl lóu gāo kōng duàn hún*

杜宇聲聲不忍聞 *dù yǔ shēng shēng bù rěn wén*

欲黃昏 *yù huáng hūn*

雨打梨花深閉門 *yǔ dǎ lí huā shēn bì mén*

---

[291] 李甲　憶王孫　宋

Text 2[292]

Yan Ren (Sung dynasty): '[On the pattern] "Magnolia flowers"'

春風只在園西畔 *chūn fēng zhǐ zài yuán xī pàn*

薺菜花繁胡蝶亂 *jì cài huā fán hú dié* luàn*

冰池晴綠照還空 *bīng chí qíng lǜ zhào huán kōng*

香徑落紅吹已斷 *xiāng jìng luò hóng chuī yǐ duàn*

意長翻恨游絲短 *yì cháng fān hèn yóu sī duǎn*

盡日相思羅帶緩 *jìn rì xiāng sī luó dài huǎn*

寶奩如月不欺人 *bǎo lián rú yuè bù qī rén*

明日歸來君試看 *míng rì guī lái jūn shì kàn*

Text 3[293]

Ouyang Xiu (1007–1072): '[On the pattern] "Treading the sedges"'

候館梅殘 *hòu guǎn méi cán*

溪橋柳細 *xī qiáo liǔ xì*

草薰風暖搖征轡 *cǎo xūn fēng nuǎn yáo zhēng pèi*

離愁漸遠漸無窮 *lí chóu jiàn yuǎn jiàn wú qióng*

迢迢不斷如春水 *tiáo tiáo bù duàn rú chūn shuǐ*

寸寸柔腸 *cùn cùn róu cháng*

盈盈粉淚 *yíng yíng fěn lèi*

樓高莫近危闌倚 *lóu gāo mò jìn wēi lán yǐ*

平蕪盡處是春山 *píng wú jìn chù shì chūn shān*

---

[292]嚴仁　木蘭花　宋

[293]歐陽修　踏莎行　宋

行人更在春山外 *xíng rén gèng zài chūn shān wài*

Notes on the texts

I include the first poem not because it has any artistic merit but because it is a medley of images you will by now be familiar with from earlier poems and so may afford you some practice.

In the second and third poems some of the images are new, but falling blossom still means what it meant in the Tang.

38.1 Sung-dynasty song-style verse

You will have noticed that whereas the second poem looks (at first sight, at least) like a normal 8x7, the other two have some shorter lines.

In the first, every line rhymes; in the second the rhyme-scheme is 'aaba,aaca'; and in the third 'abbcb,dbbeb'. In other words, none follows the familiar Tang-dynasty 'abcbdbeb' or 'aabacada'. Also, each of the latter two poems consists of two verses, with the second verse repreating the pattern of the first verse.

Clearly this is a new prosodic type. The Tang- and Sung-dynasty 詞 *cí* began as songs written for public entertainment by female singers in geisha-houses. The tunes took precedence over the lyrics in the sense that the lyrics had to be written to fit in with the phrases of different length required by the particular tune; in fact lines may be of any length from two to nine syllables.

Each different tune had its own strict pattern of metre (line-lengths), rhyme-scheme and tonal patterning; it also had a name (often several alternative names), probably referring to the lyric first sung with each tune. This pattern-name came to be used as the 'title' of the poems written to it, even though it was a purely prosodic label and did not necessarily have anything to do with the subject-matter of these poems. Once the patterns were set, poets continued to write poems (i.e. not publicly-performed songs) to fit the patterns, and this activity was called 填詞 *tián cí* 'filling in song-patterns'.

The range of content of 詞 was much narrower than that of the earlier types of verse. They tended to be lyrical, and the lonely wife (as in the three poems in this unit) was a dominant theme. Current colloquialisms of vocabulary and grammar appeared in them, and a preference for certain words and phrases (e.g. 斷魂 *duàn hún* in the first poem) gives 詞 a special atmosphere, as if written in a limited language to describe a limited (for me often claustrophobic) world of feeling, more so even than in the case of Chinese lyrical poetry in general.

UNIT 39

In this unit we sample a more advanced form of coding than we have looked at so far, namely the extended metaphor, to give you a taste of what awaits you if you delve deeper into Chinese verse. I suggest that you translate the first poem and check against the key in the usual way before looking at the paraphrase of it below. Then do the same for the second and third poems. In this way the first poem may help you decode the second and the third in turn.

Vocabulary

逼 *bī* /v/ to crowd, press against 162.9 (M 辶 'go')

側 *cè* /n/ side /a/ sideways, to one side 9.9 (M 亻 'person')

巢 *cháo* /v/ to nest 47.8 (W)

池潢 *chí huáng* /n/ ponds 85.3, 85.12 (M 氵 'water')

重 *chóng* /v/ extend range upon range (of mountains to be crossed); 重深 *chóng shēn* 'many-layered [mountains] and deep [rivers]'

翠鳥 *cuì niǎo* /n/ kingfisher 124.8 (M 羽 'feathers, wings')

冬 *dōng* /n/ winter 15.3 (M 冫 'ice')

患 *huàn* /v/ to worry about 61.7 (M 心 'heart')

嘉 *jiā* /v/ be excellent, honoured 30.11 (M 喜 'joy')

薦 *jiàn* /v/ to present to 140.13 (S)

矯矯 *jiǎo jiǎo* /v/ be elevated, outstanding, above the common herd 111.12 (S)

潔 *jié* /v/ be pure, unsullied 85.12 (M 氵 'water')

節 *jié* /n/ season 118.7 (also written 節 118.9) (M 竹 'bamboo')

橘 *jú* /n/ orange or related citrus fruit 75.12 (M 木 'tree, wood')

懼 *jù* /n/ fear 61.18 (M 忄 'heart')

慕 *mù* /v/ set one's heart upon 61.11 (M 小 'heart')

282

奈何 *nài hé* /VA/ (literally 'do-about-it what', 'What can I do about it?', i.e. 'I can do nothing about it') unfortunately, alas 37.5 (S)

求 *qiú* /v/ want, hope for, try to obtain 85.2 (S)

丸 *wán* /n/ pellet, ball; 金丸 *jīn wán* 'metal pellet' is a cross-bow (stone-bow) pellet 3.2 (X)

葳蕤 *wēi ruí* /v/ be luxuriant (of foliage) 140.9, 140.12 (M 艹 'plant')

惡 *wù* /v/ hate 61.8 (M 心 'heart')

欣欣 *xīn xīn* /v/ be vigorous, lively 76.4 (M 欠 'gape')

循環 *xún huán* /n/ cyclical movement, fortune's wheel 60.9 (M 彳 'go'); 96.13 (M 玉 'jade')

伊 *yī* /v/ be because 9.4 (S)

弋 *yì* /v/ shoot (birds with captive arrow) 56.0 (W)

遇 *yù* /v/ meet, encounter, come across 162.9 (M 辶 'go')

運命 *yùn mìng* /n/ fate, one's lot , literally 'rotating command (of Heaven)', cf. 循環 *xún huán* above 162.9 (M 辶 'go'); 30.5 (M 口 'mouth', S 令, rearranged)

珍 *zhēn* /n/ treasure, precious object 96.5 (M 玉 'jade')

指 *zhǐ* /v. point at 64.6 (M 扌 'hand')

阻 *zǔ* /v/ impede, obstruct 170.5 (M 阝 'hills')

Text 1[294]

Zhang Jiuling (678–740): 'Bewailing my lot, No. 1'

01 孤鴻海上來 *gū hong hǎi shàng lái*

02 池潢不敢顧 *chí huáng bù gǎn gù*

03 側見雙翠鳥 *cè jiàn shuāng cuì niǎo*

04 巢在三珠樹 *cháo zài sān zhū shù*

---

[294]張九齡 感遇，其一 唐1

05 矯矯珍木巔 *jiǎo jiǎo zhēn mù diān*

06 得無金丸懼 *dé* wú jīn wán jù*

07 美服患人指 *měi fú* huàn rén zhǐ*

08 高明逼神惡 *gāo míng bī* shén wù*

09 今我游冥冥 *jīn wǒ yóu míng míng*

10 弋者何所慕 *yì zhě hé suǒ mù*

Text 2[295]

Zhang Jiuling (678–740): 'Bewailing my lot, No. 2'

11 蘭葉春葳蕤 *lán yè chūn wēi ruí*

12 桂花秋皎潔 *guì huā qiū jiǎo jié*

13 欣欣此生意 *xīn xīn cǐ shēng yì*

14 自爾爲佳節 *zì ěr wéi jiā jié*

15 誰知林棲者 *shuí zhī lín qī zhě*

16 聞風坐相悅 *wén fēng zuò xiāng yuè*

17 草木有本心 *cǎo mù yǒu běn xīn*

18 何求美人折 *hé qiú měi rén zhé*

Text 3[296]

Zhang Jiuling (678–740): 'Bewailing my lot, No. 4'

19 江南有丹橘 *jiāng nán yǒu dān jú*

20 經冬猶綠林 *jīng dōng yóu lù lín*

21 豈伊地氣暖 *qǐ yī dì qì nuǎn*

---

[295]張九齡 感遇，其二 唐1
[296]張九齡 感遇，其四 唐1

22 自有歲寒心 *zì yǒu suì hán xīn*

23 可以薦嘉客 *kě yǐ jiàn jiā kè*

24 奈何阻重深 *nài hé zǔ chóng shēn*

25 運命惟所遇 *yùn mìng wéi suǒ yù*

26 循環不可尋 *xún huán bù kě xún*

27 徒言樹桃李 *tú yán shù táo lǐ*

28 此木豈無陰 *cǐ mù qǐ wú yīn*

Background note on Zhang Jiuling

One Chinese history has Zhang Jiuling saying at court: 臣嶺海孤賤, 不如仙客生于中華 [297] *chén lǐng hǎi gū jiàn, bù rú xiān kè shēng yú zhōng huá* 'I am an isolated person of low estate from the Lingnan Sea[-coast], hence inferior to [Niu] Xianke, who was born in Central China'. Lingnan corresponds roughly to modern Guangdong Province. Another history has him saying: 臣荒徼微賤, 仙客中華之士 [298] *chén huāng jiào wēi jiàn, xiān kè zhōng huá zhī shì* 'I am an insignificant and lowly person from the wild frontier, while [Niu] Xianke is a gentleman from Central China'. It may be no coincidence that the first quotation contains the two words 孤 *gū* and 海 *hǎi* that also occur in the first line of Poem No. 1.

Kingfisher feathers were prized as ornaments. The kingfisher, being a bird of the extreme south of China, could easily become associated with the mythical three-pearl tree (like a cypress, with pearls on its leaves) from somewhere to the south of China.

Paraphrase of Text 1

01 I came to the imperial court from the South China Sea, a man without connections,

02 with no ambition to become rich and powerful at others' expense.

03 There I found a pair of resplendent creatures (his political enemies Li Linfu and Niu Xianke)

04 in a position of wealth and power.

05 Being so prominently in the public eye,

06 they must go in constant fear of being plotted against.

---

[297] 玄宗開元二十四年 資214

[298] 李林甫傳 舊106

07 The more successful they seem to be, the more they will attract the hatred
     of the envious;

08 the greater their power, the more likely they are to attract the Emperor's
     displeasure.

09 But now that I am in exile, far from the court,

10 I am no longer in danger of being assassinated.

39.2 Paraphrase of Text 2

11 One man of integrity will display his talents in one way in his own season;

12 another will do so in another way at another time.

13 Such is the power of his own inward motivation

14 that he will embellish the world without needing any encouragement from
     outside.

15 Though he does not expect it, fellow-spirits

16 will hear of his merits and appreciate them.

17 He will maintain his integrity for his own inward reasons,

18 not because he hopes to be selected for office by his ruler.

39.3 Paraphrase of Text 3

19 I am a southerner now in exile in the south,

20 but I still preserve my loyalty intact.

21 This is not because it has not been put to the test,

22 but because I have the kind of integrity that can withstand adversity.

23 I should make an ideal adviser to the Emperor,

24 but alas, I'm cut off from his presence by my enemies.

25 Yet I must accept that my fate is limited to my individual personal
     experiences:

26 I cannot be sure whether the wheel of fate will turn the way I want it to. [So
     I'll just have to accept my exile and not expect fate to deal more
     kindly with me in the future.]

27 The government only thinks of employing the usual kind of bureaucrat,

28 even though a southern outsider like me would be at least as useful.

UNIT 40

In this unit we look at three examples of a poet identifying with birds, i.e. projecting his own feelings upon them, although to what extent this is a conscious process it is impossible to say. The coding in Unit 39 was clearly conscious, a deliberate literary device, but I suspect that the three examples in this unit are the kind of unconscious coding that we are familiar with in Western poetry.

Vocabulary

拔 *bá* /v/ pluck up or out 64.5 (M 扌 'hand')

蒼鷹 *cāng yīng* /n/ goshawk 196.13 (M 鳥 'bird', S like 雁 with dot on top)

滄 *cāng* /v/ blue (a spelling of 蒼 applied to the sea) 85.10 (M 氵 'water')

遲 *chí* /v/ be late, tardy, slow 162.12 (M 辶 'go')

掣 *chì* /v/ move suddenly, flash (of lightning) 64.8 (M 手 'hand')

詞 *cí* /n/ song, song-style poem 149.6 (M 言 'speak')

摧 *cuī* /v/ break; 自摧 feel shattered, downcast, feel low self-esteem 64.11 (M 扌 'hand')

點 *diǎn* /n/ dot; /v/ to dot 203.5 (M 黑 'black')

電 *diàn* /n/ lightning 173.5 (M 雨 'rain')

翻 *fān* /v/ turn over, turn in flight

行 *háng* /n/ row, line, skein (of geese) (same character as *xíng*)

翮 *hé* /n/ flight-feathers 124.10 (M 羽 'feathers')

虹霓 *hóng ní* /n/ rainbow 142.3 (M 虫 'reptile, insect'); 173.8 (M 雨 'rain')

呼 *hū* /v/ call, shout 30.5 (M 口 'mouth')

狐 *hú* /n/ fox 94.5 (M 犭 'dog')

砉然 *huò rán* /v/ swish; /a/ with a swish 112.4 (S)

擊 *jī* /v/ strike 64.13 (M 手 'hand')

激昂 *jī áng* /v/ be fierce, self-assertive, proud 85.13 (M 氵 'water'); 72.5 (S)

假 *jià* /n/ leisure, freedom; 爲假 be free, unconstrained 9.9 (M 亻 'person')

剪 *jiǎn* /v/ cut, scythe through 18.9 (M 刀 'knife')

荆棘 *jīng jí* /v/ thorns and brambles 75.8 (W)

勁 *jìng* /v/ be energetic, vigorous 19.7 (M 力 'strength')

攫 *jué* /v/ seize in the claws 64.20 (M 扌 'hand', S consists of 目 twice above 隹 and 又)

累 *léi* /n/ trammels, restraints, burdens 120.5 (M 糸 'silk')

狸 *lí* /n/ wild cat 94.7 (M 犭 'dog')

立 *lì* /v/ stand 117.0 (W)

裂 *liè* /v/ rip, rend, tear 145.6 (M 衣 'clothes')

毛 *máo* /n/ small feathers, down; fur 82.0 (W)

苗 *miáo* /n/ rice-shoots 140.5 (W)

鷗 *ōu* /n/ seagull 196.11 (M 鳥 'bird')

披 *pī* /v/ split

霹靂 *pī lì* /n/ thunderclap 173.13, 173.16 (M 雨 'rain')

飄 *piāo* /v/ float 182.11 (M 風 'wind')

凄 *qī* /v/ chilly; 凄風 the chill winds of autumn 85.8 (M 氵 'water')

且 *qiě* /c/ and

卻 *què* /v/ turn, change course; 卻思 change one's mind

群 *qún* /n/ flock, crowd 123.7 (M 羊 'sheep')

饒 *ráo* /v/ indulge, not constrain; 自饒 do as one pleases 184.12 (M 食 'eat')

任 *rèn* /v/ allow, not resist; 一任 let oneself go completely 9.4 (M 亻 'person')

溽 *rù* /v/ humid, close, muggy 85.10 (M 氵 'water')

傷 *shāng* /v/ wound, be wounded in spirit, distressed

商 *shāng* /n/ the musical note 're', associated with autumn; the attributes of autumn, such as refreshing winds and high, clear skies 30.8 (X)

捎 *shāo* /v/ skim, brush across the top of 64.7 (M 扌 'hand')

失 *shī* /v/ lose; (here) those he has lost 37.2 (S)

逝 *shì*/v/ depart, flee 162.7 (M 辶 'go')

暑 *shǔ* /n/ summer heat 72.9 (M 日 'sun')

鼠 *shǔ* /n/ rodent (rat, mouse, vole etc.) 208.0 (W)

塘 *táng* /n/ pond 32.10 (M 土 'earth')

騰 *téng* /v/ ascend, rise 187.10 (M 馬 'horse', S 朕, rearranged)

脫 *tuō* /v/ come off, moult 130.7 (M 月 'flesh')

吻 *wěn* /n/ mouth (of animal), beak (of bird) 30.4 (M 口 'mouth')

淅瀝 *xī lì* /v/ to sough with a thin, high note (of the autumn wind) 85.8, 85.16 (M 氵 'water')

戲 *xì* /v/ play 62.13 (S)

翔 *xiáng* /v/ wheel, circle (of a bird) 124.6 (M 羽 'feathers, wings')

蕭蕭 *xiāo xiāo* /v/ utter desolate cries

血 *xuè* /n/ blood 143.0 (W)

嚴 *yán* /v/ be stern, severe 30.17 (X)

炎 *yán* /v/ be scorching hot 86.4 (W)

鷹 *yīng* /n/ hawk

羽 (翼) *yǔ (yì)* /n/ feathers; wings 124.0 (W); 124.11 (M 羽 'feathers, wings')

浴 *yù* /v/ bathe 85.7 (M 氵 'water')

繒繳 *zēng zhuó* /n2/ captive arrow and the silk line attached to it 111.12
　　　(M 矢 'arrow'); 120.13 (M 糸 'silk')

爪 *zhǎo* /n/ claw 87.0 (W)

Text 1[299]

Liu Zongyuan (773–819): 'The caged goshawk'

凄風淅瀝飛嚴霜 *qī fēng xī* lì* fēi yán shuāng*

蒼鷹上擊翻曙光 *cāng yīng shàng jī* fān shù guāng*

雲披霧裂虹霓斷 *yún pī wū liè* hóng ní duàn*

霹靂掣電捎平岡 *pī* lì* chì diàn shāo píng gāng*

㸌然勁翮剪荊棘 *huò* rán jìng hé* jiǎn jīng jí**

下攫狐兔騰蒼茫 *xià jué* hú tù téng cāng máng*

爪毛吻血百鳥逝 *zhǎo máo wěn xuè* bǎi* niǎo shì*

獨立四顧時激昂 *dú* lì* sì gù shí jī* áng*

炎風溽暑忽然至 *yán fēng rù* shǔ hū* rán zhì*

羽翼脫落自摧藏 *yǔ yì* tuō luò* zì cuī cáng*

草中狸鼠足爲患 *cǎo zhōng lí shǔ zú* wéi huàn*

一夕十顧驚且傷 *yī* xī* shí* gù jīng qiě shāng*

但願清商復爲假 *dàn yuàn qīng shāng fù wéi jià*

拔去萬累雲間翔 *bá* qù wàn lèi yún jiān xiáng*

[299]柳宗元　籠鷹詞　全353

Text 2[300]

Cui Tu (late ninth century): 'The lone wild goose'

幾行歸去盡 *jǐ háng guī qù jìn*

片影獨何之 *piān yǐng dú* hé zhī*

暮雨相呼失 *mù yǔ xiāng hū shī**

寒塘獨下遲 *hán táng dú* xià chí*

渚雲低暗渡 *zhǔ yún dī àn dù*

關月冷遙隨 *guān yuè lěng yáo suí*

未必逢矰繳 *wèi bì féng zēng zhuó**

孤飛自可疑 *gū fēi zì kě yí*

Text 3[301]

Du Fu (712–770): 'The seagulls'

江浦寒鷗戲 *jiāng pǔ hán ōu xì*

無他亦自饒 *wú tā yì zì ráo*

卻思翻玉羽 *què sī fān yù yǔ*

隨意點青苗 *suí yì diǎn qīng miáo*

雪暗還須浴 *xuě àn huán xū yù*

風生一任飄 *fēng shēng yī* rèn piāo*

幾群滄海上 *jǐ qún cāng hǎi shàng*

清影日蕭蕭 *qīng yǐng rì xiāo xiāo*

My own feeling about this last poem is that Du Fu begins by envying the gulls their apparent freedom but then realises their vulnerability. The price of freedom in China's closely-knit, conformist society has always been loneliness and vulnerability.

---

[300]崔涂　孤雁　唐3

[301]杜甫　鷗　杜17

40.1 An artistic use of the 'entering tone'

I have marked all 'entering' tones in this poem, not just those which became
Mandarin first or second. I have done this not to show any regular tonal
patterning (it is an ancient-style poem, not regulated verse), but to show an
unusual artistic use of entering-tone words. In the following tonal analysis I
have used 'o' for level tone, 'x' for rising and departing tones, and 'E' for
entering tone:

```
o o E E  o o o        chai fung jit lik            fei yim söng
o o x E  o x o        chong ying söng gik          faan sü gwong
o o x E  o o x        wan pei mou lit              hung ngai dün
E E x x  o o o        pik lik jai din              saau ping gong

E o x E  x o E        waak yin ging hatjin ging gik
x E x x  o o o        haa fok wu tou               tang chong mong
x o x E  E x x        jaau mou man hüt             baak niu sai
E E x x  o E o        duk laap sei gwu             si gik ngong

o o E x  E o x        yim fung yuk sü              fat yin ji
x E E E  x o o        yü yik tüt lok               ji chöü chong
x o o x  E o x        chou jung lei sü             juk wai waan
E E E x  o x o        yat jik sap gwu              ging che söng

x x o o  x o x        daan yün ching söng          fau wai gaa
E x x x  o o o        bat höü maan löü             wan gaan chöng
```

If we analyse the percentage of each tone-class in terms of the first and
second sections of each line, we get the following:

Tone-class	First section	Second section
o (level)	14 (25%)	26 (62%)
x (rising & going)	22 (39%)	11 (26%)
E (entering)	20 (36%)	5 (12%)
Total	56 (100%)	42 (100%)

As a rough comparison, the occurrence of entering tones in the first twenty
ancient-style poems in the *Three Hundred Tang Poems* is 16.4%. Clearly there
are more than twice the average number of entering tones in the first halves of
these lines.

Entering-tone syllables ended in unexploded -*p*, -*k* or -*t*, as opposed to
syllables in the other tones, which ended in continuant -*m*, -*n*, -*ng* or a vowel;
this means that entering-tone syllables sounded more abrupt while the other
syllables sounded smoother. I have added a version in Cantonese
pronunciation above (without tones) so that you may get an idea of the
cumulative effect of the high proportion of entering-tone syllables in the first
sections of the lines.

The effect this has on me personally is to emphasize the speed and violence of the raptor, even when kept in frustrating confinement.

By contrast, we find a calm 'ooo' in the second section of four lines; this succession of level tones is particularly effective in the final line, where the hawk is soaring among the clouds, having escaped confinement.

KEY TO EXERCISES

UNIT 1

(1) Spring breeze(s)/wind(s); the breeze(s)/wind(s) of/in spring(time) etc. (2) Wind-blown flowers; flowers blown/moved etc by the wind. (3) Blossoming woods/grove(s); a woodland in bloom. (4) Woodland trees; the trees of the forest etc. (5) Birdsong; the sound/voices of birds. (6) Autumn waters/rivers/floods; the rivers etc in autumn. (7) Spring day(s). (Note: 'spring sunshine' would usually be expressed as 'spring light'.) (8) Mountain rain. Rain in/on/over the hills/mountains. (9) River breeze etc; the wind ruffling the waters etc. (10) The sounds of the night; nocturnal voices. (Note: Single versions only given from this point.) (11) A rainy night. (12) Moonlit woods. (13) Sunlight on the bamboos. (14) Bamboos on the hills. (15) Mountains and rivers. (16) The moon in springtime. (17) The sound of the wind. (18) Woodland birds. (19) Day and night. (20) Trees in autumn. (21) Water-birds. (22) Autumn in the hills. (23) The sounds of autumn. (24) An autumn day. (25) The hills in spring. (26) Springtime in the hills. (27) The sound of the mountain wind. (28) The moon shining on the autumn hills. (29) The sound of the rain. (30) The moon reflected in the water. (31) The mountains shrouded in darkness. (32) Bamboos beaten by the rain. (33) A moonlit night. (34) A bamboo-forest. (35) The flowers that bloom in the spring. (36) Sun and moon. (37) The wind in the bamboos. (38) The trees at night. (39) The birds on the mountains. (40) Woodland flowers. (41) The trees in springtime. (42) Sunlight on the mountains. (43) Rain-swept flowers. (44) The voice of the waters. (45) The moon over the mountains. (46) Bamboos and trees. (47) A rainy day. (48) A mountain tree. (49) Spring and autumn. (50) Night-birds. (51) The autumn moon. (52) Night-blooming flowers. (53) The wind rustling the bamboos. (54) Birds in the hills. (55) The rivers in springtime. (56) The sound of autumn waters. (57) The moon over the springtime woods.

UNIT 2

(1) The secluded bamboos are green. (2) The colours of late spring. (3) The full moon is white. (4) The bamboos in the valley are green. (5) Spring's colours are bright. (6) The people of the high mountains. (7) The autumn rivers are deep. (8) Flowers by the springtime river. (9) A single blossom-covered tree. (10) The floods are white. (11) This moss in the rain. (12) The sound of the river in the valley. (13) The rainy day is long. (14) The colour of the empty sky. (15) These high woods. (16) The wind's voice is high/loud.

(17) The empty valley is cold. (18) Wind across the cold river. (19) One single mountain is high. (20) The little river is green. (21) The moss in the deep woods. (22) A single cold bird. (23) Autumn skies are high. (24) The sound of secluded bamboos. (25) The chill rain goes on and on. (26) The sound of great waters. (27) The colours of the secluded flowers. (28) A single great mountain. (29) The fine rain is cold. (30) The bamboos in the rain are green. (31) The night wind is cold. (32) Birds in the blue sky. (33) The springtime hills are bright. (34) Birds on the autumn river. (35) These flowers are white. (36) The little bird is cold. (37) The high woods are deep. (38) The wind blowing across the empty sky. (39) The colour of the cold mountains. (40) The wind's voice is chill. (41) The whole sky is bright. (42) This high mountain.

UNIT 3

(1) The leaves are falling. (2) The birds return. (3) The river flows. (4) The sun has set. (5) The clouds return. (6) Someone (he, I etc) is coming. (7) (I etc) hear the voice. (8) (It etc) falls into the water (or: settles on the water). (9) (I etc) return to the hills. (10) (I etc) enter the woods. (11) (I etc) go from here. (12) I hear the sound of the wind. (13) It shines on the darkened woods. (14) It has many cold winds. (15) The moon shines on someone. (16) The leaves fall on to the water. (17) The moon sets behind the mountains. (18) I see someone coming. (19) I hear people returning. (20) The moon sets. (21) Someone returns. (22) The clouds come. (23) The sun rises. (24) The birds settle. (25) The wind comes. (26) I see the clouds. (27) It shines on the trees. (28) I emerge from the forest. (29) I came here. (30) I hear the wind. (31) I see the high mountains. (32) I return to these hills. (33) I enter the deep forest (or: I enter deep into the forest). (34) The birds settle on the trees. (35) People see the sky. (36) The birds return to the woods. (37) I hear the water falling. (38) I see the moon rise.(39) The sun is already high. (40) The sky is not yet bright (= it has not got light yet). (41) People are not few (= there are a lot of people). (42) The birds are mostly small. (43) It is white every night. (44) It is bright by day and by night. (45) The leaves have already fallen. (46) The sun has not yet risen. (47) The moon has already risen. (48) People return at night. (49) People rarely come. (50) It falls every night. (51) I returned late at night. (52) I have not yet seen anyone. (53) He has already come here. (54) The flowers are not yet numerous (= there are not many flowers yet). (55) The hill is not high. (56) The moon is already bright. (57) The hills are mostly green. (58) The water is not white. (59) It is cold day and night. (60) They are green every day. (61) The moon has not yet set. (62) He does not come home. (63) The water does not flow. (64) The clouds do not come. (65) The birds have mostly gone. (66) They come every day. (67) It flows day and night. (68) They do not go into the hills. (69) I saw the moon at night.

UNIT 4

(1) The autumn flowers are fewer every day. (2) The white sun shines on the green leaves. (3) The cold wind enters the empty valley. (4) We don't see a single person returning. (5) At night I hear the sound of the bamboo leaves. (6) The sun has already risen from the green hills. (7) At night I see the bright moon rising. (8) The sun has not yet set behind the high hills. (9) Why does this person not return? (10) Every night I hear the sound of the river. (11) The dawn birds are again singing long. (12) I was not yet aware that the day had already dawned. (13) Day and night I long think of you. (14) Why does this bird sing alone? (15) Day by day I whistle carefree alone. (16) On the autumn hills there are many cold winds. (17) Late at night I hear someone coming home. (18) The white clouds come day by day. (19) Every night I hear the sounds of autumn. (20) A cold sun shines on the mountain forests. (21) We have not yet seen the colour of the springtime hills. (22) The autumn moon shines on the darkened trees. (23) I only hear a single bird singing. (24) Only now did I realise that the sun had already set. (25) The sun's rays enter the deep woods. (26) Why not return to the high woods? (27) I only hear the echoes of the birds on the hills. (28) On what day will my beloved return? (29) The rain is so heavy that I cannot see the hills. (30) He has gone and the days are already long (= He has been gone a long time now). (31) He left here and entered a secluded valley. (32) When the sun sets the cold winds come. (33) The sun rose and shone on the high woods. (34) The night is advanced but the day has not yet broken. (35) I've come again to hear the sounds of the forest. (36) The water is deep and the birds' reflections are bright. (37) I came out of the woods and only then did I see the sun (I did not see the sun until I came out of the woods). (38) We think of (or: miss) one another but we do not see one another (or: I miss him but never see him). (39) Whistling carefree I go deep into the hills. (40) When day broke he had already gone. (41) The skies are high and the mountain trees are shedding their leaves. (42) When we came out of the woods we saw the bright moon. (43) The birds have returned but he has not yet come home. (44) The birds come and settle on the cold river. (45) Autumn comes and the birds have already gone. (46) He comes out at dawn but at night he returns to the hills. (47) When clouds come, the rain also comes. (48) I came alone and again I shall return alone. (49) The birds are singing and he is also whistling. (50) I went into the woods and only then did I hear the birds.

UNIT 5

(1) To the bamboo forest the colours of springtime come. (2) On the flood-waters white birds settle. (3) Over the green hills the white clouds drift. (4) Deep into the mountains people rarely go. (5) Somewhere I hear a singing bird. (6) Night after night I walk alone in the moonlight. (7) From the blue

hills the white sun rises. (8) In the deep forest we do not see the sun. (9) In the bamboo forest the colour of the moss is bright. (10) On the empty hills the white clouds are numerous. (11) What people live in the deep forest? (12) Where does this visitor live? (13) In the woods. (14) Beyond the waters/river. (15) In front of the mountain. (16) In the sky. (17) Among the flowers. (18) In the bamboos. (19) Beside the birds. (20) Behind the bamboos. (21) In the bamboo-grove. (22) On/above the lake. (23) In the river. (24) On the rocks. (25) Beyond the river. (26) Beneath the moon. (27) Behind the trees. (28) In the snow. (29) By the water-side. (30) Beyond the hills. (31) Before the wind. (32) At the edge of the forest. (33) In the valley. (34) Behind the bamboo-grove. (35) On the hill. (36) By the river-side. (37) In the lake.(38) White birds are asleep on the sand. (39) The waters of the lake are white at the edge of the sand. (40) A single person is walking along the edge of the lake. (41) Only now do I see the moon [reflected] in the river. (42) The traveller also returns in the rain. (43) I sit again on the rocks by the river. (44) I sit alone on the mossy rock. (45) A single leaf drifts before the wind. (46) I only think of the traveller at the edge of the sky (= far away). (47) I live alone amid the sound of waters. (48) The reflection of the moon is bright in the lake. (49) In front of the mountain the cold blossom falls. (50) We do not see those who have gone returning. (51) On the springtime waters are many drifting blossoms. (52) The autumn moon shines on the shedding trees. (53) The home-going birds enter the darkened woods. (54) With the flowing waters the blossom has already gone. (55) To the empty valley the people who come are few. (56) On the autumn hills are many fallen leaves. (57) The setting sun shines on the secluded moss. (58) At night I hear the sound of leaves falling. (59) The drifting clouds come day by day. (60) In the wind-swept woods the fallen blossom is white. (61) On the white sand are many sleeping birds. (62) To this place the visitors who come are few (= few visitors come to this place).

UNIT 6

(1) How many local people have gone but not come home! (2) What I saw and what I heard cannot be spoken about. (3) Long have you wandered at the edge of the sky (= far from home); why do you not return? (4) In the springtime breeze under a full moon I miss my old friends. (5) When will you return to your home-town next year? (6) The bird wanders among rivers and lakes and misses its native woods. (7) Why do you sit alone playing the lute for so long? (8) When the wandering birds returned the trees were not yet green. (9) How many autumn leaves have fallen on the cold hills? (10) Today I do not see last night's visitor. (11) I wonder how many years I shall live in exile among rivers and lakes? (12) This spring I wander every day in the high hills. (13) What are you thinking about as you walk alone in the chilly rain? (14) What did you see when you wandered through the mountain forests? (15) Having wandered long

beyond the river, I am very homesick (lit. my thoughts of home are many). (16) Who is able to stay silent on this matter for a long time? (17) When I heard the lute I realised for the first time that the autumn wind was cold. (18) In exile how can one not miss one's native heath? (19) On the springtime hills I hear thc birds chattering everywhere. (20) Why does this person come here again? (21) My old friend is wandering in the hills, but I don't know where. (22) How can I not miss you when I am sleeping alone? (23) Yesterday I came here and today I'm going again. (24) He has lived a long time deep in the hills, so who can know about him? (25) I wonder where we shall be at this time next year? (26) During the night there was the sound of someone playing the lute. (27) What year will we meet again as we are meeting tonight? (28) When autumn comes, how can the leaves on the trees last very long? (29) The sound of a lute in the night: I wonder who was playing? (30) I see you today, but when shall I see you again? (31) From beyond the mountains how many people return? (32) After the rain the sky is blue again. (33) He came yesterday but now he has gone. (34) Tomorrow I return to my home-town. (35) After today where will you go back to? (36) Deep in the night I heard the sound of talking. (37) When shall we meet one another again? (38) You are going home but I am not going home. (39) When will my old friend return? (40) What happened yesterday, we talk about today for the first time. (41) How long can springtime flowers endure? (42) When I came the springtime trees were green; now I am going and the autumn wind is chill. (43) Who is playing the lute in the springtime woods? (44) What does this person know? (45) Long have I wandered among the green hills. (46) Surely they come every year? (47) All I see is an exile yearning for home by the river. (48) Those who live deep in the mountains know that the wind is cold. (49) I wonder who it is, playing late at night. (50) This is surely not the sound that we heard last night. (51) Why not return again to the mountain where I live? (52) The spring blossom that I see cannot last long. (53) Since my old friend went away I have not heard from him again. (54) The spring blossom when I left has fallen when I return. (55) On the day the wanderer returns there is much cold wind. (56) On what night shall we see again the moon that we see tonight? (57) The white sands are cold where the home-going birds have settled. (58) The bright moon rises and shines on the blossom that has fallen in the water. (59) When the bright moon rises the blossom glows white. (60)Which year shall I see again the one I'm yearning for?

UNIT 7

Wang Wei (early eighth century): 'Luzhai'

> On the empty mountain I see no one,
> I only hear the distant sound (or: echo) of people talking.
> The returning sunbeams enter deep into the woods

and shine again on the green moss.

Wang Wei (early eighth century): 'Zhuliguan'

> I sit alone in a secluded bamboo-grove,
> plucking my lute and whistling long.
> Deep in the woods, nobody knows [I'm here];
> the bright moon comes and shines on me.

Meng Haoran (689–740): 'Spring dawn'

> Asleep in spring I was not aware of the dawn;
> everywhere I hear singing birds.
> The sound of wind and rain in the night:
> blossom will have fallen, I wonder how much?

UNIT 8

(1) Flow out (of). (2) Fly in(to). (3) Walk back (to). (4) Wander across. (5) Flow away. (6) Come flying, fly here. (7) Come on foot, walk here. (8) Wander away. (9) Come out. (10) Go up. (11) Come back home. (12) Go across. (13) Go/come up into the sky. (14) Go/come down to the sea. (15) Cross the hill. (16) Return to the woods. (17) Come across the river. (18) Go up the hill. (19) Come back to the valley. (20) Go into the woods. (21) Flow into the sea. (22) Fly up to the clouds. (23) Blow across the river. (24) Walk down the hill. (25) Come as far as here. (26) Travel as far as the sea. (27) Return to the river.(28) I saw someone coming down the hill. (29) A great wind blows across the river. (30) The cold snow drifts into the bamboos. (31) Last night in my sleep I heard the sound of rain. (32) I sailed a small boat alone down the great river. (33) When my old friend came back home we talked long into the night. (34) The waters of the sea rise up to the sky and the wind howls high. (35) This year there are few travellers here. (36) They fly day by day, up to the sky and down to the sea. (37) Yesterday I wandered over this side of the hill and today the far side. (38) Why will the boy not go with you? (39) All I see is the boatman sitting in his empty boat. (40) He left his home and went to live in a secluded valley. (41) The wanderer has not yet come back to his native place. (42) When the wind comes the fallen blossom flies up into the sky. (43) In the path between the bamboos the birds are singing and nobody comes here. (44) The sound of a lute reaches my boat; who, I wonder, is playing? (45) The little boat went out on the sea and never returned again. (46) All I see is the white clouds coming one after another. (47) In the blue sky the white birds fly this way and that. (48) A lonely old man rows/steers his boat across the cold river. (49) A cold moon comes and shines on the snow on the path through the pine-trees. (50) Before the wind the snow on the pines falls on to the secluded path. (51) The boatman sits and

watches the white clouds pass over. (52) The wind blows the autumn leaves across the empty hills. (53) The river water comes flowing, and goes flowing away again. (54) The visitor boarded a small boat and went across the lake. (55) It is a long time now since he went into the hills and still he has not come out. (56) The tourist has already been here a month. (57) During the night a high wind blew the leaves down. (58) The lonely old man has gone now, but the secluded path remains. (59) Where now are my old friends from my boyhood years? (60) Who is that sitting alone under the green pine-tree?

UNIT 9

(1) I go up the hill and look down over the Yangtse. (2) How long did you travel by the sea? (3) The lonely bird spends the night on the sands. (4) The fallen blossom goes with the flowing water. (5) Why not return together in the same boat? (6) I overlook the sea and watch the boats go by. (7) I walk up and down beside the river. (8) Facing into the wind I watch the rain coming. (9) A solitary old man is fishing in the autumn floods. (10) When he said goodbye the visitor wept for a long time. (11) I walked here along the edge of the wood. (12) The boy went home with the old man. (13) White clouds rest on the high mountains. (14) The shadows of the trees rest on the green moss. (15) I followed the river to the blue sea. (16) The passengers on the boat sat side by side. (17) The lonely moon is white above us. (18) I was on the point of leaving when I saw a visitor approaching. (19) Where are my teacher's footprints now? (20) I went out at dawn to gather mountain herbs. (21) How long can I survive if I'm dependent on others? (22) He is fishing from a rock beside the lake. (23) I have long been overseas and only today have I come back. (24) Above the autumn hills the bright moon follows me home. (25) On the sands the river-birds spend the night side by side. (26) While I'm away I think of you; what year shall I see you? (27) The river-birds come to spend the night beside the chill water. (28) A fellow-townsman of mine is living here but we haven't yet got together. (29) I am here today; when shall I leave? (30) Blown by the wind, the autumn leaves wander through empty woods. (31) At dawn I went out to look at the trees; the spring colours were bright. (32) A solitary old man watches the springtime while sitting on a rock. (33) What are you looking at, up there looking out over the lake every day? (34) It's chilly tonight where the river-birds pass the night. (35) The moon shines on a lonely boat resting on the white sands. (36) How many wanderers will be spending the night away from home? (37) I sit alone beneath the pine-trees watching the mountain birds. (38) My old friend has gone away; where will he be now? (39) We came here on the same day, and on the same day we depart. (40) Now he lives deep in the mountains beside a lonely pine-tree. (41) Only then did I realise that the sea-birds were following our boat. (42) At night they also spend the night on the cold waters of the sea. (43) Today I return to my native

place, but how many will still be alive? (44) The wanderer has long travelled at the edge of the sky. (45) All I see in the sky is a lone bird flying. (46) The wind is strong so I don't dare cross over sitting in my boat. (47) The snow is deep, so we should see the tracks of people walking by. (48) The little boy can't talk yet. (49) How can spring colours last a long time? (50) The night is well advanced and dawn is imminent. (51) What do you want, coming here? (52) The mountain is high and the snow is deep, so how would I dare go up! (53) When my old friend said goodbye and left, I was close to tears. (54) You should go up into the hills and gather this kind of herb. (55) You ought to know where your teacher lives. (56) People ask me why I weep; I say I'm sad about autumn. (57) I didn't dare ask my teacher what he wanted. (58) If you don't know where he is you should ask someone. (59) The old man said he didn't know when he would be back. (60) I'm only afraid the water is deep and he won't dare to cross over. (61) I'm only sad that the springtime blossom cannot last long. (62) Who says no snow will fall this year? (63) Every year when autumn comes I'm sad that the trees shed their leaves. (64) I'm constantly afraid that after you leave you won't be back for a long time.

UNIT 10

(1) Beside the river there is a high tower. (2) From a myriad trees on a thousand hills the yellow leaves come down. (3) Entering the valley I walked on till I came to a river-side, where I saw a solitary old man sitting wearing a bamboo hat. (4) Nobody knows my grief at parting today. (5) Piled-up clouds for a thousand miles enter my eye as one. (6) Who comes to gather the yellow flowers in the woods? (7) Nature has no feelings; only people have. (8) When spring comes all the birds sing. (9) Beyond the river a single lonely old man walks in the rain with a rain-cape round his shoulders. (10) I'm only afraid that beyond the mountain there will be yet more mountains. (11) I'm sad that you will long be wandering a myriad miles away. (12) An old man in a little boat on a great lake in a cold wind fishes amid the snows wearing a bamboo hat and a rain-cape. (13) I alone hear the sound of orioles singing. (14) Yesterday he was here but today there is no trace of him. (15) How many more ranges of clouded hills lie before us? (16) In my home village in a hundred years no one will know what I am feeling. (17) Nobody lives in these hundred-fold empty valleys. (18) Storey by storey I mount the high tower. (19) Who knows of the sad weeping in the high tower tonight? (20) My feelings are too deep for utterance. (21) The sea-birds sometimes spend the night on the water. (22) From a single note of the oriole we know that spring has arrived. (23) Who is sad that there have long been no footprints on the recluse's (lit. wood-dweller's) secluded path? (24) I'm only afraid that the wind will be strong and nobody will cross over. (25) Overlooking the river I let my eyes wander beyond a thousand miles. (26) He left his home to live deep in the hills, wishing only to wander beyond this world. (27) Before me is a little river and

behind me is the mountain. (28) Not yet asleep, all I could hear was rain that went on all night. (29) The autumn flood-waters in the river are wide, so how can I cross without a boat? (30) I'm only sad that there are no more storeys at the top of the tower. (31) In the bamboo-grove all I hear is the sound of ten thousand bamboos. (32) How can I tell in one day the events of a whole year away from home? (33) I hadn't realised that during the night the snow was already deep on all the hills.

UNIT 11

(1) In front of us there was a sheer cliff that we couldn't climb up. (絕壁 is a set phrase; the context is 'In front of us there was a X cliff', so only an adjective like 'sheer' will fit; 'cutting off a cliff' would not fit the context.)

(2) A lone wild goose comes flying high. (斷雁 is a set phrase; 'cutting off a wild goose' would not fit here.)

(3) Why has he left his home and gone to live on a God-forsaken mountain? ('Dwell all over the mountains' would not make sense.)

(4) You should try your best to get right up to the extreme summit. (盡力 and 絕頂 are set phrases; 窮 must be a transitive verb here because it is not usual to use two attributive verbs before a noun in verse.)

(5) At the edge of the sky I have travelled everywhere across the rivers and lakes. (If 窮 is not a verb there will be no verb in the sentence, though, as we shall see later, this is not an invalidating objection.)

(6) A solitary cloud emerges above the high woods. (In 'X cloud emerges', 斷 can only be an attributive intransitive verb since 'cut off a cloud emerges' would not make sense.)

(7) Why don't we finish off this wine tonight? (盡酒 is a set phrase; 盡 is preceded by 不, which suggests that it is a verb; also, 盡 is the only possible verb in this sentence.)

(8) When I returned the spring was almost over. (9) The flowing water never ends. (10) At night the birds' talk ceases. (11) Only now am I aware that the spring sunlight has been extinguished. (12) I've been travelling a long time and my strength is almost exhausted. (13) The sky is cold and the returning wild geese have gone out of sight. (14) Broken-hearted, I go back to my old home. (15) When, I wonder, will the Hu be exterminated? (16) When the wine was finished it was almost daybreak. (17) Human strength has a time when it comes to an end = There comes a day when our strength gives out. (18) He is gone but his tracks have not yet disappeared. (19) The fallen blossom has all vanished, carried away on the stream. (20) The woodland birds have all gone home. (21) It is late at night and the lamps have all been extinguished. (22) This lamp cannot be blown out, however strong the wind. (23) I travelled the whole length of the road by the river. (24) The bright lamp illuminates all the things on the (interior) wall. (25) This year on the borders the Hu have all been

wiped out. (26) In a cold sky the returning wild geese have almost all passed over. (27) Snow has fallen and people's tracks have all been obliterated. (28) The boat sails close to the sheer river-bank. (29) The autumn geese descend on the white sands. (30) I'm only afraid that we shall not be able to cover the whole of the road home. (31) All day I am homesick and grieve that spring is over. (32) My old friends have all disappeared and won't be coming back again. (33) The flood-waters have entered the woods and the path through the bamboos is impassable. (34) The leaves on the trees at the top of the hill have almost all been blown down. (35) Snow-clouds cover the whole sky and the moonlight is extinguished. (36) It is raining heavily today, so you should wear a rain-cape. (37) The boy sat in the boat fishing the autumn flood-waters. (38) I walked to and fro beside the wood looking at the spring blossom. (39) I weep alone in this high tower, constantly thinking of you. (40) The sun illuminates all the moss on the rocks. (41) Ahead of us are cloud-capped mountains, range after range — how many, I wonder? (42) At dawn he goes out wearing his bamboo hat to gather mountain herbs. (43) I asked the old man where my teacher was now. (44) The fallen blossom on the stream has not yet ceased to drift by. (45) I went into the woods and walked through the yellow leaves all day long. (46) The lonely wild goose has flown off to a place a thousand miles away. (47) Late at night I am not yet asleep and I hear the distant sound of a lute. (48) At this parting we weep together, our hearts close to breaking. (49) I'm only sad that my hundred years (= lifespan) will be spent in exile. (50) When will these emotions cease? (51) The gleam of the sun among the pines will soon have set out of sight. (52) There is a strong wind on the sea, so I dare not go for a sail. (53) After saying goodbye, which year shall we meet again?

UNIT 12

Wang Zhihuan (early eighth century): 'Ascending Stork Tower'

> The white sun reaches its end, resting on the mountains;
> the Yellow River flows away to the sea.
> Wishing to go to the limits of thousand-mile eyes,
> I climb a further storey of the tower.

Liu Zongyuan (773–819): 'River snow'

> On a thousand hills the birds have stopped flying;
> on a myriad paths people's tracks have been obliterated.
> A rain-caped, bamboo-hatted old man in a lonely boat
> fishes alone amid the cold river's snows.

Jia Dao (early ninth century): 'Visiting a recluse and not finding him at home'

> Beneath the pine-trees I inquired of your servant-boy;

he said his master had gone to gather herbs
somewhere among these mountains,
but the clouds were deep and he knew not where.

UNIT 14

(1) There is no way home from the long darkness (of death). (2) The moon is bright and frost (= stars) fills the sky. (3) I sit gazing at the moon with a coat around my shoulders. (4) I held up the lamp and shone it on the white wall. (5) The frosty ground is white on the opposite bank. (6) She has long spent the night alone in a cold bed. (7) Following the stream, he returned to the temple on the hill. (8) The evening birds are few in the slanting (= driving) rain. (9) The breeze carries the sound of the brook a long way. (10) The boy returned carrying a lute over his shoulder. (11) Yellow flowers face the spring sunshine. (12) I thought it was the voice of my old friend. (13) Low clouds blot out the slanting (= setting) sunlight. (14) Faint in the distance I hear the temple bell. (15) A spring breeze comes blowing and fills my gown. (16) All day I follow the stream, intoxicated by the spring blossom. (17) I go up the tower and gaze towards my home country until the darkness takes me by surprise. (18) The bird-tracks on the snow-covered ground are fewer day by day. (19) The drunken old man is on the ground and can't get up. (20) I left my home-town in boyhood and I return with a white head. (21) The land is low and the water high, and we cannot see the bank. (22) The cold trees are distant through the haze of the driving rain. (23) The low sunlight lights up the wall behind my bed. (24) I gaze ahead at the distant bank showing vaguely across the water. (25) In the darkness the lamplight is seen faintly in the distance. (26) In the evening the sound of a bell is heard by the river. (27) An old man came out of the woods carrying a long object over his shoulder. (28) He wore a large bamboo hat on his head and there was rain on his clothes. (29) You and I are both exiles in the distant south. (30) I thought the fallen blossom was overnight snow. (31) I raise my eyes and gaze afar at the wild geese faint in the distance. (32) I sit gazing at the bright moon and a longing for home arises.

UNIT 15

Li Bai (701–762): 'Self-consolation'

Sitting opposite a jug of wine I do not realise that it has got dark
and that fallen blossom fills (= covers) my gown.
Drunk, I get up and walk in the moonlight by the stream,
where the birds have gone to roost and few people remain.

Li Bai: 'Night yearning'

Before my bed, the light of the bright moon;
I thought it was frost on the ground.
Raising my head, I gaze at the bright moon;
lowering my head, I long for my old home.

Liu Changqing (eighth century): 'Seeing off [the Rev.] Lingche'

Misty grey is Bamboo Mountain Temple;
faint in the distance, the sound of the bell comes through the dusk.
With your bamboo hat on your back and the light of the setting sun upon it,
up the green mountain you return alone to your distant home.

UNIT 16

Zhang Ruoxu (seventh to eighth centuries): 'A night of blossom and moonlight on the Yangtse in springtime'

1 The tide on the springtime Yangtse stretches level to the sea;
2 the bright moon over the sea is born together with the tide.
3 It (= the moonlight) comes flooding in with the waves a thousand myriad miles;
4 where on the springtime river is there no moonlight? (= it is everywhere)

5 The river's flow snakes around meadows fragrant [with flowers];
6 when the moon shines on the blossoming trees they all seem to be [covered with] frozen rain.
7 In the air drifting hoar-frost floats imperceptibly (i.e. the moonlight seems to fill the air with a frosty haze),
8 [so that] the white sand of the islets cannot be seen.

9 The sky over the river is of one colour without a mote of dust;
10 brilliant in the void the moon's lonely wheel.
11 Who first saw the moon from a river-side?
12 In what year did a river-moon first shine upon mankind?

13 Human life goes on unending from generation to generation;
14 the river-moon is just like it (= what it was before) year after year.
15 I wonder who the river-moon is waiting for;
16 I only see the Yangtse sending the flowing waters on their way.

17 A single little white cloud (= a man away from home) has gone far, far away;

18 on the green-mapled river-bank his sadness is unbearable.
19 'At whose home tonight is the traveller in his frail craft [staying]?' [she will be asking].
20 Where on a moonlit balcony is she (=his wife) longing for him?

21 Lovely above that balcony the moon will be lingering [now];
22 it must be shining on that lonely woman's dressing-table.
23 [Its light] cannot be rolled away with the blinds in her room;
24 [when it falls] upon her fulling-block it will come back if brushed away.

25 At this moment we are gazing towards one another but hearing no news;
26 I wish I could flow with this glorious moonlight and shine upon you.
27 The wild geese fly afar, but this light would not pass [that far];
28 the fish and dragons dive and leap, making ripples in the water (a pun on 'a letter': neither geese nor fish are proving good messengers).

29 Last night by a quiet pool I dreamed of fallen blossom;
30 how sad that half-way through spring I'm not returning home.
31 The river's waters have carried the spring away until it is almost gone;
32 the settimg moon over Yangtse's pools is low again in the west.

33 The slanting moon sinks heavily, hidden in the mist from the sea;
34 [between] the North and the South the road is endless.
35 I wonder how many people are travelling home by the light of this moon;
36 the setting moon troubles my heart as it fills the river-side trees.

UNIT 17

Du Fu (712–770): 'Stars and moon by the Yangtse'

1 A sudden shower has made this autumn night even clearer;
2 the gilded waves make the jewel-strings (of stars) even brighter.
3 Now we can see how white the Milky Way actually is,
4 how clear [the water by] the bank has been all along.
5 When reflected in things the connected beads (= stars) snap;
6 climbing the void, a single mirror (= moon) rises.
7 The night-watch water-clock dims the fading light (of stars and moon),

8 the more so as the splendour of the dew condenses (and
compensates for it).

UNIT 18

Li Bai (701–762): 'Questioning the moon with a cup of wine in my hand'

1 In the blue sky there is a moon: how long has it come for?
2 I shall now stop drinking and just ask it.
3 When people reach up to pull the bright moon down they can't get
hold of it,
4 yet when the moon travels it tags along behind us.

5 Brilliant like a floating mirror, it looks down on the vermilion
palace-gates;
6 when the green mists have all been cleared away, its pure radiance
blazes forth.
7 We only see it at night coming from upon the sea;
8 how can we know (= little do we think) that at dawn it will sink out
of sight among the clouds?

9 The white hare pounds his drugs and autumn is spring again;
10 Chang'e dwells in loneliness with who (= no one) as a neighbour?
11 People today do not see the moon of ancient times
12 but tonight's moon has in the past shone upon the ancients.

13 Ancients and moderns are like flowing water,
14 as we look at the bright moon together we are all like this.
15 I only wish (= hope) that while we are in the presence of song and
wine
16 the moonlight will long shine into the golden wine-kettle.

UNIT 19

Li Bai (701–762): 'Drinking alone in the moonlight'

1 A jug of wine among the blossom,
2 I drink alone with no boon-companions.
3 I raise my cup to invite the moon [to join me];
4 my shadow opposite me will make three of us.
5 But the moon knows nothing of drinking
6 and my shadow uselessly follows my body.
7 For now I'll make do with moon and shadow as companions;
8 if I'm going to enjoy myself I must do it while spring is still here.

9 When I sing [and wag my head] the moon moves to and fro;

10 when I dance my shadow breaks and scatters.

11 While I'm [still] sober let's have fun together;

12 [when I wake up] after I've been drunk we'll each go our own way.

13 So let's join in a friendship without emotion

14 and make a date in the distant Milky Way.

UNIT 20

Du Fu (712–770): 'Full moon'

> A lonely moon is full right before my balcony;
> the chill Yangtse moves my darkened casement.
> Cast on the waves, the gold[en light] is restless;
> as it shines on my mat, the patterns remain even more [vivid].
> It is not yet waning where the empty hills are tranquil;
> it hangs high where ranked constellations are fading.
> In my old garden [back at home] the pines and cassia will be flourishing;
> ten thousand miles [apart] we share this pure radiance.

Wang Jian (eighth to ninth centuries): 'Gazing at the moon on the fifteenth night, [a poem] for Departmental Director Du'

> In the middle of the courtyard the ground is white and the trees give a roost for the crows;
> the cold dew silently wets the cassia-flowers.
> Tonight everyone is gazing at the moon's brightness;
> I wonder in whose home there is autumn yearning.

Bai Juyi (772–846): 'Village night'

> The frosted grass is misty-green and the crickets chirp sadly;
> south of the village and north of the village there are no more people walking.
> Alone I go out before the door and gaze over the countryside fields:
> the moon is bright and the buckwheat flowers are like snow.

UNIT 21

Wang Changling (early eighth century): 'Enjoying the moonlight in the South Study with my cousin Xiao and remembering Mr Cui, Assistant Prefect of Shaoxing'

As we take our ease in the South Study
the curtains are open and the moon begins to emerge.
Its pure radiance tinges the riverside trees
and [its reflection in the waves] dances in the window.
How many times has it gradually waxed and waned,
changing the present into the past with its limpid light?
For that fine man on clear Yangtse's side
songs of home will tonight be past bearing.
A thousand miles, what does it matter?
The lightest breeze will bring his fragrance.

Zhang Jiuling (678–740): 'Gazing at the moon and thinking of someone afar'

Over the sea the bright moon is born;
at the edge of the sky (= though worlds apart) we share this hour.
Parted friends hate the night for being so long;
all night long, thoughts of you arise.
I extinguish the candle to enjoy the fulness of the [moon]light;
I drape a coat around my shoulders as I feel the dew increasing.
I cannot fill my hands [with the moonlight] as a gift for you,
so I'll go back to bed and dream of a happy reunion.

Du Fu (712–770): 'Moonlit night'

The moon over Fuzhou tonight,
in her boudoir she will only be watching it alone (i.e. without me).
From far off my heart is moved to think of my little children,
who do not yet understand what remembering Chang'an means [to her].
In a fragrant mist her cloud-coiffure will be damp;
in the pure radiance her jadelike (=white) arms will be chilled.
When shall we lean [together again] at an uncurtained window,
shone upon as a couple till our tear-marks are dry?

UNIT 22

Jin Changxu (Tang, no dates): 'Spring resentment'

Drive away the orioles,
don't let them sing in the branches,
for when they sing they disturb my dreams
so that I cannot go to Liaoxi (where her husband is stationed).

Li Duan (late eighth century): 'Boudoir feelings'

The moon sets, the stars thin out, the sky begins to get light;

my lonely lamp is not yet extinguished and dreams (= sleep and then dreams

of her absent husband) will not come.

I drape a coat round my shoulders and gaze further towards the front of

the door (= out of the front door);

I am not annoyed at the magpies' glad cries in the morning (as she would

be if they had disturbed her from a dream about her husband).

Wen Tingyun (early ninth century): 'Jewelled zither grief'

On my icy mat on my silver[-ornamented] bed my dreams will not come;

the blue sky is like water and the night-clouds [float] lightly.

The cries of wild geese pass over bound for Xiao and Xiang;

in the Twelve Towers (= the boudoirs of the capital) the moon is bright by itself.

Li Shangyin (early ninth century): 'Chang'e'

In the mica screen the candle's reflection is deep;

the Milky Way gradually sets and the dawn stars drown.

Chang'e must be regretting that she stole the magical elixir;

between blue sea and blue sky, her heart night by night.

UNIT 23

Du Shenyan (late seventh century): 'In reply to a poem from Mr Lu, assistant magistrate of Jinling county, entitled "Wandering and looking afar in early spring"'

Only the official traveller

of all people is startled by Nature's renewal.

Then sunrise clouds are rosy with dawn as they emerge from the sea;

prunus and willow are green with spring when one crosses the Yangtse.

The mild air excites the golden orioles;

the cloudless light turns the green water-weed.

Suddenly hearing you sing an ancient tune,

my thoughts of going home almost soak my handkerchief.

Wu Yuanheng (late eighth century): 'Springtime arousal'

The willows are shady and the sky is clear after the small rain;

the last of the blossom has fallen, letting us see the drifting orioles.

Night-long the spring breeze wafts me fragrant dreams [of home];

my dreams pursue the spring breeze back to Luoyang.

Wang Zhihuan (early eighth century): 'Liangzhou song'

> The Yellow River rises afar into the white clouds;
> a patch of lonely city, mountains a myriad fathoms high.
> Tibetan pipes need not bewail the willows,
> for the spring breeze does not come past Jade Gate Pass.

Li Bai (701–762): 'Missing him in springtime'

> Yan grass will be like green silk threads;
> Qin mulberries lower their verdant boughs.
> The very day when you dream of coming home
> is the time when my heart is breaking.
> Spring breeze, you stranger to me,
> what business have you in my silk-gauze curtains?

UNIT 24

Wang Wei (early eighth century): 'Visiting the Temple of Accumulated Fragrance'

> I had not realised that the Temple of Accumulated Fragrance
> was several miles into the clouded peaks.
> A path through ancient trees where no one was;
> somewhere deep in the mountains the sound of a bell.
> A brook's voice sobs between precipitous rocks;
> the sunlight is cold on the blue pines.
> Towards evening, in the bend of a silent pool,
> by calm meditation I tame my poisonous dragon.

Chang Jian (early eighth century): 'Inscribed in the monks' quarters behind Broken Hill Temple'

> Clear dawn enters (or: In the clear dawn I enter) the ancient temple;
> the first sun shines on the high woods.
> A path through bamboos leads to a secluded place;
> around the monks' quarters the blossoming trees are deep.
> The mountain light cheers the birds' natures;
> the pool's reflections still my mind.
> All Nature's sounds are silent here;
> all that remains is the sound of bell and chiming-bowl.

UNIT 25

Liu Zongyuan (773–819): 'Visiting the Transcendental Master's monastery at dawn to read Buddhist scriptures'

> I draw water from the well to rinse my cold teeth;
> I clear my mind and brush my dusty clothes.
> Relaxedly holding a palm-leaf scripture,
> I walk out of the east study reading it.
>
> Nobody at all draws on the true source [within];
> empty marvels are what the world pursues.
> I hope to be able to intuit [the message behind] this ancient text
> to discover how I may repair [the damage done to] my inborn nature.
>
> My wise teacher's monastery is quiet outdoors and in;
> the colour of the moss leads on to deep bamboo thickets.
> The sun rises and traces of mist and dew remain;
> the green pine-trees look as if washed and anointed.
>
> In tranquillity I leave philosophizing behind
> and awaken to joy, my mind complete in itself.

UNIT 26

Du Fu (712–770): 'Mirror-of-the-Law Temple'

> My person being in danger, I went to another prefecture (i.e. from Huazhou to Qinzhou);
> I've done my best but in the end I am exhausted.
> With wounded spirit I've travelled deep into the mountains,
> but my sadness is broken by [the sight of] an ancient temple on a cliff.
>
> Charming is the pure green moss,
> vulnerable are the clustering cold bamboo-shoot sheaths.
> Meandering is the river at the foot of the mountain,
> limply hanging are the raindrops on the pinetrees.
>
> Disintegrating clouds obscure the pure morning;
> the first sun is hidden, then re-emerges.
> The vermilion ridge-tiles glow in the intermittent light;
> doors and windows are brilliantly coloured and every one is distinct.

Leaning on my staff, I'd forgotten my earlier plans (for today's stage
of the journey);
when I emerge from my dream it is already high noon.
Faint in the distance a cuckoo calls,
so I dare not take this narrow path (to the temple).

UNIT 27

Lu Lun (late eighth century): 'Inscribed at the pond behind the Temple of
Promoting Goodness'

Outside the window the white cranes go to roost;
it is as if I am neighbour to Mirror Lake.
How old are the trees that the moon shines on?
How many times has their blossom greeted visitors?
There is a way through the green sedge on the bank;
the mossy paths are green with no trace of dust.
I've long wished I might be allowed to find refuge here
and let this body age among the monks.

Lu Lun (late eighth century): 'Staying the night at Stone Jar Temple'

A cold lamp burns in the worship-hall, and fireflies in the grass;
a thousand forests and a myriad valleys are still and silent.
Mist thickens over the rain-pools where dragons and snakes lie
hidden;
dew moistens the empty hills and the Milky Way is bright.
In the haze and mists of twilight I am sad for the world;
in the light of coloured clouds at dawn I see the royal city.
I look back and gaze [at the temple], admire it, then weep:
when will the waves in the sea of suffering be stilled?

UNIT 28

Bai Juyi (772-846): 'The peach-blossom at Great Forest Temple'

In the ordinary world in the fourth moon the fragrant blossom is all
over;
but at this mountain temple the peach-blossom is only now in full
bloom.
I've long regretted that springtime goes away, nowhere to be found;
I hadn't realised that it gets transferred to this place.

Bai Juyi (772-846): 'For my guests when returning home in the evening at
West Lake and looking back at the temple on Lonely Hill [Island]'

A lotus-blossom temple on a pine-tree island in a willow lake;
in the evening we move our home-going oars, leaving the temple-site.
The cumquat's fruit hangs low, for the hill rain is heavy;
the palm-tree's leaves tremble, for the river breeze is cool.
The azure void['s reflection] rocks on the relaxed misted waves;
the evening sun rests on the uneven temple buildings.
As we reach the shore please look back, gentlemen:
the Penglai Palace is in the middle of the sea.

UNIT 29

Tao Yuanming (365-427): 'Back to the land, No. 1'

When young I had no taste for fitting in with the conventional world;
my nature had always been to love the hills.
By mistake I fell into the worldly trap
and once I was there I stayed for thirteen years.

The caged bird longs for its old home-woods;
the fish in the pond yearns for its old home-pool in the river.
So I reclaimed some waste land in the countryside to the south [of the
city]
and preserved my simplicity by returning to garden and field.

A square smallholding of a dozen mu (= a couple of acres),
a thatched cottage of eight or nine jian.
Elm and willow shade the eaves at the back,
peach and plum spread their branches in the front courtyard.

Dimly seen are the distant villages of people,
lazily rising is the smoke from the market-village.
A dog barks in a deep lane,
a cock crows from the top of a mulberry-tree.

No dust or din indoors or out,
just plenty of peace in the empty rooms.
I have been so long in the cage;
once more I have the opportunity to return to naturalness (= to be
myself once more).

Tao Yuanming: 'Drinking wine, No. 5'

I built a hut in an inhabited area
but without the din of carriages and horses.
You ask: 'How did you manage that?'

If the mind is distant the place becomes secluded by itself.

I gather chrysanthemums under the eastern fence;
far off in the distance I see the Southern Hills.
At sunset the mountain mists are beautiful
and flying birds accompany one another home.

There is a true consciousness (= sense of reality) in this;
if I try to explain it, all words are forgotten.

UNIT 30

Bo Daoyou (fifth century): 'A poem inspired by gathering herbs in the
mountains'

Linked peaks for several thousand miles;
tall woods girdle steep-sided plateaus.
When clouds pass over, distant mountains are obscured;
when the wind arrives, it is blocked by tangled thickets.

Thatched cottages are hidden from sight
but cocks crowing tell us there are people here.
I tread their paths with carefree steps;
everywhere I see firewood they have left.

Only now do I realise that after a hundred generations
the earliest rulers' subjects (= the Golden Age people) have been here
all this time.

Liu Zongyuan (773-819): 'Walking through an abandoned village in South
Gorge on an autumn morning'

Late autumn's frost and dew lie heavy
as I rise in the morning to walk the secluded valley.
Yellow leaves cover the bridge over the stream;
in the abandoned village there are only ancient trees.
Cold flowers are sparse and forlorn;
a hidden spring is faint and hesitant.
My worldly cunning is long forgotten,
so why should [my coming] startle the deer?

UNIT 31

Zhang Jie (late ninth century): 'The Peach[-blossom] Source'

Where sheer cliffs leaned towards one another was the gateway to the
cave;
from here a man in days gone by entered the immortals' source.
Beneath the blossom of several trees he met [dancers wearing] pearls
and kingfisher-feathers,
Laozi's descendants halfway through a song, in the midst of singing.
After taking his leave he naturally supposed that it was a dream [like
that] of the orchard-keeper;
when he came home who (= nobody) believed the old angler's tale?
In vain before the mountain the uncaring stream
still circles what once was an emerald-tree village.

Chang Jian (early eighth century): 'Going to visit Li the Ninth's estate on the
Shangsi festival'

The rain has stopped at the ferry-landing east of the willow-grove;
on Lanting anniversary I row in a light boat.
My old friend's house is on a peach-blossom bank;
right up to his garden-gate the stream's water flows.

Zhang Xu (seventh to eighth centuries): 'Peach-blossom Stream'

Faintly seen is the flying bridge through the wildland mists;
on the west side of an overhanging crag I ask [a man in] a fishing-
boat:
'Peach-blossom comes down with the flowing water all day long;
whereabouts on this pure stream is the cave?'

Li Bai (701-762): 'An answer from the hills'

You ask me what is my purpose, lodging among green hills;
I smile but do not answer, for my mind is at peace of itself.
Peach-blossom on flowing water passes into secret depths:
there is another earth and sky that is not in this world of ours.

UNIT 32

Liu Zongyuan (773-819): 'The old fisherman'

The old fisherman has spent the night under the western cliff;
at dawn he draws clear Xiang [water] and makes a fire of Chu
bamboo.
The mists disperse as the sun rises, and there is no one in sight;
with a single creak of his oar the mountains and river are green.
He turns to look at the edge of the sky as he goes down midstream;
above the cliffs, mindlessly, the clouds follow upon each other.

Qiwu Qian (early eighth century): 'Drifting on the Ruoye Stream in spring'

This atmosphere of peaceful seclusion continues uninterrupted;
on this trip I'll go along with whatever I meet by chance.
The evening breeze wafts my boat onwards
[through] a path of [floating] blossom into the mouth of the stream.

At the edge of night I turn into West Creek;
I gaze at the Southern Dipper beyond the hills.
The mist on the pools floats, swirling and merging;
the woodland moon sinks low behind me.

Life's business is in fact hazy and unpredictable;
I wish I could be an old man holding a fishing-rod.

UNIT 33

Jia Dao (779–843): 'Inscribed at Li Ning's retreat'

You live quietly with few close neighbours;
a grass-grown path leads into your overgrown garden.
The birds had gone to roost in the trees by the pond
when this old monk knocked at your moonlit door.
Crossing the bridge, I could distinguish the colours of the countryside;
the drifting rocks moved against the roots of the clouds.
I shall leave for now but I'll be back here again:
I shall not go back on my promise to see you in your retreat.

Sikong Shu (eighth century): 'Rock well'

Moss-colour covers all the spring-lit rocks;
lute-tree shade enters the chilly well.
When the recluse comes alone to draw water
he first enjoys the sun's last rays.

Lu Lun (late eighth century): 'On an old tree in the mountains'

The tall tree is lonely and chill
[from] night rains and autumn winds.
His fallen leaves rustle in the clustered bamboos;
his slanting roots clutch wandering tumbleweed.
Half immersed in the mountain's face;
constantly amid the sound of waters.
Who ever comes to this place [to visit him]?
[Through] the cloud-gates you may also reach him.

UNIT 34

Wei Yingwu (late eighth century): 'To the Taoist in the mountains of Quanjiao'

> It was cold this morning in my study in the prefecture office
> and suddenly I thought of you, hermit of the hills,
> bundling up thorn-sticks for fuel at the bottom of a ravine
> then coming home to cook your white stones.
> I was going to bring you a stoup of wine
> to cheer you up this wild, wet evening,
> but fallen leaves cover the empty hills,
> so where could I seek your footprints?

Liu Changqing (eighth century): 'Visiting the retreat of the Changshan Taoist at Nanxi'

> All the way, wherever I pass through,
> I see your footprints in the moss.
> White clouds rest on the tranquil islets;
> spring flowers block your unvisited gate.
> After the rain I look at the colour of the pinetrees;
> I follow the hill to the source of the stream.
> Brookside flowers and your meditating mind
> will look at one another, all words forgotten.

Wen Tingyun (early ninth century): 'The mountain dwelling of the recluse Lu Hu'

> At West Brook I asked [my way of] a woodcutter,
> then in the distance I recognised my host's home.
> Ancient trees had embraced the rocks with their advancing years;
> a rapid burn revealed the [bottom] sand by its clarity.
> A thousand peaks darkened as they followed [the course of] the rain;
> the single path sloped up into the clouds.
> As the sun set the flying rooks assembled
> and the hillside was filled with [the whiteness of] buckwheat flowers.

UNIT 35

Qiu Wei (eighth century): 'Going to visit a recluse in the Western Hills but not finding him at home'

> At the very top, a thatched cottage;
> all the way up, thirty *li* (= ten miles).
> I knock on the door, no servant-boy [answers];
> I peep inside: only the furniture.

If he is not [out in] his covered cart
he must be fishing in autumn floodwater.
By miscalculation we did not meet;
I tried my best, but my [attempt at a] visit has been in vain.

The colour of grass (and flowers) in the new rain;
the sound of pinetrees through evening windows.
Coming here, I feel in tune with this superbly peaceful spot;
[these things] alone are enough to cleanse my mind's hearing.

Even though we have not had the mood (= enjoyment) of guest and
host,
I've learned quite a lot about inner peace.
My mood fulfilled, only now do I descend the hill:
there's no need now to wait for him.

UNIT 36

Anon (Han dynasty): 'Three ancient poems, No. 3'

I've recently planted orchids;
among them I've used wild ginger.
All day I've gathered their flowers;
by sunset my arms are not full.

Having gathered them, who am I going to give them to?
My dear one is on a far road (= journey).
Their fragrance will easily melt away and vanish;
their glory will soon wither.

How can I tell him my yearning?
I'll send him a hug on the wind.

Anon (Han dynasty): 'Nineteen ancient poems, No. 6'

I waded the river gathering water-lilies;
in the orchid marsh are many fragrant flowers.
Having gathered them, who am I going to give them to?
My dear one is on a far road (= journey).

When he looks back towards his home
the long road stretches on for ever.
Our hearts are together but we are apart;
I shall grieve till my life is ended.

Anon (Han dynasty): 'Nineteen ancient poems, No. 9'

> In the courtyard there is a lovely tree,
> its green leaves sending forth a flood of blossom.
> I pull down a branch and break off a spray of bright blossom,
> intending to give it to my dear one.
>
> Its fragrance fills my breast and sleeves,
> [but] I cannot get it to him, for the way is too far (= long).
> Such a thing is not really worth sending as a gift:
> it's just that I'm saddened that we've been parted so long.

UNIT 37

Liu Fangping (early eighth century): 'Grieving resentfully in spring'

> [Seen through] her gauze window the sun sinks and gradually dusk [comes];
> in her golden room (cf. gilded cage) there is no one to see the traces of her tears.
> Lonely is the empty courtyard as spring is about to be late (= is nearing its end);
> pear-blossom (fills =) covers the ground but she does not open her door.

Li Shangyin (early ninth century): 'Fallen blossom'

> [Seen] from my high balcony the traveller has finally gone;
> in the little garden the blossom flies in confusion,
> unevenly [heaping] on to the winding paths,
> distantly escorting the slanting sunlight (= the setting sun).
> Heart-broken, I cannot bear to sweep it away;
> I strain my eyes, still wanting him to return.
> My blossoming heart is gone (towards =) with the spring,
> and all I get is a tear-soaked dress.

Bai Juyi (772–846): 'Saying goodbye amid the grasses of the ancient plain' (written on a given theme)

> Luxuriant are the grasses on the plain,
> withering and flourishing once every year.
> The wildfire cannot burn them out;
> the spring breeze blows them into life again.
> Their far-reaching fragrance invades the ancient road;
> their sunlit green reaches right up to the ruined city walls.
> As I once more see my prince off
> their lushness is filled with the pangs of parting.

UNIT 38

Li Jia (Sung dynasty): '[On the pattern] "Remembering my prince": a spring song'

> Luxuriant the fragrant grasses, reminding me of my prince;
> tall is the tower beyond the willows where I break my heart in vain;
> I cannot bear to hear the cuckoo calling, note after note.
> When it is almost dusk
> the rain beats the pear-blossom and my door is shut [enclosing me] deeply.

Yan Ren (Sung dynasty): '[On the pattern] "Magnolia flowers"'

> The spring breeze is only on the west side of the garden;
> the shepherd's purse flowers bloom profusely and butterflies flutter hither and yon.
> The sunlit green of the icy pond, though shone upon, is still empty;
> the fallen pink blossom on the fragrant path has all been blown away.
>
> My thoughts of you run on and on, but I'm grieved that my floating tresses are getting short;
> all day long I miss you and my silk belt grows slack (from losing weight through anxiety).
> My precious mirror is like the moon and does not lie to me;
> if you come home tomorrow you can see for yourself.

Ouyang Xiu (1007–1072): '[On the pattern] "Treading the sedges"'

> At the prospect-tower the prunus-blossom was almost over;
> at the bridge over the stream the willows were slender;
> the flower-scented breeze was warm, swinging his departing bridle.
> The sadness of parting became endless the farther he moved away
> into an unending distance like springtime floodwaters.
>
> Every inch of my tender heart [aches],
> my tears brim over on to my powdered [cheeks];
> high in the tower I cannot lean [any longer] on this precipitous balcony-rail.
> Where the open plain comes to an end are springtime hills;
> the traveller is even beyond those springtime hills.

UNIT 39

Zhang Jiuling (678–740): 'Bewailing my lot, No. 1'

> 01 A solitary wild goose comes over the sea,

02 not daring to look round at the ponds.
03 Sideways he sees a pair of kingfishers
04 nesting on a three-pearl tree.
05 High up on the top of their treasure-tree
06 can they be free of the fear of the crossbow-pellet?
07 Fine clothes [make the wearer] worry about being pointed at;
08 being exalted crowds the gods into hating one.
09 But now that I wander too far to be seen
10 what will the wildfowler set his heart upon?

Zhang Jiuling (678–740): 'Bewailing my lot, No. 2'

11 In springtime the orchid leaves are luxuriant;
12 in autumn the cassia flowers are purest white.
13 So vigorous is this energy for growth
14 that alone and unaided they create the fair seasons.
15 Little do they expect that the forest-dwellers (= recluses),
16 sensing [their fragrance on] the breeze, will [come and] sit to enjoy them.
17 Plants and trees have their own private purposes;
18 they have no desire for a beautiful woman to pluck them.

Zhang Jiuling (678–740): 'Bewailing my lot, No. 4'

19 South of the Yangtse there grows the red orange;
20 through the winter its groves remain green.
21 This is not because the climate is warm,
22 but because it has its own determination [to survive] the year's cold.
23 It would make an ideal gift for an honoured guest,
24 but alas, [the place where it grows] is obstructed by many-layered [mountains] and deep [rivers].
25 Fate is limited to what each of us encounters;
26 its cyclicality is beyond discovery.
27 People only speak of planting peaches and plums,
28 but this tree (= the orange) can provide shade just as well as these!

UNIT 40

Liu Zongyuan (773–819): 'The caged goshawk'

When chill winds are shrill and there flies a severe frost,
the goshawk (strikes =) rockets up and turns in the dawn light;
the clouds are split, the mists are torn and the rainbow severed;
[he drops like] a thunderclap and lightning-flash, and skims along the level hilltop.

With a swish his energetic flight-feathers shear through the thorn-
brakes;
downward he seizes a fox or hare, then mounts into the blue distance;
with fur on his talons and blood on his beak [he frightens] all the
birds away;
he stands alone looking all round, and then he is fierce and proud.

When scorching winds and humid summer heat suddenly arrive,
his feathers moult and fall and he is downcast and hides away;
wildcat or rodent in the grass are enough to make him anxious;
in a single night he looks round ten times, alarmed and distressed.

He only wishes that clear[-skied] autumn would again make him free,
to tear off his myriad restraints and soar among the clouds.

Cui Tu (late ninth century): 'The lone wild goose'

Several skeins have all gone home,
but, isolated figure, where will *you* go?
In the evening rain you call to them, lost;
on a chilly pond you descend alone, belated.
The islet clouds pass over low in the darkness;
the Great Wall moon follows coldly in the distance.
You will not necessarily meet the captive arrow,
but, flying alone, you should be on your guard.

Du Fu (712–770): 'The seagulls'

Along the river's edge the cold gulls play,
with no other [concerns] than doing as they please;
changing their minds, they turn their jade-white wings;
following their fancy, they dot the green rice-shoots.

When snow is dark they still must bathe;
when the wind rises, they drift, unresisting.
A few flocks over the blue sea,
pure figures daily uttering desolate cries.

VOCABULARY INDEX

The numbers refer to units, not to pages. Only vocabulary items included in the 'Vocabulary' sections are indexed here; extra vocabulary items in examples glossed *in situ* are excluded.

INDEX TO TEXTS QUOTED IN FULL

Note: An asterisk denotes an example text with a translation attached; a double asterisk denotes an example text given in translation only; all other texts are translation exercises with a translation given in the key.

331

TOPIC INDEX

333

About the Author

Born in 1931 in Holmwood, Dorking, Surrey, Archie was the eldest child of a large family. He always had a natural aptitude for languages - he won a scholarship to Dorking Grammar School, and taught himself Chinese from a book on his lap during Latin lessons, with the encouragement of a local church minister; and, aged 17, passed the London Matriculation exam in Chinese. He already excelled at Latin and German, and had a working knowledge of Greek and Russian.

He then went on to SOAS, University of London to read Chinese and graduated with a First in 1952. He was always proud that he was the first member of the family to go to university. After National Service in Germany and Korea, he became a freelance translator, translating 12 books during the late 1950s and early 1960s.

In 1961 Archie joined the University of Durham to lecture in Chinese, where he remained until his early retirement through ill-health.

He died in 2002 after completing "Chinese Through Poetry", a book which was built on a life of learning and teaching.

4545353R00210

Printed in Germany
by Amazon Distribution
GmbH, Leipzig